C000091358

sendmail® for Linux®

Richard Blum

A Division of Macmillan USA
201 West 103rd St., Indianapolis, Indiana, 46290

sendmail® for Linux®

Copyright © 2000 by Sams Publishing

All rights reserved. No part of this book shall be reproduced, stored in a retrieval system, or transmitted by any means, electronic, mechanical, photocopying, recording, or otherwise, without written permission from the publisher. No patent liability is assumed with respect to the use of the information contained herein. Although every precaution has been taken in the preparation of this book, the publisher and author assume no responsibility for errors or omissions. Nor is any liability assumed for damages resulting from the use of the information contained herein.

International Standard Book Number: 0-672-31834-2

Library of Congress Catalog Card Number: 99-66163

Printed in the United States of America

First Printing: April 2000

02   01   00   4   3   2   1

Trademarks

All terms mentioned in this book that are known to be trademarks or service marks have been appropriately capitalized. Sams cannot attest to the accuracy of this information. Use of a term in this book should not be regarded as affecting the validity of any trademark or service mark.

Linux is a registered trademark of Linus Torvalds

sendmail is a registered trademark of sendmail, Inc.

Warning and Disclaimer

Every effort has been made to make this book as complete and as accurate as possible, but no warranty or fitness is implied. The information provided is on an "as is" basis. The author and the publisher shall have neither liability nor responsibility to any person or entity with respect to any loss or damages arising from the information contained in this book or from the use of the CD or programs accompanying it.

ACQUISITIONS EDITOR
Neil Rowe

DEVELOPMENT EDITOR
Tony Amico

MANAGING EDITOR
Lisa Wilson

PROJECT EDITOR
Paul Schneider

COPY EDITOR
Mike Henry

INDEXER
Aamir Burki

PROOFREADERS
Jill Mazurczyk
Mona Brown

TECHNICAL EDITOR
Tim O'Brien

TEAM COORDINATOR
Karen Opal

MEDIA DEVELOPER
Jason Haines

COVER/INTERIOR DESIGNER
Anne Jones

COPYWRITER
Eric Borgert

EDITORIAL ASSISTANT
Angela Boley

PRODUCTION
Angela Calvert
Tim Osborne
Gloria Schurick
Mark Walchle

Overview

Contents

About the Author

Rich Blum has worked for the past 11 years as a network and systems administrator for the U.S. Department of Defense at the Defense Finance and Accounting Service. He has been using the Linux operating system since 1993 as an FTP server, TFTP server, email server, mail list server, and network monitoring device in a large networking environment. Rich currently serves on the board of directors for Traders Point Christian Schools, and is active on the computer support team at the school, supporting a Microsoft Windows NT network in the computer lab and classrooms in a small K-8 school. Rich has a Bachelors of Science degree in Electrical Engineering, and a Masters of Science in Management, specializing in Management Information Systems, both from Purdue University. When Rich is not being a computer nerd he is either playing electric bass for the church worship band, or spending time with his wife Barbara and two daughters Katie and Jessica.

Dedication

This book is dedicated to the memory of my mom, Joyce Blum, who always enjoyed reading, and always encouraged expanding one's mind through reading. "We believe that Jesus died and rose again, and so we believe that God will bring with Jesus those who have fallen asleep in him." I Thes. 4:14 (NIV)

Acknowledgments

First, all glory, honor, and praise go to God, who through His Son all things are possible, and gave us the gift of eternal life.

I would like to thank all of the great people at Macmillan for their help, support, and professionalism. Thanks to Neil Rowe, the acquisitions editor, for offering me the opportunity to write this book. Also thanks to the copy editors, Rhonda, Mary Ellen, and Mike, for their excellent work at correcting my grammatical mistakes. The technical editors of this book, Tim O'Brien and Jim Westveer, did an excellent job of pointing out my technical goofs and setting me straight. And Laura Robbins, the interior designer, did an excellent job of turning my scribbles into great pictures. The development editor, Tony Amico, gets an extra special acknowledgment. Thanks Tony for your help, support, guidance, and mentoring (both for the book and apart from it). This book would not have been possible without it.

I would also like to thank my family. My parents, Mike and Joyce Blum for the dedication and support necessary to raise children (especially me), my wife Barbara for her love, faith, and constant support, and my daughters Katie and Jessica for their love and understanding while I pined away on this book instead of playing.

And finally, I would like to thank Sister Marie Imelda, C.S.C., who back in the late 70's thought that this microcomputer craze might just catch on, and fought and struggled to teach a bunch of goofy high school kids how to program. Thanks Sister.

Tell Us What You Think!

As the reader of this book, *you* are our most important critic and commentator. We value your opinion and want to know what we're doing right, what we could do better, what areas you'd like to see us publish in, and any other words of wisdom you're willing to pass our way.

You can fax, email, or write me directly to let me know what you did or didn't like about this book—as well as what we can do to make our books stronger.

Please note that I cannot help you with technical problems related to the topic of this book, and that due to the high volume of mail I receive, I might not be able to reply to every message.

When you write, please be sure to include this book's title and author as well as your name and phone or fax number. I will carefully review your comments and share them with the author and editors who worked on the book.

Fax: 317-581-4770

Email: opsys_sams@macmillanusa.com

Mail: Mark Taber
                  Associate Publisher
                  Sams Publishing
                  201 West 103rd Street
                  Indianapolis, IN 46290 USA

Introduction

In just a few years, Internet email has gone from being a novelty to almost a necessity. Corporations spend thousands of dollars a year to implement email systems to help them communicate better both internally and externally with their customers. Email systems have changed the flow of communications in many corporations. The days of the corporate paper memo are almost over.

The next wave of the email explosion has been in the home. Many different methods are available now for home users to gain access to an Internet email account. Internet service providers (ISPs) offer many attractive packages for providing email accounts to individuals (even one for every member in the family). Also, a growing number of companies offer free email services to individuals, as long as they don't mind seeing commercials downloaded across their email systems. These days it is not uncommon to meet someone with several different personal email accounts.

Although large corporations have the resources to implement intricate email systems, many small organizations do not. There seems to be a middle ground: organizations too small to purchase large commercial email systems, but too large to implement individual ISP accounts for all their employees. This middle ground often includes nonprofit organizations, such as schools, churches, clubs, and associations. These organizations usually do not have large IS departments to implement full-scale commercial email systems.

The main purpose of this book is to help the network administrator of a small organization use tools currently available for free to implement a commercial-quality email system. If you also want to connect your email system to the Internet, details are provided regarding what you need to know to talk about email with your local ISPs. After talking with the ISPs, you can decide which ISP can connect your office Linux email system to the Internet for the best price.

Another purpose of this book is educational. Often network administrators in smaller organizations do not have the time or money to get formal training on email systems. Knowledge of the protocols used in Internet email systems is vital to properly troubleshoot email problems. Most of the commonly used protocols necessary for Internet email to operate are discussed in detail in this book. This information can be used either as training material or as reference material (or both).

The final purpose of this book is to help take some of the complication out of the sendmail program. Although many other email programs are available for the Linux environment, the sendmail program is still one of the most versatile. Many nice features are available in the sendmail program that other programs don't have. Although several very in-depth books have been written about sendmail, often it is just a matter of setting a few configuration variables to properly configure the sendmail program for a small environment. This book explains the configuration file for those readers who want to attempt in-depth changes to the sendmail program, but it also explains the bare minimum configurations needed to connect an office Linux mailserver to an ISP to provide Internet mail service to an organization.

This book uses examples for setting up a Linux mailserver for a fictitious organization. At the time of this writing, the example domain name chosen—smallorg.org—is not registered with the Internet Corporation for Assigned Names and Numbers (ICANN). If, by chance, smallorg.org is registered at the time you read this, there is no association between this book and the owner of the registered domain name. Also, all IP addresses used in this book are for example only. Where possible, public IP addresses are used and should be replaced with the IP addresses assigned to your particular organization. When that is not possible, fictitious IP addresses have been selected and are not associated with any existing IP networks. Please consult your Internet service provider before assigning IP addresses to your Linux mailserver.

I was trying to keep the focus of the book on office networks. Although many of the sendmail concepts apply to larger corporations and ISP networks, I didn't want this book to become a reference guide for ISPs. It comes close though. The chapters were written with the small office mail administrator in mind. The chapters are broken down into the following topics:

Chapters 1, "Email Principles and Services," and 2, "Using Linux As a Mailserver," present a short history and explanation of email and the role of Linux as a mailserver in a corporate email environment.

Chapter 3, "Installing Communication Devices in Linux," discusses the basic concepts of the hardware necessary for a Linux mailserver to connect to a network and to an ISP if necessary. Modems and Network Interface Cards (NICs) are items often overlooked by mail administrators, but they are nonetheless important for the mailserver.

Chapters 4, "DNS and Domain Names," through 9, "UUCP Protocol," present most of the protocols used on a mailserver. Chapter 4 deals with the topic of the Domain Name System and how to configure the Linux mailserver to use domain names and, if necessary, how to be a DNS server.

Chapter 5, "SMTP Protocol," discusses the Simple Mail Transport Protocol (SMTP), which is the backbone of the mail protocols. A basic understanding of this protocol is often helpful in troubleshooting email problems.

Chapter 6, "POP3 Protocol," describes the Post Office Protocol (POP3) used by network clients to retrieve mail messages from the Linux mailserver. This is an important protocol that, when understood, can save many hours of troubleshooting.

Chapter 7, "IMAP Protocol," presents the Interactive Mail Access Protocol (IMAP), another protocol used by network clients to access mail messages on the Linux mailserver.

Chapter 8, "PPP Protocol," discusses the Point-to-Point Protocol (PPP) used to establish a serial IP connection using the modem on the Linux mailserver. Also described are the Linux programs and utilities used to establish a PPP connection with an ISP.

Chapter 9 describes the older Unix-to-Unix Copy Protocol (UUCP). Although UUCP is an older protocol, it has become more popular in smaller networks that need only limited access to the Internet or require a more secure network connection.

Chapters 10, "The sendmail Program," and 11, "Installing and Configuring sendmail," discuss the sendmail program, its configuration, and how to use it to implement a fully functional Linux mailserver.

Chapter 12, "Installing and Configuring POP3 and IMAP," describes how to use the POP3 and IMAP programs to support network clients on the Linux mailserver.

Chapter 13, "Connecting the Mailserver to an ISP," walks office network administrators through the different scenarios involved in setting up a mailserver with an ISP.

Chapter 14, "Mailserver Administration," presents Linux topics that are required for a mail administrator to properly administer the Linux server. Items such as userid and password maintenance and log file monitoring are discussed.

Chapter 15, "Configuring LAN Clients," changes focus a little to the client workstations. Software that allows network clients to access mailboxes on the Linux mailserver is presented and described.

Chapter 16, "Supporting Dial-In Clients," discusses how to support mail users who want to dial in to the Linux mailserver from a remote location.

Chapter 17, "Mail Aliases and Masquerading," covers the specialized topics of using mail aliases and masquerading mailservers. The standard sendmail `alias.db` and `virtusertable.db` files are discussed and explained. The chapter addresses them from the point-of-view of a small organization setting up several mail spokes that funnel mail through a single corporate mail server, and how to set up the `virtusertable` on the corporate hub to handle the spokes.

Chapter 18, "Mail Lists," introduces the mail administrator to the concept of mail lists, and how to create and support them on the Linux mailserver.

Finally, Chapter 19, "IP Routing with Linux," goes a little off the mailserver path by describing how to use the Linux mailserver as a full-feature IP router, firewall, and gateway. If the Linux mailserver is on a dedicated connection to the Internet, it can also be used as the network router.

I don't argue that I don't cover every aspect of the sendmail configuration; that was not the point of this book. As I mentioned earlier, many excellent books just covering sendmail have been written. The point of this book is to help a small network administrator get just enough of the basics of sendmail—with a few examples—to get a mailserver running without getting a doctorate degree in sendmail.

Conventions Used in This Book

As you read through this book, you will notice some features that might not be recognizable. Typeface conventions are the first of these features.

- Anything that might be considered code, such as listings, appears in a `monospace` font.

  In listings, the code you type in (input) appears in **`boldface monospace`** and the output appears in standard `monospace` without bold.

- Many code-related terms within the text also appear in a `monospace` font.

- Placeholders in code appear in *`italic monospace`*.

- When a line of code is too long to fit on one line of this book, it is broken at a convenient place and continued to the next line. A code continuation character (➡) precedes the continuation of a line of code. (You should type a line of code that has this character as one long line without breaking it.)

- In many cases, a listing line is preceded by a line number. This number enables me to refer to individual lines as I discuss the text. If you are typing the code lines or snippets, you shouldn't enter that number.

A second design feature is used to enhance the text material by providing a somewhat independent flow. These short topics are subsidiary information and consist of

- Notes
- Tips
- Cautions

NOTE

Notes explain interesting or important points that can help you understand the concepts and techniques being discussed—perhaps other ways of viewing the same concept.

TIP

Tips are little pieces of information that help you in real-world situations. Tips often offer shortcuts or information to make a task easier or faster.

CAUTION

Cautions provide information about detrimental performance issues or dangerous errors. Pay careful attention to Cautions.

The last design element I employ are figures that I use to visually depict a complicated relationship between components or a complicated flow of processing. In these figures, I have standardized some visual elements. These elements consist of machines (computers, nodes), processes (programs), and files (folders). Within a machine, I might have multiple processes connected through functions and multiple files accessed by these programs. In fact, a machine might even consist of interrelated physical machines that appear as a single computer externally, such as a cluster. A machine icon will appear in figures as a box, similar to Figure IN.1.

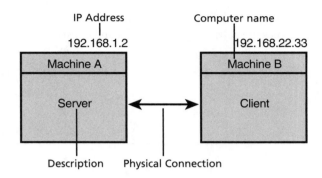

FIGURE IN.1

Any machine or computer.

In this figure, the name of the node appears in the title line, and its address, if applicable, appears outside the box—much like your home mailbox.

A process, depicted in Figure IN.2, has a similar appearance except that the corners are rounded. It, might contain subprocesses.

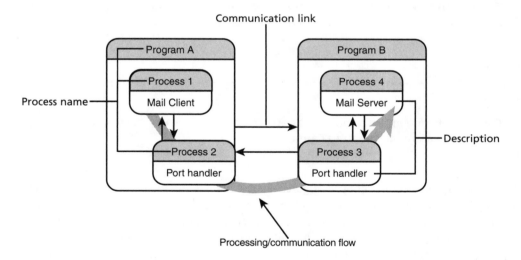

FIGURE IN.2

Any process that has no subprocesses communicating with one that does.

A file or folder looks like the elements in Figure IN.3. The concepts are almost synonymous, but the idea of a folder is just a little different. A folder brings to mind a collection of dissimilar files.

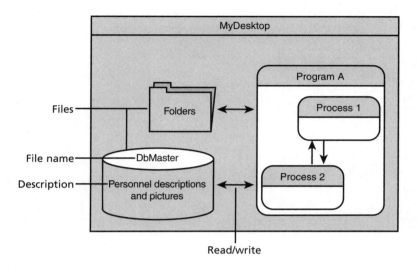

FIGURE IN.3
A file and a folder.

Introduction to Email Services and Linux

IN THIS PART

Email Principles and Services

IN THIS CHAPTER

Email systems have seen many changes over the past dozen years. From the days of sending simple text messages to the console of another user on the mainframe to sending pictures to your friends across the Internet, email systems have come a long way. To accomplish these new email tasks, many protocols had to be invented and implemented to pass both text and binary information from one person to another. Many of these protocol changes were the direct result of the rapid growth of the Internet. Just a few years ago, it was not too important for a user to need access to an Internet service provider (ISP). Now the Point-to-Point and Post Office Protocols (PPP and POP3) are mainstays of the Internet. As more people became connected, requirements for email changed. In the past, mail systems were just a small subsystem on the mainframe, taking a backseat to corporate applications. Now many ISPs devote entire systems just to service their email customers.

This chapter starts by explaining some basic history of email systems. It also explains some basic terminology used in Internet email systems to help you follow the discussions in the following chapters.

Mainframe Email Systems

Email systems themselves have been around for a long time. In the old days (the 1970s), many mainframe manufacturers implemented programs that enabled mainframe users to send messages to other users who were logged on to the same system. The message would appear on the console of the logged-on user. This system, although crude, was the beginning of the email messaging system.

The next logical step was to enable a user to send a message to another user who was not currently logged in to the system. An intricate system was devised to enable each user to have a special area, called a *mailbox,* on the mainframe. To send a message to another user, a user had to run a special mail program that enabled him to put a message in another user's mailbox. The other user could then run the mail program to check what messages were in his mailbox. Figure 1.1 shows how this system looked on the mainframe.

There were many limitations with this system. First, you could send messages only to other users on the same mainframe system. Mainframes had no means to communicate with each other. Second, messages sent could only be text messages. No binary files could be sent to another user on the mainframe.

Multi-Mainframe Email Systems

As mainframes matured, so did their communication systems. It wasn't long before mainframes could pass data between themselves on complicated communication networks. This allowed email systems to communicate between mainframes. Now a user on one mainframe could send a message to another user on a different mainframe. Figure 1.2 shows an example of this.

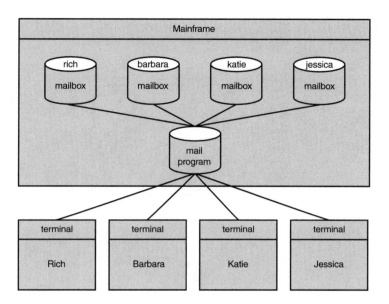

FIGURE 1.1
A mainframe email system.

With mainframe communications systems, the email program that users operated became more complicated. If a user needed to send a message to another user on a remote mainframe, the email program had to recognize this and forward the message to the mailbox of the appropriate user on the appropriate remote mainframe. Mainframe names became important, in that no two mainframes could use the same name on the same mainframe network.

Early UNIX Email Systems

In the 1980s, the UNIX operating system developed at AT&T Bell Labs was gaining popularity in the university environment. Dubbed *minicomputers*, these machines were smaller than mainframes, but had the computing power to perform complex scientific and mathematical research that university professors and students required. Still operating on mainframe principles, the UNIX system required users to log in to the system from a dumb terminal connected to the minicomputer.

The UNIX operating system changed the way software was designed and developed. Instead of large monolithic programs that performed all functions, smaller specialized programs were written that performed individual functions more efficiently. This changed the face of email systems. The email functions were now broken into different programs that performed individualized functions. Those individualized functions could then be separated from the programs, and new programs created to perform the same functions. This section describes the functions of an email system and some of the programs used to implement them.

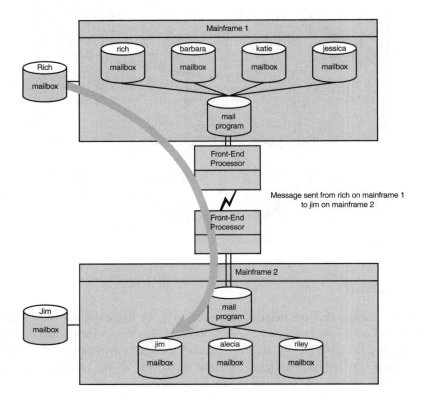

FIGURE 1.2
Mainframe email communication systems.

Mail User Agent

The UNIX email model used a local mailbox for each user to hold messages for that user. Programs became available that could interface with the mailbox format. Those programs were called Mail User Agents (MUAs). The MUAs did not receive messages from remote computers; they only displayed messages that were already placed in the user's mailbox. Throughout the years, many different MUAs have been available for the UNIX platform. The Linux operating system has borrowed many of the programs and methods used by standard UNIX systems. MUAs are no exception. All the MUA programs in the following sections are available on the Linux platform.

The mail Program

The simplest MUA available on the Linux platform is the mail program (not too original a name). The mail program uses a command-line interface to interact with the user. Commands to manipulate messages are entered at the command prompt. Listing 1.1 shows a sample mail session.

LISTING 1.1   Sample mail Program Session

```
1  [jessica@shadrach jessica]$ mail
2  Mail version 8.1 6/6/93.  Type ? for help.
3  "/var/spool/mail/jessica": 1 message 1 new
4  >N 1 rich@shadrach.smallo Sun Dec 12 17:38 13/485 "This is a test message"
5  & 1
6  Message 1:
7  From rich@shadrach.smallorg.org Sun Dec 12 17:38:09 1999
8  Received: (from rich@localhost)
9          by shadrach.smallorg.org (8.9.1a/8.9.1) id RAA00648
10         for jessica; Sun, 12 Dec 1999 17:38:08 -0500
11 Date: Sun, 12 Dec 1999 17:38:08 -0500
12 From: Rich <rich@shadrach.smallorg.org>
13 Message-Id: <199912122238.RAA00648@shadrach.smallorg.org>
14 To: jessica@shadrach.smallorg.org
15 Subject: This is a test message
16 Status: R
17
18 This is the first test message
19 This is the end of the first test message
20
21 & d
22 & q
23[jessica@shadrach jessica]$
```

Line 1 shows the email user jessica entering the mail program on the command line. Lines 2 through 4 show the mail program greeting. Line 2 displays the version of mail that is running. Line 3 displays the location of the user's home mailbox. By default, the home mailbox should be located at

```
/var/spool/mail/username
```

where username is the username of the user. Line 4 is a synopsis of the messages in the user's mailbox. This shows that one message is available to be read. Line 5 shows the command prompt the mail program uses to enable the user to input new queries. If the user types a **1**, the mail program displays the contents of the first mail message in the user's mailbox.

Lines 6 through 20 display the first mail message in its entirety. Lines 7 through 16 identify the message header. The message header is a standard format that is used to identify information regarding the source and destination of the mail message. This header information is often useful when trying to troubleshoot email problems.

Lines 8 through 10 show the `Received` by header field information. Each node that the message traverses to get from the sender to the recipient adds a `Received` by header field. This is one method to use to track messages. For example, in one instance, mail messages were taking more than an hour to get from one host to another. By examining the `Received` by header fields of the received message, it was determined that one particular host along the relay path was queuing messages and not delivering them for approximately 55 minutes. After this information was determined, the offending host administrator was contacted and the problem was resolved. This problem was solved by observing the date and time parts of the `Received` by field.

Lines 18 and 19 are the message body. Much like the mainframe email systems, UNIX email systems allow only text mail messages. However, to compensate for this, UNIX systems provide a method to convert binary files to ASCII text files for email purposes, and then to convert the ASCII text file back into the binary file.

The pine Program

The beginning of the graphical revolution brought programs that could utilize terminal screen graphics to display information. The pine program is one program available to read a user's mailbox that graphically displays the messages on the console screen. Figure 1.3 shows a sample pine session screen.

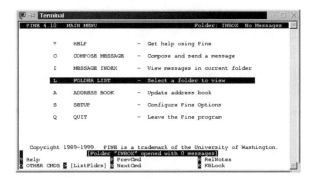

FIGURE 1.3
The UNIX pine program.

The pine program lists all the messages available in the user's INBOX folder, which is the location where new mail messages are stored for the user. Additional folders can be created to enable the user to store and manipulate messages based on content.

X Window Programs

Almost all Linux distributions support the graphical X Window environment. This allows fancier graphical programs to run on either the Linux server console or remotely from an X Window workstation on the network. The Netscape Communicator program includes an email system that enables the user to read messages from his mailbox and send messages through the Linux server. Figure 1.4 shows the mail screen from the Netscape mail program.

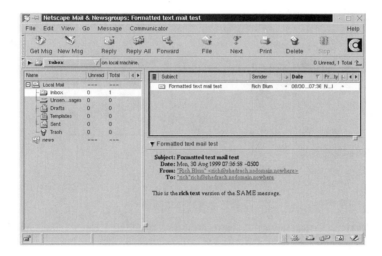

FIGURE 1.4
The Netscape mail program main screen.

Mail Transfer Agent

With the MUA responsible for displaying only the email messages already in the user's mailbox, a new type of program was needed whose job was to get the messages to the mailbox. The Mail Transfer Agent (MTA) was created to accomplish just that job. MTAs are responsible for sending messages from one user to another user. Those users can be on the same system or they can be on remote systems. The MTA is responsible for routing the mail message to the remote system through any means possible. Often there can be several email systems between the sending host and the destination host. Figure 1.5 shows an example of how MTAs communicate to transfer a message.

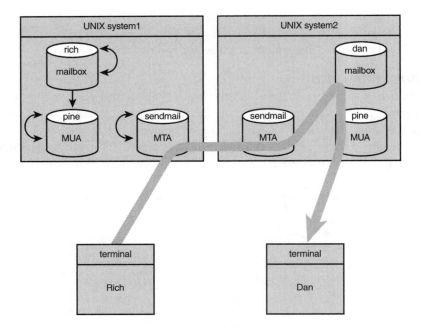

FIGURE 1.5
Using MTAs to route a message to its destination.

If the MTA cannot find a direct path to the destination MTA, it must attempt to determine the next best place to send the message or return an undeliverable message. Each MTA along a path must take responsibility for passing the message along to the final destination or it must return an undeliverable message to the originating sender.

The Linux operating system has several different MTA programs available. Each has features that make it different from the rest. This section identifies a few of the more commonly used MTA programs available.

The sendmail Program

The sendmail program is the most popular MTA program available for the Linux platform. It is maintained by the sendmail Consortium (http://www.sendmail.org), as well as being supported by the sendmail, Inc. corporation.

The sendmail program is the most robust and versatile MTA program available. Because of its versatility, it is also one of the most complicated to configure. sendmail gets its configuration settings from a standard configuration file. It is not uncommon for this file to be a few hundred lines in length. Within the configuration file are parameters that control how sendmail handles incoming messages and routes outgoing messages.

Incoming messages are run through a complicated series of rules that can be used to filter messages from the system. The rules used for filtering are also stored in the configuration file (hence the large file size). Messages can be checked for header content and handled according to either the source or destination information available. Outgoing messages must be routed to the proper location for delivery. sendmail must be configured according to the method used to connect the mailserver to the Internet. Often a Linux mailserver for a small office is configured to pass all outgoing messages to the ISP, which can then relay the messages to their proper destinations. This method is called using a "smart host."

The purpose of this book is to take some of the complication out of the sendmail program. There are many nice features available in the sendmail program. Although several very in-depth books have been written about sendmail, often it is just a matter of setting a few configuration variables to properly configure the sendmail program for a small environment. This book explains the configuration file for those readers who want to attempt in-depth changes to the sendmail program, but it will also explain the bare minimum configurations needed to connect an office Linux mailserver to an ISP to provide Internet mail service to an organization.

The smail Program

The smail program is another popular MTA program available for the Linux platform. It is maintained by the GNU Project (http://www.gnu.org). The GNU Project is a major software contributor to Linux, and will be discussed more in detail in Chapter 2, "Using Linux As a Mail Server."

The smail program uses many of the same features as the sendmail program, but is much easier to configure. A standard smail configuration file requires fewer than 20 lines of configuration code, which is many fewer than sendmail requires.

One of the nice features of smail is its ability to forward mail messages without using mail queues. The sendmail program places all messages in a queue file to queue them for delivery. For low-volume mailservers, queuing becomes an unnecessary delay. The smail program attempts to deliver the message immediately without placing the messages in a queue. This works great for low-volume mailservers, but unfortunately, this method can get bogged-down in high-volume mailservers. To compensate, the smail program is configurable to use mail queues such as sendmail to handle large volumes of mail.

The qmail Program

The qmail program is another MTA program available for Linux. Dan Bernstein (http://www.qmail.org) maintains it. It is reported to be the most secure email package available on the Linux platform. To support its high level of security, qmail uses several userids and groups that must be configured on the Linux system. Each userid is used as the owner of a restricted area on the Linux server. This enables qmail to restrict access to the mail messages from outside intruders, while allowing access by a user to his mailbox.

Another nice feature of qmail is the method it uses to store messages. Both sendmail and smail use the standard ASCII text method of storing messages in both mail queues and mailboxes. The qmail program uses a nonstandard method of writing messages to the queues and mailboxes. This method allows for greater recovery in case of a system crash. Often, if the Linux system crashes when a message is being either retrieved or stored, the message (and sometimes the mailbox) can become corrupt and unreadable. The qmail program has improved the chances of maintaining the integrity of the mail message.

The exim Program

The University of Cambridge (`http://www.exim.org`) maintains the exim program. exim has recently gained popularity because of its ability to be easily configured to restrict hackers and spammers. *Hackers* are people who attempt to break into sites using well-known security holes in software. *Spammers* are people who send out mass quantities of (usually) unwanted emails, mostly for advertisement purposes.

The exim program contains several configuration files that can contain addresses of known hackers and spammers to restrict any messages from those sites to the mailserver. After a hacker or spammer has been identified, his address can be added to the configuration files to prevent any more messages from that address from being received.

LAN-Based Email Systems

In the late 1980s, the computer world was again dramatically changed with the invention of the personal computer. PCs started popping up in corporations, replacing the dumb terminals that were used to communicate with mainframes and minicomputers.

Many organizations utilize some type of Large Area Network (LAN) -based network server that allows network workstations to share disk space on the network fileserver. This has created a new type of email server that utilizes the shared network disk space.

Modern email packages, such as Microsoft Exchange, Novell GroupWise, and IBM Lotus Notes, utilize programs that access a common disk area to contain the user mailboxes. The mailboxes are often contained within a single database. To access the database, the MUA programs running on the workstations must be able to read and parse the mailbox database. This method almost always uses a proprietary protocol to access the mailboxes in the database.

The MTA programs often become quite complicated in this environment. Because the email systems use special databases, the method of sending messages to remote systems depends on what the remote system is. If the remote system is the same email system as the sending system, the same proprietary protocol can be used to transfer the message. If the remote system is a different type of email system, the MTA must be able to convert the message to a standard format and use a standard email protocol (discussed later) to send the message. Figure 1.6 shows an example of a proprietary email system on a network.

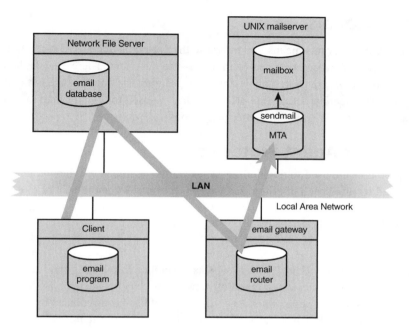

FIGURE 1.6

A LAN-based proprietary email system.

Often with LAN-based email systems, separate workstations are required to route messages between destinations. This increases the chance of failure because additional hardware and software besides the email server are now involved in the email transfer.

Another possible problem with proprietary email systems is the mail database. Because all messages are stored in one database, the database increases in proportion to the number of messages saved on the system. It is not uncommon to see databases of more than 1GB in size for a small organization. Often in this situation, the database becomes corrupt and a database recovery routine must be run. If the routine is unsuccessful, all the messages in the database are lost. UNIX-based systems keep individual mailboxes for each user. If one mailbox becomes corrupt, only one user loses her messages, but the rest of the users are unaffected.

Proprietary LAN-based email systems are very popular, but they tend to be very expensive. As the mail administrator, you should weigh all the pros and cons involved with purchasing a proprietary email system. Often the same functionality can be obtained by using the Linux mailserver with open source programs.

Email Protocols

Using open source programs means you must use the protocols that are required to transfer mail messages both between hosts and from the host to the client. There are standard protocols used by open source programs that allow any open program to communicate with any other open program. This section defines the protocols that are used to transfer mail messages. Each protocol is discussed in greater detail later in the book.

Mail Transfer Agent Protocols

The MTA protocols are used to transfer messages from one email host to another. Each protocol can be used by any host, either to initiate a connection to a remote host or to accept a connection from a remote host. This section describes the two most popular MTA protocols available for the Linux platform.

UUCP

The UNIX-to-UNIX-CoPy (UUCP) protocol was developed in the early days of the UNIX operating system. It was used as a method of transferring data between UNIX hosts using low-cost modems and standard phone lines. Over the years, it has been replaced by other protocols that utilize high-bandwidth LAN and WAN connections to transfer data.

With the popularity of Internet service providers utilizing UNIX systems to support dial-in customers, UUCP has made a small comeback. It is possible to connect a remote office to an ISP by using a low-cost UUCP connection for Internet email applications. For small offices looking for inexpensive email, this could be the answer. Figure 1.7 shows a sample UUCP network configuration.

The UUCP protocol is supported on Linux by using the Taylor uucp program. The uucp program uses configuration files to identify remote hosts to connect to for transferring mail messages. The ISP UUCP host can be identified in the sendmail program as the smart host, so all outbound mail messages from the Linux mailserver will be forwarded via UUCP to the ISP. Chapter 9, "UUCP Protocol," discusses this process in detail.

SMTP

The Simple Mail Transfer Protocol (SMTP) was developed as a protocol for hosts to transfer mail messages using the Internet. By using a common protocol, any type of host can connect to and transfer mail to any other type of host across the Internet. The power of the SMTP protocol is its simple command structure (that's why they called it *simple*). It is easy for software developers to create an MTA program that communicates with other hosts using SMTP. Standard SMTP commands solicit standard SMTP replies. All the MTA program must do is observe the reply codes to determine whether a mail transfer was successful. Figure 1.8 shows an example of an SMTP connection.

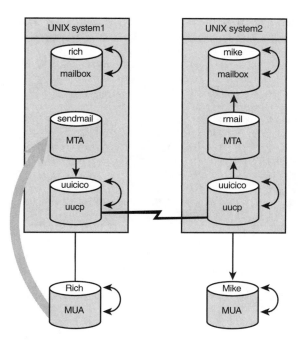

FIGURE 1.7

A sample UUCP connection.

The SMTP protocol uses hostnames to identify hosts for email purposes. With the large quantity of hosts available on the Internet, a method of uniquely identifying each host became necessary. The Domain Name System (DNS) was developed to create domains (or zones) that can be controlled by a nameserver. It is the responsibility of the nameserver to maintain a database mapping the hostnames in the domain to the actual IP addresses. A host can determine the IP address for another host by using the DNS protocol to connect to the proper nameserver for the remote domain. A hierarchy was developed to help hosts find the proper DNS host responsible for a particular domain.

The SMTP protocol also requires an IP connection to connect to remote hosts. With hosts directly connected to the Internet this is not a problem. The typical small office network is not directly connected to the Internet. This becomes a problem.

To solve this problem, ISPs offer a method to connect the office mailserver to the Internet for short periods of time to transfer mail messages. The Point-to-Point Protocol (PPP) is used to connect the Linux mailserver to the Internet via a standard modem on a standard phone line. After a PPP session is established, IP packets can be transferred between the Linux mailserver and the Internet. The SMTP protocol can then be used to transfer any mail messages that have accumulated in the mail queues, both outgoing from the Linux mailserver and incoming from the ISP. Chapter 5, "SMTP Protocol," discusses this in more detail. Figure 1.9 shows an example of this.

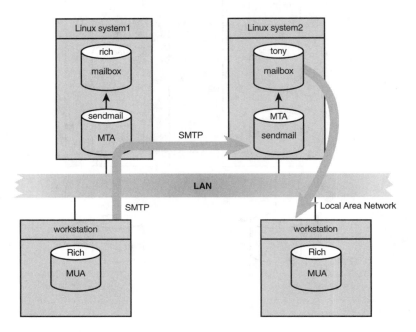

FIGURE 1.8
A sample SMTP connection.

Mail User Agent Protocols

When the mail user is on the Linux mailserver's console, the standard MUA programs listed earlier can directly access the mailbox to retrieve mail messages. However, in a small office environment it would be impractical for each user to log in to the Linux server console to read mail messages. To compensate for this, two different MUA protocols have been developed to enable a remote client to access his mailbox on a Linux server. This section describes those protocols.

POP3

The simplest MUA protocol is the Post Office Protocol (POP). Currently the POP protocol is in its third version, thus the name POP*3*. The POP3 protocol allows a remote network client to retrieve messages from a mailbox on a Linux mailserver. Each message must be downloaded to the client workstation to be read. Often the message is deleted from the mailbox when it is download to the workstation. This presents a problem for clients that connect to the mailserver from two or more workstations. The messages are downloaded to the workstation that the user used to connect at that particular moment. This results in messages being scattered among different workstations. Chapter 6, "POP3 Protocol," discusses this protocol in detail. Figure 1.10 shows an example of a client using the POP3 protocol.

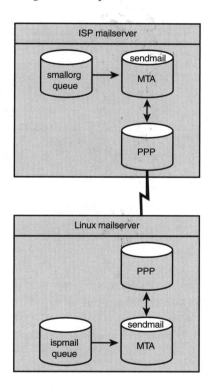

FIGURE 1.9

A sample PPP connection to the Internet.

IMAP

To solve the problem that POP3 causes by scattering mail messages, the Interactive Mail Access Protocol (IMAP) was developed. IMAP allows the client to create folders on the mailserver, and to place messages in those folders for storage. A session can be created to an IMAP server from any workstation and access the same folders and mailboxes. The messages are downloaded to the workstation only for display purposes. The messages are kept on the mailserver in the folder in which they were placed.

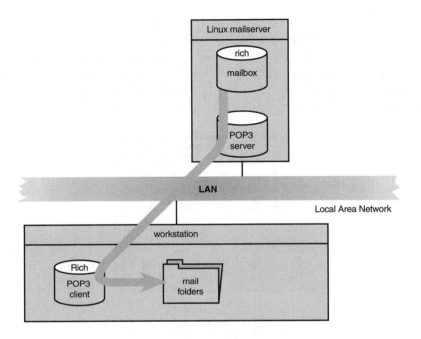

FIGURE 1.10
A sample POP3 session.

Keeping messages on the mailserver does present a problem to the mail administrator in that disk space on the mailserver can quickly fill up. It is up to the mail administrator to implement a policy to manage disk space for the server. Chapter 7, "IMAP Protocol," describes the IMAP process in more detail. Figure 1.11 shows an example of a client using the IMAP protocol to retrieve mail messages.

Summary

This chapter discusses the history and theory behind using email in the office environment. Email began as simply allowing users on the same mainframe system to send messages to one another. As mainframes began communicating with other mainframes, email grew to be a solution for communicating with remote users. The UNIX environment included email support from the start. UNIX email systems are divided into two types of programs: Mail Transfer Agents (MTAs) and Mail User Agents (MUAs). MTAs are responsible for delivering a message to another user, either locally on the same UNIX machine or remotely to another UNIX machine. The MUA programs are responsible for allowing a remote client to access his mailbox on a mailserver via the network. LAN-based email systems rely on shared disk space on network fileservers. These systems use a proprietary protocol to store messages in a large database of mailboxes on the system. Often, external devices are required to route messages from the database to another host on the network. As open systems matured, open network protocols were developed to create a standard method for transferring information across the Internet. The UUCP and SMTP protocols were developed to help MTAs transfer messages in a standard method to remote hosts. Clients can use MUA software that utilizes the standard POP3 and IMAP protocols to retrieve messages from the mailserver.

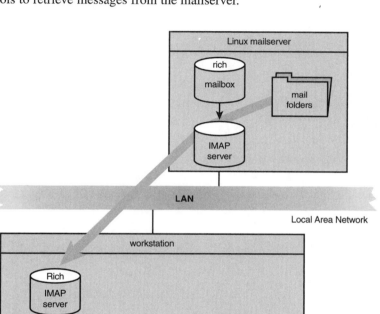

FIGURE 1.11

A sample IMAP session.

Using Linux As a Mailserver

IN THIS CHAPTER

With the widespread use of Linux, many system administrators are experimenting with various Linux configurations for various purposes. Although many system administrators use Linux to replace Microsoft Windows operating systems at the desktop, the real power of Linux is in performing server functions.

To use a Linux server as a mailserver, you must first have a basic understanding of the Linux operating system. The Linux operating system has been in development for several years, with many new features added at every new release. This chapter is not intended to teach the Linux operating system. This chapter describes some of the features of the Linux operating system so that a system administrator with some familiarity with the Linux operating system will be able to configure the necessary software to create a mailserver.

The term *Linux operating system* is somewhat of a misnomer. Many pieces and parts make up the standard Linux operating system. At the heart of the operating system is the kernel. Linus Torvalds is credited with creating and maintaining the Linux kernel. The kernel, by itself, is not very useful. For the operating system to do anything exciting, there must be application programs and a way to run them. Fortunately for Linus, the GNU Project was already in action.

The goal of GNU, which stands for GNU's Not UNIX, was to create an open UNIX environment without the problems of the current UNIX licensing wars. It turned out that the GNU Project had source code for lots of UNIX utilities laying about, but no operating system kernel on which to implement them (the GNU Project is working on its version of a UNIX kernel, hurd). Linus, on the other hand, had a UNIX-like kernel without many UNIX utilities to use. The combination of the two forces created the Linux operating system. By combining the Linux kernel with the GNU UNIX utilities, a fully functional UNIX-like operating system was born. The following sections describe the details involved in the Linux kernel, some of the major GNU Project UNIX utilities, and the companies attempting to combine the pieces into what are called Linux distributions.

The Linux Kernel

The operating system kernel is the core of the system. The kernel must control the hardware and software on the system, allocating hardware when necessary, and executing software when required. The Linux kernel takes most of its functionality from the UNIX world. Linus Torvalds states that his work on the Linux kernel was a result of his studying the MINIX operating system, which itself was an attempt by Andrew Tanenbaum to reproduce the UNIX operating system on an IBM-compatible PC.

The UNIX kernel comprises functions to control the various hardware and software elements within the computer system. The kernel is primarily responsible for system memory management, software program management, hardware management, and filesystem management. The following sections describe each of these functions in more detail.

Memory Management

One of the primary functions of the operating system kernel is memory management. Not only does the kernel manage the physical memory available on the PC, but it can also create and manage *virtual memory*, or memory that does not actually exist. The kernel does this by using space on the hard disk (called the *swap space*) and swapping memory locations back and forth from the hard disk to the actual physical memory. This allows the system to think there is more memory available than what physically exists. The memory locations are grouped into blocks called *pages*. Each page of memory is located in either the physical memory or the swap space. The kernel must maintain a table of the memory pages that indicates which page is where.

The kernel copies memory pages that have not been accessed for a period of time to the swap space area on the hard disk. When a program wants to access a memory page that has been swapped out, the kernel must swap out a different memory page and swap in the required page from the swap space.

To use virtual memory, you must create a swap space on the hard disk. This is often done during system installation. The `fdisk` command is used to partition the installed hard drive on the system. The format of the `fdisk` command is

```
fdisk [option] [device]
```

where `device` is the hard disk device being partitioned. Linux uses a naming standard for hard disk devices. Table 2.1 shows the Linux hard disk naming standard.

TABLE 2.1   Linux Hard Disk Devices

Device	Description
`/dev/hd[a-h]`	IDE disk drives
`/dev/sd[a-p]`	SCSI disk drives
`/dev/ed[a--d]`	ESDI disk drives
`/dev/xd[ab]`	XT disk drives

The first available drive of a particular type is labeled as drive a, the second one drive b, and so on. Within a particular drive, partitions are numbered starting at partition 1. Listing 2.1 shows a sample partition from a Linux system.

LISTING 2.1   Sample `fdisk` Partition Listing

```
1  [root@shadrach root]# /sbin/fdisk /dev/sda
2
3  Command (m for help): p
4
5  Disk /dev/sda: 64 heads, 32 sectors, 521 cylinders
6  Units = cylinders of 2048 * 512 bytes
7
8     Device Boot    Start      End    Blocks   Id  System
9  /dev/sda1             1      460    471024   83  Linux native
10 /dev/sda2           461      521     62464    5  Extended
11 /dev/sda5           461      521     62448   82  Linux swap
12
13 Command (m for help): q
14 [root@shadrach root]#
```

Line 1 shows the `fdisk` command being run on the first SCSI disk on the Linux system: `/dev/sda`. The fdisk program is an interactive program that enables the system administrator to manipulate the partition table on the disk drive. Line 3 shows the command used to print the current partition table. Lines 5 through 11 show the information from the disk partition table. Line 11 shows the partition available on the hard drive for the Linux swap area.

After a swap area has been created on a hard drive, the Linux kernel must know that the swap area is available and activate it. The swapon program is used to activate memory page swapping. The `swapon` command sets up the virtual memory information in the kernel. This information is lost when the Linux server is rebooted. This means that the `swapon` command must be executed at every boot. Most Linux distributions allow the `swapon` command to be run from a startup script when the system boots.

The current status of the Linux virtual memory can be determined by viewing the special `/proc/meminfo` file. Listing 2.2 shows a sample `/proc/meminfo` entry.

LISTING 2.2   Sample `/proc/meminfo` File

```
1  [root@shadrach /proc]# cat meminfo
2            total:    used:    free:  shared: buffers:  cached:
3  Mem:  31535104 29708288  1826816 31817728  3051520 15773696
4  Swap: 63942656  2838528 61104128
5  MemTotal:     30796 kB
6  MemFree:       1784 kB
7  MemShared:    31072 kB
8  Buffers:       2980 kB
9  Cached:       15404 kB
10 SwapTotal:    62444 kB
```

```
11 SwapFree:     59672 kB
12 [root@shadrach /proc]#
```

Line 1 shows the Linux command used to view the /proc/meminfo file. Lines 2 through 11 show the output from the meminfo file. Line 3 shows that this Linux server has 32MB of physical memory. It also shows that approximately 18MB is not currently being used. Line 4 shows that there is approximately 64MB of swap space memory available on this system. This corresponds with line 11 in Listing 2.1 that showed a 64MB swap space partition on the /dev/sda hard drive.

By default, each process running on the Linux system has its own private memory area. One process cannot access memory being used by another process. No processes can access memory used by the kernel processes. To facilitate data sharing, shared memory segments can be created. Multiple processes can read and write to a common shared memory area. The kernel must maintain and administer the shared memory areas. The Linux ipcs command can be used to view the current shared memory segments on the Linux system. Listing 2.3 shows the output from a sample ipcs command.

LISTING 2.3 Sample ipcs Command Output

```
1  [root@shadrach /proc]# ipcs -m
2
3  ------ Shared Memory Segments --------
4  key         shmid      owner      perms      bytes      nattch      status
5  0x00000000 0           rich       600        52228      6           dest
6  0x395ec51c 1           oracle     640        5787648    6
7
8  [root@shadrach /proc]#
```

Line 1 shows the ipcs command using the -m option to display only the shared memory segments. Lines 3 through 6 show the output from this command. Each shared memory segment has an owner that created the segment. Each segment also has a standard UNIX permission setting that sets the availability of the segment to other users. The key value is used to enable other users to gain access to the shared memory segment.

Process Management

The Linux operating system handles programs as processes. The kernel controls how processes are managed in the system. The kernel creates the first process, called the init process, to start all other processes on the system. When the kernel starts, the init process is loaded into virtual memory. As each process is started, it is given an area in virtual memory to store data and code that will be executed by the system.

When the `init` process starts, it reads the file `/etc/inittabs` to determine what other processes it must start on the system. The Linux operating system uses an `init` system that utilizes run levels. A run level can be used to direct the `init` process to run only certain types of processes. There are five `init` run levels in the Linux operating system.

At run level 1, only the basic system processes are started, along with one console terminal process. This is called *single-user mode*. Single-user mode is most often used for filesystem maintenance. The standard `init` run level is 3. At this run level most application software, such as network support software, is started. Another popular run level in Linux is run level 5. This is the run level at which the X Window software is started. Notice how the Linux system can control the overall system functionality by controlling the `init` run level. By changing the run level from 3 to 5, the Linux system can change from a console-based system to an advanced, graphical X Window system.

To view the currently active process on the Linux system, you can use the `ps` command. The format of the `ps` command is

```
ps [options]
```

where `options` is a list of options that can modify the output of the `ps` command. Table 2.2 shows the available options.

TABLE 2.2   `ps` Command Options

Option	Description
l	Uses the long format to display
u	Uses user format (shows username and start time)
j	Uses job format(shows process GID and SID)
s	Uses signal format
v	Uses vm format
m	Displays memory information
f	Uses forest format (displays processes as a tree)
a	Shows processes of other users
x	Shows processes without displaying controlling terminal
S	Shows child CPU and time and page faults
c	Command name for `task_struct`
e	Shows environment after command line and a +
w	Uses wide output format
h	Does not display the header
r	Shows running processes only

Option	Description
n	Shows numeric output for USER and WCHAN
txx	Shows the processes controlled by terminal ttyxx
O	Orders the process listing using sort keys k1, k2, and so on
Pids	Shows only the specified PIDs

Many options are available to modify the ps command output. A sample output is shown in Listing 2.4.

LISTING 2.4 Sample ps Command Output

```
1  [rich@shadrach rich]$ ps ax
2    PID TTY      STAT    TIME COMMAND
3      1 ?        S       0:03 init [5]
4      2 ?        SW      0:00 [kflushd]
5      3 ?        SW      0:00 [kpiod]
6      4 ?        SW      0:02 [kswapd]
7    232 ?        S       0:00 portmap
8    278 ?        S       0:00 syslogd
9    288 ?        S       0:00 klogd
10   301 ?        S       0:00 /usr/sbin/atd
11   314 ?        S       0:00 crond
12   327 ?        S       0:00 inetd
13   340 ?        SW      0:00 [lpd]
14   369 ?        S       0:00 sendmail: accepting connections on port 25
15   383 ?        S       0:00 gpm -t ms
16   396 ?        S       0:01 httpd
17   415 ?        S       0:13 xfs
18   435 tty1     SW      0:00 [mingetty]
19   436 tty2     SW      0:00 [mingetty]
20   437 tty3     SW      0:00 [mingetty]
21   438 tty4     SW      0:00 [mingetty]
22   439 tty5     SW      0:00 [mingetty]
23   440 tty6     SW      0:00 [mingetty]
24   441 ?        S       0:05 /etc/X11/prefdm -nodaemon
25   488 ?        S       0:00 kwmsound
26   578 ?        S       1:01 ora_pmon_test1
27   580 ?        S       0:07 [oracle]
28   582 ?        S       0:11 ora_lgwr_test1
29   584 ?        S       3:34 ora_ckpt_test1
30   586 ?        S      19:38 ora_smon_test1
31   588 ?        S       0:00 ora_reco_test1
```

continues

2

**USING LINUX AS
A MAILSERVER**

LISTING 2.4 continued

```
32   590 ?        S      0:00 ora_s000_test1
33   592 ?        S      0:00 [oracle]
34   594 ?        S      0:00 ora_arc0_test1
35  9102 ?        S      0:00 kwmsound
36  9710 ?        S      0:26 /usr/X11R6/bin/X
37 18854 ?        S      0:05 /oracle/product/8.1.5/bin/tnslsnr LISTENER -i
38 19607 ?        S      0:00 httpd
39 19608 ?        S      0:00 httpd
40 19609 ?        S      0:00 httpd
41 19610 ?        S      0:00 httpd
42 19611 ?        S      0:00 httpd
43 19657 ?        S      0:00 httpd
44 19658 ?        S      0:00 httpd
45 19659 ?        S      0:00 httpd
46 24844 ?        S      0:00 kwmsound
47 24905 ?        S      0:00 -:0
48 25357 ?        S      0:00 in.telnetd
49 25358 pts/0    S      0:00 login -- rich
50 25359 pts/0    S      0:00 -bash
51 25404 pts/0    R      0:00 ps ax
52 [rich@shadrach rich]$
```

Line 1 shows the ps command as entered on the command line. Both the a and x options are used for the output to display all processes running on the system. The first column in the output shows the process ID (or PID) of the process. Line 3 shows the init process started by the kernel. The init process is assigned PID 1. All other processes that start after the init process are assigned PIDs in numerical order. No two processes can have the same PID.

The third column shows the current status of the process. Table 2.3 lists the possible process status codes.

TABLE 2.3 Process Status Codes

Code	Description
D	Uninterruptible sleep
R	Runnable
S	Sleeping
T	Traced or stopped
Z	A defunct (zombie) process
W	Process has no resident pages
<	High-priority process

Code	Description
N	Low-priority task
L	Process has pages locked into memory

The process name is shown in the last column. Processes in square brackets ([ ]) are processes that have been swapped out of memory to the disk swap space due to inactivity. For example, lines 18 to 23 show the `mingetty` process running on the virtual console sessions on the Linux server. Because no users have logged in to the virtual sessions, they are inactive, and are thus swapped out. If a user logs in to a virtual session, the corresponding `mingetty` process is swapped back into memory to execute. This creates a small performance problem for the application. Lines 26 through 34 show the processes required for an Oracle database server. You can see that some of the processes have been swapped out, whereas others have not.

Device Driver Management

Another responsibility for the kernel is hardware management. Any device with which the Linux system must communicate needs driver code inserted inside the kernel code. The driver code allows the kernel to pass data back and forth to the device. Two methods are used for inserting device driver code in the Linux kernel.

In the past, the only way to insert a device driver code was to recompile the kernel. Each time a new device was added to the system, the kernel code had to be recompiled. This process became more inefficient as Linux supported more hardware. A better method has been developed to insert driver code into the kernel. Kernel modules were developed to allow driver code to be inserted into a running kernel and also to be removed from the kernel when the device is no longer being used. The section "Kernel Modules" later in the chapter describes this process in more detail.

Hardware devices are identified on the Linux server as special device files. The three different classifications of device files are

- Character
- Block
- Network

Character files are for devices that can handle data only one character at a time. Most types of modems are created as character files. Block files are for devices that can handle data in large blocks at a time, such as disk drives. Network files are used for devices that use packets to send and receive data. This includes network cards and the special loopback device that allows the Linux system to communicate with itself using common network programming protocols.

Device files are created in the filesystem as nodes. Each node has a unique number pair that identifies it to the Linux kernel. The number pair includes a major and a minor device number. Similar devices are grouped into the same major device number. The minor device number is used to identify the device within the major device numbers. Listing 2.5 shows an example of device files on a Linux server.

LISTING 2.5   Sample Device Listing from a Linux Server

```
 1  [rich@shadrach /dev]$ ls -al sda* ttyS*
 2  brw-rw----  1 root      disk      8,   0 May   5  1998 sda
 3  brw-rw----  1 root      disk      8,   1 May   5  1998 sda1
 4  brw-rw----  1 root      disk      8,  10 May   5  1998 sda10
 5  brw-rw----  1 root      disk      8,  11 May   5  1998 sda11
 6  brw-rw----  1 root      disk      8,  12 May   5  1998 sda12
 7  brw-rw----  1 root      disk      8,  13 May   5  1998 sda13
 8  brw-rw----  1 root      disk      8,  14 May   5  1998 sda14
 9  brw-rw----  1 root      disk      8,  15 May   5  1998 sda15
10  brw-rw----  1 root      disk      8,   2 May   5  1998 sda2
11  brw-rw----  1 root      disk      8,   3 May   5  1998 sda3
12  brw-rw----  1 root      disk      8,   4 May   5  1998 sda4
13  brw-rw----  1 root      disk      8,   5 May   5  1998 sda5
14  brw-rw----  1 root      disk      8,   6 May   5  1998 sda6
15  brw-rw----  1 root      disk      8,   7 May   5  1998 sda7
16  brw-rw----  1 root      disk      8,   8 May   5  1998 sda8
17  brw-rw----  1 root      disk      8,   9 May   5  1998 sda9
18  crw-------  1 root      tty       4,  64 Nov  29 16:09 ttyS0
19  crw-------  1 root      tty       4,  65 May   5  1998 ttyS1
20  crw-------  1 root      tty       4,  66 May   5  1998 ttyS2
21  crw-------  1 root      tty       4,  67 May   5  1998 ttyS3
22  [rich@shadrach /dev]$
```

Line 1 shows the ls command being used to display all the entries for the sda and ttyS devices. The sda device is the first SCSI hard drive and the ttyS devices are the standard IBM PC COM ports. Lines 2 through 17 show all the sda devices created on the sample Linux system. Not all are actually used, but they are created in case the administrator needs them. Lines 18 through 21 show all the created ttyS devices.

The fifth column shows the major device node number. Notice that all the sda devices have the same major device node (8) and all the ttyS devices use 4. The sixth column shows the minor device node number. Each device within a major number has its own unique minor device node number.

The first column indicates the permissions for the device file. The first character of the permissions indicates the type of file. Notice that the SCSI hard drive files are all marked as block (b) files, whereas the COM port device files are marked as character (c) files.

To create a new device node, you can use the `mknod` command. The format of the `mknod` command is

```
mknod [OPTION] NAME TYPE [MAJOR MINOR]
```

where `NAME` is the filename and `TYPE` is the filetype (character or block). The `OPTION` parameter has only one usable option. The `-m` option enables you to set the permissions of the file as it is created. You must be careful to select a unique major and minor device node number pair.

Filesystem Management

Unlike some other operating systems, the Linux kernel can support different types of filesystems to read and write data to hard drives. Currently, 15 different filesystem types are available on Linux. The kernel must be compiled with support for all filesystem types that the system will use. Table 2.4 lists the filesystems that Linux can use to read and write data.

TABLE 2.4   Linux Filesystems

Filesystem	Description
affs	Amiga filesystem
ext	Extended filesystem
ext2	Second extended filesystem
hpfs	OS/2 high-performance filesystem
iso9660	ISO 9660 filesystem (CD-ROMs)
minix	MINIX filesystem
msdos	Microsoft FAT16
ncp	NetWare filesystem
nfs	Network File System
proc	Access to system information
smb	Samba SMB filesystem
sysv	Older UNIX filesystem
ufs	Solaris and SunOS filesystem
umsdos	UNIX-like filesystem that resides on top of MS-DOS
vfat	Windows 95 filesystem
xia	Similar to ext2, not used

2

USING LINUX AS A MAILSERVER

Any hard drive that Linux accesses must be formatted using one of the filesystem types listed in Table 2.4. Formatting a Linux filesystem is similar to formatting an MS-DOS type disk. The operating system must build the necessary filesystem information onto the disk before the disk can be used to store information. Linux uses the `mkfs` command to format filesystems. The format of the `mkfs` command is

```
mkfs [ -V ] [ -t fstype ] [ fs-options ] filesys [ blocks ]
```

where `fstype` is the type of filesystem to use and `blocks` is the number of blocks to use. The default filesystem type is `ext2`, and the default block count is all blocks available on the partition.

The Linux kernel interfaces with each filesystem using the Virtual File System (VFS). This provides a standard interface for the kernel to communicate with any type of filesystem. VFS caches information in memory as each filesystem is mounted and used.

Kernel Modules

As mentioned previously, in older versions of the Linux kernel, adding new drivers for devices was not an easy task. The entire kernel had to be recompiled with the new drivers inserted. Fortunately, this problem has been fixed. Now the Linux kernel supports *modules*, drivers that can be inserted and removed from the kernel as it is running. This was a major breakthrough in the Linux kernel development.

Modules can be inserted into the running kernel using the `insmod` command. The format of the `insmod` command is

```
insmod [ -fkmpsxXv ] [ -o module_name ] object_file [ symbol=value ... ]
```

The insmod program attempts to link the module code specified by `object_file` into the running kernel. Table 2.5 shows the command-line options that can be used with `insmod`.

TABLE 2.5 `insmod` **Command-Line Options**

Option	Description
-f	Attempts to load even if it does not match the kernel version
-k	Sets the auto-clean flag
-m	Outputs a load map
-o	Explicitly names the module
-p	Probes the module
-s	Outputs everything to `syslog`
-v	Uses verbose mode
-X	Exports all the module's external symbols
-x	Does not export all the module's external symbols

The insmod program links the module code to the kernel code, but this is only a temporary addition. When the Linux server is rebooted, the old kernel loads without the added modules. The solution to this problem is the modprobe program.

The modprobe program can load a set of modules into the kernel based on a set of configuration files. The formats of the modprobe command are

```
modprobe module.o [symbol=value ...]
modprobe -t tag pattern
modprobe -a -t tag pattern
modprobe -l [ -t tag ] pattern
modprobe -r module
modprobe -c
```

The first format of the modprobe command is used to load an individual module into the kernel. If the module requires any parameters, they can be entered on the command line. The -t option allows modprobe to load all modules that match a particular tag within a pattern list. The -r option is used to remove a particular module from the kernel.

The list of modules can be placed in a file accessible at boot time. On Mandrake Linux version 6.0, the location of the modules file is /lib/modules/2.2.9-19mdk/modules.dep.

This file contains a list of all the modules that the modprobe command will attempt to install into the kernel at boot time. The depmod program can be used to add or delete modules from the modules file.

Another important configuration file for modprobe is the /etc/conf.modules file. This configuration file determines the behavior of the modprobe program. Table 2.6 shows the configuration lines that can be used in this file.

TABLE 2.6 /etc/conf.modules **File Commands**

Command	Description
keep	Directs modprobe to add any paths defined to the conf file instead of replacing them
path=MOD_PATH	Specifies directory in which to search for modules
path[tag]=MOD_PATH	Specifies a tag for the modules located in the directory
alias module real-name	Specifies an alias to use to refer to the module name
pre-install module command	Executes command before module is installed
install module command	Executes command when module is installed
post-install module command	Executes command after module is installed
pre-remove module command	Executes command just before module is removed
remove module command	Executes command while module is removed
post-remove module command	Executes command after module is removed

2

USING LINUX AS A MAILSERVER

A sample `/etc/conf.modules` file is shown in Listing 2.6.

LISTING 2.6   Sample `/etc/conf.modules` File

```
1   alias scsi_hostadapter aic7xxx
2   alias eth0 3c59x
3   alias parport_lowlevel parport_pc
4   pre-install pcmcia_core /etc/rc.d/init.d/pcmcia start
```

Lines 1 through 3 define aliases for generic devices that are loaded in the modules list. Each generic device points to the real name of the module file that will be loaded. Line 4 shows a program that should be run before the `pcmcia` module is loaded.

Kernel Versions

The development of the Linux kernel has taken on a very rapid pace. Linus Torvalds maintains strict control over the Linux kernel, although he accepts change requests from anyone, anywhere. There have been many advances in the Linux kernel design over the years, such as the addition of modules.

The kernel developers use a strict version control system. The format of a kernel release is

`linux-a.b.c`

where a is the major release number, b is the minor release number, and c is the patch number. Currently, a convention has been established where odd-numbered minor releases are considered developmental releases, and even-numbered minor releases are considered stable production releases.

At the time of this writing, the current stable production release of the Linux kernel is 2.2.13, whereas the current development release is 2.3.31. Although version 2.2.13 is the current kernel release, most Linux distributions have not released versions using this kernel.

To determine the kernel version your Linux system is using, you can use the `uname` command with the `-a` option. Listing 2.8 shows an example of this command using a Mandrake 6.0 Linux system.

LISTING 2.7   Sample `uname -a` Output

```
1   [rich@shadrach rich]$ uname -a
2   Linux shadrach.smallorg.org 2.2.9-19mdk #1 Wed May 19 19:53:00 GMT 1999
➥   i586 unknown
3   [rich@shadrach rich]$
```

The output from the `uname` command is shown in line 2. The third field shows the specific Linux kernel version used. In the case of this example, it is using the 2.2.9 kernel that was compiled specifically for the Mandrake Linux distribution, thus the extra added `-19mdk` information.

It is possible to download newer versions of the kernel to install in a running Linux system. You must have the kernel source code files, which are usually available for download from the Linux Kernel Archives at `http://www.kernel.org`. Compiling and installing a new kernel is not for the beginner. Numerous steps are involved in the process. If you decide to upgrade your Linux kernel, please read all the documentation that comes with the kernel source code and any tips provided by your specific Linux distribution support group.

> **CAUTION**
>
> Installing a new Linux kernel falls under the category of "if it ain't broke, don't fix it." If your Linux server is not experiencing any problems, don't attempt to install a new kernel just because it is newer. Many Linux distributions are fine-tuned to work with a specific kernel; changing only the kernel can result in unpredictable results.

Linux Libraries

The Linux operating system depends heavily on the C programming language. The kernel, many device drivers, and almost all the utilities were written using the C language. It is not surprising that most of the application programs written for the Linux platform were also written using the C programming language.

One feature of the C programming language is the capability for a program to load code segments from a library file as the program is running. Most computer users familiar with the Microsoft Windows operating system are familiar with the use of DLLs. Program code that can be shared among several programs can be compiled into a common library (DLL file). When a program executes, it can load the DLL file into memory as it needs to use the library functions found in the file.

The Linux operating system uses a similar technique. In Linux, the `lib` prefix denotes library files. A library table keeps track of all the shared libraries registered on the system. A common problem in the Microsoft Windows environment is when one program updates a DLL file, another program that needed the older version of the DLL stops working. In Linux, this is not a problem because the library table can maintain multiple separate copies of the same library file for programs to access.

The file /etc/ld.so.conf contains the list of libraries that are inserted into the library table. You can display the current library table on your Linux system by using the ldconfig command. Listing 2.8 shows a sample partial output from the ldconfig command on a Mandrake 6.0 Linux system. This is only a partial listing because, as shown in line 2, 534 different libraries are registered on this Linux system.

LISTING 2.8 Sample ldconfig Partial Output

```
 1  [rich@shadrach rich]$ /sbin/ldconfig -p
 2  534 libs found in cache `/etc/ld.so.cache' (version 1.7.0)
 3          libzvt.so.2 (libc6) => /usr/lib/libzvt.so.2
 4          libzvt.so.2 (libc6) => /usr/lib/libzvt.so.2
 5          libz.so.1 (libc6) => /usr/lib/libz.so.1
 6          libz.so.1 (libc6) => /usr/lib/libz.so.1
 7          libx11amp.so.0 (libc6) => /usr/X11R6/lib/libx11amp.so.0
 8          libxml.so.0 (libc6) => /usr/lib/libxml.so.0
 9          libxml.so.0 (libc6) => /usr/lib/libxml.so.0
10          libvgagl.so.1 (libc6) => /usr/lib/libvgagl.so.1
11          libvgagl.so.1 (libc5) => /usr/i486-linux-libc5/lib/libvgagl.so.1
12          libvgagl.so.1 (libc6) => /usr/lib/libvgagl.so.1
13          libvgagl.so (libc6) => /usr/lib/libvgagl.so
14          libvgagl.so (libc6) => /usr/lib/libvgagl.so
15          libvga.so.1 (libc6) => /usr/lib/libvga.so.1
16          libvga.so.1 (libc5) => /usr/i486-linux-libc5/lib/libvga.so.1
17          libvga.so.1 (libc6) => /usr/lib/libvga.so.1
18          libvga.so (libc6) => /usr/lib/libvga.so
19          libvga.so (libc6) => /usr/lib/libvga.so
20          libuulib.so.5 (libc6) => /usr/lib/libuulib.so.5
21          libuulib.so.5 (libc6) => /usr/lib/libuulib.so.5
22          libuulib.so (libc6) => /usr/lib/libuulib.so
23          libuulib.so (libc6) => /usr/lib/libuulib.so
```

Each Linux implementation requires that a version of the standard C library is installed. The standard C library contains many of the commonly used functions for the system. This is where Linux has had a checkered past. In the early days of Linux, the Linux C library was tightly coupled with the kernel. Changes in the kernel required C library changes, and vice versa. The first version of the Linux C library was called libc1. This version was improved with the versions libc2, libc3, and libc4. These libraries were used to create many Linux utilities and application programs during the early years of Linux.

After awhile, Linux developers decided that the old C library method was not good. Not only was the library too closely related to the Linux kernel, but it also produced executable files in an older executable format called a.out. Most newer POSIX-type systems had already converted to an Executable and Linking Format (ELF) that proved to be faster and more efficient. The next version of the C library—libc5—implemented the ELF executable format. Programs compiled using the libc5 library would not run on older Linux systems that still were using the a.out-style libraries. However, older programs compiled on the a.out-style would execute fine on the new libc5 systems. This created the first round of confusion in the Linux application world.

At the same time that the libc5 library was being developed and used, the GNU Project developed its own library that was not tied to a specific kernel. The GNU Project's C library was called glibc. With the libc5 library working so well, no one really continued work on the glibc library.

After a period of dormancy, programmers revisited the glibc code. They thought it could be made better than the libc5 library. One advantage that glibc had was its independence from any particular operating system or kernel. Out of the effort of those programmers came the glibc 2.0 library.

Many Linux distributors decided to bundle the new glibc 2.0 code with their new Linux distributions. Unfortunately, many Linux distributors decided to keep the libc5 library with the new kernel. This quickly became confusing.

The Linux distributions that used the glibc 2.0 library also included the libc5 library for backward compatibility. Remember that Linux maintains a table of library files, so using two separate C libraries at the same time is possible. Because of this, many Linux applications continued to use the libc5 library for compatibility purposes.

Netscape's Communicator and Corel's WordPerfect are two applications that continued to be written using the libc5 library and could be used on almost every Linux distribution. Some Linux application programmers decided to take advantage of features of the new glibc 2.0 library and released versions of their software for that platform. Star Division's StarOffice 5.0 and Oracle's Oracle8 database software are two applications that use the glibc 2.0 library. These applications will not run on Linux distributions that exclusively use the libc5 library.

It would be bad enough if the story ended there. Recently the GNU Project released the glibc 2.1 library. What complicated things is that some functions were changed from the glibc 2.0 library, so some applications written with the glibc 2.0 library (such as StarOffice 5.0) crash when run on a Linux system using the glibc 2.1 library.

2

**USING LINUX AS
A MAILSERVER**

> ## Linux Libraries
>
> If, after reading this section, you are concerned about your Linux system, don't be. For applications distributed in source code (such as all the mailserver programs discussed in this book), compile the code using whichever C library your system uses and that code will run just fine. For applications distributed in binary format, just remember to use the version that is released for the C library on your Linux system (libc5, glibc 2.0, or glibc 2.1).

If you do not know which library your Linux distribution is using, you can find out by looking for the libraries in the /lib directory. Table 2.7 shows the different C libraries that might be present on a Linux system.

TABLE 2.7   List of Linux C Libraries

Library	Description
libc.so	libc1 a.out library
libc.so.2	libc2 a.out library
libc.so.3	libc3 a.out library
libc.so.4	libc4 a.out library
libc.so.5	libc5 ELF library
libc.so.6	Symbolic link to a glibc library
libc-2.0.x.so	glibc 2.0 ELF library
libc-2.1.x.so	glibc 2.1 ELF library

The GNU Project

The GNU Project was created in 1984 to create a free UNIX-like operating system. It is responsible for maintaining open source versions of many common UNIX utilities. Without the GNU Project, the Linux operating system would not be very exciting. Most of the core pieces of the Linux operating system are products of the GNU Project. This section describes three programs that are crucial to the operation of the Linux mailserver: the bash shell, the gcc compiler, and the make utility.

GNU bash

The kernel requires some kind of macro processor to enable a user to execute commands (programs) on the system. In the UNIX world, that macro processor is called the *shell*. The most common shell in the UNIX environment is the Bourne shell, named after its creator, Stephen Bourne. The Bourne shell is a program that runs as a process on the system, and has an interactive session that enables the user to enter commands at a command prompt. The commands can be executable programs, internal shell commands, or a program file that contains shell commands (called a *script file*). The shell launches executable programs by creating a new process and running the program within that new process. This allows every program that runs from the shell to have its own process on the system.

The GNU Project developers knew that it was crucial to have a good open source shell to use with an open source UNIX-like operating system. The shell program they developed was called bash, for Bourne-Again SHell. The bash shell is compatible with the original Bourne shell (called sh). The bash shell also includes features from other shells that have been developed in the UNIX environment—the C shell (csh) and the Korn shell (ksh). bash has become the default shell for Linux systems. The current version of bash at the time of this writing is version 2.03.

The shell a user utilizes after logging in to the Linux system is determined by the user's entry in the /etc/passwd file. A typical record in this file looks like this:

```
riley:x:504:506:Riley M.:/home/riley:/bin/bash
```

Colons are used to separate the fields in the record. The first field identifies the user login name. The second field is a placeholder for the user password. This particular Linux system uses shadow passwords, so the real password is encrypted and placed in a separate file. The third and fourth fields are the userid and groupid for the user. The fifth field is the text identifier for the user. The sixth field identifies the user's default, or home, directory when he logs in to the system. The last field identifies the default shell for the user. This points to the location of the bash shell executable file on the server.

The bash shell has several different configuration files that can be used to modify the features of the shell as a user logs in. When bash is invoked as a shell from a login process, any commands present in the /etc/profile file are executed. This occurs for all users who specify the bash shell as the default login shell in the password file. Listing 2.9 shows the default /etc/profile file from a Mandrake 6.0 Linux system.

2

USING LINUX AS
A MAILSERVER

LISTING 2.9 Sample `/etc/profile` File

```
1   # /etc/profile
2
3   # System wide environment and startup programs
4   # Functions and aliases go in /etc/bashrc
5
6   PATH="$PATH:/usr/X11R6/bin"
7   PS1="[\u@\h \W]\\$ "
8
9   # In bash2 we can't define a ulimit for user :-(
10  [ "$UID" = "0" ] && {
11  ulimit -c 1000000
12  }
13
14  if [ `id -gn` = `id -un` -a `id -u` -gt 14 ]; then
15      umask 002
16  else
17      umask 022
18  fi
19
20  USER=`id -un`
21  LOGNAME=$USER
22  MAIL="/var/spool/mail/$USER"
23
24  HOSTNAME=`/bin/hostname`
25  HISTSIZE=1000
26  HISTFILESIZE=1000
27  export PATH PS1 HOSTNAME HISTSIZE HISTFILESIZE USER LOGNAME MAIL
28
29  for i in /etc/profile.d/*.sh ; do
30      if [ -x $i ]; then
31          . $i
32      fi
33  done
34
35  unset i
```

The main thing the `/etc/profile` file does is create new environment variables for the shell to identify special characteristics for the session that can be used by application programs running in the shell. Line 22, the MAIL environment variable, is of special interest to the mail administrator. It points the user's mail program to the proper mailbox for the user.

After the common `/etc/profile` program is executed, bash looks for three more configuration files in the user's default (home) directory. If they exist, the `.bash_profile`, `.bash_login`, and `.profile` files are executed, in order. Each of these files should be located in the user's home directory, so these files can be specific for a particular user. One final configuration file is available for use: `.bash_logout`. This script file is executed when the user logs out of the interactive session. By using a combination of script files, the system administrator can fine-tune the bash shell for each user on the system.

GNU gcc

If you plan to install software programs that are distributed in source code, you must be able to compile the code to create an executable file. To do this, you need the proper compiler. All the Linux programs described in this book are written in the C programming language. This requires that a C compiler is installed on your Linux server. The most common C compiler package for Linux is the GNU C compiler (gcc).

The gcc package has itself had quite an interesting past. The GNU Project team developed gcc and released version 1 in early 1990. The GNU Project continued development of gcc, creating version 2.0 and continuing with improvements until version 2.8 was released in 1997. At the same time, another group of developers was working on a C++ compiler called egcs (pronounced "eggs"). After gcc 2.8, both projects were combined into the egcs project and egcs 1.0 was released. egcs 1.0 combined both the C and C++ compilers into one package.

Unfortunately, the egcs project was short-lived (only getting up to version 1.1). Now both the gcc and egcs projects have been rolled into the gcc project again. At the time of this writing, the current version of gcc is version 2.95. This version supports both C and C++ compilers. To complicate things even more, Linux distributions often still call this distribution egcs version 2.95. I hope this confusion will clear up soon.

To determine the version of gcc your Linux distribution uses, you can use the `--version` option as follows:

```
[rich@shadrach rich]$ gcc --version
pgcc-2.91.66
[rich@shadrach rich]$
```

The sample Mandrake 6.0 Linux system shown is using gcc version 2.91 with patch level 66.

make

Large C and C++ projects often become complicated. There are several different source code files, each with several different header files. Compiling individual source files creates multiple object files that must be linked together in specific combinations to create executable files. Maintaining the source, object, and executable files is often a difficult job. To simplify this task, most C and C++ compilers utilize a make program. The job of the make program is to control the creation of executable files, based on changes made to the source code files or to variables in a standard make configuration file.

The GNU Project has a version of make that is compatible with the gcc compiler. At the time of this writing, the current version available is version 3.78.1.

The meat and potatoes of the make utility is the Makefile. The Makefile specifies how the make utility compiles the source code to create the executable program(s). A sample Makefile is shown in Listing 2.10.

LISTING 2.10   Sample Makefile

```
1   # Makefile -- Make file for test program
2   #
3
4   # Edit the following for your installation
5
6   CC   =   gcc
7   #====================================
8
9   # Compiler and linker flags
10
11  CFLAGS   =    -O
12  LFLAGS   =    -O
13
14  # This program's object code files
15
16  OBJS     =    test.o
17
18  # File dependencies
19
20  all:     test
21
22  objs:    $(OBJS)
23
24  clean:
25       rm -f $(OBJS)
26       rm -f test
27
28  test: $(OBJS)
29       $(CC) -o $@ $(LFLAGS) $(OBJS) $(LIBS)
30
31  test.o:   test.c
32       $(CC) -c $(CFLAGS) -o $@ $<
```

Lines 6, 11, 12, and 16 show the use of variables within the Makefile. The user can change these values to the appropriate values for the system. Line 18 declares the make targets for the system. Each target can be run individually by specifying the target name as a parameter on the make command line. For example, to run the `clean` target, which removes any old object and executable files, you can type

```
make clean
```

To create just the object files for the test program, you can type

```
make objs
```

If you type only **make** at the command line, the `all` target will be executed, which builds the executable file `test`.

Linux Distributions

If your head is starting to spin thinking about all the variables required to complete a Linux system, don't worry. Fortunately for us, lots of very smart people packaged the different pieces together for us. A prepackaged set of the Linux operating system is called a *Linux distribution*.

Many Linux distributions are available both for purchase and for free download. Often people question how a company can charge for free software. The GNU Project License provides an answer to this. Its motto is "free" as in "free speech," not "free beer." A Linux distributor is free to charge whatever price he feels the public will pay to purchase a distribution package. The "free" part comes in because the distribution packages contain the source code for all the software and you are free to modify anything you want. Most Linux distributors offer free (as in "free beer") versions of their distribution packages as a public service.

The main chore of the Linux distributor is to mix and match the various releases of the kernel, shell, and other Linux utilities into a compatible operating system. This is often not an easy job. Each utility must be carefully configured and placed in the distribution so that it can be seamlessly installed with the operating system.

Most often Linux distributors package programs so that they can be installed and removed individually without affecting the operating system as a whole. Many distributions use the Red Hat RPM distribution packaging method. The RPM program can package into a single distribution file all the files necessary for a program to operate. The RPM program can then install or remove an entire software package with one command.

Table 2.8 shows a list of some of the more common Linux distributions available at the time of this writing and how those distributions package the kernel and C libraries.

TABLE 2.8   Sample Linux Distribution Matrix

Distribution	Kernel	GLIBC
Caldera OpenLinux 2.3	2.2.10	2.1.1
Debian Linux 2.1	2.0.36	2.1
Mandrake 6.1 Linux	2.2.13pre	2.1.1
Red Hat 6.1 Linux	2.2.12	2.1.2
Slackware 7.0	2.2.13	2.1.2
SuSe 6.2 Linux	2.2.10	2.1.1

As shown in Table 2.8, most of the current Linux distributions are fairly close in the various release levels of the kernel and C libraries. When selecting a Linux distribution to use for an office Linux server, make sure it meets any software version requirements necessitated by the application software you plan to use.

Summary

The main ingredient of a Linux mailserver is the Linux operating system. Many parts make up a Linux server, but the core of the server is the Linux kernel. The kernel controls many facets of the operating system, including memory management, process management, device management, and filesystem management. Besides the kernel, many utilities are required for the operating system. The GNU Project team has created a large library of UNIX-compatible utilities that run on the Linux kernel. The bash shell provides an interactive session for users to start programs. The gcc compiler enables users to create new executable programs using the C and C++ programming languages. The make utility is used by prepackaged programs to distribute the source code needed to build the executable program. Many Linux distributions are available that include in one package all the required utilities, along with a particular Linux kernel. Beginners to Linux are often confused by the multitude of Linux distributions available. If you are purchasing a new Linux package for a business, many distributions cater to business users by offering advanced support packages

Installing Communication
Devices in Linux

IN THIS CHAPTER

An email server is worthless unless it can communicate with remote hosts and client workstations. The Linux mailserver uses two different types of communication devices to accomplish this.

The Linux mailserver must establish an IP connection with the Internet service provider (ISP) to send and receive mail from the Internet. A modem is used to establish a serial connection with the ISP. After the serial connection is established, the Linux mailserver can use the Point-to-Point Protocol (PPP) to transmit and receive IP packets. Chapter 8, "PPP Protocol," describes this process in more detail.

Besides the Internet connection, the Linux mailserver must also establish communications with the local office workstations to allow clients to connect to the mailserver to read and send email messages. The easiest way to establish connectivity with the office workstations is via an office Local Area Network (LAN). Several different types of LANs can be installed in small offices. The type that seems to be the most popular is the Ethernet LAN. Ethernet technology allows workstations to connect to the LAN at 10 or 100Mbps using network interface cards (NICs). For the Linux mailserver to connect to the office Ethernet LAN, it must also have a NIC installed and configured properly.

This chapter discusses the steps necessary to ensure that the Linux mailserver can communicate with both the local office workstations and the ISP. First, an overview of communication hardware is presented. Then installing and configuring network interface cards are described. Finally, installing and configuring different types of modems are discussed.

Communication Devices and Linux

Modems and NICs are hardware devices that are connected to the PC, often by using internal boards plugged into the motherboard. These devices must be recognized by the Linux operating system before they work properly. Several layers of Linux drivers and software are necessary for these devices to work. Figure 3.1 shows a diagram of the hardware and software layers necessary for these devices.

As shown in Figure 3.1, each communication device must interface with the Linux kernel. As discussed in the previous chapter, the kernel is responsible for controlling the interfaces to the hardware devices. This is usually accomplished with loadable drivers, called *modules*, that can be installed at boot time using scripts. The kernel must know the hardware settings of the devices to be able to communicate with them.

After the Linux kernel recognizes and configures the communication devices, software must be available to access the device. In the case of a mailserver, the common software layer is the TCP/IP software.

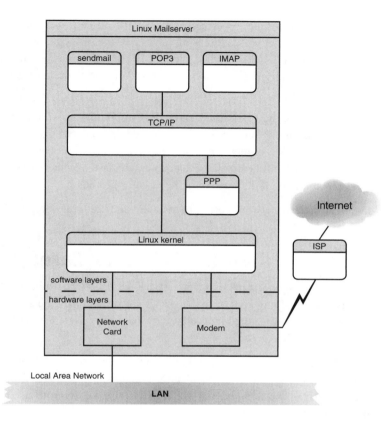

3

INSTALLING
COMMUNICATION
DEVICES IN LINUX

FIGURE 3.1

A diagram of Linux communication device layers.

The Linux TCP/IP software allows programs to send TCP/IP packets via the network card and
modem to remote devices based on IP addresses. For the TCP/IP software to operate properly,
a valid set of IP parameters must be configured. The parameters necessary for an IP connection
are

- IP address
- IP subnet mask
- IP default router
- DNS nameservers

The IP address uniquely identifies the Linux mailserver on the office IP network. The IP subnet mask identifies the local IP network addressing scheme of the office network. This enables the Linux mailserver to determine when it must forward IP packets to a router to reach remote hosts. The default router the mailserver uses to forward packets to remote hosts must also be configured.

The last parameter required for the Linux mailserver IP configuration is a Domain Name System (DNS) nameserver. The IP network scheme is based on numerical addresses. The DNS system equates a hostname with a numerical IP address. This allows users and programs to refer to remote hosts by their DNS hostnames rather than having to remember IP addresses. The DNS nameserver returns the IP address for a given DNS hostname.

The next section describes how network cards are installed and configured on the Linux mailserver.

Installing and Configuring Network Cards

The Linux operating system supports many different types of NICs. Most Linux distributions can autodetect an installed NIC and configure the kernel software during the software installation process. If the NIC was not installed before the original Linux system installation, it must be manually configured into the kernel.

The ifconfig program is used to manually install and configure network cards in the Linux system. Several Linux distributions include a graphical X Window program to assist in setting the parameters that ifconfig sets. The Red Hat and Mandrake Linux distributions use the netcfg program to configure installed network cards.

This section first describes how Linux uses the ifconfig program in the boot process to recognize and configure the network card, and then it describes both the ifconfig and netcfg programs in more detail.

Configuring Network Cards in the Boot Process

After the network card has been properly configured (either manually or automatically), the Linux server can communicate with other devices on the office network. There is only one problem: When the Linux server is rebooted, the network device information will be lost. The `ifconfig` command is used to enter the information for the network devices into a table in the kernel. The kernel table is rebuilt from configuration scripts when the server is rebooted.

The ifconfig program requires a script file to run at boot time to re-enter the `ifconfig` commands necessary to get the network card working. All Linux distributions include script files that are used at boot time to load programs. Unfortunately, different Linux distributions have different ways of running the script files. The Mandrake, Caldera, and Red Hat Linux distributions use the UNIX Sys V `init` method, which is discussed here.

The Sys V initialization method is a very complicated series of script files. The initialization process is divided into run levels. Each run level executes a set of scripts to initialize certain devices for the run level. Figure 3.2 demonstrates the script layout used by Linux to load run level configuration information when booting.

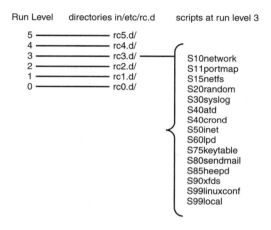

FIGURE 3.2
The Linux boot process steps.

The /etc/rc.d directory contains the scripts that are run depending on the current init run level of the system. A normal Linux server should operate in either run level 3 (for console mode) or 5 (for X Window mode). Both run levels use the same network initialization script, S10network, which can be found in the /etc/rc.d/rc3.d and /etc/rc.d/rc5.d directories. The S10network script starts the network functions for the server. It uses another script, called ifup, which attempts to start any network interfaces that were configured to start at boot time. The ifup script is located in the /etc/sysconfig/network-scripts directory.

Each configured network interface on the Linux system is assigned a file in the /etc/sysconfig/network-scripts directory. The /dev/eth0 device is assigned the file ifcfg-eth0. Listing 3.1 shows the file created for the eth0 device on a sample Linux system.

LISTING 3.1   Sample /etc/sysconfig/network-scripts/ifcfg-eth0 File

```
1   DEVICE=eth0
2   IPADDR=192.168.1.1
3   NETMASK=255.255.255.0
4   NETWORK=192.168.1.0
5   BROADCAST=158.18.1.255
6   ONBOOT=yes
7   BOOTPROTO=none
```

The `ifcfg-eth0` file defines environment variables that are used in the `ifup` script to start the interface. The line in the `ifup` script that uses these variables looks like this:

```
ifconfig ${DEVICE} ${IPADDR} netmask ${NETMASK} broadcast ${BROADCAST}
```

The format of the `ifconfig` command line in the `ifup` script is exactly as if it were entered at the command prompt manually.

If you are creating a script yourself for a new network interface, it does not need to be as complicated and involved and the ones generated by Red Hat. All that is needed is the `ifconfig` lines necessary to start the network interface. If you already know the device name and IP address information, you do not need to use environment variables and separate configuration files. Just a simple line in the `S10network` script file suffices.

Using ifconfig

The ifconfig program is standard in the Linux operating system. It is used to identify and configure network devices in the Linux system.

There are two modes of operation for using the ifconfig program:

```
ifconfig [interface]
```

```
ifconfig interface [aftype] options | address ...
```

The first mode is the report mode. This mode allows the system administrator to extract configuration information from the installed network devices. The second mode is the configure mode. This mode allows the system administrator to set or change configuration parameters for the network devices. The following sections describe these modes in detail.

Report Mode

In report mode, ifconfig lists information about either a single network interface or all the installed network interfaces. The information presented is a mixture of hardware and software parameters for the device, as well as some operational information. Each network device requires several parameters to operate. Figure 3.3 shows an example of a network device on a Linux system.

As shown in Figure 3.3, one set of parameters for the network device is the hardware configuration. The hardware interrupt and the base address are used to identify the network card to the Linux system, and must be unique. The next set of parameters is the software network parameters. For the Linux system to properly communicate on an IP network, it must have the proper IP parameters. This includes a unique IP address as well as the proper subnet mask and broadcast address for the network.

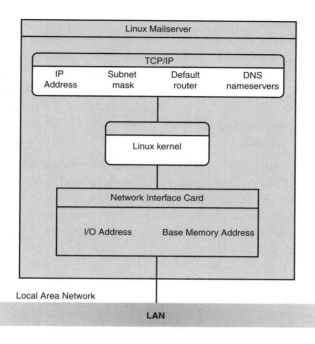

FIGURE 3.3

The network device components.

Listing 3.2 shows an example of using the report mode format of the ifconfig command.

LISTING 3.2   Sample ifconfig Command Output

```
1  [alex@shadrach alex]$ /sbin/ifconfig
2  eth0      Link encap:Ethernet  HWaddr 00:A0:24:9C:69:02
3            inet addr:192.168.1.1  Bcast:192.168.1.255  Mask:255.255.255.0
4            UP BROADCAST RUNNING MULTICAST  MTU:1500  Metric:1
5            RX packets:7948525 errors:0 dropped:0 overruns:0 frame:0
6            TX packets:22003 errors:0 dropped:0 overruns:0 carrier:0
7            collisions:72 txqueuelen:100
8            Interrupt:11 Base address:0x8400
9
10 lo        Link encap:Local Loopback
11           inet addr:127.0.0.1  Mask:255.0.0.0
12           UP LOOPBACK RUNNING  MTU:3924  Metric:1
13           RX packets:38 errors:0 dropped:0 overruns:0 frame:0
14           TX packets:38 errors:0 dropped:0 overruns:0 carrier:0
15           collisions:0 txqueuelen:0
16
17 [alex@shadrach alex]$
```

In Listing 3.2, line 1 shows the ifconfig command as typed at the command prompt. You might have to include the complete pathname for the command if you are not logged in as the root user. Lines 2 through 8 show the first network device found on the system. The first Ethernet NIC card is usually labeled as device eth0. Line 2 shows the Ethernet hardware, or MAC, address of the network card. Each network card has a unique MAC address. This enables devices to properly identify other devices on the network at the Ethernet packet layer. Line 3 shows the IP address information for the network device. This network card has been assigned the IP address 192.168.1.1 and is using a subnet mask of 255.255.255.0.

Lines 4 through 8 give statistics and information for the network card. These values are often handy as troubleshooting tools when you are experiencing network problems with the Linux system. Line 4 gives basic information about the status of the network device. If the network device is properly running, you should see the UP and RUNNING messages as shown in Line 4. Lines 5 through 7 can also be used for troubleshooting. If you cannot communicate with other devices, but see the TX (transmit) and RX (receive) packet counts increasing, that usually indicates that the server is connected to the network, but the IP address might be invalid. If you see a large number of errors and collisions, it is a good indication that you have a network media problem, such as a bad cable or defective network hub.

Lines 10 through 15 show information for the second network device found on the Linux system. The lo device is a special device called the loopback device. A *loopback device* is used as an internal network connection in the Linux system to enable the operating system to communicate with itself by using standard network protocols. The IP address shown in Line 11, 127.0.0.1, is the standard IP address for loopback devices. It cannot be used as a network address on a LAN.

Configure Mode

Configuring the ifconfig program enables you to modify information regarding network devices. The interface being configured must be specified. After the interface, the address family (aftype) may be listed. The address family is used for displaying and decoding all protocol addresses in ifconfig. Table 3.1 shows the available address families that can be used.

TABLE 3.1   ifconfig Address Families

Address Family	Description
inet	TCP/IP (default family)
inet6	Ipv6
ax25	AMPR packet radio
ddp	AppleTalk Phase 2
ipx	Novell IPX
netrom	AMPR packet radio

If no address family is specified, the default `inet` family is assumed. After the address family, various ifconfig options can be listed. Table 3.2 shows the options available for use with `ifconfig`.

TABLE 3.2 `ifconfig` Command Options

Option	Description
`interface`	Specifies the device to modify
`up`	Causes the interface to attempt to become active
`down`	Causes the interface to attempt to become inactive
`[-]arp`	Enables (or disables) the ARP protocol
`[-]promisc`	Enables (or disables) promiscuous mode
`[-]allmulti`	Enables (or disables) multicast capability
`metric N`	Specifies the interface metric used for routing
`mtu N`	Specifies the maximum transfer unit
`dstaddr address`	Sets the remote IP address on a point-to-point link
`netmask addr`	Sets the IP subnet mask
`add addr/prefixlen`	Adds an IPv6 address to the interface
`del addr/prefixlen`	Removes an IPv6 address from the interface
`tunnel a.b.c.d`	Creates a new SIT (IPv6 to IPv4) device
`irq addr`	Sets the IRQ address of the device
`io_addr addr`	Sets the I/O address of the device
`mem_start addr`	Sets the starting address of shared memory for the device
`media type`	Sets the physical medium type used by the device
`[-]broadcast [addr]`	Sets the IP broadcast address, or sets (or clears) the broadcast flag for the interface
`[-]pointtopoint [addr]`	Enables (or disables) point-to-point mode using `addr` for the remote IP address
`hw class addr`	Sets the hardware class and address for the device
`multicast`	Sets the multicast flag
`address`	Sets the IP address of the device
`txqueuelen length`	Sets the transmit queue length of the device

3

INSTALLING COMMUNICATION DEVICES IN LINUX

As shown in Table 3.2, many command-line parameters can be used by the ifconfig program to configure the network device. Multiple parameters can be entered on a single command line.

> ### `ifconfig` Command Format
>
> The ifconfig program uses a slightly different command-line format than you might be used to. Command-line options are listed without the customary leading dash (-).

Setting NIC Parameters

The proper hardware parameters must be configured using `ifconfig` for the Linux system to recognize the network card. If the NIC card uses jumpers to set these values, installing the NIC is easy. If you cannot determine the IRQ and I/O address values, you might need to boot the server with an MS-DOS boot disk and run the NIC's diagnostic program to set the values that the NIC will use. Maybe someday network card manufacturers will include a Linux executable version of their diagnostic programs.

A sample `ifconfig` command line could look like this:

```
ifconfig eth0 irq 9 io_addr 0x310
```

The command shown sets the `/dev/eth0` device to a NIC that is configured with IRQ 9 and base I/O address `310` (in hexadecimal). After this command is entered at the command line, an entry is made into the kernel table for this network device, and the Linux system will recognize the network card. For the Linux system to remember the settings, this `ifconfig` command should be placed in a boot script as described previously.

Assigning IP Addresses

After the hardware parameters are configured, the Linux system must have an IP address and subnet mask configured to communicate properly on the office network.

The ifconfig program can also be used to assign an IP address and subnet mask to the interface. A sample of this command is

```
ifconfig eth0 192.168.1.1 netmask 255.255.255.0 broadcast 192.168.1.255
```

This command defines the IP address of the `/dev/eth0` device to `192.168.1.1`, with a subnet mask of `255.255.255.0`. To verify that the addresses have been configured, you can type the `ifconfig` command alone at the command prompt to display the new information. Again, for Linux to use these parameters on subsequent boots, a boot script must be created with the `ifconfig` command.

Using netcfg

Before you go off trying to write a new init script to start the ifconfig program, there is an easier way. Many Linux distributions include a graphical X Window program that handles most of the unpleasantness of configuring the network interfaces and writing init scripts. Both Red Hat

Linux and Mandrake Linux use the netcfg program. Caldera OpenLinux uses the Caldera Open Administrator System (COAS) to perform the same network functions as netcfg.

The format of the `netcfg` command is simple:

```
netcfg
```

That's all. You must be the root user for netcfg to configure the network interfaces. Figure 3.4 shows the main window that will appear.

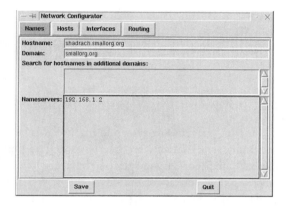

FIGURE 3.4

The main netcfg window.

The first window that appears is the Names window. This window enables you to change the configured hostname, domain, and DNS nameservers configured for the Linux system. Multiple nameservers can be configured for the system. Linux allows up to three nameservers to be specified.

If you click the Hosts button, the window shown in Figure 3.5 appears. The Hosts window enables you to modify the /etc/hosts file on the Linux server. By default, the loopback address and the local IP address of the server should be present. The address `localhost` is a special name for the loopback IP address `127.0.0.1`. Additional hostnames can be added to the /etc/hosts file from this window. If any commonly used hostnames will be used by your clients, you can add them to the /etc/hosts file to help speed up DNS lookups. Chapter 4, "DNS and Domain Names," describes the function of the /etc/hosts file in more detail.

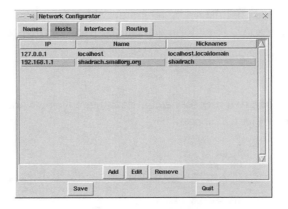

FIGURE 3.5
The Hosts netcfg window.

If you click the Interfaces button, the window shown in Figure 3.6 appears. The Interfaces window enables you to add, remove, and edit network interfaces to the Linux system. The first interface listed is the loopback interface. If you select an interface and click the Edit button, the Edit Ethernet/Bus Interface window appears. From this window, you can set the IP address and subnet mask for the interface. Also, you can specify whether this interface should be activated at boot time. If your network supports assigning IP addresses automatically using either the BOOTP or DHCP protocol, you can also specify that as the boot protocol. Each answer will be automatically added to the `ifcfg-eth0` script file described in the "Configuring Network Cards in the Boot Process" section. This is much easier than adding the network interface scripts manually.

Installing Modems

For most Linux mailservers, the modem is the gateway to the outside world. Unless your mailserver is connected to a LAN that is connected to the Internet, you must provide a connection to an Internet service provider for the mailserver to forward mail. That connection requires some kind of serial modem device. Today there are lots of different types of modems to choose from. This section describes how Linux communicates with modems, and gives some insights into how different types of modems can be used with Linux.

Linux Serial Ports

Most network administrators are familiar with the way the Microsoft MS-DOS and Windows operating systems interact with serial ports on IBM-compatible computers. The IBM-compatible architecture supports serial devices as COM ports. The ports are numbered 1 through 4, with each port having a separate IRQ and I/O address pair.

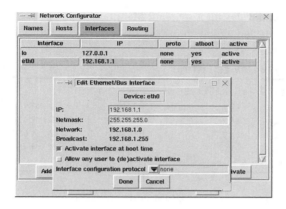

FIGURE 3.6
The Interfaces netcfg window.

Linux recognizes the same COM ports, but does not use the same naming convention. In Linux, they are called tty devices. Specifically, they are located at /dev/ttySx, where x is the number of the communication port. Unfortunately, Linux uses a different numbering scheme than Microsoft. Linux starts numbering serial ports at port 0, not port 1. Table 3.3 shows how the Linux serial ports match with MS-DOS serial ports.

TABLE 3.3 Linux Serial Ports

MS-DOS	Linux	IRQ	I/O Address
COM1	ttyS0	4	0x3f8
COM2	ttyS1	3	0x2f8
COM3	ttyS2	4	0x3e8
COM4	ttyS3	3	0x2e8

Multiport Serial Cards

Linux can also support multiport serial devices. These devices contain multiple serial ports that may share a single IRQ. They use special software drivers to differentiate between ports. In this situation, Linux continues the naming convention with ttyS4 and continues for as many ports as are available. Often these devices require special drivers in the Linux kernel which are normally supplied by the multiport manufacturer.

Listing 3.3 shows the ttyS*x* devices for a standard Mandrake Linux system on an IBM-compatible PC with two COM ports and a modem using COM4.

LISTING 3.3   `/dev/ttySx` Device Listing

```
1  [alex@shadrach /dev]$ ls -al ttyS*
2  crw-------  1 root     tty       4,  64 Nov 29 16:09 ttyS0
3  crw-------  1 root     tty       4,  65 May  5  1998 ttyS1
4  crw-------  1 root     tty       4,  66 May  5  1998 ttyS2
5  crw-------  1 root     tty       4,  67 May  5  1998 ttyS3
6  [alex@shadrach /dev]$
```

Listing 3.3 shows that although only three COM ports are used in the PC, by default, the Linux system created entries for all four basic COM ports. Attempting to use device ttyS2 would produce an error.

Linux also supports a mirror set of devices named `/dev/cuax` for each `/dev/ttySx` device. The purpose of the cua devices is to simplify the programming required to control the devices. The cua devices allow programs to connect to the device without a DCD signal being present. A DCD signal is a signal provided by the modem indicating that a connection is present. This feature is used mainly for dial-out software because no connection will be present when dialing out. Thus, the Linux convention was started to use cua for dial-out programs and ttyS for dial-in programs. Listing 3.4 show the cua devices on the same Mandrake Linux system used in Listing 3.3.

LISTING 3.4   `/dev/cuax` Device Listing

```
[alex@shadrach /dev]$ ls -al cua*
crw-------  1 root     root      5,  64 May  5  1998 cua0
crw-------  1 root     root      5,  65 May  5  1998 cua1
crw-------  1 root     root      5,  66 May  5  1998 cua2
crw-------  1 root     root      5,  67 May  5  1998 cua3
[alex@shadrach /dev]$
```

When using both dial-in and dial-out programs, modem locking becomes a problem. It has been found that it is easier to write the controlling software for the ttyS type of devices rather than to maintain code for two different types of device names for the same device.

> ### tty versus cua
>
> If the cua devices are present on your Linux distribution, avoid using them. Many software programs now produce a warning message when cua device names are used, indicating that they may be deprecated in future Linux kernels. It is best to refer to the serial lines by their tty names.

Another special device that may be present is the /dev/modem device. This is a symbolic link to the cua device to which the modem is connected. It was intended to simplify programs that need to communicate with the modem by creating a standard device with which to communicate. Many Linux distributions create this link when the operating system is first installed as part of the setup program. In the Red Hat and Mandrake Linux distributions, if you install a modem later, you can use the modemtool X Window program to create the /dev/modem link. Figure 3.7 shows the modemtool program window.

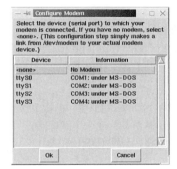

FIGURE 3.7
The modemtool utility.

The setserial Command

The setserial command is used to set and modify the configuration information for the individual serial ports on the Linux system. Each port that Linux uses must be configured with the setserial command. As shown in Listing 3.3, the four standard COM ports are configured by default. If you are using a modem that does not use standard IRQ or I/O port settings, or are using multiport serial devices, you must use the setserial program to properly configure the serial ports for Linux.

There are two formats of the `setserial` command. They are

```
setserial [-abqvVW] device [parameter 1 [arg] ] ...
```

```
setserial -g [-abv] device1 ...
```

The `-g` option is used to retrieve information regarding the listed devices. Listing 3.5 shows the output from using the `setserial` command on the sample Linux system.

LISTING 3.5   Sample Output from `setserial`

```
1   [root@shadrach rich]$ /sbin/setserial -g /dev/ttyS0 /dev/ttyS1 /dev/ttyS2
➥ /dev/ttyS3
2   /dev/ttyS0, UART: 16550A, Port: 0x03f8, IRQ: 4
3   /dev/ttyS1, UART: 16550A, Port: 0x02f8, IRQ: 3
4   /dev/ttyS2, UART: unknown, Port: 0x03e8, IRQ: 4
5   /dev/ttyS3, UART: 16550A, Port: 0x02e8, IRQ: 3
6   [root@shadrach rich]$
```

In Listing 3.5, line 1 shows the `setserial` command entered using the `-g` option to display the serial port information. You must be the root user to be able to run the `setserial` command. Lines 2 through 5 show the output of the command for the Linux system. Each line shows the information for a single serial port. Notice in line 4 that the unused ttyS2 port produces an "unknown" UART type. This might be misleading because in reality it does not exist.

You can modify the output from the setserial program by using one of the three available command-line options. The default output is the `-v` option, which produces the output shown in Listing 3.5. The `-b` option produces a summarized version of the output. An example of this output is

```
/dev/ttyS0 at 0x03f8 (irq = 4) is a 16550A
```

This produces the same information but in a compact method. The `-a` option can be used to produce a verbose output. An example of this output is

```
/dev/ttyS0, Line 0, UART: 16550A, Port: 0x03f8, IRQ: 4
Baud_base: 115200, close_delay: 50, divisor: 0
closing_wait: 3000, closing_wait2: infinite
Flags: spd_normal skip_test auto_irq session_lockout
```

The `-a` option displays values for the internal parameters used by Linux to control the device. These parameters can be set and modified by using the first format of the `setserial` command that was shown. Table 3.4 shows the parameters available to use with the `setserial` command.

TABLE 3.4 `setserial` Command-Line Parameters

Parameter	Description
port N	Sets the I/O port number of the device.
irq N	Sets the hardware IRQ of the device.
uart type	Sets the UART type of the device.
autoconfigure	Attempts to autodetect the serial device information.
auto_irq	Attempts to determine the IRQ of the serial device.
^auto_irq	Does not attempt to determine the IRQ of the serial device during autoconfigure.
skip_test	Skips the UART test during autoconfigure.
^skip_test	Does not skip the UART test during autoconfigure.
baud_base	Sets the base baud rate of the serial device; normally the clock rate divided by 16.
spd_hi	Uses 57.6kb when the application requests 38.4kb.
spd_vhi	Uses 115kb when the application requests 38.4kb.
spd_cust	Uses a custom divisor to set the speed when the application requests 38.4kb; set to the `baud_base` divided by the divisor.
spd_normal	Uses 38.4kb when the application requests 38.4kb.
divisor	Sets the `spd_cust` value.
sak	Sets the Break key as the Secure Attention Key.
^sak	Disables the Secure Attention Key.
fourport	Sets the device as an AST Fourport card.
^fourport	Disables AST Fourport configuration.
close_delay D	Sets the amount of time that DTR should remain low on a line after the device is closed, in hundredths of a second; default is **50**.
closing_wait D	Sets the amount of time that the kernel should wait for data to be transmitted from the serial port while closing the port, before the receiver has been disabled, in hundredths of a second. Default is none, for wait indefinitely.
closing_wait2 D	Sets the amount of time that the kernel should wait for data to be transmitted from the serial port while closing the port, after the receiver has been disabled, in hundredths of a second. Default is **30**.
session_lockout	Locks out the dial-out port (cua) access by other sessions when in use.
^session_lockout	Does not lock out the dial-out port access by sessions when in use.
pgrp_lockout	Locks out the dial-out port (cua) access by other processes when in use.

continues

3

INSTALLING COMMUNICATION DEVICES IN LINUX

TABLE 3.4 continued

Parameter	Description
^pgrp_lockout	Dos not lock out the dial-out port access by other processes when in use.
hup_notify	Notifies a process waiting on the dial-out line when it is available.
^hup_notify	Does not notify a process waiting on the dial-out line when it is available.
split_termios	Treat the termios settings used by the dial-out and dial-in devices as separate.
^split_termios	Does not treat the termios settings used by the dial-out and dial-in devices as separate.
callout_nohup	If the serial port is opened as a dial-out device, does not hang up the tty when carrier detect is dropped.
^callout_nohup	If the serial port is opened as a dial-out device, hangs up the tty when carrier detect is dropped.

The `setserial` command must always identify the device on which it is operating. If the default IRQ and I/O address for the port are being used, they can be omitted from the command line. After that, parameters can be entered on the command line in any order. A sample `setserial` command looks like the following:

```
setserial /dev/ttyS3 autoconfigure auto_irq skip_test
```

This command attempts to autodetect the serial device in COM4.

---

setserial Scripts

Just as with the ifconfig program, entries made by the setserial program in the kernel table disappear when the Linux server is rebooted. Thus, the `setserial` command should be executed for each COM port present in the server at each boot time. Because this is a common function, most Linux distributions include init scripts to run the `setserial` command.

Linux Serial Port Init Scripts

The default location for the setserial scripts is the `/etc/rc.d/rc.serial` file. Most Linux distributions include a generic version of this script that can be edited for the particular server configuration. The script contains many lines for special situations such as multiport serial boards and specially configured modem cards. Listing 3.6 shows an excerpt from a sample `rc.serial` script.

LISTING 3.6   Excerpt from an `/etc/rc.d/rc.serial` Script

```
1   STD_FLAGS="session_lockout"
2   SETSERIAL=/sbin/setserial
3   WILD=false
4   SUMMARY=true
5
6   echo -n "Configuring serial ports...."
7
8   ###############################################################
9   #
10  # AUTOMATIC CONFIGURATION
11  #
12  # Uncomment the appropriate lines below to enable auto-configuration
13  # of a particular board.  Or comment them out to disable them....
14  #
15  ###############################################################
16
17  # Do AUTOMATIC_IRQ probing
18  #
19  AUTO_IRQ=auto_irq
20
21  # These are the standard COM1 through COM4 devices
22  #
23  SetSerial /dev/ttyS0 ${AUTO_IRQ} skip_test autoconfig ${STD_FLAGS}
24  SetSerial /dev/ttyS1 ${AUTO_IRQ} skip_test autoconfig ${STD_FLAGS}
25  SetSerial /dev/ttyS2 ${AUTO_IRQ} skip_test autoconfig ${STD_FLAGS}
26  SetSerial /dev/ttyS3 ${AUTO_IRQ} autoconfig ${STD_FLAGS}
27
28  ###############################################################
29  #
30  # MANUAL CONFIGURATION
31  #
32  # If you want to do manual configuration of one or more of your
33  # serial ports, uncomment and modify the relevant lines.
34  #
35  ###############################################################
36
37  # These are the standard COM1 through COM4 devices
38  #
39  #SetSerial /dev/ttyS0 uart 16450 port 0x3F8 irq 4 ${STD_FLAGS}
40  #SetSerial /dev/ttyS1 uart 16450 port 0x2F8 irq 3 ${STD_FLAGS}
41  #SetSerial /dev/ttyS2 uart 16450 port 0x3E8 irq 4 ${STD_FLAGS}
42  #SetSerial /dev/ttyS3 uart 16450 port 0x2E8 irq 3 ${STD_FLAGS}
43
44  echo "done."
```

3

INSTALLING COMMUNICATION DEVICES IN LINUX

continues

LISTING 3.6   continued

```
45
46 ###########################################################
47 #
48 # Print the results of the serial configuration process
49 #
50 ###########################################################
51
52 if [ -n "$SUMMARY" ]; then
53   SetSerial -bg /dev/ttyS?
54
55   if [ '/dev/ttyS??' != /dev/ttyS?? ]; then
56     SetSerial -bg /dev/ttyS??
57   fi
58 fi
```

In Listing 3.6, lines 23 through 26 use setserial commands that attempt to autodetect the first four serial ports in the server. If you prefer that the server does not attempt to autodetect the serial ports, you can comment out these lines and uncomment lines 39 through 42. Lines 39 through 42 use the specific IRQ and I/O port addresses for each serial port in the setserial command. If you are using a modem configured with a nonstandard IRQ and I/O port setting, you can customize the appropriate setserial command to the proper values.

Linux Modem Support

Many different types of modems that can be used with the Linux server are available on the market. Unfortunately, many types of modems are also available on the market that cannot be used with the Linux server. The choice of modem can make the difference between a simple installation and a nightmare. This section describes what to look for in a modem if you are either purchasing a new modem to use or are trying to use one that has been lying around for awhile.

External Modems

Standard external modems are fairly safe to use with Linux. This type of modem connects to the Linux server COM port with a standard 9- or 25-pin modem cable, which can be purchased at nearly every computer store. At the time of this writing, the current standard for modems is the V.90 specification, which calls for a modem speed of 56kbps. Unfortunately, most of the time this speed is never realized in actual transmissions. The 56kbps speed is accomplished using advanced data compression and signaling techniques. On normal voice-grade telephone lines, the quality of the signal is not adequate for these advanced techniques to operate. It is common to connect at speeds around 38.4kbps when using a 56kbps modem. Nonetheless, it is still beneficial to use a V.90 modem to benefit from the advanced error correction methods that are used.

When using a high-speed modem, you can set the speed at which the modem communicates with the server using the internal modem registers. If this speed is not set, the modem attempts to connect to the server at the same speed that the remote modem connected, which can vary, depending on the phone line and remote modem. By setting the modem interface speed to a standard 115200bps, you can configure the serial port on the Linux server to a standard value. This is discussed in more detail later in the chapter.

Internal Modems

Internal modems are not as easy to work with. There are many pitfalls to using internal modems with Linux. First, avoid modems that are advertised as WinModem compatible. These modems are specially designed to work with the Microsoft Windows 95 and 98 operating systems. They do not include the proper interface hardware and will not work with Linux. They rely on software within Windows 95 and 98 to operate.

PCI modems are another problem to watch for with internal modems. PCI is a bus architecture that allows devices to be automatically configured at boot time. Depending on the devices installed, a single device can obtain any IRQ and I/O port setting for any given boot process. At the time of this writing, the Linux 2.2 kernel is not configured to properly handle PCI modems. There are rumors in the Linux community that the next version of the kernel will include advanced PCI card support. If a newer version of the Linux kernel is available, you might check this feature out.

Currently, if you have a PCI modem, you can try to get Linux to recognize it manually. At boot time, the PCI card settings are displayed by the system BIOS. Watch what IRQ is assigned to the modem card at boot time, and run the setserial program manually with the appropriate IRQ value. Although ugly, this method has been known to work.

Normal ISA type internal modems will work fine. Most often these modems include jumpers that can be configured to install the modem on a specific COM port. Remember not to use a COM port that is currently on the server as an external port. Also, be careful about what else is plugged into the existing COM ports. Those devices might be used at the same time as the modem. Many servers have pointer devices plugged into COM1 (such as a mouse). Remember from Table 3.3 that COM1 shares the same IRQ as COM3. If you install the internal modem as COM3, you will not be able to use the mouse and the modem at the same time. Ouch. To solve this problem, you should install the modem as the COM4 port. Of course, if you also have another device plugged into COM2, this might not be a solution. This is exactly the scenario that forces you to use nonstandard configurations for serial ports. You must pick an IRQ that is

3

INSTALLING
COMMUNICATION
DEVICES IN LINUX

not being used by any other devices on the system. Often, IRQs 9, 10, and 11 can be used for this purpose.

ISA Plug-and-Play Modems

One oddity in the IBM-compatible PC world is ISA plug-and-play devices. The precursor to PCI, they bridge the ISA and PCI worlds by using the ISA bus architecture, but attempt to autoconfigure IRQ and I/O ports at boot time. Much like the PCI situation, Linux cannot automatically detect and use ISA PnP modems.

Thankfully, there is some help. The isapnptools programs were written by Peter Fox to solve this problem. The isapnp program can read a configuration file that specifies the ISA PnP devices in the server, and configure them in the Linux kernel. If you do not know the configuration of the ISA PnP devices, don't worry: The pnpdump program can query them and attempt to create the configuration file automatically.

The format of the pnpdump program is

```
pnpdump [ --config ] [ --script[=outputfile] ] [ --reset ]
        [ --ignorecsum ] [ --showmasks ] [ --dumpregs ] [ [ devs ] readport ]
```

By default, the pnpdump program scans the ISA PnP cards and displays their resource data to the standard output. pnpdump resets the internal PnP serial numbers on all PnP cards and then isolates each card for examination. The devs parameter can be used to specify a number of devices you want pnpdump to scan. Using this technique, the PnP cards are not isolated and reset. However, a readport must be provided that matches the value stored in the BIOS.

Also by default, pnpdump displays the resource data for PnP cards, but comments out the configuration lines. By using the --config parameter, you can cause pnpdump to create a configuration file that the isapnp program can use to configure the ISA PnP modem card. Listing 3.7 shows excerpts from the configuration file created by the pnpdump --config command for a Linux system with an ISA PnP modem.

LISTING 3.7   Sample pnpdump --config Output

```
1  # $Id: pnpdump.c,v 1.16 1998/10/09 22:19:06 fox Exp $
2  # This is free software, see the sources for details.
3  # This software has NO WARRANTY, use at your OWN RISK
4  #
5  # For details of this file format, see isapnp.conf(5)
6  #
7  # For latest information on isapnp and pnpdump see:
8  # http://www.roestock.demon.co.uk/isapnptools/
9  #
10 # Compiler flags: -DREALTIME
```

```
11 #
12 # Trying port address 0203
13 # Board 1 has serial identifier 5b 10 0d 6a 0e 24 00 8c 0e
14 # Board 2 has serial identifier c5 00 00 11 11 01 00 36 10
15
16 # (DEBUG)
17 (READPORT 0x0203)
18 (ISOLATE PRESERVE)
19 (IDENTIFY *)
20 (VERBOSITY 2)
21 (CONFLICT (IO FATAL)(IRQ FATAL)(DMA FATAL)(MEM FATAL)) # or WARNING
22
23 # Card 2: (serial identifier c5 00 00 11 11 01 00 36 10)
24 # Vendor Id DAV0001, Serial Number 4369, checksum 0xC5.
25 #     Version 1.0, Vendor version 1.0
26 #     ANSI string -->DAVICOM 336PNP MODEM<--
27 #
28 # Logical device id DAV0336
29 #     Device support I/O range check register
30 #     Device supports vendor reserved register @ 0x39
31 #     Device supports vendor reserved register @ 0x3a
32 #     Device supports vendor reserved register @ 0x3d
33 #
34 # Edit the entries below to uncomment out the configuration required.
35 # Note that only the first value of any range is given, this may be changed
36 # if required. Don't forget to uncomment the activate (ACT Y) when happy
37
38 (CONFIGURE DAV0001/4369 (LD 0
39
40 # Multiple choice time, choose one only !
41
42 #     Start dependent functions: priority acceptable
43 #        Logical device decodes 16 bit IO address lines
44 #              Minimum IO base address 0x02f8
45 #              Maximum IO base address 0x02f8
46 #              IO base alignment 8 bytes
47 #              Number of IO addresses required: 8
48   (IO 0 (SIZE 8) (BASE 0x02f8))
49 #     IRQ 3.
50 #              High true, edge sensitive interrupt (by default)
51   (INT 0 (IRQ 3 (MODE +E)))
52
53 (NAME "DAV0001/4369[0]{DAVICOM 336PNP MODEM}")
54
55 #     End dependent functions
56   (ACT Y)
```

continues

3
INSTALLING
COMMUNICATION
DEVICES IN LINUX

LISTING 3.7 continued

```
57 ))
58 # End tag... Checksum 0x00 (OK)
59
60 # Returns all cards to the "Wait for Key" state
61 (WAITFORKEY)
```

Listing 3.7 is just a partial listing of the complete file generated by pnpdump. The pnpdump program generates all possible combinations of settings, but uncomments only the settings it thinks will work with the PnP card. The output of the pnpdump program can be redirected to a file to store the PnP card configurations:

```
pnpdump --config > /etc/isapnp.conf
```

The /etc/isapnp.conf file is the default location where the isapnp program looks to obtain configuration information. After the configuration file is created, the isapnp program can be run. The format of the isapnp command is

```
isapnp conffile
```

where conffile is an alternative location of the configuration file. After the isapnp program is run, the Linux system should recognize the PnP modem as a device. To finish the job, you must run the setserial program on the serial port that the PnP modem is configured for.

Like the setserial program, information generated by the isapnp program is placed in the kernel tables and is lost when the system is rebooted. As with the setserial program, the isapnp program can be run from an init script at boot time. Many Linux distributions allow for the isapnp program to be run whenever the /etc/isapnp.conf file is present. Remember that the setserial program must be run after the isapnp program to properly configure the ISA PnP modem serial port.

ISDN Modems

ISDN technology was available for several years with no significant uses. Now, with the Internet producing bandwidth-hungry remote users, ISDN modems have become more popular with Internet service providers and organizations that want higher speed remote network access.

ISDN modems can provide two 64kbps digital data channels. Both channels can be combined to produce an effective 128kbps bandwidth for data. This is ideal for small organizations wanting to provide interactive Internet service to the desktops for Web browsing, file transfers, and email service.

ISDN modem support in Linux has also been a recent (and ongoing) development. The most recent Linux kernel at the time of this writing (2.2) includes basic ISDN support. Future kernels are promised to contain more ISDN support. Most of the ISDN development work has been coming out of Germany from the SuSe Linux group. It has created the ISDN4Linux toolkit, which can be used to set up an ISDN modem on a Linux server. The ISDN4Linux toolkit contains many useful utilities for configuring the Linux server to use an ISDN modem. Table 3.5 lists the available utilities.

TABLE 3.5   ISDN4Linux Toolkit Utilities

Utility	Description
isdnctrl	General link-level setup utility
iprofd	Daemon for realizing AT&W0 on ttyI's
icnctrl	Setup utility for icn driver
telesctrl	Setup utility for teles driver
hisaxctrl	Setup utility for HiSax driver
pcbitctrl	Setup utility for pcbit driver
avmcapictrl	Setup utility for avmb1 driver
actctrl	Setup utility for act2000 driver
eiconctrl	Setup utility for eicon driver
divertctrl	Setup utility for dss1 diversion services
imon	Ncurses-based monitoring utility
imontty	tty-based monitoring utility
isdnlog	ISDN connection logging utility
ipppstats	syncPPP statistics utility
xisdnload	xload-like monitor
isdnmon	Tcl/Tk based monitoring utility
vbox	Answering machine/voice mailbox
ipppd	Daemon needed for syncPPP and MPP

3

INSTALLING COMMUNICATION DEVICES IN LINUX

Several documents are available with the ISDN4Linux toolkit that describe the necessary steps to install and configure ISDN modems on Linux servers. Because Linux ISDN support is still in its infancy, there is no doubt that it will improve in future Linux releases.

Controlling Modems in Linux

After the modem serial port is configured, Linux must run a separate program to monitor the line and recognize when it is being used. Several programs can be used to control the serial port device, but the most common one is the getty program. The getty program allows the modem to be work as both a dial-in and dial-out line. When dialing-in, getty accepts the incoming call and passes the session to the login program to validate a userid and password entered from the remote client.

The format of the getty command is

```
getty [-d defaults_file] [-a] [-h] [-r delay] [-t timeout] [-w waitfor]
       ➥line [speed [type [lined]]]
```

The getty program is often started by the init program to monitor the modem line at all times. For the getty program to be started by init, it must be present in the /etc/inittab file. The inittab file contains the programs that will be started by the init process when it starts at boot time. The format for using the getty command in the inittab file is

```
s1:345:respawn:/sbin/getty ttyS0 38400 vt100
```

The first field is a label that uniquely identifies the entry in the inittab file. The second field is a list of the init run levels in which the program will be started. This process will start in run levels 3, 4, and 5. The third field contains information that the init program uses on how to run the program. The respawn keyword instructs the init program that if the original getty program stops, init will start it again. This is necessary to allow getty to monitor the modem after a connection has finished.

The fourth field is the getty command line with its parameters. This example shows the getty program monitoring /dev/ttyS0 (COM1), with the port speed set to 38400bps. This allows the modem to be set to a constant interface speed. The last parameter specifies the terminal emulation type used for the line. The getty program can produce a greeting when the modem line becomes active. The terminal emulation type is necessary to properly format the greeting message.

Summary

For the Linux mailserver to communicate with other hosts and workstations, it must have communication devices installed. To communicate with other workstation on the local office network, there must be an Ethernet Network Interface Card (NIC) installed. The ifconfig program can be used to configure the necessary IP address information on the NIC. There are also graphical X Window–based programs available for configuring the NIC. The netcfg program is one example that is used on Mandrake and Red Hat Linux distributions. For the mailserver to communicate with the remote Internet service provider, it must be able to interface with some type of modem. Many different types of modems can be used by the Linux server. External V.90 modems are the easiest to configure and use provided that the Linux server contains at least one standard COM port. Internal modems can be used if they are standard ISA type modems. PCI modems are difficult to configure, but can work. The isapnp Linux program can be used to help configure ISA plug-and-play type modems. After the modem is installed, the setserial program must be run for Linux to recognize the serial port as a valid device. After Linux recognizes the device, the getty program can be used to monitor the device for incoming and outgoing connections.

3

INSTALLING COMMUNICATION DEVICES IN LINUX

DNS and Domain Names

IN THIS CHAPTER

What's in a name? Plenty if you are a Montague, or are using the Internet. How would you react if your favorite product was advertised on television with the statement, "visit our Web site at 198.182.196.56 for more information"? Would you make it as far as your PC before forgetting the address? I wouldn't.

Unfortunately humans don't process numbers as well as computers. To compensate for that, systems administrators have used names to identify their computer systems. The domain name system (DNS) was developed to aid humans in easily locating computer names on the Internet. The use of DNS is vital in properly processing email. If you choose to let your ISP handle your domain name and email, you might not need to know the details about DNS configurations, but it might not be a bad idea to know how DNS works in general (just in case of any problems). This chapter discusses where DNS came from, why it is so vital to email operations, and how you can configure your Linux server to use it either as a client or as a DNS server.

History of Computer Names

Back in the old days when the Internet was small (just a few hundred computers), it wasn't too complicated to locate another computer. Each Internet computer had a database of hostnames and IP addresses. Internet hostnames could be anything the administrator desired—Fred, Barney, Acct1, anything. There was a central clearinghouse for keeping track of new computer names and addresses. Once a week or so, a system administrator would download a new copy of the current database. Of course this system did have its drawbacks. When someone brought a new computer online, he needed to search the database to make sure that nobody had already used the clever new hostname he wanted to use. It didn't take system administrators long to figure out that this method was on a collision course with progress. As the Internet grew, so did the database. As the database grew, so did the time it took to download and search it. It was also starting to get difficult to come up with a unique hostname. Something had to be changed, and it was.

Domain Names

The method that was agreed upon was the domain name system (DNS). DNS uses a hierarchical distributed database to break up the hostname's database. That's a catchy phrase to say that now no one computer has to maintain the entire database of Internet devices. The database is distributed among multiple computers, called DNS servers, on the Internet. For client computers to locate another computer on the Internet, they only need to find the nearest DNS server and query for the IP address of the remote computer. In order to implement this system, a new protocol was invented to pass the DNS information from the DNS server to the client, as well as software created for DNS server computers to implement the new database system.

DNS Structure

The structure of a hierarchical database is similar to an organization chart with nodes connected in a tree-like manner (the hierarchical part). The top node is called the *root*. The root node does not explicitly show up in addresses, so it is called the nameless node. Multiple categories were created under the root level to divide the database into pieces called domains. Each domain contains DNS servers that are responsible for maintaining the database of computer names for that area of the database (the distributed part). Figure 4.1 shows a diagram of how the DNS domains are distributed.

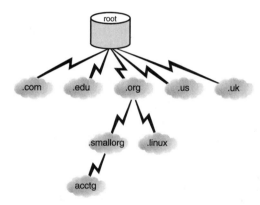

FIGURE 4.1

A diagram of the Internet domain name system.

The first (or top) level of distribution is divided into domains based on country codes. Additional top level domains for specific U.S. organizations were created to prevent the .us domain from getting overcrowded. The domain name is appended to the end of the computer hostname to form the unique Internet hostname for that computer. This is the popular hostname format that we are now familiar with. Table 4.1 shows how the top level DNS domains are laid out.

TABLE 4.1   DNS Top Level Domain Names

Name	Description
.com	U.S. commercial organizations
.edu	U.S. educational institutions
.gov	U.S. government organizations
.mil	U.S. military sites
.net	U.S. Internet providers

continues

TABLE 4.1   continued

Name	Description
.org	U.S. non-profit organizations
.us	other U.S. organizations
.ca	Canadian organizations
.de	German organizations
(other country codes)	Other countries' organizations

As the Internet grows, the top level domains are each divided into subdomains, or zones. Each zone is an independent domain in itself, but relies on its parent domain for connectivity to the database. A parent zone must grant permission for a child zone to exist and is responsible for the child zone's behavior (just like in real life). Each zone has at least two DNS servers that maintain the DNS database for the zone.

The original specifications stipulated that the DNS servers for a single zone must have separate connections to the Internet and be housed in separate locations for fault-tolerance purposes. Because of this stipulation, many organizations rely on other organizations to host their secondary and tertiary DNS servers.

Hosts within a zone add their domain name to their hostname to form their unique Internet name. Thus, computer 'fred' in the smallorg.org domain would be called fred.smallorg.org. It becomes a little confusing because a domain can contain hosts as well as zones. For example, the smallorg.org domain can contain host fred.smallorg.org, as well as grant authority for zone acctg.smallorg.org to a subdomain, which in turn can contain another host barney.acctg.smallorg.org. Although this simplifies the database system, it makes finding hosts on the Internet more complicated. Figure 4.2 shows an example of a domain and an associated subdomain.

Internet Domain Names

In the past few years, Internet domain names have become a hot topic. In the past, one single corporation controlled all U.S. domain names in the .com, .net, and .org domains—the Internic Corporation. Recently, a nonprofit organization—the Internet Corporation for Assigned Names and Numbers (ICANN)—was created to control this process. ICANN is now responsible for the management of all U.S. domain names. The purchase of a domain name can now be made from multiple vendors, not just one company. All domain names must be cleared by the ICANN for use in the U.S. domains.

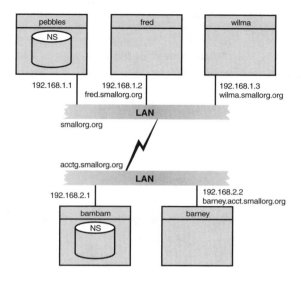

FIGURE 4.2

A sample domain and subdomain on the Internet.

DNS allows for three different scenarios to occur in finding an IP address using the DNS system:

1. A computer that wants to communicate with another computer in the same zone queries the local DNS server in the zone to find the address of the remote computer. The local DNS server should have the address of the remote computer in its local database and return the IP address.

2. A computer that wants to communicate with a computer in another zone queries the local DNS server in its zone. The local DNS server realizes the requested computer is in a different zone and queries a root-level DNS server for the answer. The root DNS server then walks the tree of DNS servers to find the local zone DNS server and gets an IP address for the remote computer. It then passes the address to the local DNS server, which in turn passes the information it receives to the requesting computer. Part of the information that is returned with the IP address of the remote computer is a time to live (TTL) value. This instructs the local DNS server that it can keep the IP address of the remote computer in a local name cache for the amount of time of the TTL value. This will speed up any subsequent name requests.

3. A computer that wants to communicate with the same remote computer in another zone queries the local DNS server in its zone. The local DNS server checks its name cache, and if the TTL value has not expired, the server sends the IP address of the remote computer to the requesting client computer. This is considered a non-authoritative response,

4

DNS AND DOMAIN NAMES

as the local DNS server is assuming that the remote computer's IP address has not changed since it was last checked.

In all three instances, the local computer only needs to know the IP address of its local DNS server to find the IP address of any computer on the Internet. It is the job of the local DNS server to find the proper IP address for the given hostname. The local computer's life is now much simpler. Figure 4.3 shows a diagram of how these different functions operate.

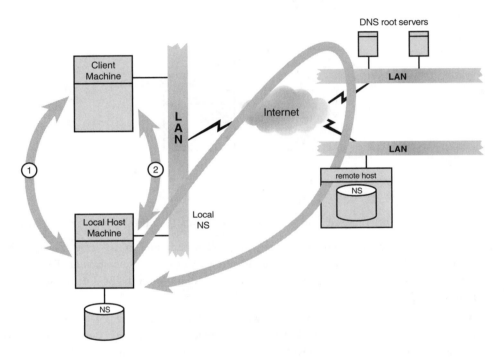

FIGURE 4.3

A diagram of different DNS resolution methods.

As the DNS tree grows, new requirements are made on DNS servers. As mentioned, parent DNS servers are required to know the IP addresses of their children zone DNS servers to properly pass DNS queries on to them for resolution. The tricky part comes into play with the lower-level zone DNS servers. In order for them to properly process DNS queries, they have to be able to start their name searches somewhere in the DNS tree. When the Internet was in its infancy, most of the name searches were for local hostnames. The bulk of the DNS traffic was able to stay local to the zone DNS server or, at worst, its parent. However, with the increased popularity of the Internet and Web browsing, more DNS requests were made for remote hostnames. When a DNS server did not have the hostname in its local database, it would need to query a remote DNS server.

The most likely candidate for the remote DNS server is a top level domain DNS server that has the knowledge to work its way down the tree until it finds the responsible zone DNS server for the remote host and returns the result to the local DNS server. This puts a great deal of stress on the root servers. Fortunately there are quite a few of them, and they do a good job of distributing the load. The local DNS servers communicate with the top level domain DNS servers using the DNS protocol that is discussed later in this chapter.

DNS is a two-way street. Not only is it useful for finding the IP address of a computer based on its hostname, but it is also useful for finding the hostname of a computer based on its IP address. Many Internet Web and FTP sites restrict access based on a client computer's domain. When the connection request is made from a client, the host server passes the IP address of the client to the DNS server as a reverse DNS query. If the client's DNS zone database is configured correctly, the client's hostname should be returned to the server, which in turn can decide whether to grant access to the client.

DHCP and DNS

If your organization uses Dynamic Host Configuration Protocol (DHCP) to dynamically assign IP addresses to workstations, you might have to create DNS records for all possible DHCP addresses that can be assigned by the server. Often a generic hostname can be assigned to each address, such as station1.smallorg.org.

DNS Database Records

Each DNS server is responsible for keeping track of the hostnames in its zone. To accomplish this, the DNS server must have a method of storing host information in a database that can be queried by remote machines. The DNS database is a text file that consists of resource records (RRs) that describe computers and functions in the zone. The Linux server must run a DNS server software package—usually named—to communicate the DNS information from the database to remote DNS servers. The named program is discussed in detail later in this chapter.

The DNS server's database first has to declare the zone that it is responsible for. Then, it must declare each host computer in its zone. Finally, the database can declare special information for the zone, such as email and name servers. Resource record formats were created to track all the information required for the DNS server. Table 4.2 shows some of the basic RRs that a DNS database could contain. DNS database design has become a hot topic lately with researchers who want to add more information to the database, as well as increase the security of the information that is there. New record types are constantly being added to the DNS database. The record types in Table 4.2 represent the core records needed to establish a zone in the DNS database.

TABLE 4.2 DNS Database Resource Record Types

Record Type	*Description*
SOA	Start of Authority
A	Internet address
NS	Name Server
CNAME	Canonical name (nickname)
HINFO	Host Information
MX	Mail Server
PTR	Pointer

Each domain DNS server should contain resource records for the hosts in the domain. There should be one SOA record for the domain listed at the top of the database. Any other resource records for the domain can be added in any order after that. Figure 4.4 demonstrates how the DNS database would look for the sample network that was shown previously in Figure 4.2. The next section describes the DNS records in more detail.

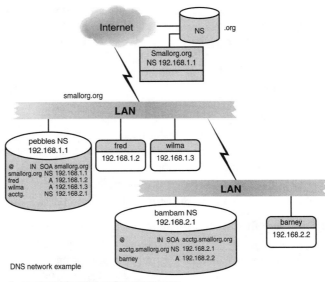

FIGURE 4.4

The DNS records for the sample network.

Start of Authority Record (SOA)

Each database starts with an SOA record that defines the zone in which the database resides. The format for the SOA record is

```
domain name      [TTL] [class] SOA origin person (
                       serial number
                       refresh
                       retry
                       expire
                       minimum)
```

`domain name` is the name of the zone that is being defined (the @ sign can be used as a placeholder to signify the computer's default domain).

`TTL` is the time (in seconds) that a requesting computer will keep any DNS information from this zone in its local name cache. This value is optional.

`class` is the protocol that is being used (which in our case will always be class `IN` for Internet). This value is optional and will default to `IN`.

`origin` is the name of the computer where the master zone database is located. Be careful to include a trailing period . after the hostname, or your local domain name will be appended to the hostname (unless of course you want to use that feature).

`person` is an email address of a person responsible for the zone. This is a little different than usual because the @ sign is already used to signify the default domain name, so it can't be used in the mail address. Instead, use a period . in place of the @ sign. For example, instead of using `sysadm@smallorg.org`, you would use `sysadm.smallorg.org`. If there are any periods . in the name part, they must be escaped out by using a backslash \. An example of this is the address `john.jones@smallorg.org`. This address translates to `john\.jones.smallorg.org`.

`serial number` is a unique number that identifies the version of the zone database file. Often the date created plus a version count is used (such as 199908051).

`refresh` is the time (in seconds) that a secondary DNS server should query a primary DNS server to check the SOA serial number. If it is different, it will request an update to its database. Specifying one hour (3,600 seconds) is common for this value.

`retry` is the time (in seconds) that a secondary DNS server should retry after a failed refresh attempt.

`expire` is the time (in seconds) that a secondary DNS server can use the data retrieved from the primary DNS server without getting refreshed. This value should usually be large, such as 3,600,000 (about 42 days).

`minimum` is the time (in seconds) that should be used as the `TTL` in all RRs in this zone. Usually 86,400 (1 day) is a good value.

Internet Address Record (A)

Each host in the zone defined by the database should have a valid `A` record to define its hostname to the Internet. The format for the `A` record is

```
host    [TTL]    [class]    A    address
```

`host` is the fully qualified hostname for the computer (including the domain name).

`address` is the IP address of the computer.

Canonical Name (CNAME)

Besides a normal hostname, many computers also have nicknames. This is useful if you want to identify particular services without having to rename computers in your domain, such as `www.smallorg.org`. The `CNAME` record links nicknames with the real hostname. The format of the `CNAME` record is

```
nickname    [TTL]    [class]    CNAME    host name
```

Name Server Record (NS)

Each zone should have at least two DNS servers. `NS` records are used to identify these servers to other DNS servers trying to resolve hostnames within the zone. The format of an `NS` record is

```
domain    [TTL]    [class]    NS    server
```

`domain` is the domain name of the zone that the DNS server is responsible for. If it is blank, the `NS` record refers to the zone defined in the `SOA` record.

`server` is the hostname of the DNS server. There should also be an associated `A` record to identify the IP address of the DNS server.

Host Information Record (HINFO)

Additional information about a computer can be made available to DNS servers by using the `HINFO` record. The format of the `HINFO` record is

```
host    [TTL]    [class]    HINFO    hardware    software
```

`host` is the hostname of the computer the information applies to.

`hardware` is the type of hardware the computer is using.

`software` is the OS type and version of the computer.

Pointer Record (PTR)

In addition to an A record, each computer in the zone should also have a PTR record. This allows the DNS server to perform reverse queries from the IP address of the computer. Without this information, remote servers could not determine the domain name where your computer is located. The format of a PTR record is

```
IN-ADDR name     [TTL]     [class]     PTR     name
```

IN-ADDR name is the reverse DNS name of the IP address. If that sounds confusing, it is. This name allows the DNS server to work its way backward from the IP address of the computer. The IN-ADDR.ARPA address is a special domain to support gateway location and Internet address-to-host mapping. Inverse queries are not necessary because the IP address is mapped to a fictitious hostname. The IN-ADDR name of a computer with IP address 192.168.0.1 would be 1.0.168.192.IN-ADDR.ARPA.

name is the hostname of the computer as found in the A record.

Mail Server Record (MX)

Most important (at least as far as we mail administrators are concerned) are the MX records. They instruct remote mail servers where to forward mail for your zone. The format of the MX record is

```
name    [TTL]    [class]    MX    preference    host
```

name is the zone name (or the SOA zone if it is blank). This can also be a hostname if you want to redirect mail for a particular host in your network.

preference is an integer signifying the order in which remote servers should try connecting if multiple mail servers are specified—0 being the highest preference with decreasing preference for increasing numbers. This is used to create primary and secondary mail servers for a zone. When a remote mail server queries the DNS server for a mail server responsible for the zone, the entire list of servers and preferences are sent. The remote mail server should attempt to connect to the highest priority mail server listed, and if that fails, continue down the list by preference.

host is the hostname of the mail server. There should also be an associated A record to identify the IP address of the mail server.

A Sample DNS Database for a Domain

If you allow your ISP to host your domain name and email, they will have records in their DNS database identifying your domain to the Internet. The SOA record will identify your domain name, but point to the ISP's host as the authoritative host. The NS records for your domain will point to your ISP's DNS servers, and your MX records will point to your ISP's mail servers. As far as the rest of the Internet is concerned, these computers are part of your network, even though they do not really exist on "your" network. Listing 4.1 shows a sample of how your ISP might define your zone definitions in its DNS database.

LISTING 4.1   DNS Zone Database Entry

```
1   smallorg.org  IN   SOA    master.isp.net. postmaster.master.isp.net (
2                                 1999080501    ;unique serial number
3                                 8H         ; refresh rate
4                                 2H         ;retry period
5                                 1W         ; expiration period
6                                 1D)         ; minimum
7
8              NS    ns1.isp.net.    ;defines primary name server
9              NS    ns2.isp.net.    ; defines secondary name server
10
11             MX    10 mail1.isp.net.   ; defines primary mail server
12             MX    20 mail2.isp.net.   ; defines secondary mail server
13
14   www    CNAME    host1.isp.net    ;defines your www server at the ISP
15   ftp    CNAME    host1.isp.net    ; defines your FTP server at the ISP
16
17   host1.isp.net   A    10.0.0.1
18
19   1.0.0.10.IN-ADDR.ARPA     PTR    host1.isp.net    ; pointer address for
  ➥reverse DNS
```

Lines 1-6 show the SOA record for your new domain. The ISP points your domain name smallorg.org to the ISP server master.isp.net. Lines 8 and 9 define the primary and secondary DNS servers that will be used to resolve your hostnames (again, belonging to the ISP), and lines 11 and 12 define the primary (mail1.isp.net) and secondary (mail2.isp.net) mail servers that will receive and spool mail for your domain. Lines 14 and 15 define nicknames for services in your domain. The hostname www.smallorg.org is a nickname that points to the ISP server that hosts your Web pages. The address ftp.smallorg.org is also a nickname that points to the same ISP server that also hosts your FTP site. This is a service that most ISPs provide to customers who cannot afford to have a dedicated connection to the Internet, but want to provide Web and FTP services to their customers. Lines 17 and 19 provide the Internet IP address information so that remote clients can connect to this server. Often PTR records, such as the one shown in line 19, are placed in a separate database file on the server to help simplify the databases. In this example with just one PTR record that is not a problem, but often there can be dozens of them.

When a DNS server has a valid database installed, it must be able to communicate with other DNS servers to resolve hostname requests from clients and to respond to other DNS servers' queries about hosts in its zone. The DNS protocol was invented to accomplish that.

DNS Protocol

The DNS protocol serves two functions in life. It allows client computers to query a DNS server for an IP address or a hostname, and it allows DNS servers to communicate with each other and pass DNS database information back and forth. It uses a standard request/response format, where the client submits a request packet, and the server returns a response packet with either the information from the database, or an error message stating the reason the query could not be processed. The DNS protocol uses either TCP or UDP well-known ports 53 to communicate, although UDP has become the preferred method of transportation across the Internet. The DNS packet contains five main sections—header, question, answer, authority, and additional information. Figure 4.5 shows the basic structure for a DNS packet.

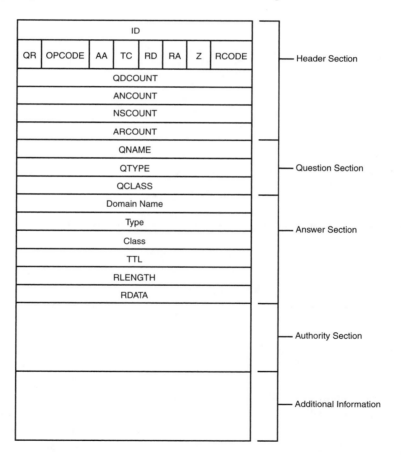

4

DNS AND DOMAIN NAMES

FIGURE 4.5

A DNS protocol packet description.

Header Section

The header section contains information identifying the packet and its purpose. It gives the basic information regarding whether the packet is a request or response packet, and how much of each type of data is contained in the packet. The layout of the header section is shown in Table 4.3.

TABLE 4.3   DNS Packet Header Section

Bit	Description
0-15	ID
16	QR
17-20	OPCODE
21	AA
22	TC
23	RD
24	RA
25-27	Z
28-31	RCODE
32-47	QDCOUNT
48-63	ANCOUNT
64-79	NSCOUNT
80-95	ARCOUNT

The ID bits specify a unique 16-bit identification number for the request packet. The response packet from the server will use the same identification number so that the client can match the response to the query. The QR bit signifies whether the packet is a query (0) or a response (1). The OPCODE section determines the type of query—standard query (0), inverse query (1), or server status request (2).

The next four bits determine the characteristics of the packet. The AA bit is set when the response is authoritative (the data came directly from the DNS server responsible for the zone). Non-authoritative answers come from DNS servers that might have the RR information in their cache from previous DNS look ups. This information is considered non-authoritative because there is a possibility that it could be wrong. The TC bit is set when the packet data had to be truncated to fit the packet into the transportation medium. This is possible when using the UDP protocol, which limits the packet size to 512 bytes. The RD bit is set when a client desires the server to pursue the query recursively. If this is set, the DNS server will query other DNS servers to obtain the answer. If it is not set, the DNS server will just return whatever information it has for the query. The RA bit is set to tell the client that recursion is available on the server. The Z bits are not used at this time, but are reserved for future use.

The RCODE bits are used in response packets. They indicate the status of the response—no errors (0), query format errors (1), internal errors that prevented the server from processing the query (2), the name requested in the query does not exist (3), the server does not support the query type (4) or the server has refused to process the query (5).

The last four items are 16-bit numbers that are used as counters. They count the number of resource records returned in the packet. QDCOUNT is the number of queries (more than one query can be encapsulated in a packet). ANCOUNT is the number of answer RRs in the answer section. NSCOUNT is the number of DNS server RR records in the authority section, and ARCOUNT is the number of RRs in the additional information section.

Question Section

The question section contains the queries that the client wants to have answered by the DNS server. A single DNS packet can contain multiple queries. The number of queries present is indicated by the QDCOUNT parameter in the header section. The question section consists of three parts—a list of domain names to resolve, the type of records the client wants returned, and the class of the query. The list of domain names is what the client wants to have resolved into IP addresses. As there can be multiple names listed, a specific format is used to list the names. Each name is preceded by a one-byte value that is the length of the name. The end of the list is signified by a length value of 0. Following the text section, a two-byte QTYPE record is added. This signifies what kind of information the client wants to receive about the listed domains. These values are the same as the DNS RR types. For finding the email server for a domain, you would use the MX record type. The last part of the question section is the QCLASS area, which defines the class of the query, which in our case is always IN for Internet.

Answer, Authority, and Additional Information Sections

The next three sections in the DNS packet have the same record format. They each return data using the resource record format that is used in the DNS database. The answers contain the DNS database RR information available to the server for the resources asked for by the client. If the AA bit in the header is not set, the authority section lists other DNS servers that the client can query to obtain authoritative answers. Again, authoritative answers come from the DNS servers that are responsible for the zone in which the requested hostname is contained. Any other responses are considered non-authoritative as their information might have been obtained from an outdated name cache on a DNS server. The additional information section will list any related RRs that the DNS server felt were relevant to the query.

4

DNS AND DOMAIN NAMES

An example would be if you request the MX information for a domain, the answer section will contain the MX records, and the additional information section might contain the A records for the servers listed in the answer section. That way, you would know the hostname and IP address of the mail server for the domain in just one DNS query.

The format of a resource record in a DNS packet is shown in Table 4.4.

TABLE 4.4 Answer, Authority, and Additional Record Formats

Section	Description
Names	The variable-length domain name string that pertains to the resource record
TYPE	The RR type that pertains to the record
CLASS	The RR class that pertains to the record
TTL	The 32-bit TTL value of the record
RDLENGTH	The 16-bit length of the data record
RDATA	The variable-length string that describes the record

The RDATA values in the answer section provide the results for the requested query. For MX records, the format is different from a simple text string. The preference value is added to the string as well as the mail server name.

Name Compression

In situations where multiple records are returned as a response, there could be duplication of text data. An example would be if there were two NS records returned—one for ns1.isp.net and another for ns2.isp.net. It would be more efficient to return the answer as ns1 and ns2 in domain isp.net. In an attempt to minimize packet size during the DNS query, the DNS protocol implements a method of using this type of compression of the information in the packet. A shorthand method was devised to indicate duplicate domain information. A pointer system was implemented to track the duplicate information and transmit a minimum amount of bytes. As previously discussed, the first byte in the names section is a one-byte integer signifying the length of the domain name. To implement name compression, the meaning of the top two bits of this value has been changed. If the top two bits are both zero, the byte has the same meaning as before—the length of the domain name. If the top two bits are both ones, the value becomes a pointer to an offset in the names section that signifies the remainder part of the domain name to tack onto the name.

DNS and Email

Computers must follow a set process to properly deliver email, and knowing how that process works sometimes helps out when it comes time to troubleshoot email problems. When a remote client tries to send an email message to prez@smallorg.org, several steps are taken before the message is sent:

1. The local DNS server for the client must first determine which computer in smallorg.org to send the email to. It does this by looking for a MX record for the smallorg.org domain.

2. If the local DNS server does not contain any information in its local database or name cache, it must traverse the Internet searching for an answer. The first stop would be one of the top level domain DNS servers. That server would not have your MX record, but it would know how to get to a DNS server for the .org domain.

3. That server, in turn, would not have your information, but would (or at least should) know the IP address of a DNS server for the smallorg.org domain, and query it for an appropriate MX record. If one or more MX records exist, they are sent back up the chain until they get to the requesting client computer.

4. When the client has the address(es) in hand, it must then try and establish an SMTP connection (see Chapter 5, "SMTP Protocol") to the primary mail server for the smallorg.org domain.

5. If that connection fails, it will then try the secondary mail server address returned in the answer section, and so on until it either establishes a connection, or runs out of servers to try. At this point, it is up to the client's mail program what to do next. Most will try the same process again a few hours later, up to a set point when it will finally give up.

If your domain database is not configured correctly, the DNS search for your mail host will fail, and the client will not be able to deliver the mail message. Remember that at no point in the DNS process was the mail message sent. The purpose of this process is that the remote client can find the IP address of a computer that would accept mail messages for the smallorg.org domain. When it finds an address, it can then (hopefully) initiate an SMTP mail session.

Linux as a DNS Client

If you do not have a dedicated connection to the Internet, you should not use your Linux server as a DNS server for your domain. If someone tried sending email to you at three o'clock in the morning and your Linux server was not up and connected to the Internet, she might not be able to resolve your domain name and send your message. Most ISPs provide a DNS server for their clients that is continually connected to the Internet. The ISP's DNS server directs the remote client to the proper email server for your domain. Again, if your network is not directly connected to the Internet, most likely the ISP will accept the email messages and spool them to be picked up later by your Linux mailserver when it is convenient.

If the Linux server has a dedicated connection to the Internet but you still want the ISP to host your DNS domain records, the Linux server can be configured to use the ISP DNS server to resolve remote hostnames. The following sections describe how to configure the Linux server to do this.

Configuring DNS Client Files

Three files are needed to use your Linux server as a DNS client to resolve hostnames. All three files are normally located in the /etc directory. They are `resolv.conf`, `hosts`, and `host.conf`.

Hostname Resolver File

The `/etc/resolv.conf` file is used to tell Linux the DNS server where you want to send your DNS queries. You can list up to three DNS servers. The second and third entries will be used as backup if no response is received from the first (primary) server. If you have a local DNS server in your network, you should use that as your primary, although it isn't required. If you access other computers in your local network by name, it would increase performance to specify the local DNS server because it would have the name resolution quickly. If you just use DNS to access remote computers, there probably won't be much of any performance increase. You can also specify a default domain name to use when looking up domain names. If your domain is `smallorg.org`, you can specify that as the default domain to search in. That way if you need the IP address for hostname `fred.smallorg.org`, you can specify 'fred', and Linux will automatically append the `smallorg.org` to it. Unfortunately that can work against you. The DNS software will automatically append `smallorg.org` to *everything* that it tries to resolve. If you try connecting to `www.linux.org`, it will first attempt to find `www.linux.org.smallorg.org`. When that fails, it will try `www.linux.org`. Listing 4.2 shows a sample `/etc/resolv.conf` file used in a Linux client.

LISTING 4.2   Sample `/etc/resolv.conf` File

```
1    search smallorg.org
2    nameserver 10.0.0.1
3    nameserver 10.0.0.2
4    nameserver 10.0.0.3
```

Line 1 shows the search statement that defines the default domain to use in all DNS queries. Remember that this will slow down queries for hosts not in your domain because the search text is appended to all queries. Lines 2-4 show the primary, secondary, and tertiary DNS servers that service this Linux client. Most often they are the DNS servers assigned to you by your ISP, although you are free to try other DNS servers if you want to (unless of course your ISP filters out DNS requests).

hosts File

Another method of resolving hostnames is to use a local host database, much like what was previously done on the Internet. The /etc/hosts file contains a list of hostnames and related IP addresses. Listing 4.3 shows a sample /etc/hosts file for a Linux client. At the minimum, this should contain your local hostname and IP address, as well as the common loopback address 127.0.0.1 for internal communications on the Linux server. If there are remote hosts that you regularly access, you could find their IP addresses and manually enter them into the /etc/hosts file. Then every time you accessed those hostnames, Linux would have the addresses on hand and not have to perform a DNS lookup. This greatly improves the connection time.

LISTING 4.3 Sample /etc/hosts File

```
1  127.0.0.1    localhost
2  192.168.0.1    shadrach.smallorg.org
3  10.0.0.1     mail1.isp.net
4  10.0.0.2     mail2.isp.net
5  10.0.0.3     fred.otherplace.com
```

Lines 1 and 2 show the IP addresses used for the local Linux server. Lines 3–5 show IP addresses for commonly used computers on your network. This allows the Linux server to access these sites by name quicker than by using DNS.

The localhost Name

All Linux computers include a special hostname called localhost. This name always points to the special IP address 127.0.0.1, which is associated with a special network device called the loopback device. This name and address allow internal processes to communicate with other processes on the same system using network programming. Many programs are configured to use the localhost address. Changing localhost to point to anything else could change the behavior of those programs.

4

DNS AND DOMAIN NAMES

DNS Resolution File

The /etc/host.conf file specifies the methods and order that Linux can attempt to resolve hostnames. Listing 4.4 shows a sample /etc/host.conf file.

LISTING 4.4 Sample /etc/host.conf File

```
1  order    hosts,bind
2  multi on
```

Line 1 lists the order in which hostnames should be resolved. This shows that first Linux will look up the hostname in its /etc/hosts file, and then attempt to use DNS (bind) if it is not found.

Linux Client DNS Utilities

Numerous utilities have been written for Linux that help system administrators find DNS information for remote hosts and networks. The Internet Software Consortium has created the Berkeley Internet Name Domain (BIND) package for UNIX systems, which includes three of my favorite and often-used utilities: host, nslookup, and dig. On most Linux distributions, these programs come pre-built in the software distribution. The Red Hat and Mandrake Linux distributions package these together in the bind-utils RPM package.

These utilities often come in handy when trying to troubleshoot email problems on the Internet. Often a customer will copy an email address incorrectly and get his email rejected. Of course he will indicate that he is 100 percent sure that he is using the proper address, and can't understand why the message is getting rejected. With a little DNS work, you can determine if the host part of the email address is correct or a typo.

host

The host program does basic DNS name resolution. The format of the host command is as follows:

```
host [-l] [-v] [-w] [-r] [-d] [-t querytype] [-a] host [server]
```

By default, host will attempt to resolve the hostname host by using the default DNS server specified in the /etc/resolv.conf file. If server is added, host will attempt to use that instead of the default DNS server. By adding additional parameters to the command line, the output and behavior of host can be modified. These parameters are shown in Table 4.5.

TABLE 4.5 host Command Parameters

Parameter	Description
-l	Lists the complete domain info
-v	Uses verbose output format
-w	Makes host wait for response
-r	Turns off recursion
-d	Turns on debugging
-t querytype	Specifies definite query type
-a	Retrieves all DNS records

The -l option can be used to find information about all the hosts listed in a domain. This is often used with the -t option to filter particular types of information (such as -t MX, which returns all the MX records for a domain). Unfortunately in this day of security awareness, it is often difficult to use the -l option because many DNS servers will refuse attempts to access all the host information contained in the database. If you are trying to get information from a slow DNS server (or a slow link to the network), you might want to try the -w parameter. This tells the host program to wait forever for a response to the query. By default, it will time out after about one minute.

One useful parameter is -r. This tells the DNS server to return only information regarding the query that it has in its own local DNS database. The DNS server will not attempt to contact a remote DNS server to find the information.

This is useful in determining whether your DNS server is properly caching DNS answers. First, try resolving a hostname using the -r parameter. If no one else has gone there, you should not get an answer back from your DNS. Then try it without the -r parameter. You should get the normal DNS information back, as the local DNS server was allowed to contact a remote DNS server to retrieve the information. Next, try the host command again with the -r parameter. You should now get the same information that you received from the previous attempt. This means that the DNS server did indeed cache the results from the previous DNS query in its local name cache. If you did not receive any information back, your local DNS server did not cache the previous response. You should have noticed a significant decrease in time that it took to respond with an answer from cache than when it responded after doing the DNS query on the network.

By default, host attempts to produce its output in human readable format. For example, a typical output is shown in Listing 4.5. If you use the -v option, the output changes to resemble the normal RR format found in the DNS database. This can be useful in trying to debug a DNS problem with the configuration of the DNS server.

LISTING 4.5   Sample host Output

```
1  [rich@shadrach rich]$host www.linux.org
2  www.linux.org has address 198.182.196.56
3  www.linux.org mail is handled (pri=20) by router.invlogic.com
4  www.linux.org mail is handled (pri=30) by border-ai.invlogic.com
5  www.linux.org mail is handled (pri=10) by mail.linux.org
6  [rich@shadrach rich]$
```

Line 1 shows the basic format for using the host command—just add the hostname you are interested in finding information on. Lines 2–5 show the output from the command. First, line 2 shows that the DNS server was able to resolve the hostname into an IP address. Then,

4

DNS AND DOMAIN NAMES

lines 3–5 show that the hostname has three different mail server (MX) records that show computers that can accept email for that host. Notice that host also lists the preference (OK, maybe they got it a little confused with priority) of each mail server. If you were sending mail to a person at this host, you would first attempt to send mail to the priority 10 computer (mail.linux.org). If the host command fails, you can try a different DNS server to send the query to by specifying its address after the hostname address on the command line. This is a good technique to use if you think your DNS server is not behaving properly.

nslookup

The nslookup program is an extremely versatile tool that can be used in a variety of trouble-shooting situations. There are two modes that nslookup can be run under. In non-interactive mode, it behaves much like the host command discussed previously. The interactive mode is where all the fun can be found. It can give more detailed information about remote computers and domains because you can change options as you traverse the DNS database. The basic format of the nslookup command is

```
nslookup [-option ...] [host-to-find | -[server]]
```

If you enter the host-to-find parameter on the command line, nslookup operates in non-interactive mode and returns the result of the query similar to the host command. If no arguments are given, or the first argument is a hyphen -, nslookup will enter into interactive mode. If you want to use a different DNS server, you can specify that using the -server argument, where server is the IP address of the DNS server to use. Otherwise nslookup will use the default DNS server as listed in the /etc/resolv.conf file.

There are three ways to change option settings in the nslookup program. One way is to list them as options in the nslookup command line. Another way is to specify them on the interactive command line when nslookup starts by using the set command. The third way is to create a file in your $HOME directory called .nslookuprc and enter one option per line. A list of options available is shown in Table 4.6.

TABLE 4.6   nslookup Options

Option	Description
all	Prints current values of options
class	Sets the DNS class value (default=IN)
[no]debug	Turns debugging mode on (or off) (default = nodebug)
[no]d2	Turns exhaustive debugging mode on (or off) (default = nod2)
domain=name	Sets the default domain name to name
srchlist=name1/name2...	Changes the default domain name to name1 and the search list to name1, name2, and so on

Option	Description
[no]defname	Appends the default domain name to a single component lookup request
[no]search	Appends the domain names in search list to the hostname (default = search)
port=value	Changes TCP/UDP port to value (default = 53)
querytype=value	Changes type of information requested to type value (default = A)
type=value	Same as querytype
[no]recurse	Tells name server to query other servers to obtain an answer (default=recurse)
retry=number	Sets number of retries to number (default = 4)
root=host	Changes name of root server to host (default = ns.internic.net)
timeout=number	Changes initial timeout interval to wait for a reply to number (default = 5 seconds)
[no]vc	Always uses a virtual circuit (default = novc)
[no]ignoretc	Ignores packet truncation errors (default = noignoretc)

Listing 4.6 shows a sample nslookup session used to get information for host www.linux.org. The default parameters return the IP address for the hostname. This example demonstrates changing the parameters to find the mail servers for the domain.

LISTING 4.6   Sample nslookup Session

```
1   [katie@shadrach katie]$ nslookup
2   Default Server:  ns1.isp.net
3   Address:   10.0.0.1
4
5   > www.linux.org
6   Server:  ns1.isp.net
7   Address:   10.0.0.1
8
9   Non-authoritative answer:
10  Name:    www.linux.org
11  Address:  198.182.196.56
12
13  > set type=MX
14  > www.linux.org
15  Server:  ns1.isp.net
16  Address:   10.0.0.1
```

4

DNS AND
DOMAIN NAMES

continues

LISTING 4.6   continued

```
17
18  Non-authoritative answer:
19  www.linux.org    preference = 20, mail exchanger = router.invlogic.com
20  www.linux.org    preference = 30, mail exchanger = border-ai.invlogic.com
21  www.linux.org    preference = 10, mail exchanger = mail.linux.org
22
23  Authoritative answers can be found from:
24  linux.org        nameserver = NS0.AITCOM.NET
25  linux.org        nameserver = NS.invlogic.com
26  router.invlogic.com     internet address = 198.182.196.1
27  border-ai.invlogic.com  internet address = 205.134.175.254
28  mail.linux.org  internet address = 198.182.196.60
29  NS0.AITCOM.NET  internet address = 208.234.1.34
30  NS.invlogic.com internet address = 205.134.175.254
31  > exit
32  [katie@shadrach katie]$
```

Line 5 shows the query for the hostname www.linux.org. Lines 6 and 7 show the DNS server used to process the query, and lines 9–11 show that the server contained a non-authoritative answer for the IP address. Obviously someone must have accessed this site before and its IP address was still in the DNS server's local name cache. In line 13, the option is set to return information on the mail servers in the domain. Lines 18–30 show the information returned by the DNS server. Lines 18–21 show the answer section of the DNS packet, which again indicates that the answer is non-authoritative, and lists the three mail servers responsible for the www.linux.org hostname. Lines 23–30 show the information in the authoritative and additional sections in the DNS packet. Lines 23–25 show that there are two DNS servers that are authoritative for the linux.org domain, and would have the RR records for www.linux.org. Lines 26–30 show the additional information section, listing IP addresses for hostnames contained in the responses. If you want to extend this example, you could change the default DNS server to one of the authoritative DNS servers listed (by using the server command) and retry the MX query to see if the information has changed at all from the information returned from the non-authoritative DNS server.

dig

The dig program uses a simple command-line format to query DNS servers regarding domain information. The format for the dig command is as follows:

```
dig [@server] domain [query-type] [query-class] [+query-option]
➥ [-dig-option] [%comment]
```

`server` is an optional DNS server that you can specify. By default, `dig` will use the DNS server defined in the `/etc/resolv.conf` file. You can specify the `server` option by using either an IP address in numeric dot notation, or as a hostname. If you use a hostname for the `server` option, `dig` will use the default DNS server to resolve the hostname, and then use that DNS server to find the information on the domain.

`query-type` is the `RR` type information that you are requesting, such as the `A`, `SOA`, `NS`, and `MX` records. A query-type of any can be used to return all information available about a domain.

`query-class` is the network class of information that you are requesting. The default is Internet (`IN`), which is the type of information we are looking for.

`+query-option` is used to change an option value in the DNS packet, or to change the format of the `dig` output. Many of these options shadow options available in the `nslookup` program. Table 4.7 shows the query-options available to use.

TABLE 4.7 dig query options

Option	Description
[no]debug	Turns on (off) debugging
[no]d2	Turns on (off) extra debugging
[no]recurse	(Doesn't) use recursive lookups
retry=#	Sets number of retries
time=#	Sets timeout length
[no]ko	Keeps open option (implies vc)
[no]vc	(Doesn't) use virtual circuit
[no]defname	(Doesn't) use default domain name
[no]search	(Doesn't) use domain search list
domain=NAME	Sets default domain name to NAME
[no]ignore	(Doesn't) ignore truncation errors
[no]primary	(Doesn't) use primary server
[no]aaonly	Authoritative query only flag
[no]cmd	Echoes parsed arguments
[no]stats	Prints query statistics
[no]Header	Prints basic header
[no]header	Prints header flags
[no]ttlid	Prints TTLs
[no]cl	Prints class info

4

**DNS AND
DOMAIN NAMES**

continues

TABLE 4.7 continued

Option	Description
[no]qr	Prints outgoing query
[no]reply	Prints reply
[no]ques	Prints question section
[no]answer	Prints answer section
[no]author	Prints authoritative section
[no]addit	Prints additional section
pfdef	Sets to default print flags
pfmin	Sets to minimal print flags
pfset=#	Sets print flags to #
pfand=#	Bitwise AND prints flags with #
pfor=#	Bitwise OR prints flags with #

-dig-option is used to specify other options that affect the operation of dig. Table 4.8 shows some of the other options available to fine-tune the dig command and its output.

TABLE 4.8 dig operation options

Option	Description
-x	Specifies inverse address mapping in normal dot notation
-f	Reads a file for batch mode processing
-T	Time in seconds between batch mode command processing
-p	Port number to use
-P	After a response, issues a ping command
-t	Specifies type of query
-c	Specifies class of query
-envsav	Specifies that the dig options should be saved to become the default dig environment

A sample dig session output is shown in Listing 4.7. As you can see, the dig program produces the same information as host and nslookup, but shows more detail on how and where the answers came from.

LISTING 4.7   Sample dig Output

```
1  [jessica@shadrach jessica]$ dig www.linux.org
2
3  ; <<>> DiG 8.1 <<>> www.linux.org
4  ;; res options: init recurs defnam dnsrch
5  ;; got answer:
6  ;; ->>HEADER<<- opcode: QUERY, status: NOERROR, id: 6
7  ;; flags: qr aa rd ra; QUERY: 1, ANSWER: 1, AUTHORITY: 2, ADDITIONAL: 2
8  ;; QUERY SECTION:
9  ;;       www.linux.org, type = A, class = IN
10
11 ;; ANSWER SECTION:
12 www.linux.org.          12H IN A        198.182.196.56
13
14 ;; AUTHORITY SECTION:
15 linux.org.              12H IN NS        ns.invlogic.com.
16 linux.org.              12H IN NS        ns0.aitcom.net.
17
18 ;; ADDITIONAL SECTION:
19 ns.invlogic.com.        12H IN A         205.134.175.254
20 ns0.aitcom.net.         1d23h31m17s IN A  208.234.1.34
21
22 ;; Total query time: 335 msec
23 ;; FROM: shadrach to SERVER: default - 10.0.0.1
24 ;; WHEN: Sun Aug 22 15:45:45 1999
25 ;; MSG SIZE  sent: 31  rcvd: 145
26
27 [jessica@shadrach jessica]$
```

Linux as a DNS Server

If you have a direct full-time connection to the Internet, you might want to host your own DNS server for your domain. You can do this with your Linux server. Alternatively, you could also use your Linux server as a local DNS server in name caching mode. This would save some network time on DNS requests in that your Linux server will implement its local name cache, and then use it to answer future DNS requests (within the TTL limit of the information).

The popular UNIX DNS package mentioned previously in the client section—the Berkley Internet Name Domain (BIND) by the Internet Software Consortium—also contains software for implementing a DNS server. The DNS server software program is called named. Many Linux distributions contain the named program in a canned binary package. The current Red Hat 6.0 distribution uses the bind-8.2-6.i386.rpm package to install the named program and its related configuration files. If you don't have a pre-built binary package, or you want to use the latest version of BIND, you can download the source code from the Internet Software Consortium at ftp.isc.org. The current version at the time of this writing is BIND 8.2.1. You must have the GCC compiler installed on your Linux server to be able to compile the new software.

Compiling BIND

Currently, the source code for the BIND package can be downloaded as file `ftp://ftp.isc.org/src/8.2.1/bind-src.tar.gz`. The steps involved in compiling a new `named` program are as follows:

1. Unpack the file into a work directory by typing

   `tar -zxvf bind-src.tar.gz`

2. Change to the newly created `src` directory

3. Type **`make clean`**

4. Type **`make depend`**

5. Type **`make`** to produce the binaries

6. Type **`make install`** to place the binaries and configuration files in the appropriate directories

After BIND has been installed by either compiling the source or installing a binary distribution, you can start configuring the `named` configuration files for the specific situation you want.

Using named as a Workstation Cache Server

The easiest way to use the `named` program is as a way to cache DNS responses on your local Linux server for future requests. First, you must configure the `/etc/named.conf` file for your local computer. Listing 4.8 shows what the `/etc/named.conf` file would look like to use it as a cached DNS server.

LISTING 4.8   Sample DNS `/etc/named.conf` File for Caching DNS Server

```
1  options {
2          directory "/var/named";
3  };
4
5    zone "." {
6            type hint;
7            file "root.cache";8
9  };10
11
12   zone "localhost" {
```

```
13          type master;
14          file "pri/localhost";
15  };
16
17  zone "0.0.127.in-addr.arpa" {
18          type master;
19          file "pri/127.0.0";
20  };
```

Lines 1–3 define options that are used in the named program. Line 2 shows that the default directory for the configuration files will be in the /var/named directory. Lines 5–7 define the 'root' domain definitions. As discussed previously, each DNS server must know the address of the root servers to be able to query the DNS tree. Line 7 indicates that the file which contains the root server addresses is file /var/named/root.cache. This file can be produced by using the dig command:

dig @f.root-servers.net . ns >> root.cache

Listing 4.9 shows a sample /var/named/root.cache file.

LISTING 4.9 Sample DNS /var/named/root.cache File

```
1   ; <<>> DiG 8.2 <<>> @f.root-servers.net . ns
2   ; (1 server found)
3   ;; res options: init recurs defnam dnsrch
4   ;; got answer:
5   ;; ->>HEADER<<- opcode: QUERY, status: NOERROR, id: 10
6   ;; flags: qr aa rd; QUERY: 1, ANSWER: 13, AUTHORITY: 0, ADDITIONAL: 13
7   ;; QUERY SECTION:
8   ;;      ., type = NS, class = IN
9
10  ;; ANSWER SECTION:
11  .                       6D IN NS        G.ROOT-SERVERS.NET.
12  .                       6D IN NS        J.ROOT-SERVERS.NET.
13  .                       6D IN NS        K.ROOT-SERVERS.NET.
14  .                       6D IN NS        L.ROOT-SERVERS.NET.
15  .                       6D IN NS        M.ROOT-SERVERS.NET.
16  .                       6D IN NS        A.ROOT-SERVERS.NET.
17  .                       6D IN NS        H.ROOT-SERVERS.NET.
18  .                       6D IN NS        B.ROOT-SERVERS.NET.
19.                       6D IN NS        C.ROOT-SERVERS.NET.
20  .                       6D IN NS        D.ROOT-SERVERS.NET.
21  .                       6D IN NS        E.ROOT-SERVERS.NET.
22  .                       6D IN NS        I.ROOT-SERVERS.NET.
```

continues

4

**DNS AND
DOMAIN NAMES**

LISTING 4.9   continued

```
23 .                          6D IN NS        F.ROOT-SERVERS.NET.
24
25 ;; ADDITIONAL SECTION:
26 G.ROOT-SERVERS.NET.        5w6d16h IN A    192.112.36.4
27 J.ROOT-SERVERS.NET.        5w6d16h IN A    198.41.0.10
28 K.ROOT-SERVERS.NET.        5w6d16h IN A    193.0.14.129
29 L.ROOT-SERVERS.NET.        5w6d16h IN A    198.32.64.12
30 M.ROOT-SERVERS.NET.        5w6d16h IN A    202.12.27.33
31 A.ROOT-SERVERS.NET.        5w6d16h IN A    198.41.0.4
32 H.ROOT-SERVERS.NET.        5w6d16h IN A    128.63.2.53
33 B.ROOT-SERVERS.NET.        5w6d16h IN A    128.9.0.107
34 C.ROOT-SERVERS.NET.        5w6d16h IN A    192.33.4.12
35 D.ROOT-SERVERS.NET.        5w6d16h IN A    128.8.10.90
36 E.ROOT-SERVERS.NET.        5w6d16h IN A    192.203.230.10
37 I.ROOT-SERVERS.NET.        5w6d16h IN A    192.36.148.17
38 F.ROOT-SERVERS.NET.        5w6d16h IN A    192.5.5.241
39
40 ;; Total query time: 10 msec
41 ;; FROM: power.rc.vix.com to SERVER: f.root-servers.net   192.5.5.241
42 ;; WHEN: Thu Jun  3 14:55:57 1999
43 ;; MSG SIZE   sent: 17  rcvd: 436
```

Lines 26–38 show the IP addresses of the root level servers as of June 1999. You will have to update this file (every 5 weeks, 5 days, and 16 hours according to the TTL values) to make sure that your DNS server forwards DNS queries to the proper root level servers.

Back in the /etc/named.conf file in Listing 4.8, you also defined two zones that your DNS server will be responsible for. Each zone must also have its own definition file. Lines 10–13 show the definition for the localhost zone. It is defined in file /var/named/pri/localhost. Listing 4.10 shows an example of what this file would look like.

LISTING 4.10   Sample /var/named/pri/localhost DNS File

```
1  ;localhost.
2  @                in      soa     localhost. postmaster.localhost. (
3                                   1993050801      ;serial
4                                   3600            ;refresh
5                                   1800            ;retry
6                                   604800          ;expiration
7                                   3600 )          ;minimum
8
9                           ns      localhost.
10
11                          a       127.0.0.1
```

As can be seen in Listing 4.10, the `localhost` file defines the SOA for your Linux server, stating that it is its own DNS name server (line 9), and gives the loopback address as its IP address (line 11). The last section in the `/etc/named.conf` file is the reverse lookup zone for your Linux server. Lines 17–19 in Listing 4.8 define the `0.0.127.in-addr.arpa` zone, and point to configuration file `/var/named/pri/127.0.0`. Listing 4.11 shows what this file would look like.

LISTING 4.11   Sample `/var/named/pri/127.0.0` DNS File

```
1   ; 0.0.127.in-addr.arpa
2   @               in      soa     localhost. postmaster.localhost. (
3                                   1993050801      ;serial
4                                   3600            ;refresh
5                                   1800            ;retry
6                                   604800          ;expiration
7                                   3600  )         ;minimum
8
9                           ns      localhost.
10
11  1                       ptr     localhost.
```

Line 11 in Listing 4.11 defines the loopback address `127.0.0.1` as the localhost address.

The final piece of the puzzle is to change the `/etc/reslov.conf` file to point to the local Linux server. By specifying the loopback address (`127.0.0.1`) as the primary nameserver, Linux will "query itself" for DNS name resolutions. This completes the DNS configuration for the workstation. By running `named` as a background process, your Linux server will be able to respond to DNS queries, and cache the responses in memory to answer future requests quicker.

Using named As a Zone DNS Server

The final example will be using your Linux server as a full-blown DNS server for your domain. This will use the same `named` configuration files as in the previous example, but will add two additional zones to the `/etc/named.conf` file shown in Listing 4.8. The new zones will define your domain for the `named` program. Listing 4.12 shows the additional sections that will be added to the `/etc/named.conf` file.

LISTING 4.12   Additional `/etc/named.conf` Sections

```
1   zone smallorg.org {
2       type master
3       file "pri/smallorg.org";
4   };
5
```

continues

LISTING 4.12   continued

```
6  zone 0.168.192.in-addr.arpa {
7      type master;
8      file "pri/192.168.0";
9  };
```

Much like the other example, the zone sections define the type of zone DNS server this will be
(the master, or primary), and what files the zone definitions will be found in. Listing 4.13
shows a sample zone definition for the smallorg.org zone file.

LISTING 4.13   Sample /etc/named/pri/smallorg.org DNS File

```
1  @       IN      SOA     master.smallorg.org. postmaster.smallorg.org. (
2                          199802151           ; serial, todays date + todays
↪serial #
3                          3600                ; refresh, seconds
4                          1800                ; retry, seconds
5                          604800              ; expire, seconds
6                          3600)               ; minimum, seconds
7
8                  NS      master              ; name server
9                  MX      10 mail.smallorg.org.      ; Primary mail server
10                 MX      20 mail.isp.net.   ; Secondary mail server
11
12 localhost       A       127.0.0.1
13 master          A       192.168.0.1
14 mail            A       192.168.0.2
```

Now you're halfway to hosting your domain. Next you must create the DNS database file for
your reverse domain address as listed in the /etc/named.conf file in Listing 4.12. Listing 4.14
shows an example of what this file would look like.

LISTING 4.14   Sample /etc/named/pri/192.168.0 DNS File

```
1  @       IN      SOA     master.smallorg.org. postmaster.smallorg.org. (
2                          199802151 ; Serial, todays date + todays serial
3                          3600      ; Refresh
4                          1800      ; Retry
5                          604800    ; Expire
6                          3600)     ; Minimum TTL
7                  NS      master
8
9  1               PTR     master.smallorg.org.
10 2               PTR     mail.smallorg.org.
```

These configuration files will allow your named program to respond properly to DNS queries for your domain. Of course, this assumes that you have properly registered your domain with the Internet Network Information Center (NIC), and that the root DNS servers for the proper first level domain (.org in this example) has pointers to the IP address of your Linux server that is serving as your DNS server.

> **CAUTION**
>
> One final word of caution. The examples in this chapter use fictitious IP addresses for example purposes. To host your own domain, you must have a valid IP address space on the Internet as assigned by the Internet Assigned Numbers Authority (IANA) and use a valid IP address for your DNS server so other Internet computers can connect to it. Also, your domain must be properly registered with ICANN before any DNS queries will work on your domain. If you choose to let your ISP host your domain, you can use the public IP address network of 192.168.0.0 to assign IP addresses to hosts on your network, but these hosts cannot use a valid domain name in your domain.

Summary

This chapter discusses the domain name system (DNS) and how it relates to email. Each computer connected to the Internet has a unique hostname and a unique IP address. The DNS database system matches the hostnames and IP addresses together. The database is distributed among many different servers on the Internet, so no one server has to maintain the list of all computers. You can find a remote computer's IP address by its hostname by sending a DNS query to a DNS server. That server has the capability of walking the DNS tree to find the database record that relates the hostname to the IP address, or vice versa. Many domains use their domain name as a generic email address. Your email server must know how to use DNS to find a server responsible for receiving email messages for the domain.

SMTP Protocol

IN THIS CHAPTER

In the previous chapter, you learned how to locate another computer on the Internet using host-names and DNS servers. Now that you know where the other computer is, you might want to actually be able to do something with it. This chapter explains how to send a message to a user on the remote computer from your computer. The Simple Mail Transfer Protocol (SMTP) has been used since 1982 to relay email messages and attachments to many different types of computer systems. Its ease of use and portability made it the standard protocol used to transfer messages between computer systems on the Internet. To have an understanding of how email works, you should get to know SMTP.

SMTP Protocol Description

The SMTP protocol was designed to work on many different types of transport media. The most common transport medium is the Internet, using a TCP/IP connection on port 25. Many Linux distributions will automatically install an SMTP package when the IP services are installed. A common troubleshooting technique to use to check if a remote server is running an SMTP server package is to telnet to TCP port 25 and see if you get a response. You can test this out on your own Linux server by telneting to hostname localhost using port 25. Listing 5.1 shows a sample telnet session to a Linux server running an SMTP package.

LISTING 5.1   Sample telnet Session to Port 25

```
1  [jessica@shadrach jessica]$ telnet localhost 25
2  Trying 127.0.0.1...
3  Connected to localhost.
4  Escape character is '^]'.
5  220 shadrach.smallorg.org ESMTP Sendmail 8.9.3/8.9.3;
        ➥Wed, 25 Aug 1999 18:35:33 -0500
6  QUIT
7  221 shadrach.smallorg.org closing connection
8  Connection closed by foreign host.
9  [jessica@shadrach jessica]$
```

Line 1 shows the telnet command format using host localhost and TCP port 25. Line 5 shows a typical response if your Linux server has an SMTP software package installed. The first number is a three-digit response code. This code can be used for troubleshooting purposes if mail is not being transferred properly. Next, the hostname of the SMTP server, and a description of the SMTP software package that the server is using are displayed. This server is using the common sendmail SMTP software package that is maintained and distributed by the send-mail Consortium. Line 6 shows how you can close the telnet connection by typing the word QUIT followed by pressing the ENTER key. The SMTP server should send you a closing message and kill the TCP connection. As you can tell from this example, the SMTP protocol uses simple ASCII text commands, and returns three-digit reply codes with optional ASCII text messages. The SMTP protocol is defined in Internet Request For Comment (RFC) document number 821 maintained by the Internet Engineering Task Force (IETF) published on August 21, 1982. Several modifications have been made to the SMTP protocol over the years, but the basic protocol commands still remain in use.

Basic SMTP Client Commands

When a TCP session has been established and the SMTP server acknowledges the client by sending a welcome banner (as shown in Listing 5.1), it is the client's responsibility to control the connection between the two computers. The client accomplishes this by sending special commands to the server. The server should respond accordingly to each command sent. RFC 821 defines the basic client commands that an SMTP server should recognize and respond to. Since then, there have been several extensions to the SMTP protocol that not all servers have used. This section documents the basic SMTP keywords that are defined in RFC 821. The section "Extended SMTP" covers some of the new extensions that have been implemented by several SMTP software packages.

The basic format of an SMTP command is

```
command [parameter]
```

where command is a four-character SMTP command and parameters are optional qualifying data for the command. Table 5.1 shows the basic SMTP commands that are available. The following sections describe the commands in more detail.

TABLE 5.1   SMTP Basic Commands

Command	Description
HELO	Opening greeting from client
MAIL	Identifies sender of message
RCPT	Identifies recipients
DATA	Identifies start of message
SEND	Sends message to terminal
SOML	Send-or-Mail
SAML	Send-and-Mail
RSET	Resets SMTP connection
VRFY	Verifies username on system
EXPN	Queries for lists and aliases
HELP	Requests list of commands

continues

5

SMTP PROTOCOL

TABLE 5.1   continued

Command	Description
NOOP	No operation—does nothing
QUIT	Stops the SMTP session
TURN	Reverses the SMTP roles

HELO Command

This is not a typo. By definition, SMTP commands are four characters long, thus the opening greeting by the client to the server is the HELO command. The format for this command is

```
HELO domain name
```

The purpose of the HELO command is for the client to identify itself to the SMTP server. Unfortunately, this method was devised in the early days of the Internet before mass hacker break-in attempts. As you can see, the client can be identified as whatever it wants to use in the text string. That being the case, most SMTP servers use this command just as a formality. If they really need to know the identity of the client, they will try to use a reverse DNS lookup of the client's IP address to determine the client's DNS name. In fact, for security reasons many SMTP servers will refuse to talk to hosts whose IP addresses do not resolve to a proper DNS hostname. By sending this command, the client indicates that it wants to initialize a new SMTP session with the server. By responding to this command, the server acknowledges the new connection, and should be ready to receive further commands from the client.

People Clients Versus Host Clients

In SMTP you must remember to differentiate between people and hosts. When creating a new mail message the email user is the client of his local host. Once the user sends his message, he is no longer the client in the SMTP process. His local host computer takes over the process of mailing the message and now becomes the client as far as SMTP is concerned. When the local host contacts the remote host to transfer the message using SMTP, it is now acting as the client in the SMTP process. The HELO command identifies the local host name as the client, not the actual sender of the message. This terminology often gets confusing.

MAIL Command

The MAIL command is used to initiate a mail session with the server after the initial HELO command is sent. It identifies from whom the message is being sent. The format of the MAIL command is

```
MAIL reverse-path
```

The `reverse-path` argument not only identifies the sender, but it also identifies how to reach the sender with a return message. If the sender is a user on the client computer that initiated the SMTP session, the format for the `MAIL` command would look something like this:

```
MAIL FROM:rich@shadrach.smallorg.org
```

Notice how the `FROM` section denotes the proper email address for the sender of the message, including the full hostname of the client computer. This information should appear in the text of the email message in the `FROM` section (but more on that later). If the email message has been routed through several different systems between the original sender and the desired recipient, each system will add its routing information to the `<reverse-path>` section. This documents the path that the email message traversed to get to the server. Often, mail from clients on private networks has to traverse several mail relay points before getting to the Internet. The `reverse-path` information is often useful in troubleshooting email problems, or in tracking down emailers who are purposely trying to hide their identity by bouncing their email messages off of several unknowing SMTP servers.

RCPT Command

The `RCPT` command defines who the recipients of the message are. There can be multiple recipients for the same message. Each recipient is normally listed in a separate `RCPT` command line. The format of the `RCPT` command is

```
RCPT forward-path
```

The `forward-path` argument defines where the email is ultimately destined. This is usually a fully qualified email address, but could be just a username that is local to the SMTP server. For example, the following `RCPT` command

```
RCPT TO:haley
```

would send the message to user `haley` on the SMTP server computer that is processing the message. Messages can also be sent to users on other computer systems that are remote from the SMTP server to which the message is sent. For example, sending the following `RCPT` command

```
RCPT TO:riley@meshach.smallorg.org
```

to the SMTP server on computer `shadrach.smallorg.org` would cause `shadrach.smallorg.org` to make a decision. Because the user is not local to `shadrach`, it must decide what to do with the message. There are three possible actions that `shadrach` could take with the message. They are as follows:

- shadrach could forward the message to the destination computer and return an OK response to the client. In this scenario, shadrach would add its hostname to the <reverse-path> of the MAIL command line to indicate that it is part of the return path to route a message back to the original sender.

- shadrach would not forward the message, but would send a reply to the client specifying that it was not able to deliver the message, but verified that the address of meshach.smallorg.org was correct. Thus the client could then try to resend the message directly to meshach.smallorg.org.

- Finally, shadrach would not forward the message, and would send a reply to the client specifying that this operation is not permitted from this server. It would be up to the system administrator at shadrach to figure out what happened and why.

In the early days of the Internet, it was common to run across computers that used the first scenario and blindly forwarded email messages across the world. Unfortunately, that technique became popular with email spammers. Spammers are people who do mass mailings across the Internet for either fun or profit. They often use unsuspecting SMTP servers that blindly forward email messages in an attempt to disguise the origin of their mail messages. To combat this situation, most mail system administrators have either completely turned off mail forwarding, or have at least limited email forwarding to hosts within their domain. Many ISPs allow their customers to relay email from their mail servers, but restrict outside computers from that privilege.

In the case of multiple recipients, it is up to the client how to handle situations in which some of the recipients are not acknowledged. Some clients will abort the entire message and return an error to the sending user. Some will continue sending the message to the recipients that are acknowledged and list the recipients that aren't acknowledged in a return message.

DATA Command

The DATA command is the meat-and-potatoes of the SMTP operation. After the MAIL and RCPT commands are hashed out, the DATA command is used to transfer the actual message. The format of the DATA command is

DATA

Anything after that command is treated as the message to transfer. Usually the SMTP server will add a timestamp and the return-path information to the head of the message. The client indicates the end of the message by sending a line with just a single period. The format for that line is

<CR><LF>.<CR><LF>

When the SMTP server receives this sequence, it knows that the message transmission is done, and should return a response code to the client indicating whether the message is accepted.

There has been much work done on the format of the actual DATA messages. Technically there is no wrong way to send a message, although work has been done to standardize a method (see the "Message Formats" section). Any combination of valid ASCII characters will be transferred to the recipients. Listing 5.2 shows a sample session sending a short mail message to a local user on an SMTP server.

LISTING 5.2   Sample SMTP Session

```
 1  [rich@shadrach rich]$ telnet localhost 25
 2  Trying 127.0.0.1...
 3  Connected to localhost.
 4  Escape character is '^]'.
 5  220 shadrach.smallorg.org ESMTP Sendmail 8.9.3/8.9.3;
➥Wed, 25 Aug 1999 19:34:02 -050
 6  HELO localhost
 7  250 shadrach.smallorg.org Hello localhost [127.0.0.1], pleased to meet you
 8  MAIL FROM:rich@localhost
 9  250 <rich@localhost>... Sender ok
10  RCPT TO:rich
11  250 <rich>... Recipient ok
12  DATA
13  354 Enter mail, end with "." on a line by itself
14  This is a short, but sweet, mail message.
15  .
16  250 QAA01619 Message accepted for delivery
17  QUIT
18  221 shadrach.smallorg.org closing connection
19  Connection closed by foreign host.
20  You have mail in /var/spool/mail/rich
21  [rich@shadrach rich]$ mail
22  Mail version 8.1 6/6/93.  Type ? for help.
23  "/var/spool/mail/rich": 1 message 1 new
24  >N  1 rich@shadrach.smallor  Wed Aug 25 19:34   11/409
25  &1
26  Message 1:
27  From rich@shadrach.smallorg.org  Wed Aug 25 19:34:46 1999
28  Date: Wed, 25 Aug 1999 19:34:24 -0500
29  From: rich@shadrach.smallorg.org
30
31  This is a short, but sweet, mail message.
32
33  &x
34  [rich@shadrach rich]$
```

Listing 5.2 shows a typical SMTP exchange between two hosts. Line 12 shows the client entering the DATA command, and line 13 shows the response returned by the SMTP server. Lines 14 and 15 show the text message sent by the client. Line 15 is the terminating period indicating the end of the message to the server. As you can see in lines 20–33, the SMTP server transferred the message to the local user's mailbox account exactly as the server received it. Also note how in lines 28 and 29 the SMTP server included a timestamp and the return path information in the text of the email message.

Much work has been done in an attempt to standardize the format of Internet mail messages. RFC 822 specifies a standard format for sending text mail messages between hosts. The section "Message Formats" covers some of these features.

SEND Command

The SEND command is used to send a mail message directly to the terminal of a logged in user. This command only works when the user is logged in, and usually pops up as a message much like the UNIX write command works. This command does have a serious drawback. It is an easy way for an external user to determine who was logged into a computer system at any given time without having to log into the system. Hackers have exploited this "feature" by searching the Internet for unsuspecting victims' user IDs and when they are logged in. Because it is such a security threat, most SMTP software packages do not implement this command anymore.

SOML Command

The SOML command stands for SEND or MAIL. If the recipients are logged onto the computer system, it behaves like the preceding SEND command. If not, it behaves like the MAIL command and sends the message to the recipients' mailbox. The "exploit-ability" of this command has made it another victim of the Internet world, and it is often not implemented on newer SMTP server packages.

SAML Command

The SAML command stands for SEND and MAIL. This command tries to cover both bases by both sending a message to the terminal of a logged in user, as well as placing the message in the users' mailbox. Again, the "exploit-ability" of this command has rendered it unsafe to implement.

RSET Command

The RSET command is short for reset. If the client somehow gets confused by the responses from the server and thinks that the SMTP connection has gotten out of sync, it can issue the RSET command to return the connection back to the HELO command state. Thus any MAIL, RCPT, or DATA information entered will be lost. Often this is used as a "last ditch effort" when the client either has lost track of where it was in the command series, or did not expect a particular response from the server.

VRFY Command

The VRFY command is short for verify. You can use the VRFY command to determine if an SMTP server can deliver mail to a particular recipient before entering the RCPT command mode. The format of this command is

VRFY username

When received, the SMTP server will determine whether the user is on the local server. If the user is local to the server, it will return the full email address of the user. If the user is not local, the SMTP server can either return a negative response to the client, or indicate that it is willing to forward any mail messages to the remote user—depending on whether the SMTP server will forward messages for the particular client.

The VRFY command can be a very valuable troubleshooting tool. Often users incorrectly type a username or hostname in an email message, and don't know why their mail message did not get to where they wanted it to go. Of course the first thing they will do is complain about the lousy mail system, and then contact you—the mail administrator. As the mail administrator, you can attempt to verify the email address in two ways. First, use the DNS host command to determine if the domain name is correct and has a mail server associated with it. Then, you can telnet to port 25 of the mail server and use the VRFY command to determine if the user name is correct. Listing 5.3 shows an example of using the VRFY command to check the validity of usernames.

LISTING 5.3 Example of the VRFY Command

```
1  [riley@shadrach riley]$ telnet localhost 25
2  Trying 127.0.0.1...
3  Connected to localhost.
4  Escape character is '^]'.
5  220 shadrach.smallorg.org ESMTP Sendmail 8.9.3/8.9.3;
➥ Thu, 26 Aug 1999 19:20:16 -050
6  HELO localhost
7  250 shadrach.smallorg.org Hello localhost [127.0.0.1], pleased to meet you
8  VRFY rich
9  250 <rich@shadrach.smallorg.org>
10 VRFY prez@mechach.smallorg.org
11 252 <prez@mechach.smallorg.org>
12 VRFY jessica
13 550 jessica... User unknown
14 QUIT
15 221 shadrach.smallorg.org closing connection
16 Connection closed by foreign host.
17 [riley@shadrach riley]$
```

5

SMTP PROTOCOL

Lines 8 through 13 show the VRFY commands tried and the results. Line 8 shows an attempt to VRFY a local user rich. The SMTP server's response in line 9 shows that the username was indeed valid, and returns the full email address to the client. Line 10 shows a different approach. On line 10, the client attempts to VRFY a username on a remote computer. The response in line 11 from shadrach shows a different result code than the result in line 9. The next section, "Server Responses," discusses the meaning of this code in greater detail, but the upshot is that shadrach is telling the client that it is willing to forward mail to the username prez at the remote computer meshach.smallorg.org. Line 12 shows an attempt to VRFY a non-existent username. The response from the SMTP server in line 13 is fairly self-explanatory.

Much like some of the other useful commands, the VRFY command has the capability of being exploited by hackers. Because of this, many sites do not implement the VRFY command. This will seriously impede your ability to troubleshoot bad email addresses.

EXPN Command

The EXPN command is short for expand. This command queries the SMTP server for mail lists and aliases. Mail lists are handy ways of sending mass mailings to groups of people with just one address. Chapter 18, "Mail Lists," looks at the topic of mail lists more in depth. Mail aliases can be used to disguise the real username in an email address. Chapter 17, "Mail Aliases and Masquerading," covers aliases more in depth. The format of the EXPN command is

```
EXPN mail-list
```

where mail-list is the name of the mail list or alias. The SMTP server will either return an error code if the client does not have privileges to see the list, or the complete mailing list, one email address per line.

HELP Command

The HELP command is used to return a list of SMTP commands that the SMTP server will understand. Most all SMTP software packages will understand and process the basic RFC 821 commands listed here (except of course ones that contain security issues). Where differences occur are with the extended SMTP options. Listing 5.4 shows the output from a HELP command issued to a Linux server running the sendmail SMTP package version 8.9.3.

LISTING 5.4 SMTP HELP Command Output

```
1  [katie@shadrach katie]$ telnet localhost 25
2  Trying 127.0.0.1...
3  Connected to localhost.
4  Escape character is '^]'.
5  220 shadrach.smallorg.org ESMTP Sendmail 8.9.3/8.9.3;
➥ Thu, 26 Aug 1999 19:50:57 -050
6  HELO localhost
```

```
7  250 shadrach.smallorg.org Hello localhost [127.0.0.1], pleased to meet you
8  HELP
9  214-This is Sendmail version 8.9.3
10 214-Topics:
11 214-      HELO    EHLO    MAIL    RCPT    DATA
12 214-      RSET    NOOP    QUIT    HELP    VRFY
13 214-      EXPN    VERB    ETRN    DSN
14 214-For more info use "HELP <topic>".
15 214-To report bugs in the implementation send email to
16 214-      Sendmail-bugs@Sendmail.org.
17 214-For local information send email to Postmaster at your site.
18 214 End of HELP info
19 HELP RCPT
20 214-RCPT TO: <recipient> [ <parameters> ]
21 214-      Specifies the recipient.  Can be used any number of times.
22 214-      Parameters are ESMTP extensions.  See "HELP DSN" for details.
23 214 End of HELP info
24 HELP VRFY
25 214-VRFY <recipient>
26 214-      Verify an address.  If you want to see what it aliases
27 214-      to, use EXPN instead.
28 214 End of HELP info
29 QUIT
30 221 shadrach.smallorg.org closing connection
31 Connection closed by foreign host.
32 [katie@shadrach katie]$
```

As shown in Listing 5.4, there are two levels of help available. By sending the HELP command alone, the SMTP server will give a brief overview of all of the available commands. By sending the HELP command with an argument that is another SMTP command, the server will return a more detailed description of the command, including any parameters that are required.

NOOP Command

The NOOP command is short for no operation. This command has no effect on the SMTP server other than for it to return a positive response code. This is often a useful command to send to test connectivity without actually starting the message transfer process.

QUIT Command

The QUIT command does what it says. It indicates that the client computer is finished with the current SMTP session and wants to close the connection. It is the responsibility of the SMTP server to respond to this command and to initiate the closing of the TCP connection. If the server receives a QUIT command in the middle of an email transaction, any data previously transferred should be deleted and not sent to any recipients.

TURN Command

The TURN command is not implemented on SMTP servers today for security reasons. It is part of the RFC 821 standard because it was a great idea that, unfortunately, was exploited by hackers. The TURN command idea was modified in the extended SMTP RFCs, and it is discussed in the section "Extended SMTP." It is described here as a background reference for the extended SMTP version ETRN.

The purpose of the TURN command is to allow two-way mail transfer between two computers during one TCP connection. Normally, the SMTP protocol sends mail in only one direction for each connection. The client host is in control of the transmission medium, and directs the actions of the server by the SMTP commands that are sent. Mail can only be sent from the client to the server. It would be desirable for a computer to make contact with an SMTP server, and not only be able to send mail to the server, but also be able to receive any mail that the server had waiting to send back to the client.

As discussed previously, the server uses the domain name indicated by the HELO command text string to identify the client it is talking to. The idea of the TURN command is to allow the SMTP server to switch roles with the client and send any mail destined for the client's domain name to the client. The problem with this idea was the reliance by the SMTP server that the client was actually who it says it was. If a hacker connected to the SMTP server and identified himself as another computer domain name, the server would unknowingly send all the mail messages destined for that domain name to the hacker. Ouch!

Server Responses

For each command that the client sends to the SMTP server, the server must reply with a response message. As you can see from Listings 5.2 and 5.3, response messages are made up of two parts. The first part is a three-digit code that is used by the SMTP software to identify whether the command was successful, and if not, why. The second part is a text string that helps humans understand the reply. Often the text string is passed on by the SMTP software and displayed to the user as part of a response message.

Usually a space separates the code from the text string. In the case of multi-line responses (such as the HELP and EXPN commands in Listing 5.4), a dash (-) separates the code from the text on all but the last line, which conforms to the normal pattern of using a space. This helps the client host identify when to expect more lines from the server. There are four different groups, or categories, of reply codes. The following sections explain these codes.

Error SMTP Response Codes

Table 5.2 shows the response codes for error conditions that could occur from various problems in the SMTP transaction.

TABLE 5.2   SMTP Error Response Codes

Code	Description
500	Syntax error, command not recognized
501	Syntax error in parameters
502	Command not implemented
503	Bad sequence of commands
504	Command parameter not implemented

SMTP error responses are not overly descriptive. They just give a general idea of what might have gone wrong in the SMTP process. When troubleshooting mail problems, it is helpful to be able to watch the actual SMTP transactions and watch for command errors if you are communicating with an unfamiliar SMTP server. Often 500, 502, and 504 errors occur when trying to implement extended SMTP commands with older SMTP software servers.

Informational SMTP Response Codes

The next category of response codes is informational codes. Informational codes are used to display additional information about a command. Table 5.3 shows these codes.

TABLE 5.3   SMTP Informational Response Codes

Code	Description
211	System status, or system help
214	Help message

As shown in Listing 5.4, the 214 response code is used when displaying output from the HELP command. When there are multiple lines of output, a dash is used after the response code to signify that more lines are coming. The last line uses a space to separate the response code from the text.

Service SMTP Response Codes

Another response code category is the service codes. Service codes are used to mark the status of the SMTP service in the connection. Table 5.4 shows these codes.

TABLE 5.4   SMTP service Response Codes

Code	Description
220	Service ready
221	Service closing transmission channel
421	Service not available

Each of these response codes will include the hostname of the SMTP server in the text string portion, as well as the text description. The 421 response code is a little misleading. Many mail administrators think that this response code is returned when there is no SMTP software available on the remote server. Although this can happen, usually this response code means that there is an SMTP server, but it is not accepting mail messages at the time. Sometimes this is the case if a server locks its file system to perform nightly data backups. The SMTP server would be unable to store mail messages on the locked file system, so the SMTP server shuts down temporarily while the backup is running. Trying to connect to the same server a little later in the evening would result in a successful transaction.

Action SMTP Response Codes

The last response code category relates to replying to SMTP client actions. Table 5.5 shows the action codes used in an SMTP transaction.

TABLE 5.5   SMTP Action Response Codes

Code	Description
250	Requested mail action OK, completed
251	User not local, will forward to <forward-path>
354	Start mail input: end with <CRLF>.<CRLF>
450	Requested mail action not taken: mailbox unavailable
451	Requested action aborted: error in processing
452	Requested action not taken: insufficient system storage
550	Requested action not taken: mailbox unavailable
551	User not local: please try <forward-path>
552	Requested mail action aborted: exceeded storage allocation
553	Requested action not taken: mailbox name not allowed
554	Transaction failed

Action codes are a result of the SMTP server trying to perform a function requested by the client, such as MAIL, RCPT, and DATA commands. They return the status of the requested action so that the client will know what actions to take next in the SMTP process.

SMTP server response codes are often "behind-the-scenes" players in the SMTP world. Some email client packages will forward any error response codes that they receive back to the sender of the email. When this happens, it is easy to check the response codes against the code lists to determine what went wrong. Sometimes it is difficult to determine what went wrong with an email message that does not get processed properly. A return email message does not get routed back properly to the client, so no error text is sent to the user. Often the mail administrator has to resort to using network analyzers to watch the actual TCP packets on the LAN to see the response codes that are coming from the SMTP server. Remember that the SMTP data packets are ASCII text, so they are easy to read and decode.

Message Formats

Listing 5.2 shows a simple example of an SMTP session. The format of the message was extremely basic—just one line of text. As shown in the example, the resulting email message was functional, but not too exciting. Today's email messages are much more complex, and users are beginning to expect that level of complexity from their email service. Niceties such as Subject, CC:, and BCC: lines are now the norm in email text. RFC 822 describes a standard email message format that most SMTP systems implement to somewhat "standardize" the look and feel of email. Simple one-line text messages are now unacceptable in the business world.

Standard RFC 822 Header Fields

RFC 822 specifies splitting the message into two separate parts. The first part is called the header. Its job is to identify the message. The second part is the body of the message. The header consists of data fields that can be used whenever additional information is needed in the message. The header fields should appear before the text body of the message, and should be separated by one blank line. Header fields do not need to appear in any particular order, and the message can have multiple occurrences of any header field. Figure 5.1 shows how a basic RFC 822 compliant message would look.

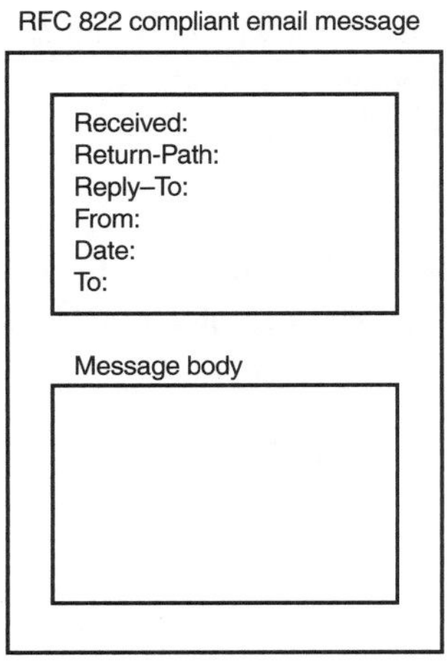

FIGURE 5.1
The RFC 822 message format.

Received Header Field

The format for the received header field is as follows:

```
Received:
    from host name
    by host name
    via pysical-path
    with protocol
    id message-id
    for final e-mail destination
```

The received header field is used to identify the SMTP servers that were used to relay the email message from the originating sender to the destination. Each server will add a new received field to the email message identifying specific details about itself. The subfields in the received header field further identify the path, protocol, and computers that were used in transferring the email message.

Return-path Header Field

The return header field format is as follows:

```
Return-path: route
```

The last SMTP server in the relay chain adds the return field to the message. Its purpose is to identify the route that was taken to pass the message to the destination server. If the message was sent directly to the destination server, there will be only one address in this field. Otherwise, this will list the path that was taken to transfer the message.

Originator Header Fields

The originator field shows the address from where the message originated. This is extremely useful on messages that have been bounced around several times on private networks before making it to the Internet. The format of this field is

```
Reply-To: address
```

The originator field is a small subset of the full-blown authentic header field. This serves as an easier way for smaller SMTP packages to implement this feature without having to implement a full-blown authentic header field.

Resent Header Field

The resent header field identifies an email message that for some reason had to be resent from the client. The format for this field is

```
Resent-Reply-To: address
```

Authentic Header Fields

The authentic header fields identify the sender of the email message. The format of the authentic field is

```
From:    user-name
Sender:  user-name
```

The From: field identifies the author of the original message. Usually the from and sender fields are the same user, so only one is needed. If the situation should occur where the sender of the email is not the original author, both can be identified for return mail purposes.

Resent-authentic Header Fields

The resent-authentic header identifies the sender of an email message that for some reason had to be resent by the client. The format for this is

```
Resent-From:   user-name
Resent-Sender: user-name
```

The resent-from and resent-sender fields behave just like the from and sender authentic fields. They just signify that the email message was resent from the client for some unknown reason.

Dates Header Fields

The dates header fields are used to timestamp the message as the client sends it to the server. The format for the date field is

```
Date:        date-time
Resent-Date: date-time
```

The date header field will pass the data information in the message header exactly as it is entered in the original message. This is useful for tracking message times in responses, especially multiple responses.

Destination Header Fields

The destination header fields identify email addresses that are the intended recipients of the mail message. These fields are purely informational. The SMTP server will not send a message to a user mailbox unless there has been a RCPT command issued for that user (see the "Basic SMTP Client Commands" section). The formats for the destination fields are

```
To: address
Resent-To: address
cc: address
Resent-cc: address
bcc: address
Resent-bcc: address
```

The To:, CC:, and BCC: fields have set a standard in the way email is processed. Most email packages now use this terminology to classify the recipients of a message. The To: field is intended for the main recipient of the message. The CC: fields, much like in a memo, are recipients that should receive a "copy" of the message. One new item that email has brought into the world is the term BCC:, or blind carbon copy. A blind carbon copy is a recipient that will receive a copy of the message, but whose address won't show up on the message for other people to see (sneaky). There has been some debate in computer ethics circles over the ethics of such a tactic, but practically every email package in use today implements this feature.

Optional Header Fields

Optional header fields are fields that further identify the message to the SMTP server, but are not required for a message to be RFC 822 compatible. These fields are some of the niceties mentioned earlier that many email customers have now come to expect to see. The formats of some of the optional header fields are

```
Message-ID:  message-id
Resent-Message-ID:  message-id
In-Reply-To: message-id
References: message-id
Keywords: text-list
Subject: text
Comments:  text
Encrypted: word
```

The most useful and often used optional header field is the Subject field. Most email packages allow the sender to include a one-line subject that identifies the email message for the recipient. This text string is often used in the email client package when listing multiple email messages. Other optional header fields help further identify the email message. The message-id fields give it a unique message ID that can be referred to in return messages. The encrypted field indicates if the email message has been encrypted for security purposes, and the keyword field offers keywords that can be used when searching for specific content in multiple messages.

Using the RFC 822 format in an SMTP Mail Transaction

A sample SMTP mail transaction using full RFC 822 message formats is shown in Listing 5.5.

LISTING 5.5   Sample SMTP RFC 822 Message Transaction

```
1  [rich@shadrach rich]$ telnet localhost 25
2  Trying 127.0.0.1...
3  Connected to localhost.
4  Escape character is '^]'.
5  250 shadrach.smallorg.org Hello localhost [127.0.0.1], pleased to meet you
6  MAIL FROM:rich@localhost
```

```
 7  250 rich@localhost... Sender ok
 8  RCPT TO:rich
 9  250 rich... Recipient ok
10  DATA
11  354 Enter mail, end with "." on a line by itself
12  Return-Path:rich@localhost
13  received: from localhost by localhost with TCP/IP id 1 for Richard Blum
14  Reply-to:rich@localhost
15  From:rich
16  Date:8/27/99
17  To:rich
18  cc:jessica
19  cc:katie
20  bcc:barbara
21  bcc:haley
22  Message-ID:1
23  Subject:Test RFC 822 message
24
25  This is a test message sent from the local host to rich.
26  This message is a little larger, and sweet.
27  .
28  250 PAA02866 Message accepted for delivery
29  QUIT
30  221 shadrach.smallorg.org closing connection
31  Connection closed by foreign host.
32  You have new mail in /var/spool/mail/rich
33  [rich@shadrach rich]$ mail
34  Mail version 8.1 6/6/93.  Type ? for help.
35  "/var/spool/mail/rich": 1 message 1 new
36  >N  1 rich@shadrach.smallo  Fri Aug 27 18:50  18/622    "Test RFC 822
➥message"
37  &1
38  Message 1:
39  From rich@smallorg.org  Fri Aug 27 18:50:21 1999
40  From: rich@shadrach.smallorg.org
41  Reply-to: rich@shadrach.smallorg.org
42  Date: 8/27/99
43  To: rich@shadrach.smallorg.org
44  cc: jessica@shadrach.smallorg.org
45  cc: katie@shadrach.smallorg.org
46  Subject: Test RFC 822 message
47
48  This is a test message sent from the local host to rich.
49  This message is a little larger, and sweet.
50
51  &x
52  [rich@shadrach rich]$
```

This example is similar to the example in Listing 5.2, but notice the differences. Lines 12–23 show the RFC 822 header fields that were used for the message. Line 36 shows how the email reader package has used the RFC 822 subject field as a short description of the email message. Lines 39–46 show how the header fields were displayed by the email reader package in the message. One thing that stands out is the missing BCC: fields. The BCC: fields are for identifying blind carbon copies. Those are recipients of the message that other recipients shouldn't know got copies (tricky). It makes sense that those fields do not show up in the email reader. Another obvious difference is the date line. Line 28 in Listing 5.2 shows a complete date that was automatically added by the email package. Line 42 in Listing 5.5 shows the date as it was set by the RFC 822 message. This email reader package allowed the RFC 822 field to override its automatic field insertion.

MIME and Binary Data

You might have noticed that the DATA command is the only way to transfer messages to the SMTP server. You might also have noticed that the DATA command only allows for ASCII text lines to be entered. You are probably wondering how you can email those great digital pictures to all of your relatives if SMTP mail only sends text messages. The answer is simple. The client's email program must convert the binary data message into an ASCII text message before it passes it on to the SMTP program. Then of course the recipient's email program must be able to convert the ASCII text message back into the binary data message that was originally sent. That is much easier said than done.

Several years before SMTP was invented, UNIX system administrators were sending binary data using ASCII text mail programs. The method they used to convert binary data into ASCII text was called uuencode and uudecode. The uu stands for UNIX-to-UNIX, a protocol suite that was invented to help transfer data between UNIX computers using modems (see Chapter 9, "UUCP Protocol"). When SMTP became popular, it was natural for UNIX system administrators to use these existing utilities for transferring binary data within an SMTP message across the Internet. Many older email packages still use this method for encoding binary data to send via SMTP. Unfortunately many newer email packages don't include this capability.

---

uuencoded Messages

If you receive a binary file that used the uuencode coding method and your emailer can't decode it, don't worry, you can save the entire message as a text file and use a separate uudecode program to extract the binary file. All Linux distributions come with the uudecode utility, and many DOS and Windows versions of uudecode are available also.

The reason many newer email packages don't use uuencode is because an Internet standard for encoding binary data had been created. RFCs 2045 and 2046 describe the Multipurpose Internet Mail Extensions (MIME) format. MIME is more versatile than uuencode. It identifies the type of binary file that was converted, as well as passes additional information about the file to the decoder. MIME enables binary data to be directly incorporated into a standard RFC 822 message. Five new header fields were defined to identify binary data types embedded in the RFC 822 message. Email packages that can handle MIME messages must be able to process these five new header types. Figure 5.2 demonstrates how this fits together in a standard email message.

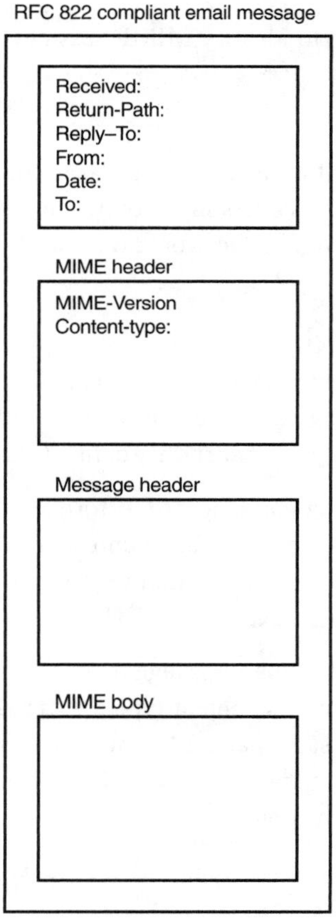

RFC 822 compliant email message

```
Received:
Return-Path:
Reply–To:
From:
Date:
To:
```

MIME header

```
MIME-Version
Content-type:
```

Message header

MIME body

FIGURE 5.2

The MIME message header fields.

MIME-Version Header Field

The first additional header type identifies the version of MIME that the sender used to encode the message. Currently this value is always 1.0.

Content-Transfer–Encoding

The content-transfer–encoding header field identifies how the binary data embedded in the message is encoded into ASCII text. There are currently seven different ways to encode the binary data, but the most common is the base64 type. This method encodes the binary data bay mapping six-bit blocks of data to eight-bit blocks of printable ASCII text.

Content-ID

The content-ID header field is used to identify MIME sessions with some unique identification code when using multiple contents.

Content-Description

The content-description header field is an ASCII text description of the data to help identify it in the text of the email message. This comes in handy when sending binary data such as word processing documents or graphic images that would otherwise be unidentifiable by their base64 encoding.

Content-Type Header Field

The content-type header field is where the action is. This field identifies the data that is enclosed in the MIME message. Currently there are seven basic classes of content-type identified by MIME. Each type has different subtypes that further define the type of data in the message.

The `text` content-type identifies data that is in ASCII format and should be able to be read as is. There are two subtypes—`plain`, which signifies unformatted ASCII text, and `enriched`, which signifies formatting features similar to a rich-text format. Many newer email packages can display the email message in rich-text format (RTF).

The `message` content-type allows the email package to send RFC 822 messages within a single RFC 822 message. The subtypes for this content-type are `rfc822`, which specifies a normal embedded RFC 822 formatted message, `partial`, which allows for breaking up long email messages into separate bodies, and `external-body`, which allows for a pointer that points to an object that is not within the email message.

The `image` content-type defines embedded binary data streams that represent graphic images. Currently two subtypes are defined—`jpeg` and `gif`.

The `video` content-type defines embedded binary data streams that represent video data. The only subtype defined at this time is the `mpeg` format.

The audio content-type defines embedded binary data streams that represent audio data. Currently its only subtype is basic, which defines a single-channel ISDN mu-law encoding at an 8kHz sample rate.

The application content-type is used to identify embedded binary data that represents application data, such as spreadsheets, word processor documents, and other applications. Currently there are two formal subtypes defined—postscript and octet-stream. Often the octet-stream subtype is used when embedding application-specific data, such as Microsoft Word documents and Microsoft Excel spreadsheets.

The multipart content-type identifies messages that contain different data content-types combined in one message. This format is common in email packages that can present a message in a variety of ways, such as ASCII text, HTML, and audio formats. A boundary identifier separates each content type, and each content type is identified with its own content-type header field. The multipart content-type has four subtypes.

The mixed subtype identifies that each of the parts are independent of one another and all should be presented to the recipient in the order they were sent. The parallel subtype identifies that each of the parts are independent of one another and can be presented to the recipient in any order. The alternative subtype identifies each of the parts that represent different ways of presenting the same data. The best method available for the recipient is used. The digest subtype identifies the same method as the mixed subtype, but specifies that the body of the message is always in RFC 822 format.

Listing 5.6 demonstrates the use of content-type definitions in a multipart email message.

LISTING 5.6   Sample SMTP Multipart MIME Message Session

```
1  [rich@shadrach rich]$ telnet localhost 25
2  Trying 127.0.0.1...
3  Connected to localhost.
4  Escape character is '^]'.
5  220 shadrach.smallorg.org ESMTP Sendmail 8.9.3/8.9.3;
➥Mon, 30 Aug 1999 07:36:58 -050
6  HELO localhost
7  250 shadrach.smallorg.org Hello localhost [127.0.0.1], pleased to meet you
8  MAIL FROM:rich@localhost
9  250 rich@localhost... Sender ok
10 RCPT TO:rich
11 250 rich... Recipient ok
12 DATA
13 354 Enter mail, end with "." on a line by itself
14 From:"Rich Blum" <rich@localhost>
```

continues

5

SMTP PROTOCOL

LISTING 5.6   continued

```
15 To:"rich"<rich@localhost>
16 Subject:Formatted text message test
17 MIME-Version: 1.0
18 Content-Type: multipart/alternative; boundary=bounds1
19
20 --bounds1
21 Content-Type: text/plain; charset=us-ascii
22
23 This is the plain text part of the message that can be read by simple
24 e-mail readers.
25
26 --bounds1
27 Context-Type: text/entriched
28
29 This is the <bold>rich text</bold> version of the <bigger>SAME</bigger>
↪message.
30
31 --bounds1--
32 .
33 250 MAA04305 Message accepted for delivery
34 QUIT
35 221 shadrach.smallorg.org closing connection
36 Connection closed by foreign host.
37 You have new mail in /var/spool/mail/rich
38 [rich@shadrach rich]$
```

The sample message shown in Listing 5.6 shows a two-part MIME message. Line 18 shows the content-type definition for the entire message. The multipart/alternative type indicates that there are multiple content-types included in this message, and that they are separated by the boundary identifier bounds1. The first content-type starts at line 21 and is a simple plain ASCII text message that can be read by virtually any email reader.

The second content-type starts at line 27 and is a fancier enriched text message that uses the standard rich text format for the message. Because the MIME content-type specified for the message was multipart/alternative, it is up to the discretion of the email reader which content-type version of the message to present. Figure 5.3 shows a sample of how a Netscape mail reader would display the message. Notice how the plain ASCII text part of the message was discarded, and the enriched text part was presented to the reader. In a normal email message, both parts would have the same message. I made them different here to show which version the email reader would use.

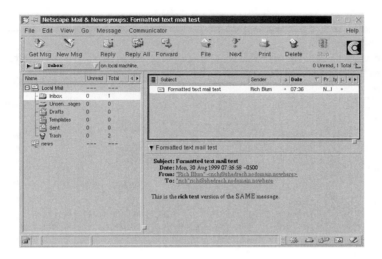

FIGURE 5.3
Using Netscape mail to read a MIME multipart message.

Extended SMTP

Since its invention in 1982, SMTP has performed well in transporting messages between computers across the Internet. As it got older, system administrators began to recognize its limitations. Instead of trying to replace a standard protocol that was in use all over the world, work was done to try and improve the basic SMTP protocol by keeping the original specifications and adding new features.

RFC 1869 was published in 1995 and defined a method of extending the capabilities of SMTP, calling it "SMTP Service Extensions."

Extended SMTP is implemented by replacing the original SMTP greeting (HELO) with a new greeting command—EHLO. When an SMTP server receives this command, it should realize that the client is capable of sending extended SMTP commands. Listing 5.7 shows a sample EHLO session and the commands that are available.

LISTING 5.7 Extended SMTP Commands

```
1  [katie@shadrach katie]$ telnet localhost 25
2  Trying 127.0.0.1...
3  Connected to localhost.
4  Escape character is '^]'.
5  220 shadrach.smallorg.org ESMTP Sendmail 8.9.3/8.9.3;
➥  Mon, 30 Aug 1999 16:36:48 -050
```

continues

LISTING 5.7 continued

```
 6 EHLO localhost
 7 250-shadrach.smallorg.org Hello localhost [127.0.0.1], pleased to meet you
 8 250-EXPN
 9 250-VERB
10 250-8BITMIME
11 250-SIZE
12 250-DSN
13 250-ONEX
14 250-ETRN
15 250-XUSR
16 250 HELP
17 HELP DSN
18 214-MAIL FROM: <sender> [ RET={ FULL ‖ HDRS} ] [ ENVID=<envid> ]
19 214-RCPT TO: <recipient> [ NOTIFY={NEVER,SUCCESS,FAILURE,DELAY} ]
20 214-                     [ ORCPT=<recipient> ]
21 214-    SMTP Delivery Status Notifications.
22 214-Descriptions:
23 214-    RET     Return either the full message or only headers.
24 214-    ENVID   Sender's "envelope identifier" for tracking.
25 214-    NOTIFY  When to send a DSN. Multiple options are OK, comma-
26 214-            delimited. NEVER must appear by itself.
27 214-    ORCPT   Original recipient.
28 214 End of HELP info
29 HELP ETRN
30 214-ETRN [ <hostname> | @<domain> | #<queuename> ]
31 214-    Run the queue for the specified <hostname>, or
32 214-    all hosts within a given <domain>, or a specially-named
33 214-    <queuename> (implementation-specific).
34 214 End of HELP info
35 QUIT
36 221 shadrach.smallorg.org closing connection
37 Connection closed by foreign host.
38 [katie@shadrach katie]$
```

Line 6 shows the new extended SMTP EHLO command used to connect to the SMTP server. Lines 7–16 show the server's response. Notice that the server indicates that more commands are available now that it is in "extended" mode. One of the new groups of commands is the Delivery Status Notification options. These options can be used on the MAIL and RCPT commands to indicate the delivery status of a particular email message for the client. One command that we are extremely interested in as mail administrators is the ETRN command.

The TURN SMTP command was briefly mentioned earlier. This command is extremely useful, but not very secure. To compensate for that, RFC 1985 defines a new method of implementing the TURN command that is more secure. The ETRN command allows an SMTP client to issue a request for the SMTP server to initiate another SMTP connection with the client to transfer messages back to it. This differs from the original TURN command in that the ETRN command is just a request to start another SMTP session, not to transfer data on the existing session. This way, the SMTP server can then contact the client computer using the normal DNS hostname resolution methods. This does not rely on who the client computer says it is. If a hacker establishes an unauthorized SMTP connection and issues an ETRN command, the SMTP server will just start an SMTP connection with the real client and send any mail—no harm done. The format for the ETRN command is

```
ETRN name
```

where name can be either an individual hostname, or a domain name if you are requesting mail for an entire domain. The ETRN command is a valuable tool for the mail administrator. If you elect to have an ISP spool mail for your email server, you might use this method to notify the ISP when you are ready to receive your spooled mail. There are several different ways to accomplish this. One way is to use a canned Perl program that is supplied with the sendmail SMTP software package that connects to your ISP and issues the ETRN command for your domain. When the ISP's mail server receives this command, it will initiate another SMTP connection with your SMTP server (on the same PPP link) and transfer all mail that it has in the mail queue for your domain.

SMTP on Linux

For a Linux server to implement SMTP, it must run software capable of understanding the SMTP protocol. Several different software packages are available for Linux that implement both the SMTP client and server protocols. Some packages are more robust than others, whereas some are easier to configure than others. Your choice of which SMTP package to use will depend on several variables that you will need to evaluate. This section lists some of the more popular SMTP software packages available for Linux to help you get a feel for what to expect.

sendmail

sendmail is the granddaddy of all SMTP software packages. It has been used for many years in the UNIX environment. It is produced and supported by the sendmail Consortium (`http://www.sendmail.org`). At the time of this writing the current version available is version 8.9.3. Version 8.10 is in beta testing and may be available soon, so watch the Web site for details on newer releases.

sendmail is the most robust of the SMTP software packages around. Because of this robustness, it is also the most difficult to configure. Fortunately there are many guides and help documents available to help the mail administrator properly install and configure it. Most Linux distributions use sendmail as the default SMTP package when an SMTP package is installed. When this is the case, a fairly generic configuration file is generated that allows the Linux server to send and receive SMTP messages assuming that it is directly connected to the Internet. If this does not fit your situation, you must change the sendmail configuration file to meet your specific requirements.

Configuring sendmail can be quite an experience. Entire books are dedicated to just configuring and running sendmail. The sendmail Consortium also has devoted a Web site to helping mail administrators understand and configure sendmail. One nice feature about sendmail is that it contains a skeleton configuration file and uses an automated system to generate a specific configuration file from the skeleton. All you need to do is create a text file that includes the features and options of sendmail that you want to implement. Listing 5.8 shows a sample sendmail text file that can be used to generate a configuration file.

LISTING 5.8 Sample sendmail Definition File

```
1   divert(-1)
2   divert(0)dnl
3   include(`../m4/cf.m4')dnl
4
5   OSTYPE(`linux')
6
7   FEATURE(`allmasquerade')dnl
8   FEATURE(`masquerade_envelope')dnl
9   FEATURE(`always_add_domain')dnl
10  FEATURE(`nodns')dnl
11  FEATURE(`nocanonify')dnl
12  FEATURE(`local_procmail')dnl
13  FEATURE(`uucpdomain')dnl
14
15  MAILER(`smtp')dnl
16  MAILER(`uucp')dnl
17  MAILER(`procmail')dnl
18
19  define(`SMART_HOST', `uucp-dom:mail.isp.net')dnl
```

When the definition file is finished, it needs to be processed by the m4 macro processor program. The format for using the m4 program is as follows:

```
m4 mailhost.m4 > Sendmail.cf
```

This command will generate a `sendmail.cf` configuration file from the features and options you configured in the definition file. Chapter 11, "Installing and Configuring sendmail," discusses this process in greater detail.

Another nice thing about sendmail is its wide distribution. Many Internet sites use it, so when a bug or security hole is found, it is quickly fixed. In the spring of 1999, a well-known email virus named Melissa came on the Internet scene. It was a typical Microsoft Word macro virus in that it launched itself from a Microsoft Word document. What made it atypical was that it used the host computer's Microsoft Outlook email package to send bogus email copies of itself to other unsuspecting victims in the address book of the infected client. Even though the virus did not affect the sendmail program directly, programmers were able to define a filter to add to a sendmail configuration to ensure that any sendmail SMTP server would not forward an email that contained the Melissa virus. Pretty neat!

qmail

The `qmail` software package written by Dan Bernstein is a total replacement for the sendmail package. Its main focus is on security and reliability—two very impressive goals. Dan has put up a `qmail` server on the Internet and has offered $1,000 to anyone who could compromise the security of the SMTP functions on it. As of the date of this writing, no one has claimed the prize money. `qmail` also touts an improved method of writing mail messages to a user's mailbox using a new mailbox format that is less susceptible to crashes. Maybe the best feature of `qmail` is its ease of configuration. It uses simple ASCII text files to configure features. It is a good choice for a simple mail server site.

The current version of `qmail` is version 1.03. Currently no Linux distribution comes with a precompiled `qmail` package, so if you decide to use it you must download it from the `qmail` site at `http://www.qmail.org` and compile it yourself (but that's half the fun of Linux).

When it is downloaded and compiled, you must install it. To support the high level of security that it does, `qmail` must be installed and run using its own separate user ID and groups. Actually, it uses two different groups and seven different user IDs. `qmail` uses the `/var/qmail` directory to hold its binary and configuration files. If your Linux distribution installed sendmail, you must make sure that it is uninstalled (or at least disabled) so that `qmail` can take control of the SMTP TCP port to receive incoming SMTP requests. Also, the `qmail` install instructions describe the steps you must take to ensure that the `qmail` daemon is properly started on boot ups and stopped on shutdowns.

smail

The `smail` package is an SMTP software implementation offered by the GNU Project, which is responsible for publishing many free Linux utilities. The GNU project has many download mirror sites available to obtain the current release of `smail`, which at the time of this writing is at release level 3.2. Also, some Linux distributions include `smail` as a binary install package.

`smail` has become popular with many mail administrators who want an SMTP package that has some of the flexibility of sendmail, but is easier to configure. In fact, sites that use the UUCP protocol to transfer mail need to do little else than add their domain name to the configuration file. The main configuration file for `smail` is `/usr/lib/smail/config`. Listing 5.9 shows a sample config file for `smail`.

LISTING 5.9   Sample `smail` Configuration File

```
 1  #
 2  #list all domain names this host will accept mail for
 3  hostnames=mail.smallorg.org:smallorg.org:mail
 4  #
 5  #describe our advertised domain name
 6  visible_name=smallorg.org
 7  #
 8  #identify our default SMTP gateway to the Internet
 9  smart_path=mail.isp.net
10  smart_transport=smtp
11  #
12  #list domains we are authoritative for
13  auth_domains=smallorg.org
```

That's it—a 13-line configuration file (including comments) for routing all outbound email messages to a default SMTP host.

One of the nice features of `smail` is its capability to deliver mail messages immediately without queuing them for delivery. This method speeds up mail delivery, but could cause some problems with high mail volume. To solve that problem, `smail` also can be configured to resort to mail queuing much like sendmail does.

exim

The `exim` SMTP program was developed at the University of Cambridge under the GNU General Public License. It is available for most flavors of UNIX, including Linux. The current version available for use is 3.02. Its capability of restricting SMTP messages from spammers and hackers has helped its popularity in the Linux community. It has several configuration files that can restrict or permit access based on hostnames, IP addresses, and domain names. More information about this software package can be found at the `exim` Internet Web site `http://www.exim.org`.

Summary

The Simple Mail Transfer Protocol (SMTP) allows computers to transfer messages from a user on one computer to a user (or multiple users) on another computer using a standard method. The SMTP protocol is defined in RFC 821, and defines a standard set of commands that are used to identify the mail sender and recipients, as well as transfer the message. The actual message can be in any form, but a standard format has been set forth in RFC 822. This format provides for two different sections—the message header and the message body. The message header contains fields that identify important parts of the message such as the sender, recipients, subject, and comments. Binary data must be encoded into an ASCII text stream before it can be sent via the SMTP protocol. An Internet standard has been implemented for encoding and transferring binary data within a standard RFC 822 message. RFCs 2045 and 2046 describe new RFC 822 header fields that help identify the binary data encoding as well as its purpose. Linux supports the SMTP protocol with several different software implementations. The sendmail software package is standard on many different UNIX platforms. A version of sendmail has been ported to the Linux environment. Other Linux SMTP packages include `qmail`, `smail`, and `exim`, which incorporate improvements and/or ease-of-use to the sendmail SMTP software package.

POP3 Protocol

IN THIS CHAPTER

The previous chapter describes how to send mail to a user at a remote computer using the SMTP protocol. Back in the old days (the 1980s), that user would have to sit at a terminal, log in to the host computer, and read his mail message via a character-based text email processor. Now things are different. Computer users want to have the freedom of reading their mail from anywhere at any time, as well as having fancy GUI interfaces to do that. If the user cannot be at the Linux server using X Window to view the email, the next best thing is to let her connect to the Linux server via a network to read her mailbox using a client software package on her local PC. One protocol that allows a client to read email messages on a remote server is defined in RFC 1939 and is called the Post Office Protocol (POP). Currently, the POP protocol is at version 3, thus the new name POP3.

Description of the Post Office Protocol

Much like the SMTP protocol (described in Chapter 5, "SMTP Protocol") the POP3 protocol is a command-based protocol. The POP3 server listens for connection requests on TCP port 110, and it responds by issuing a banner line indicating that it is ready for commands. One method of determining if a host is running a POP3 server is to `telnet` to port 110 and see if you get a POP3 greeting banner. Listing 6.1 shows an example of this.

LISTING 6.1 Sample POP3 Client Session

```
1  [frank@shadrach frank]$ telnet localhost 110
2  Trying 127.0.0.1...
3  Connected to localhost.
4  Escape character is '^]'.
5  +OK POP3 localhost v7.59 server ready
6  QUIT
7  +OK Sayonara
8  Connection closed by foreign host.
9  [frank@shadrach frank]$
```

Line 1 shows an example of using the `telnet` command to attempt a connection to the POP3 TCP port on the local computer. Line 5 shows the response banner that the POP3 server issued to identify itself. Line 6 shows a POP3 command issued by the client to log off of the server, and line 7 shows the clever exit message issued by the POP3 server. When the connection is terminated, the POP3 server will initiate closing the TCP connection. Under normal circumstances, the client should respond by closing the TCP connection.

In a POP3 session, the first step for the client would be to log into the server. There are several different methods to do this. After logging in to the POP3 server, the client can query the server to see if there are any mail messages in the mailbox assigned to the user ID that the client logged in with. It is not the intent of the POP3 protocol to allow the client to do extensive manipulation of the messages in its mailbox. The POP3 protocol can simply send a list of messages to the client and transfer each message individually for the client to manipulate locally.

POP3 Authentication Methods

After the POP3 client has established a TCP connection to the server, it must be able to identify itself to the server so that the server can know it is sending the right email messages to the right user. The original method of POP3 authentication uses a user ID/password command set. Unfortunately, this method uses a clear text transmission of the user ID and password to log into the server. This method is not preferred, especially if you are connecting to a remote server where your packets will traverse unknown networks. To provide an alternative for this problem, RFC 1734 describes a more secure method of logging into a POP3 server using the AUTH command. The following sections describe both methods of authentication, as well as a third, newer method called APOP.

USER/PASS Commands

The USER/PASS command combination is the easiest to implement, but again, the most dangerous to use. Each time a client wants to log in to the POP3 server to check mail, her complete user ID and password are transmitted across the network in plain ASCII text format. Ouch! The format for these commands is

```
USER username
PASS password
```

The username parameter must be a valid user ID for the host POP3 server. The password parameter must also be the server password associated with that user ID. Listing 6.2 shows a sample POP3 session with a client using the USER/PASS combination.

LISTING 6.2   Sample USER/PASS POP3 Client Log In

```
1   [melanie@shadrach melanie]$ telnet localhost 110
2   Trying 127.0.0.1...
3   Connected to localhost.
4   Escape character is '^]'.
5   +OK POP3 localhost v7.59 server ready
6   USER melanie
7   +OK User name accepted, password please
8   PASS toybox
9   +OK Mailbox open, 0 messages
10  QUIT
11  +OK Sayonara
12  Connection closed by foreign host.
13  [melanie@shadrach melanie]$
```

Line 6 shows the client sending the USER command with her user ID in plain text. The POP3 server responded, asking for the matching password for the user ID. Line 8 shows the client sending her password. After the password is received, the user ID/password combination is compared for validity. One security feature of POP3 is that it won't immediately tell the client if a user ID is invalid until after the password is entered, thus a hacker can't easily use a POP3 server to find valid user IDs on the host system. Listing 6.3 shows the difference between a valid user with a bad password, and an invalid user.

LISTING 6.3   Example of POP3 Login Attempts

```
1  [rich@shadrach rich]$ telnet localhost 110
2  Trying 127.0.0.1...
3  Connected to localhost.
4  Escape character is '^]'.
5  +OK POP3 localhost v7.59 server ready
6  USER rich
7  +OK User name accepted, password please
8  PASS hello
9  -ERR Bad login
10 USER baduser
11 +OK User name accepted, password please
12 PASS hello
13 -ERR Bad login
14 QUIT
15 +OK Sayonara
16 Connection closed by foreign host.
17 [rich@shadrach rich]$
```

Line 6 shows a valid user login, with the invalid password attempt on line 8. The POP3 server's response is shown on line 9, and is purposely generic. Next, on line 10, a login attempt with an invalid user ID is shown, with the POP3 server's response shown on line 13. Notice that both situations produce the same error message from the server. In this case, the use of generic error messages helps prevent a hacker from using the POP3 server to find valid user IDs on the system. Of course the downside is that it is not very helpful for mail administrators trying to troubleshoot connection problems with the host.

Using clear text user IDs and passwords in the POP3 connection is even more dangerous if the client logs in to the POP3 server several times a day (or hour) to check for new mail messages. Many email client packages can be configured to check for new mail at regular intervals. This is a great opportunity for a hacker with a network analyzer to capture user IDs and passwords. To compensate for this situation, RFC 1939 provides some relief with the APOP command.

APOP Command

The client can use the APOP command in place of the USER/PASS combination to log in to the POP3 server. The APOP command allows the client to log in to the server without sending a plain text version of the password. Instead, the APOP command uses an MD5 encrypted version of the password. The format of the APOP command is

```
APOP name digest
```

where name is the normal user ID the client wants to log in as. The digest parameter allows the client to send an MD5 encoded digest value to the server to authenticate who it is. The MD5 encryption algorithm was invented by Ron Rivest and is described in RFC 1321. It uses a hashing algorithm to combine a known message with a shared secret word that only both entities should know. The result of the hashing algorithm is the digest parameter supplied by the client. Obviously, for this to work, both the client and server must have a predetermined secret word to use for the algorithm. The known message is supplied by the POP3 server on the greeting banner issued when the TCP connection is established. The known message is usually a message-id followed by the hostname of the POP3 server. An example APOP session is illustrated in Listing 6.4.

LISTING 6.4   Sample APOP Session

```
1  [chris@shadrach chris]$ telnet meshach 110
2  Trying 198.162.0.5...
3  Connected to meshach.smallorg.org.
4  Escape character is '^]'.
5  +OK POP3 server ready <1896.698370952@meshach.smallorg.org>
6  APOP chris c4c9334bac560ecc928e58001b3e22fb
7  +OK maildrop has 1 message (369 octets)
8  QUIT
9  +OK Sayonara
10 Connection closed by foreign host.
11 [chris@shadrach chris]$
```

Line 5 shows the greeting banner displayed by the POP3 server. The known message shows the timestamp and the hostname within angle brackets. The entire value is used for the known message. Line 6 shows the APOP command using the user ID and the MD5 hash value of the known message and the shared secret. The actual text password is never transmitted across the network. Without the knowledge of the shared secret word, it would be extremely difficult to break the MD5-encoded password for this client.

The APOP command is not a required command for a POP3 server to support. The easiest way to determine if a POP3 server supports the APOP command is to observe the greeting banner when you connect to the server. As can be seen in Listing 6.1, the POP3 server on the sample

Linux server does not supply the necessary message for the MD5 algorithm. A client would not be able to use the APOP method of logging into this server. In fact, trying to use the APOP command produces a negative response error message from the server.

AUTH Command

Another method of secure user identification is the AUTH command described in RFC 1734. The AUTH command has been adapted from the newer IMAP protocol (see Chapter 7, "IMAP Protocol") that has more functionality in handling mailbox messages than the POP3 protocol. The format of the AUTH command is

```
AUTH mechanism
```

where mechanism is a method of authenticating the user that the client can negotiate with the server. When an authentication method is agreed upon, the actual user ID authentication will take place.

The client initiates the negotiation method. The client first issues an AUTH command with the highest level of authentication encryption that it can support. If the server does not support that encryption technique, a negative response will be sent to the client. The client can then issue another AUTH command with a different mechanism specified. This negotiation can go back and forth until the client and server find a common authentication encryption technique, or they resort to using the USER/PASS technique. Listing 6.5 shows a sample AUTH negotiation session with a POP3 server.

LISTING 6.5 Sample AUTH Negotiation Session

```
1  [matthew@shadrach matthew]$ telnet localhost 110
2  Trying 127.0.0.1...
3  Connected to localhost.
4  Escape character is '^]'.
5  +OK POP3 localhost v6.50 server ready
6  AUTH KERBEROS_V4
7  -ERR Bad authentication
8  AUTH GSSAPI
9  -ERR Bad authentication
10 AUTH SKEY
11 -ERR Bad authentication
12 AUTH
13 +OK Supported authentication mechanisms:
14 LOGIN
15 .
16 AUTH LOGIN
17 + VXNlciBOYW1lAA==
18 xxxxxxxxx
```

```
19 + UGFzc3dvcmQA
20 xxxxxxxxx
21 -ERR Bad authentication
22 USER matthew
23 +OK User name accepted, password please
24 PASS apple
25 +OK Mailbox open, 0 messages
26 QUIT
27 +OK Sayonara
28 Connection closed by foreign host.
29 [matthew@shadrach matthew]$
```

Lines 6 through 11 show the client attempting to negotiate some standard IMAP authentication techniques with the POP3 server, all of which fail. Line 12 shows the client issuing an AUTH command with no parameters. The server responds by listing the authentication methods it supports in lines 14 and 15. Line 16 shows the client attempting to use the LOGIN authentication method supported by the server. Line 17 shows the encrypted response from the server to the AUTH command. Unfortunately the client was unable to log in with the LOGIN authentication method, and had to resort to using the USER/PASS combination in lines 22 through 25.

POP3 Client Commands

When the POP3 client has successfully logged in to the server, it enters the transaction mode. It must issue commands to control the transfer of messages from the server to the client. Each command will solicit a specific POP3 action from the server.

STAT

The STAT command has no parameters. It is used to obtain a "drop listing" from the POP3 server. The drop listing is a formatted line of text that indicates the current status of the mailbox. The line is formatted in the following way:

```
+OK nn mm
```

The format of the STAT response is standard to allow email clients to parse the response for the information. The nn value represents the total number of messages in the user's mailbox. Messages that have been marked as deleted are not counted in this value, however, messages that have already been read are counted. The mm value represents the total byte count of the messages represented by the count number. The STAT command is often used to quickly check on the status of the mailbox by the email client program. By logging in and issuing a STAT command, the email package can compare the message count number to the value obtained at the last mail check. If the number is different, the email package can then proceed further in obtaining the messages. The only problem with this method is that the email client has no idea how many of the messages have been downloaded previously that were not deleted.

LIST

The LIST command is used to obtain a *scan listing* of the mailbox. A scan listing is a brief synopsis of the mailbox contents that includes the message number and its size in bytes. The LIST command issued with no parameters displays the scan listing of all the messages in the mailbox. By including a message number as a parameter, the LIST command will display the scan listing for that individual message. A sample LIST command session is shown in Listing 6.6.

LISTING 6.6   Sample LIST Command

```
1  [alex@shadrach alex]$ telnet localhost 110
2  Trying 127.0.0.1...
3  Connected to localhost.
4  Escape character is '^]'.
5  +OK POP3 localhost v6.50 server ready
6  USER alex
7  +OK User name accepted, password please
8  PASS tarzan
9  +OK Mailbox open, 2 messages
10 LIST
11 +OK Mailbox scan listing follows
12 1 355
13 2 465
14 .
15 LIST 1
16 +OK 1 355
17 LIST 2
18 +OK 2 465
19 LIST 3
20 -ERR No such message
21 QUIT
22 +OK Sayonara
23 Connection closed by foreign host.
24 [alex@shadrach alex]$
```

Line 10 shows the client issuing the LIST command with no parameters to the server. The server responds in lines 12 through 14 first with a positive acknowledgment in line 11, and then the individual message scan listings in lines 12 and 13. In some POP3 server implementations, the positive acknowledgment response will include the STAT output to summarize the messages, but the client software cannot count on that being the case (as shown by this listing). Lines 15 and 17 show the client issuing a LIST command for individual messages, with the server's responses shown in lines 16 and 18. Line 19 shows the client issuing a LIST command for a nonexistent message number. The server responds with a negative response in line 20.

RETR

The RETR command is used to retrieve the text of individual messages from the mailbox. The parameter used with this command is a message number as returned by the LIST command described previously. If the message number is valid, the server will respond with a positive acknowledgment line and the complete text of the message followed by a terminating character (a single period on a line by itself). The message sent to the client should be the full RFC 822–formatted message contained in the mailbox on the server as received by the host software (often SMTP). The POP3 server will not format or manipulate the message in any way. The job of the POP3 server is to transfer the message in its entirety to the client. A sample RETR command session is shown in Listing 6.7.

LISTING 6.7   Sample RETR Command

```
1   [rich@shadrach rich]$ telnet localhost 110
2   Trying 127.0.0.1...
3   Connected to localhost.
4   Escape character is '^]'.
5   +OK POP3 localhost v6.50 server ready
6   USER rich
7   +OK User name accepted, password please
8   PASS guitar
9   +OK Mailbox open, 2 messages
10  LIST
11  +OK Mailbox scan listing follows
12  1 355
13  2 465
14  .
15  RETR 1
16  +OK 355 octets
17  Return-Path: <rich>
18  Received: (from rich@localhost)
19          by shadrach.smallorg.org (8.8.7/8.8.7) id KAA00648
20          for rich; Thu, 2 Sep 1999 10:15:25 -0500
21  Date: Thu, 2 Sep 1999 10:15:25 -0500
22  From: rich@shadrach.smallorg.org
23  Message-Id: <199909021515.KAA00648@shadrach.smallorg.org>
24  To: rich@shadrach.smallorg.org
25  Subject: Message 1
26  Status:  O
27
28  This is test message 1
29  .
30  QUIT
31  +OK Sayonara
32  Connection closed by foreign host.
33  [rich@shadrach rich]$
```

Line 15 shows the client issuing the RETR command for message number 1. Lines 16 through 27 show the POP3 server sending the message text in its entirety to the client. It is the responsibility of the client to have a storage buffer large enough to store the message after it receives it (that's why the LIST command returns the size of the message).

DELE

The DELE command is used for deleting messages from the mailbox on the server. Its single parameter is the message number as identified from the LIST command. Actually, the DELE command does not delete the message, it just marks it for deletion. The actual deletion of the message will not take place until the session is properly terminated with the QUIT command described later. Care must be taken when using the DELE command in that the message numbering system must be closely watched. Listing 6.8 shows the results from deleting a message from the scan listing.

LISTING 6.8   Results from Using the DELE Command

```
1  [rich@shadrach rich]$ telnet localhost 110
2  Trying 127.0.0.1...
3  Connected to localhost.
4  Escape character is '^]'.
5  +OK POP3 localhost v7.59 server ready
6  USER rich
7 +OK User name accepted, password please
8  PASS guitar
9  +OK Mailbox open, 3 messages
10 LIST
11 +OK Mailbox scan listing follows
12 1 377
13 2 387
14 3 396
15 .
16 DELE 1
17 +OK Message deleted
18 LIST
19 +OK Mailbox scan listing follows
20 2 387
21 3 396
22 .
23 QUIT
24 +OK Sayonara
25 Connection closed by foreign host.
26 [rich@shadrach rich]$ telnet localhost 110
27 Trying 127.0.0.1...
28 Connected to localhost.
```

```
29 Escape character is '^]'.
30 +OK POP3 localhost v7.59 server ready
31 USER rich
32 +OK User name accepted, password please
33 PASS guitar
34 +OK Mailbox open, 2 messages
35 LIST
36 +OK Mailbox scan listing follows
37 1 387
38 2 396
39 .
40 QUIT
41 +OK Sayonara
42 Connection closed by foreign host.
43 [rich@shadrach rich]$
```

Line 10 shows the client issuing a LIST command to check if any messages are in his mailbox. Lines 11 through 15 indicate that three messages are available. In line 16, the client issues a DELE command to delete message number 1 (again, it will actually only be marked for deletion). Line 17 shows the confirmation of the action by the POP3 server. The new scan listing from the server, shown in lines 20 and 21, now show only messages 2 and 3 available for downloading. The client decides to terminate the POP3 session at that point.

Lines 26 through 42 show a second POP3 session initiated by the client. In this session, a new LIST command is issued in line 35. As before, the POP3 server indicates that two messages are available in the mailbox. However, notice that with the new POP3 session, the server renumbered the messages. The message that used to be message 2 is now message 1, and the message that used to be message 3 is now message 2.

This example shows that message numbers are not static entities. The message numbers are valid only for the current POP3 session. Any attempt by the client to use the message numbers between POP3 sessions will almost always end up with unexpected results. The UIDL command mentioned in a later section is an optional command that some POP3 servers support in an attempt to uniquely identify messages between sessions.

NOOP

The NOOP command does what is says—nothing. After receiving a NOOP command, the POP3 server will respond with a positive response. This command can be used to determine the connectivity of the POP3 server. It might only be issued after establishing a session by logging into the server.

RSET

The RSET command will reset the session back to the start of the session after the authentication of the client with the server (the client will not have to log in again). The important thing to know about the RSET command is that it will cause the server to unmark any messages marked for deletion. The messages unmarked will return to the scan listing with their original message numbers.

QUIT

The QUIT command is used to terminate the POP3 session. When the server receives a QUIT command, it will actually delete any messages marked for deletion from the user's mailbox and terminate the TCP session. If the POP3 session should terminate before the client issues a QUIT command, any messages marked for deletion are restored and not deleted.

TOP

The TOP command is an optional POP3 command that servers might choose to implement. The TOP command is a handy way for the client to get a brief synopsis of messages available in the mailbox. It will return the RFC 822 header fields for a message, along with a designated number of lines from the body of the message. The TOP command has two parameters that are both required. The format of the TOP command is

```
TOP msg n
```

where msg is the message number from a LIST scan listing, and n is an integer representing the number of lines from the message body that will be displayed. Email clients often use this command to obtain Subject header fields of messages to display in a list of messages without having to download the entire text of the messages. Listing 6.9 shows an example of the TOP command being used.

LISTING 6.9   Sample of the TOP Command

```
1   [rich@shadrach rich]$ telnet localhost 110
2   Trying 127.0.0.1...
3   Connected to localhost.
4   Escape character is '^]'.
5   +OK POP3 localhost v7.59 server ready
6   USER rich
7   +OK User name accepted, password please
8   PASS guitar
9   +OK Mailbox open, 5 messages
10  LIST
11  +OK Mailbox scan listing follows
12  1 387
13  2 396
14  3 374
15  4 375
16  5 383
17  .
```

```
18 TOP 1 0
19 +OK Top of message follows
20 Return-Path: <rich>
21 Received: (from rich@localhost)
22         by shadrach.smallorg.org (8.9.3/8.9.3) id MAA00496
23          for rich; Thu, 2 Sep 1999 12:35:51 -0500
24 Date: Thu, 2 Sep 1999 12:35:51 -0500
25 From: rich@shadrach.smallorg.org
26 Message-Id: <199909021735.MAA00496@shadrach.smallorg.org>
27 To: rich@shadrach.smallorg.org
28 Subject: Test message 1
29 Status:   O
30
31 .
32 TOP 4 10
33 +OK Top of message follows
34 Return-Path: <rich>
35 Received: (from rich@localhost)
36         by shadrach.smallorg.org (8.9.3/8.9.3) id NAA00588
37          for rich; Thu, 2 Sep 1999 13:32:35 -0500
38 Date: Thu, 2 Sep 1999 13:32:35 -0500
39 From: rich@shadrach.smallorg.org
40 Message-Id: <199909021832.NAA00588@shadrach.smallorg.org>
41 To: rich@shadrach.smallorg.org
42 Subject: Sample message #4
43 Status:
44
45 This is the fourth sample message.
46 .
47 QUIT
48 +OK Sayonara
49 Connection closed by foreign host.
50 [rich@shadrach rich]$
```

Line 10 shows the client issuing the LIST command to obtain the list of mail message numbers from the POP3 server. When the client has the message numbers, it can begin using the TOP command to display the RFC 822 header field information from each message. Line 18 shows the client requesting the information for message 1, with no lines from the message body. The server response is shown in lines 19 through 31. In line 32, the client requests the first 10 lines of message 4. Because the message body only has one line, the server responds by displaying the entire header and message body.

UIDL

The UIDL command is another optional POP3 server command. Its purpose is to uniquely identify messages in the mailbox between POP3 sessions. As previously shown for the LIST command, messages are normally sequentially numbered during the POP3 session. When a client terminates one session and begins another, the messages are renumbered sequentially. Thus, if the client had ten messages in her mailbox and deleted message six during a POP3 session, the next POP3 session would have nine messages renumbered one through nine. This is not an easy way for the email client software to keep track of messages.

To solve this problem, some POP3 servers implement the UIDL, or "unique-id listing" command. Each message is assigned a unique character string ID consisting of from 1 to 70 printable ASCII characters. That ID will remain with the message for as long as it is in the mailbox. Often the UIDL of the message is obtained by performing a hash algorithm on the message header. Using this technique, it is possible for two identical copies of the same message to have the same UIDL. The client email software should be capable of recognizing this situation and handling it accordingly. Listing 6.10 shows an example of listing and deleting messages identified by a UIDL.

LISTING 6.10   Sample of the UIDL Command

```
1   [rich@shadrach rich]$ telnet localhost 110
2   Trying 127.0.0.1...
3   Connected to localhost.
4   Escape character is '^]'.
5   +OK POP3 localhost v7.59 server ready
6   USER rich
7   +OK User name accepted, password please
8   PASS guitar
9   +OK Mailbox open, 3 messages
10  LIST
11  +OK Mailbox scan listing follows
12  1 370
13  2 371
14  3 370
15  .
16  UIDL
17  +OK Unique-ID listing follows
18  1 37cabbcb00000009
19  2 37cabbcb0000000a
20  3 37cabbcb0000000b
21  .
22  DELE 1
23  +OK Message deleted
24  LIST
25  +OK Mailbox scan listing follows
26  2 371
27  3 370
```

```
28 .
29 UIDL
30 +OK Unique-ID listing follows
31 2 37cabbcb0000000a
32 3 37cabbcb0000000b
33 .
34 QUIT
35 +OK Sayonara
36 Connection closed by foreign host.
37 [rich@shadrach rich]$ telnet localhost 110
38 Trying 127.0.0.1...
39 Connected to localhost.
40 Escape character is '^]'.
41 +OK POP3 localhost v7.59 server ready
42 USER rich
43 +OK User name accepted, password please
44 PASS guitar
45 +OK Mailbox open, 2 messages
46 LIST
47 +OK Mailbox scan listing follows
48 1 371
49 2 370
50 .
51 UIDL
52 +OK Unique-ID listing follows
53 1 37cabbcb0000000a
54 2 37cabbcb0000000b
55 .
56 QUIT
57 +OK Sayonara
58 Connection closed by foreign host.
59 [rich@shadrach rich]$
```

Line 16 shows the client issuing the UIDL command to display the unique IDs of the messages in the mailbox. Lines 17 through 21 show the server's response with the unique IDs for each message. In line 22, the client deletes message number 1. Lines 30 through 33 show that the remaining message UIDLs have not changed. In the next POP3 session, lines 47 through 50 show that the messages have been renumbered for the new session, but lines 52 through 55 show that the UIDL numbers for the remaining messages have stayed the same between POP3 sessions. Thus the client can identify messages between POP3 sessions.

POP3 Server Responses

As shown in the sample POP3 sessions earlier in the chapter, every command the client sends to the POP3 server generates a response from the server. The format of the server responses is

`result text`

where `result` is a result code returned by the POP3 server, and `text` is a text message describing the results of the command.

There are two results that can be returned by the POP3 server. The `+OK` message indicates a successful command result, and an `-ERR` message indicates an unsuccessful command result.

Details of the command result are contained in the text portion of the return message. Multi-line responses are allowed. The end of a multi-line response is indicated with a single period (`.`) on a line by itself.

Linux POP3 Implementations

Several software packages are available for Linux that implement POP3 clients and servers. This section discusses three popular packages used in many Linux distributions.

Linux as a POP3 Client

By far the most popular POP3 client package for Linux is the fetchmail program written by Eric Raymond. Calling it a POP3 program is actually a misnomer because it does much more than just POP3 client functions. It can retrieve messages from a mailbox on a remote host using the POP3, IMAP4, or SMTP `ETRN` protocols. However, with the popularity of POP3 mail services being offered by ISPs, fetchmail has become the standard software package for many Linux users wanting to retrieve their POP3 Internet mail. fetchmail automatically determines which protocols the remote server supports and attempts to choose the best method to transfer messages. After it downloads the message, it will attempt to pass it to the local mail processor on the Linux server for delivery to the local user.

One use of fetchmail that is becoming popular is downloading mail for an entire domain using a single ISP mailbox. The ISP configures its sendmail to forward any message sent to any user at a domain to a single user ID. For example, any messages sent to `prez@smallorg.org`, `viceprez@smallorg.org`, or `janitor@smallorg.org` are forwarded by the ISP to the account `maildrop@smallorg.org`. The Linux mail server for `smallorg.org` then uses fetchmail and POP3 to download the messages for `maildrop@smallorg.org`. Although each message is sent to the same mailbox, they all have different values in the RFC 822 To: header field (see the section "Message Formats" in Chapter 5, "SMTP Protocol"). The fetchmail program can be configured to forward each of the received messages to the appropriate local mailbox on the

Linux server based on the To: header field values. Although this is an extremely popular technique (especially with servers running Windows POP3 utilities), it is not generally recommended because important RFC 822 header information can be lost in the process. The best method to use is the SMTP ETRN method described in Chapter 13, "Connecting the Mailserver to an ISP." This method preserves the proper RFC 822 header fields in the messages.

Installing fetchmail

Because of its popularity, many Linux distributions come with a binary package for fetchmail. If your distribution did not include a fetchmail package, or you want to use the most current version (currently 5.0.7), you can download the fetchmail source code from the fetchmail home page at `http://tuxedo.org/~esr/fetchmail/`. You should have a current version of the GNU gcc compiler, as well as a current copy of the flex program installed on your Linux system. After the source code is downloaded, you can unpack it into a working directory by typing the following:

```
tar -zxvf fetchmail-5.0.7.tar.gz
```

This will create a subdirectory named `fetchmail-5.0.7` with the source code and related files needed for compiling. The steps necessary to create the fetchmail executable are

1. Run the configure program. configure checks for compiler-specific options available on your Linux distribution necessary for the proper creation of the Makefile. The configure program will perform tests of libraries, include files, and compiler options and output the results as it goes along. If you want to customize your fetchmail implementation, you can use the `configure` parameters to change parts of the program, such as leaving out IMAP or SMTP support if they are not needed to produce a smaller binary footprint.

2. Run the make utility to process the Makefile created in the previous step. This will compile the source code pieces and produce two binary files—`fetchmail` and `fetchmailconf`.

3. As the 'root' user, run `make install` to place the executables in the proper location so that any user on the Linux system can use them without permissions problems (unless, of course, you do not want any user to be able to use them).

After the executables are created and installed, you must create a configuration file for each fetchmail user so that fetchmail can properly connect to the remote server and retrieve your mail.

Configuring fetchmail

Each `fetchmail` user requires a configuration file. The location of the configuration file is `$HOME/.fetchmailrc`. When fetchmail runs, it checks for the existence of this file and complains if it is not found, using the following message:

```
fetchmail: no mailservers have been specified.
```

The .fetchmailrc file is a standard ASCII text file defining what server fetchmail should connect to, what protocol(s) to use, and what user ID and password method it should use to retrieve the mail messages. The format of the configuration file takes a kind of odd form—half configuration and half narrative. A sample .fetchmailrc file is shown in Listing 6.11.

LISTING 6.11 Sample .fetchmailrc File

```
1  # Configuration created Fri Sep  3 09:16:53 1999 by fetchmailconf
2  set postmaster "rich"
3  set bouncemail
4  set properties ""
5  poll 10.0.0.1 with proto POP3
6          user "rich" there with password "guitar" is rich here
```

Lines 5 and 6 set the fetchmail configuration parameters for the user ID "rich." The remote host address, protocol, user ID, and password are all configured in this file. In line 6, fetchmail will match the remote user "rich" with the local Linux user ID "rich." This can be changed if necessary, but be careful with this because it could get extremely confusing.

An easier way to configure the .fetchmailrc file is to use the fetchmailconf configuration X Window program. This is a graphical program that queries for the necessary configuration pieces for fetchmail. Table 6.1 shows which lines the fetchmailconf dialogs generate in the .fetchmailrc file.

TABLE 6.1 .fetchmailrc Lines Generated by fetchmailconf

fetchmailconf window	*.fetchmailrc lines*
Novice configurator	poll, frequency
Host configurator	poll, proto, user
User configuration	password, properties

Figure 6.1 shows the main screen for fetchmailconf.

To use the configuration features, press the Configure fetchmail button. This produces the fetchmail configurator menu shown in Figure 6.2.

By choosing the Novice Configuration option, fetchmailconf will assist you in setting the parameters for the POP3 server you connect to. The first screen queries you for the address of the POP3 server(s) and how frequently you want to poll them for new mail. If a polling frequency is selected, fetchmail will run in background mode and poll the sites as desired. This won't work if you are using a dial-in connection to the ISP though. If this is your situation, choose a poll frequency of 0 and create a shell script that dials the ISP and runs fetchmail once; then use that script in a cron file to execute at the desired frequency. Figure 6.3 shows a sample Novice configurator screen.

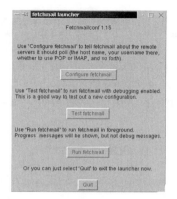

FIGURE 6.1
The main fetchmail screen.

FIGURE 6.2
The fetchmail configurator screen options.

FIGURE 6.3
The fetchmail novice configurator main screen.

After entering the address of the POP3 server, you can edit parameters for it by highlighting the address and clicking the Edit button. This produces the host configuration screen. Here you can configure the protocol required to connect to the remote server. You can even let fetchmail query the remote server, determine which protocols the remote server supports, and choose the best one by pressing the Probe for Supported Protocols button. Also, you can configure the list of user IDs for which you want fetchmail to retrieve mailr. Figure 6.4 shows the host configuration screen.

FIGURE 6.4

The fetchmail host configuration screen.

By highlighting an individual user ID and pressing the Edit button, you can configure the parameters required to connect to the server as the user. Figure 6.5 shows the fetchmail user configuration screen.

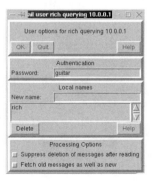

FIGURE 6.5

The fetchmail user configuration screen.

The user configuration screen allows you to configure the password required for the user ID to log into the POP3 server. Also, there are two check boxes to select other options for the user account. The first box determines if fetchmail will delete all messages in the mailbox after downloading them. This option saves disk space on the server, but if the user connects to the server via multiple PCs, this could cause confusion because different mail messages would then be scattered among the different PCs. The second option, Fetch Old Messages as Well as New, allows fetchmail to use the POP3 UIDL feature to attempt to identify messages already downloaded and not download them again. This is a nice feature in that if users use multiple PCs to check their mailbox, each PC could not delete the mailbox messages, but only download new messages since the last download. Although this solves the multiple PC mail problem, it does not solve the disk space issue associated with keeping all mail messages on the server.

Using fetchmail

When the `.fetchmailrc` configuration file is completed, you can use the fetchmail program to retrieve mail from the POP3 server. In interactive mode, all that is needed is to type the command **fetchmail**. This will cause fetchmail to read the configuration file, log in to the configured servers, and transfer the mail messages to the appropriate user ID on the local Linux computer. fetchmail can also be used with command-line parameters that alter its behavior. Table 6.2 shows some of the options that are available for using fetchmail in POP3 mode.

TABLE 6.2   fetchmail Command-Line Options

Option	Description
-V	Displays the version of fetchmail
-c	Checks for mail without downloading any messages
-s	Silent mode—suppresses output
-v	Verbose mode—extra output
-a	Retrieves all messages from server
-k	Keeps messages on the remote server after they have been downloaded
-K	Deletes messages on the remote server after they have been downloaded (default)
-F	Flush—deletes old messages before retrieving new messages
-p	Specifies a transfer protocol
-U	Uses the UIDL to identify messages
-P	Uses a different TCP port
-t	Sets a different timeout value

fetchmail can also be used as a daemon by specifying the poll frequency in the configuration file. This allows fetchmail to run in the background and check for new mail messages on a regular basis.

Linux as a POP3 Server

Linux also supports POP3 server implementations to give remote users the ability to check and retrieve mail messages on the local host. Each email user must have his own user ID on the Linux server, and each user ID should have access to a single mailbox. The server can then run POP3 server software as a background process to watch the network for POP3 connections. Figure 6.6 shows how the POP3 server software interacts on the Linux server, allowing remote users to access their mailbox on the Linux server.

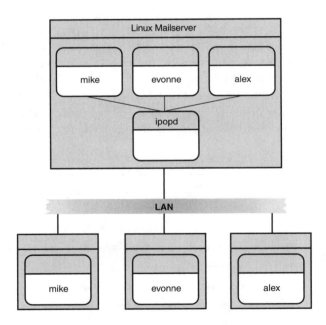

FIGURE 6.6
Linux mailserver running POP3 server software.

ipopd

ipopd is the default POP3 server software available for Linux systems. The ipopd program is part of the IMAP software project maintained by the University of Washington. The IMAP software project includes both POP3 and IMAP server implementations. Many Linux distributions include this software as a binary distribution package. The current version shipped with Red Hat 6.0 is imap-4.5-3.

The ipopd software contains implementations for both the POP3 protocol and its older brother—POP2. All new email client software now implements the POP3 protocol, so the POP2 software is obsolete. The POP3 program is called ipop3d, and is called from the inetd server software. The /etc/inetd.conf file should already contain a file for POP3 mail, but is probably commented out. The line should look like the following:

```
pop-3   stream  tcp     nowait  root    /usr/sbin/tcpd  ipop3d
```

The ipop3d program is normally installed in the /usr/sbin subdirectory on the Linux server.

qpopper

The qpopper program is a POP3 server implementation originally written at Berkeley, but currently maintained by Qualcomm. It is included as a binary package with many Linux distributions, or the latest version (2.53) can be downloaded from the Eudora Web site at http://www.eudora.com/free/servers.html. One nice feature of qpopper over the standard ipopd program is its capability to support APOP connections using a special database of user IDs. The two binary executables installed for qpopper are in.qpopper and popauth.

The in.qpopper program is a replacement for the ipop3d program normally used in Linux POP3 servers. The /etc/inetd.conf file must be modified to run this program when a client established a TCP connection on port 110. The /etc/inetd.conf line to use qpopper should look like this:

```
pop3    stream  tcp     nowait  root    /usr/sbin/tcpd  in.qpopper
```

After restarting the inetd process, the in.qpopper program should be ready to accept new POP3 connections.

The popauth program allows qpopper the capability to accept APOP connections from clients. It creates a user database in the /etc/pop.auth file, and uses utilities to add and delete user IDs to the database. To add a new user ID to the database, use the command

```
popauth -user username
```

This creates a new entry for user ID username in the database. To delete users, use the command

```
popauth -delete username
```

To obtain a list of users in the database, you can use the command

```
popauth -list
```

After a user ID is in the pop.auth database, the user can use a POP3 client program that implements the APOP authentication method to connect to the qpopper server.

> ## Mail Server Philosophy
>
> Maintaining an email server can be a complicated adventure. Mail administrators must make several political and philosophical decisions for the proper operation of the mail server in a multiuser environment. Rules for proper mail procedures must be established before turning users loose on the server.
>
> One of the biggest concerns for the mail administrator is the accumulation of email messages on the local server. Most email servers are limited in the amount of disk space available to store mail messages. The POP3 protocol does not specifically mention the deletion of mail messages after retrieval. It is at the discretion of the mail user to decide whether mail messages should be deleted from the server after downloading them to their local PC.
>
> One method to solve this problem is to impose a strict disk space limit on each user's mailbox. When the user's mailbox has reached its imposed limit, the user cannot receive any more mail messages. This method often becomes politically impossible to implement.
>
> Another solution is to impose a rule regarding the retention of messages on a per-message basis. Rules regarding the deletion of read messages after a certain number of days will sometimes help, but are often complicated and difficult to implement.
>
> Many POP3 client packages can use the UIDL command to identify messages in the mailbox and download only new messages, saving download time. Unfortunately some older POP3 clients do not implement the UIDL command, and thus, must download all messages every time they connect to the server. One way to minimize this problem is to delete every message after downloading it. But then that causes another problem.
>
> The problem of deleting messages as soon as they are downloaded is magnified when users must use more than one PC to view their mail. This often occurs when users are allowed to connect from home to view their email (discussed in Chapter 16, "Supporting Dial-in Clients"), as well as viewing their email from their office PCs. Whichever PC they download their message from is where the message will reside. This results in "splitting" their mailbox onto two separate and distant computers—something that most (if not all) users do not appreciate.

Summary

After mail has been transferred to the Linux SMTP server, users must be able to connect to the server to retrieve their mail. The Post Office Protocol Version 3 (POP3) is used to download the messages to the user's local PC, so they can be read using graphical email packages. The POP3 protocol is not as robust as newer protocols used, but its simplicity in configuration and use make it a common tool in use today for mail transfers. Software is available for Linux to implement the POP3 protocol both as a server and as a client. The ipopd and qpopper programs are used to provide POP3 server functionality to a Linux server so users can retrieve their mail messages remotely from the server. The fetchmail program is used to allow a Linux server to act as a POP3 client and retrieve mail messages from a remote POP3 server, often the ISP mail server that spools mail messages for the Linux mail server. Unfortunately the POP3 protocol has its limitations, and over the years a trend is starting toward more advanced mail retrieval programs such as IMAP, covered in the next chapter.

IMAP Protocol

7

IN THIS CHAPTER

The previous chapter discusses the POP3 protocol—a popular way of retrieving email messages from a remote server. Although the POP3 protocol is easy to implement, it does have its drawbacks. Mainly, it lacks any serious message-handling capabilities. Messages are usually downloaded in mass from the mail server, and then deleted from the server. This technique is good for the ISP hosting the mail server because it saves on required disk space, but for the mail user, this could get confusing. By downloading the messages, they become "tied-down" to the PC in which the download was performed. If your users only retrieve mail from a single workstation on the network, that might not be a problem, but if they need to access their mailbox from home as well as from work, this gets to be a big problem. This means that their mailbox messages get split between two workstations located in different areas. Ouch!

To compensate for this situation, a new protocol was devised. The Internet Message Access Protocol (IMAP) was developed at the University of Washington so that email users can access their mailboxes from multiple locations without splitting their mail between workstations. This is accomplished by maintaining the mailbox on the mail server and allowing the client PC to manipulate the messages on the server. Of course the downside to this scenario is that the Linux mail server must maintain all of the mail on its own disk. This can lead to some scary disk space situations for the mail administrator. Care must be taken when administering an IMAP server so that the system does not max out on disk space and not be able to store new messages.

This chapter outlines the IMAP protocol and demonstrates how it is implemented in a Linux environment. The current version of IMAP is version 4 revision 1, or IMAP4rev1 for short. It is fully described in RFC 2060.

Description of the Internet Mail Access Protocol

Just like its cousin POP3, IMAP uses a client/server command method of transferring messages from the server to the client. The client establishes a TCP connection to port 143 of the server to initiate the connection. The server should respond with a greeting banner. Listing 7.1 shows a sample IMAP session.

LISTING 7.1   Sample IMAP Session

```
1   [jessica@shadrach jessica]$ telnet localhost 143
2   Trying 127.0.0.1...
3   Connected to localhost.
4   Escape character is '^]'.
5   * OK shadrach.smallorg.org IMAP4rev1 v12.250 server ready
6   a001 LOGOUT
7   * BYE shadrach.smallorg.org IMAP4rev1 server terminating connection
```

```
8   a001 OK LOGOUT completed
9   Connection closed by foreign host.
10  [jessica@shadrach jessica]$
```

Line 1 shows a telnet session to TCP port 143 (the default IMAP port). Line 5 shows the greeting banner presented by the IMAP server. Line 6 shows the LOGOUT command issued by the client to the server to close the session. The server then sends a termination banner in line 7, and then closes the TCP session with the client.

Each command from the client must start with a unique identifier that tags the command. The server can use this identifier when responding to the command, so the client will know which command the server is responding to in the case of multiple commands being processed. The identifier is usually a short alphanumeric string that is generated by the client. Line 6 in Listing 7.1 shows that the client chose the tag a001 to represent the first identifier. If more commands had been sent by the client, the next identifier used would be a002. Often, client command identifiers will increment sequentially throughout the IMAP session to simplify things.

When the client establishes a connection, it starts out in an un-authenticated state. For the client to be allowed to perform any operations with the mailbox, it must first authenticate itself with the server. After the client has authenticated itself to the host, it can issue IMAP commands to manipulate mail messages on the server. The IMAP protocol supports each user having multiple mailboxes on a server. The client can read, transfer, and delete messages to and from any mailbox that he has access to on the server. This is a vast improvement over the POP3 protocol.

IMAP Authentication Methods

Also like its cousin POP3, IMAP allows several methods to authenticate a client—some more secure than others. Unlike POP3 clients, IMAP clients often keep established sessions open for extended periods of time while they process their messages. Thus the user ID and password pair are not transferred across the network several times each hour as with POP3. Nonetheless, it is still beneficial to transmit userid and password information using an encrypted method if possible.

LOGIN

The LOGIN command allows the client to use plain text userids and passwords to log in to the IMAP server. Although this is not necessarily the best method to use, sometimes it is the only method that a client and server can agree on. Listing 7.2 shows a sample IMAP logon session using the LOGIN command.

7

IMAP PROTOCOL

LISTING 7.2   Sample LOGIN Command Session

```
 1  [katie@shadrach katie]$ telnet localhost 143
 2  Trying 127.0.0.1...
 3  Connected to localhost.
 4  Escape character is '^]'.
 5  * OK localhost IMAP4rev1 v12.250 server ready
 6  a001 LOGIN katie boxcar
 7  a001 OK LOGIN completed
 8  a002 LOGOUT
 9  * BYE shadrach.smallorg.org IMAP4rev1 server terminating connection
10  a002 OK LOGOUT completed
11  Connection closed by foreign host.
12  [katie@shadrach katie]$
```

Line 6 shows the IMAP user katie logging in to the server with the LOGIN command. Line 7 shows the server response. Note how the server includes the command identifier code (a001) from the client's command to tag the response.

AUTHENTICATE

The AUTHENTICATE command allows a client to use alternative methods to log in to the IMAP server without having to send a plain text userid/password pair. The implementation of individual authentication methods is optional, and not all IMAP servers support the same set of methods. When the client issues a valid AUTHENTICATE command, the server responds with a base64 encoded challenge string. It is the responsibility of the client to respond to the challenge with a base64 encoded response string. If the IMAP server does not support the authentication method proposed by the client, it will respond with a NO response message. The client must attempt to negotiate a common authentication method, falling back to the LOGIN method as a last resort. Listing 7.3 shows a sample AUTHENTICATE session.

LISTING 7.3   Sample AUTHENTICATE Session

```
 1  [riley@shadrach riley]$ telnet localhost 143
 2  Trying 127.0.0.1...
 3  Connected to localhost.
 4  Escape character is '^]'.
 5  * OK localhost IMAP4rev1 v12.250 server ready
 6  a1 AUTHENTICATE KERBEROS_V4
 7  a1 NO AUTHENTICATE KERBEROS_V4 failed
 8  a2 AUTHENTICATE GSSAPI
 9  a2 NO AUTHENTICATE GSSAPI failed
10  a3 AUTHENTICATE LOGIN
11  + VXNlciBOYU1lAA==
12  *
```

```
13 a3 NO AUTHENTICATE LOGIN failed
14 a4 LOGIN riley firetruck
15 a4 OK LOGIN completed
16 a5 LOGOUT
17 * BYE shadrach.smallorg.org IMAP4rev1 server terminating connection
18 a5 OK LOGOUT completed
19 Connection closed by foreign host.
20 [riley@shadrach riley]$
```

Lines 6 through 9 show failed attempts by the client to negotiate common IMAP authentication methods. Line 10 shows a successful method. The server responds by issuing a base64 encoded challenge in line 11. However, the client aborts the login attempt in line 12 and resorts to a LOGIN command in line 14.

IMAP Client Protocol

When the client is authenticated with the IMAP server, it can begin manipulating messages. The IMAP protocol provides a large number of commands used to read, move, and delete mail messages from within different mailboxes on the server. Remember the IMAP protocol provides that all the messages reside on the server. Downloading messages is purely for display purposes; no messages should be stored on the client.

The default mailbox for a client is called the INBOX. All new messages appear in the INBOX. The client has the ability to create new mailboxes (sometimes called folders by email client software) to move messages from the INBOX to other areas to reduce clutter.

Each message is assigned a unique identifier (UID) to identify it in the mailbox. The UID should persist between sessions so that the IMAP client software can properly identify messages. Each mailbox has a unique identifier validity tag (UIDVALIDITY). The UIDVALIDITY tag should persist between sessions only if the UIDs of the messages in the mailbox remain the same. If there are any different UIDs in the mailbox, the UIDVALIDITY value for the mailbox should become larger for the next IMAP session. This allows clients the ability to quickly determine if anything has changed since the last time a mailbox was opened.

Each message is also tagged with flags that indicate the status of the message. A flag might be session only or permanent. Permanent flags might be changed by the client and will persist between sessions. Session-only flags will apply only for the current IMAP session. Table 7.1 shows different flags available for mail messages.

7

IMAP PROTOCOL

TABLE 7.1 IMAP Mail Message Flags

Flag	Description
\Seen	Message has been read
\Answered	Message has been answered
\Flagged	Message if marked as urgent
\Deleted	Message has been deleted
\Draft	Message is not in final form
\Recent	New mail in mailbox

A mail message can have zero or more flags associated with it. The flag information is transferred with the message to the client. It is the responsibility of the client to handle the flag accordingly.

The following sections define the IMAP commands that a client can issue to the IMAP server. Although the RFC shows IMAP commands in uppercase, it appears that most IMAP servers will accept commands in either upper- or lowercase. The server should respond to every command with the information requested, or a negative response if the command is not formatted properly or not supported.

SELECT

The SELECT command is used to select an active mailbox. By default, no mailboxes are selected for use when the client first authenticates to the server. The client must select a mailbox to work in. Usually the first mailbox selected is the special INBOX mailbox where new messages are placed. The format of the SELECT command is

SELECT mailbox

where mailbox is the text name of the desired mailbox. Only one mailbox can be active at a time per IMAP connection. If the mailbox exists and the client has proper access to it, the server responds with a multiline response describing the status of the mailbox. A sample SELECT session is shown in Listing 7.4.

LISTING 7.4 Sample SELECT Session

```
1   [alex@shadrach alex]$ telnet localhost 143
2   Trying 127.0.0.1...
3   Connected to localhost.
4   Escape character is '^]'.
5   * OK localhost IMAP4rev1 v12.250 server ready
6   a1 LOGIN alex drums
7   a1 OK LOGIN completed
```

```
8  a2 SELECT INBOX
9  * 2 EXISTS
10 * 1 RECENT
11 * OK [UIDVALIDITY 936033227] UID validity status
12 * OK [UIDNEXT 3] Predicted next UID
13 * FLAGS (\Answered \Flagged \Deleted \Draft \Seen)
14 * OK [PERMANENTFLAGS (\* \Answered \Flagged \Deleted \Draft \Seen)]
       ➥ Permanent fs
15 * OK [UNSEEN 2] first unseen message in /var/spool/mail/alex
16 a2 OK [READ-WRITE] SELECT completed
17 a3 LOGOUT
18 * BYE shadrach.smallorg.org IMAP4rev1 server terminating connection
19 a3 OK LOGOUT completed
20 Connection closed by foreign host.
21 [alex@shadrach alex]$
```

In line 8, user alex issues the SELECT command for the special mailbox INBOX. The server response is shown in lines 9 through 15. Line 9 shows that two messages exist in the mailbox, and line 10 shows that there is one new message for alex. Line 11 shows the UIDVALIDITY value for the mailbox, and line 12 shows the next available UID that will be used in the mailbox. Both of these values were discussed in the "IMAP Client Protocol" section.

Lines 13 and 14 show the flags settings supported by the mailbox for both session-only (line 13) and permanent (line 14) use. The client is allowed to change the status of these flags for each message in the mailbox if it so desires. The IMAP command used to change flags for individual messages is the STORE command discussed later.

Line 15 also provides important information. It shows that at least one message in the mailbox is flagged as UNSEEN and provides the UID identifier for the first unseen message. This enables the email client to know which message to download to view without having to download the entire mailbox. Another useful piece of information provided is the location of the message. It shows that the unseen message is in the /var/spool/mail/alex directory. This is where the Linux mail program places new mail for users.

Line 16 shows the client's status in the mailbox. The status indicates the permissions that the client has in the mailbox. The current status of this client is read/write capabilities. This client will be able to read any message and write any new message in the mailbox. Alternatively, a client can be granted read-only status and thus cannot add or delete any messages in the mailbox.

EXAMINE

The EXAMINE command is used to open the mailbox in read-only mode. The server response to the EXAMINE command is the same as for the SELECT command. The command-line parameter for EXAMINE is the name of the mailbox to open. When a mailbox is opened using the EXAMINE command, no manipulation of the messages is allowed. Thus you cannot add or remove flags from messages.

CREATE

The CREATE command is used to create a new mailbox on the IMAP server for the client. The pathname of the new mailbox will follow normal Linux pathname specifications. A mailbox name with no path will be created in the $HOME directory of the client. For example, if the client's home directory is /home/haley, and she issues a CREATE command to create a mailbox called stuff/junk, the new mailbox created on the Linux server will have the pathname /home/haley/stuff/junk. This example assumes a Linux server that uses the / character as the hierarchy separator; this is not always the case with other IMAP servers.

> ### Folders Versus Mailboxes
>
> Some IMAP clients use the term *folder* to refer to new mailboxes. Some IMAP clients also allow users to create folders several layers deep, so use caution when creating new folders (mailboxes). It is easy to get lost in a chain of pathnames.

Listing 7.5 shows a sample IMAP session that creates a new mailbox and makes it the active mailbox for a user.

LISTING 7.5 Sample CREATE IMAP Session

```
1  [alex@shadrach alex]$ ls -l
2  total 0
3  [alex@shadrach alex]$ telnet localhost 143
4  Trying 127.0.0.1...
5  Connected to localhost.
6  Escape character is '^]'.
7  * OK localhost IMAP4rev1 v12.250 server ready
8  a1 LOGIN alex drums
9  a1 OK LOGIN completed
10 a2 CREATE stuff/junk
11 a2 OK CREATE completed
12 a3 SELECT stuff/junk
13 * 0 EXISTS
14 * 0 RECENT
15 * OK [UIDVALIDITY 936998958] UID validity status
16 * OK [UIDNEXT 1] Predicted next UID
17 * FLAGS (\Answered \Flagged \Deleted \Draft \Seen)
18 * OK [PERMANENTFLAGS (\* \Answered \Flagged \Deleted \Draft \Seen)]
```

```
          ➥Permanent fs
19 a3 OK [READ-WRITE] SELECT completed
20 a4 LOGOUT
21 * BYE shadrah.smallorg.org IMAP4rev1 server terminating connection
22 a4 OK LOGOUT completed
23 Connection closed by foreign host.
24 [alex@shadrach alex]$ ls -lR
25 .:
26 total 1
27 drwx------    2 alex      alex             1024 Sep 10 16:29 stuff
28
29 stuff:
30 total 1
31 -rw-------    1 alex      alex              516 Sep 10 16:29 junk
32 [alex@shadrach alex]$
```

Line 1 shows our test user Alex listing the contents of his empty home directory. In line 3, he establishes a `telnet` connection to the local IMAP server. After logging in, Alex issues a CRE-ATE command in line 10 to create a new mailbox in his system. In line 11, the server responds positively by indicating that the new mailbox has been created. Alex then tries to use the new mailbox by issuing a SELECT command for the new mailbox name in line 12. The IMAP server responds in lines 13 through 19 showing the relevant information for the new mailbox (there are no new or old messages in the new mailbox—imagine that!). After being satisfied that the new mailbox actually does exist, Alex then proceeds to log out of the IMAP server. To complete this example, our hero performs another listing of his home directory in line 24. Lines 25 through 31 show the results—a new directory named `stuff`, and a new file under the directory named `junk`. Notice that the new mailbox is a file, not a directory. Messages placed in this mailbox will be appended to this file as they come in.

DELETE

The DELETE command refers to mailboxes, not messages. The IMAP server will attempt to delete the mailbox name specified as the argument to the DELETE command. Again, standard Linux pathnames apply to the argument, relative to the $HOME directory location unless preceded with a leading /. Messages in deleted mailboxes are lost and gone forever.

RENAME

The RENAME command allows the client to change the name of a mailbox. The RENAME command uses two parameters. The first parameter is the name of the mailbox that you want to change. The second parameter is the new mailbox name. The standard rules for pathnames applies for both parameters. Remember that pathnames without a leading / are relative to the $HOME directory of the logged in user. Listing 7.6 shows an example of renaming a mailbox.

LISTING 7.6   Sample RENAME Command Session

```
1  [alex@shadrach alex]$ ls -lR
2  .:
3  total 1
4  drwx------    2 alex     alex            1024 Sep 10 16:48 stuff
5
6  stuff:
7  total 1
8  -rw-------    1 alex     alex             918 Sep 10 16:44 junk
9  [alex@shadrach alex]$ telnet localhost 143
10 Trying 127.0.0.1...
11 Connected to localhost.
12 Escape character is '^]'.
13 * OK localhost IMAP4rev1 v12.250 server ready
14 a1 login alex drums
15 a1 OK LOGIN completed
16 a2 rename stuff/junk newbox
17 a2 OK RENAME completed
18 a3 select newbox
19 * 1 EXISTS
20 * 0 RECENT
21 * OK [UIDVALIDITY 936998958] UID validity status
22 * OK [UIDNEXT 2] Predicted next UID
23 * FLAGS (\Answered \Flagged \Deleted \Draft \Seen)
24 * OK [PERMANENTFLAGS (\* \Answered \Flagged \Deleted \Draft \Seen)]
        ➥ Permanent flags
25 a3 OK [READ-WRITE] SELECT completed
26 a4 logout
27 * BYE shadrach.smallorg.org IMAP4rev1 server terminating connection
28 a4 OK LOGOUT completed
29 Connection closed by foreign host.
30 [alex@shadrach alex]$ ls -lR
31 .:
32 total 2
33 -rw-------    1 alex     alex             918 Sep 10 16:44 newbox
34 drwx------    2 alex     alex            1024 Sep 12 13:59 stuff
35
36 stuff:
37 total 0
38 [alex@shadrach alex]$
```

Line 1 shows our user Alex displaying the contents of his home directory. As from the last example, he has a mailbox stuff/junk that created a subdirectory stuff and a file junk. In line 9, Alex establishes an IMAP session with the localhost. After the usual formalities, Alex issues the RENAME command in line 16, renaming his old stuff/junk mailbox to a new name newbox. Line 17 shows the IMAP server's positive response to the command. In line 18, Alex tries to make the new mailbox active by issuing the SELECT IMAP command. The server responds with the current information for the new box. One important thing to see here is on line 19. Previously, Alex had stored a message in the stuff/junk mailbox. Line 19 shows that the new mailbox, newbox, has one message in it. This shows that renaming a mailbox does not change the contents of the mailbox, just the name. After disconnecting the IMAP session, Alex performs another listing of his home directory. Much to his surprise, the stuff directory is still there, but the junk file has vanished. The IMAP server properly deleted the junk file from the stuff/junk mailbox, but left behind the stuff subdirectory, which is now empty. Line 33 shows that the new mailbox was created as a new file named newbox.

SUBSCRIBE

The SUBSCRIBE command is used to add a mailbox to the list of active mailboxes for the client. The SUBSCRIBE command uses a single parameter, which is the mailbox that you want to add. The current active mailboxes can be listed using the LSUB command described later. The mailbox does not necessarily have to exist for it to be added to the active mailbox list. This feature can be used to add active mailboxes that don't yet exist, or mailboxes that get deleted when they are empty.

UNSUBSCRIBE

The UNSUBSCRIBE command is used to remove a mailbox from the list of active mailboxes for the client. The UNSUBSCRIBE command uses a single parameter, which is the mailbox that you want to remove from the list. The mailbox itself is not deleted, just removed from the client's active list. The current active mailboxes can be listed using the LSUB command described later.

LIST

The LIST command is used to obtain a list of mailboxes available to the client. The LIST command uses two parameters. The format of the LIST command is

```
LIST reference mailbox
```

where reference is the directory where the mailbox names will be relative to. If you use an empty string ("") for this parameter, the mailboxes listed will be relative to your $HOME directory. The second parameter, mailbox is the mailbox name that you want to list. This value can include wildcard characters much like a normal directory listing. If the mailbox name is an empty string (""), the server will return the hierarchy delimiter (/ for Linux) and the root name of the reference parameter. Listing 7.7 shows a sample LIST session.

LISTING 7.7   Sample LIST Session

```
1  [alex@shadrach alex]$ telnet localhost 143
2  Trying 127.0.0.1...
3  Connected to localhost.
4  Escape character is '^]'.
5  * OK localhost IMAP4rev1 v12.250 server ready
6  a1 login alex drums
7  a1 OK LOGIN completed
8  a2 create new/anotherbox
9  a2 OK CREATE completed
10 a3 list "" *
11 * LIST (\NoInferiors) "/" .Xdefaults
12 * LIST (\NoInferiors \UnMarked) "/" .bash_logout
13 * LIST (\NoInferiors \UnMarked) "/" .bash_profile
14 * LIST (\NoInferiors \UnMarked) "/" .bashrc
15 * LIST (\NoSelect) "/" stuff
16 * LIST (\NoInferiors \UnMarked) "/" .mailboxlist
17 * LIST (\NoInferiors \UnMarked) "/" .bash_history
18 * LIST (\NoInferiors) "/" newbox
19 * LIST (\NoSelect) "/" new
20 * LIST (\NoInferiors) "/" new/anotherbox
21 * LIST (\NoInferiors) NIL INBOX
22 a3 OK LIST completed
23 a4 logout
24 * BYE shadrach.smallorg.org IMAP4rev1 server terminating connection
25 a4 OK LOGOUT completed
26 Connection closed by foreign host.
27 [alex@shadrach alex]$
```

Line 8 shows our test user Alex issuing a CREATE command to create a new mailbox for our example. In line 10, he issues a LIST command with the parameters " " and *. The first parameter indicates that the mailbox names specified will be relative to his $HOME directory. The second parameter is the * wildcard character, indicating that he wants to obtain a listing of all mailboxes in his $HOME directory. Lines 11 through 22 show the IMAP server's response to the LIST command. The IMAP server sends a listing that shows a whole lot more than just mailboxes. The IMAP server assumes that every file in Alex's $HOME directory is related to the mail system. Although this is somewhat true, there is a problem with hidden configuration files. Alex was created as a normal Linux user on this system. Thus, his $HOME directory was created using the template that is found in /etc/skel. This created a few configuration files used for things such as the bash shell and X Window. Unfortunately, these files come across the IMAP server as mailboxes.

> **CAUTION**
>
> If you are creating user IDs on a Linux system for purely email purposes, you should try to avoid using the normal user creation techniques, or at least remember to remove the standard configuration files that are often created by default.

Another thing that Listing 7.7 shows is how the LIST command displays the mailboxes that it lists. Lines 11 through 21 show the mailboxes that the IMAP server thinks are on the server. Notice how the files listed show the mailbox flag \NoInferior, which indicates that there are no mailboxes under this name. Also, notice how the subdirectories stuff and new (in lines 15 and 19) have the \NoSelect flag, indicating that they cannot be activated using the SELECT command. Also notice how in line 21 the LIST command automatically lists the INBOX mailbox, even though no file actually exists in the $HOME directory for this mailbox.

LSUB

The LSUB command is used to correct the problem previously described with the LIST command. Although the LIST command returns everything that is in a client's $HOME directory, the LSUB command lists only the mailboxes that have been tagged as being active for the client using the SUBSCRIBE command previously described. The parameters for the LSUB command are a reference name and a mailbox name. Like the LIST command described previously, the reference parameter points to the directory in which the mailbox names are relative to ($HOME if ""), and the mailbox parameter is the mailbox you want to list (including wildcard characters).

Mailboxes can be added to the active mailbox list using the SUBSCRIBE command and removed from the active list by using the UNSUBSCRIBE command, also described earlier. These commands also can be used to allow an IMAP client to implement the network news feature. Each network newsgroup is implemented as a separate mailbox on the server that can be SUBSCRIBED to. Now many email clients also include software to access network news and IMAP does not need to perform these services. Listing 7.8 shows a sample LSUB session.

LISTING 7.8 Sample LSUB Command Session

```
1   [alex@shadrach alex]$ telnet localhost 143
2   Trying 127.0.0.1...
3   Connected to localhost.
4   Escape character is '^]'.
5   * OK localhost IMAP4rev1 v12.250 server ready
6   a1 login alex drums
7   a1 OK LOGIN completed
```

continues

LISTING 7.8   continued

```
8   a2 subscribe new/anotherbox
9   a2 OK SUBSCRIBE completed
10  a3 lsub "" *
11  * LSUB () "/" stuff/junk
12  * LSUB () "/" newbox
13  * LSUB () "/" new/anotherbox
14  a3 OK LSUB completed
15  a4 logout
16  * BYE shadrach.smallorg.org IMAP4rev1 server terminating connection
17  a4 OK LOGOUT completed
18  Connection closed by foreign host.
19  [alex@shadrach alex]$
```

Line 8 shows Alex adding a new mailbox created in the last example to his list of subscribed mailboxes. In line 10, he issues the LSUB command to see what mailboxes he has subscribed to. Notice that the LSUB parameters point to his $HOME directory and use the * wildcard character to list all the mailboxes under his $HOME directory. The IMAP server's response is shown in lines 11 through 14. This response differs greatly from the LIST response shown in Listing 7.7. Only mailboxes that Alex had subscribed to are listed. Also notice line 11. The stuff/junk mailbox had been successfully renamed back in Listing 7.6. What happened? Remember that subscribing to a mailbox does not necessarily mean that the mailbox is still available. The LSUB command keeps any previously subscribed mailboxes in its active list regardless of the actual mailbox status. This allows for mailboxes to be temporarily deleted when they are empty and re-created when they get messages, without the clients having to re-subscribe to them.

STATUS

The STATUS command is used to request the current status of a mailbox. The first parameter for this command is the name of the mailbox. The second parameter is a list of items the client wants to receive information on enclosed in parentheses (). The STATUS command can be used to obtain mailbox information without having to issue the SELECT or EXAMINE commands to actually open the mailbox.

The items that the STATUS command can retrieve information on are shown in Table 7.2.

TABLE 7.2   STATUS Command Data Items

Item	Description
MESSAGES	Total number of messages in mailbox
RECENT	Number of messages in mailbox flagged with the \RECENT flag
UIDNEXT	Next available UID to assign to a new message

Item	Description
UIDVALIDITY	The UID validity identifier for the mailbox
UNSEEN	Number of messages in mailbox not flagged with the \SEEN flag

A sample IMAP session using the STATUS command is shown in Listing 7.9.

LISTING 7.9   Sample STATUS Command

```
1  [alex@shadrach alex]$ telnet localhost 143
2  Trying 127.0.0.1...
3  Connected to localhost.
4  Escape character is '^]'.
5  * OK localhost IMAP4rev1 v12.250 server ready
6  a1 login alex drums
7  a1 OK LOGIN completed
8  a2 status inbox (messages recent unseen)
9  * STATUS inbox (MESSAGES 1 RECENT 0 UNSEEN 0)
10 a2 OK STATUS completed
11 a3 status newbox (messages uidnext unseen)
12 * STATUS newbox (MESSAGES 1 UNSEEN 0 UIDNEXT 2)
13 a3 OK STATUS completed
14 a4 logout
15 * BYE shadrach.smallorg.org IMAP4rev1 server terminating connection
16 a4 OK LOGOUT completed
17 Connection closed by foreign host.
18 [alex@shadrach alex]$
```

Line 8 shows Alex issuing the STATUS command asking for information about the total number of messages, the number of recent messages, and the number of unseen messages from the special INBOX mailbox. Line 9 shows the IMAP server response to the command. Line 11 shows another STATUS command issued by Alex for another mailbox. Notice the IMAP server response in line 12. The server responded with the information requested for the mailbox, but not in the order that it was requested. The IMAP server will always use a consistent order in returning the information. The order is MESSAGES, RECENT, UNSEEN, UIDNEXT, and UIDVALIDITY.

APPEND

The APPEND command is an interesting addition to the IMAP command family. Normally, the IMAP protocol is used exclusively for reading mail from mailboxes. The APPEND command gives the IMAP protocol the ability to send messages to a mailbox by appending the message to the end of the mailbox file. This is an extremely tricky and dangerous practice, and it is not recommended as a normal replacement for using SMTP software to deliver messages. It's more of a "nice-to-have" feature of IMAP just in case the need arises. The basic format of the APPEND command is

```
APPEND mailbox [(flags)] [date/time string] {message size} message
```

This is an awkward command to implement (end even more awkward to try and simulate). Listing 7.10 shows an attempt to push a message into a mailbox. Of course the client needs read/write capabilities for the mailbox.

LISTING 7.10   Sample APPEND Command Session

```
 1  [alex@shadrach alex]$ telnet localhost 143
 2  Trying 127.0.0.1...
 3  Connected to localhost.
 4  Escape character is '^]'.
 5  * OK localhost IMAP4rev1 v12.250 server ready
 6  a1 login alex drums
 7  a1 OK LOGIN completed
 8  a2 create testbox
 9  a2 OK CREATE completed
10  a3 append testbox (\SEEN) {23}
11  + Ready for argument
12  This is a test message.
13  a3 OK APPEND completed
14  a4 select testbox
15  * 1 EXISTS
16  * 1 RECENT
17  * OK [UIDVALIDITY 937242636] UID validity status
18  * OK [UIDNEXT 2] Predicted next UID
19  * FLAGS (\Answered \Flagged \Deleted \Draft \Seen)
20  * OK [PERMANENTFLAGS (\* \Answered \Flagged \Deleted \Draft \Seen)]
        ➥ Permanent fs
21  a4 OK [READ-WRITE] SELECT completed
22  a5 logout
23  * BYE shadrach.smallorg.org IMAP4rev1 server terminating connection
24  a5 OK LOGOUT completed
25  Connection closed by foreign host.
26  [alex@shadrach alex]$ mail -f testbox
27  Mail version 8.1 6/6/93.  Type ? for help.
28  "testbox": 2 messages
29  >   1 MAILER-DAEMON@shadra  Mon Sep 12 19:11   12/516    "DON'T DELETE THIS
                                                        ➥ MES"
30      2 alex@shadrach.smallo  Mon Sep 12 19:11    8/128
31  & 2
32  Message 2:
33  From alex@shadrach.smallorg.org Mon Sep 12 19:11:18 1999 -0500
```

```
34
35 This is a test message.
36 Status: RO
37 X-Status:
38 X-Keywords:
39 X-UID: 1
40
41 & q
42 [alex@shadrach alex]$
```

Line 8 shows Alex creating a brand new empty mailbox for testing. Line 10 shows the APPEND command in action. The message appended will be flagged as seen, and will be 23 bytes long. The message size includes all CR-LF combinations in the message, with the exception of the terminating CR-LF at the end of the last line entered. For our example, Alex used a very simple message. After pressing Enter, the IMAP server responded with a positive response, and prompted Alex to enter the "argument" for the APPEND command in line 11. Alex responded by typing the message. The new message was successfully added to the client's mailbox. Line 14 shows Alex issuing a SELECT command to activate the testbox mailbox. The server response to the SELECT command gives us some information. Notice that line 15 shows there is now one message in the mailbox, and line 16 shows that it is flagged as recent. However, the SELECT command did not give Alex an UNSEEN message UID, so all the messages in the mailbox are flagged as seen. This corresponds to the APPEND command, where Alex used the \SEEN flag for the appended message. To double check things, Alex exits the IMAP server, and uses his local Linux mail program to check the testbox mailbox. Line 26 shows Alex issuing the mail -f testbox Linux command to read the mail in the testbox mailbox. Line 30 shows that there is indeed a message in the mailbox with no subject line. By displaying the message, we can see that this message was sent using the APPEND command, although the IMAP server tried to make a normal message out of the test text. Had this been a real message, Alex (or his email package) would have sent a properly formatted RFC 822 message, and the IMAP server would have handled it properly.

CHECK

The CHECK command is used to initiate a checkpoint for the mailbox. Any pending operations, such as writing data from server memory to disk, should be performed to place the mailbox in a consistent state. The CHECK command does not use any parameters.

CLOSE

The CLOSE command does what it says—it closes the mailbox. When a mailbox is closed, any messages tagged with the \DELETED flag are physically removed from the mailbox. The CLOSE command is also implicitly performed on an open mailbox when a new mailbox is opened.

Also, an open mailbox is implicitly closed when a LOGOUT command (described later) is issued. The CLOSE command does not use any parameters.

EXPUNGE

The EXPUNGE command is used to remove all messages in a mailbox tagged with the \DELETED flag without closing the mailbox. The EXPUNGE server response is a list of the new status of the mailbox. Listing 7.11 is a sample EXPUNGE session.

LISTING 7.11   Sample EXPUNGE Session

```
1  [alex@shadrach alex]$ telnet localhost 143
2  Trying 127.0.0.1...
3  Connected to localhost.
4  Escape character is '^]'.
5  * OK localhost IMAP4rev1 v12.250 server ready
6  a1 login alex drums
7  a1 OK LOGIN completed
8  a2 select newbox
9  * 6 EXISTS
10 * 0 RECENT
11 * OK [UIDVALIDITY 937243866] UID validity status
12 * OK [UIDNEXT 8] Predicted next UID
13 * FLAGS (\Answered \Flagged \Deleted \Draft \Seen)
14 * OK [PERMANENTFLAGS (\* \Answered \Flagged \Deleted \Draft \Seen)]
       ➥ Permanent flags
15 * OK [UNSEEN 1] first unseen message in /home/alex/newbox
16 a2 OK [READ-WRITE] SELECT completed
17 a3 store 1 +flags \DELETED
18 * 1 FETCH (FLAGS (\Deleted))
19 a3 OK STORE completed
20 a4 store 2 +flags \DELETED
21 * 2 FETCH (FLAGS (\Deleted))
22 a4 OK STORE completed
23 a5 status newbox (messages unseen)
24 * STATUS newbox (MESSAGES 6 UNSEEN 6)
25 a5 OK STATUS completed
26 a6 expunge
27 * 1 EXPUNGE
28 * 1 EXPUNGE
29 * 4 EXISTS
30 * 0 RECENT
31 a6 OK Expunged 2 messages
32 a7 status newbox (messages unseen)
33 * STATUS newbox (MESSAGES 4 UNSEEN 4)
34 a7 OK STATUS completed
```

```
35 a8 logout
36 * BYE shadrach.smallorg.org IMAP4rev1 server terminating connection
37 a8 OK LOGOUT completed
38 Connection closed by foreign host.
39 [alex@shadrach alex]$
```

Line 8 shows Alex selecting the mailbox named newbox. Lines 9 through 16 show the IMAP server's response with the information pertinent to the mailbox. Line 9 shows that there are six messages in the mailbox. In lines 17 and 20, Alex uses the STORE command (discussed later) to flag the first two messages as \DELETED. After flagging the two messages, Alex issues a STATUS command in line 23 for the mailbox. Line 24 shows that the IMAP server still sees six messages in the mailbox, even though two of them are now marked for deletion. In line 26, Alex issues the EXPUNGE command to remove the messages marked for deletion. The server response in lines 27 through 31 show that two messages were expunged (deleted), and four messages still exist. This is verified by issuing a STATUS command on the mailbox again in line 32. The server responds by showing only four messages remaining in the mailbox.

SEARCH

The SEARCH command is a very powerful tool in the IMAP command arsenal. The SEARCH command searches messages in an active mailbox based on search criteria and displays the matching message numbers. The format for the SEARCH command is

SEARCH [CHARSET specification] (search criteria)

where CHARSET specification consists of the word CHARSET followed by a registered CHARSET symbol set. The default CHARSET is US-ASCII, so this parameter is usually omitted. The search criteria parameter specifies keys and values to search for in the messages as shown in Table 7.3.

TABLE 7.3 SEARCH Command Defined Search Keys

KEY	*Description*
<message set>	Messages with message numbers corresponding to the specified message sequence number set
ALL	All messages in the mailbox
ANSWERED	Messages with the \ANSWERED flag set
BCC <string>	Messages that contain the specified string in the BCC header field
BEFORE <date>	Messages whose internal date is before the date specified

continues

7

IMAP PROTOCOL

TABLE 7.3 continued

KEY	*Description*
BODY <string>	Messages that contain the specified string in the body of the message
CC <string>	Messages that contain the specified string in the CC header field
DELETED	Messages with the \DELETED flag set
DRAFT	Messages with the \DRAFT flag set
FLAGGED	Messages with the \FLAGGED flag set
From <string>	Messages that contain the specified string in the From header field
HEADER <field name> <STRING>	Messages that contain the specified header field name and specified string in that field
KEYWORD <flag>	Messages with the specified keyword set
LARGER <n>	Messages with a size larger than n
NEW	Messages with the \RECENT flag set but not the \SEEN flag set
NOT <search key>	Messages that don't contain the search key specified
OLD	Messages that do not have the \RECENT flag set
ON <date>	Messages whose internal date is the specified date
OR <searchkey 1><searchkey2>	Messages that contain either search key
RECENT	Messages that have the \RECENT flag set
SEEN	Messages that have the \SEEN flag set
SENTBEFORE <date>	Messages whose Date header field is before the date specified
SENTON <date>	Messages whose Date header field is on the specified date
SENTSINCE <date>	Messages whose Date header field is on or after the specified date
SINCE <date>	Messages whose internal date is on or after the date specified
SMALLER <n>	Messages whose message size is smaller than n
TEXT <string>	Messages that contain the specified string in either the header or body
UID <message set>	Messages whose UID corresponds to the message set specified
UNANSWERED	Messages that do not have the \ANSWERED flag set
UNDELETED	Messages that do not have the \DELETED flag set
UNDRAFT	Messages that do not have the \DRAFT flag set
UNFLAGGED	Messages that do not have the \FLAGGED flag set
UNKEYWORD <flag>	Messages that do not have the specified keyword set
UNSEEN	Messages that do not have the \SEEN flag set

As you can see from Table 7.3, there are many things you can search for in messages. This command is extremely handy when trying to find specific messages in mailboxes that have become cluttered. Listing 7.12 shows a short example of using the SEARCH command.

LISTING 7.12   Sample SEARCH Command Session

```
1  [alex@shadrach alex]$ telnet localhost 143
2  Trying 127.0.0.1...
3  Connected to localhost.
4  Escape character is '^]'.
5  * OK localhost IMAP4rev1 v12.250 server ready
6  a1 login alex drums
7  a1 OK LOGIN completed
8  a2 select inbox
9  * 2 EXISTS
10 * 0 RECENT
11 * OK [UIDVALIDITY 936999597] UID validity status
12 * OK [UIDNEXT 5] Predicted next UID
13 * FLAGS (\Answered \Flagged \Deleted \Draft \Seen)
14 * OK [PERMANENTFLAGS (\* \Answered \Flagged \Deleted \Draft \Seen)]
        ➥ Permanent fs
15 * OK [UNSEEN 1] first unseen message in /var/spool/mail/alex
16 a2 OK [READ-WRITE] SELECT completed
17 a3 search header subject test
18 * SEARCH 1 2
19 a3 OK SEARCH completed
20 a4 search header subject another
21 * SEARCH 2
22 a4 OK SEARCH completed
23 a5 search unseen
24 * SEARCH 1 2
25 a5 OK SEARCH completed
26 a6 logout
27 * BYE shadrach.smallorg.org IMAP4rev1 server terminating connection
28 a6 OK LOGOUT completed
29 Connection closed by foreign host.
30 [alex@shadrach alex]$
```

Lines 17, 20, and 23 show examples of using the SEARCH command. Lines 18, 21, and 24 show the IMAP server's response to the SEARCH command. The response will produce a list of message numbers that match the search criteria. If no matches are found, the server will return the word SEARCH with no UIDs.

FETCH

The FETCH command is used for retrieving the text of the mail message. This is used for display purposes only. Unlike POP3, the IMAP client does not retain a copy of the message on the client PC. It is the responsibility of the server to maintain the messages in mailboxes. The format of the FETCH command is

```
FETCH <message set> <data item names>
```

where <message set> is a list of message numbers you want to retrieve, and <data item names> is a list of data items from each message you want to retrieve.

The message set can be a single message number, a list of specific numbers separated by commas, or a range of numbers separated by a colon. The IMAP server will return the specified data items for all the messages in the message set.

The data item names is a complex specification of pieces of the message that can be returned individually. Three special macros return specific message information: ALL, BODY, and BODY[section].

The ALL data item does not return the entire message as you might expect, but a formatted synopsis of the message that includes the flags set, the internal date, and the message envelope. The IMAP client can parse this standard message into the relevant parts to display information about the message.

The BODY data item does not return the actual text of the body, but a synopsis of the type of text and the size of the body. Again, the IMAP client can parse this information to provide more detailed information to the user about the message.

The BODY[section] macro can be used to return individual pieces of the message. RFC 2060 lists each of the specific RFC 822 message parts that can be used in this section. Two of the most common are HEADER and TEXT. The BODY[HEADER] macro will return the complete header of the message. You can get even more precise by specifying only certain header fields, such as BODY[HEADER.FIELDS (SUBJECT)] to return the Subject header field of a message. Multiple fields can be displayed by separating them with spaces within the parentheses.

The BODY[SECTION] macro can also be modified by using the <partial> field. The <partial> field consists of two numbers separated by a period. The first number is a starting position octet in the data output that you want to display. The second number is the number of octets from the data output you want to display. This feature can be used to further format the desired output. For example, if you want to display only the first 10 characters in the message body of message 1, you would use the following command:

```
FETCH 1 BODY[TEXT]<0.10>
```

This command fetches the first 10 characters of the body section defined as "text". If less than 10 characters were in the message body, the whole body would then be displayed. Listing 7.13 shows more examples of using the FETCH command.

LISTING 7.13   Sample FETCH Command Session

```
1  [alex@shadrach alex]$ telnet localhost 143
2  Trying 127.0.0.1...
3  Connected to localhost.
4  Escape character is '^]'.
5  * OK localhost IMAP4rev1 v12.250 server ready
6  a1 login alex drums
7  a1 OK LOGIN completed
8  a2 select inbox
9  * 6 EXISTS
10 * 0 RECENT
11 * OK [UIDVALIDITY 937321060] UID validity status
12 * OK [UIDNEXT 7] Predicted next UID
13 * FLAGS (\Answered \Flagged \Deleted \Draft \Seen)
14 * OK [PERMANENTFLAGS (\* \Answered \Flagged \Deleted \Draft \Seen)]
      ➥ Permanent flags
15 a2 OK [READ-WRITE] SELECT completed
16 a3 fetch 3:5 body[header.fields (date from subject)]
17 * 3 FETCH (BODY[HEADER.FIELDS ("DATE" "FROM" "SUBJECT")] {112}
18 Date: Tue, 14 Sep 1999 10:09:50 -0500
19 From: alex@shadrach.smallorg.org
20 Subject: This is the first test message
21
22 )
23 * 4 FETCH (BODY[HEADER.FIELDS ("DATE" "FROM" "SUBJECT")] {113}
24 Date: Tue, 14 Sep 1999 10:10:04 -0500
25 From: alex@shadrach.smallorg.org
26 Subject: This is the second test message
27
28 )
29 * 5 FETCH (BODY[HEADER.FIELDS ("DATE" "FROM" "SUBJECT")] {112}
30 Date: Tue, 14 Sep 1999 10:10:26 -0500
31 From: alex@shadrach.smallorg.org
32 Subject: This is the third test message
33
34 )
35 a3 OK FETCH completed
36 a4 fetch 4 body[text]
37 * 4 FETCH (BODY[TEXT] {42}
38 This is the second test message for IMAP
```

continues

LISTING 7.13   continued

```
39 )
40 a4 OK FETCH completed
41 a5 logout
42 * BYE shadrach.smallorg.org IMAP4rev1 server terminating connection
43 a5 OK LOGOUT completed
44 Connection closed by foreign host.
45 [alex@shadrach alex]$
```

Lines 16 and 36 show samples of using the FETCH command to retrieve message data. Line 16 requests the header Date, From, and Subject fields from messages 3 through 5. Lines 17 through 35 show the IMAP server's response to the command, listing the data requested for each message requested. Line 36 requests the text of the body from message 4. Lines 37 through 40 show the IMAP server's response by displaying the text of the message body.

By default, the BODY[SECTION] data item alters the message by setting the \SEEN flag. If you want to look at a part of the message without flagging it as being seen, you can substitute the BODY[SECTION] data item with BODY.PEEK[SECTION]. This performs the same function as the BODY[SECTION] data item without setting the \SEEN flag for the message.

STORE

The STORE command is used to alter information associated with the message. The format of the STORE command is

```
STORE <message set> <data item name> <data item value>
```

where message set is a list of message numbers to perform the STORE operation on. There are currently only two data item types available for the STORE command. FLAGS identifies a list of flags that are set for the message. FLAGS.SILENT identifies a list of flags that are set for the message also, but with this option, the IMAP server does not return the new value as part of the response.

The behavior of the two data items can be further modified by preceding them with either a plus sign (+) or a minus sign (-). The plus sign signifies that the data item value will be added to the message, whereas the minus sign signifies that the data item value will be removed from the message.

Listing 7.11 shows a good example of using the STORE command to set flags for messages. Line 18 shows setting the \DELETED flag for message 1 in the active mailbox. Notice how the flags parameter was preceded by a plus sign (+). You could use a minus sign (-) to remove the \DELETED flag from the message (a way to undelete a message before the next checkpoint takes effect). Remember, when a message is flagged as \DELETED, it is not actually removed from the mailbox until a checkpoint is performed on the mailbox using either the CHECK, EXPUNGE, SELECT, or LOGOUT commands.

COPY

The COPY command is used to copy messages from one mailbox to another. The format for the COPY command is

COPY <message set> <mailbox name>

where message set is a list of messages you want to copy from the active mailbox, and mailbox name is the mailbox you want the messages to go to.

There is no move command defined in IMAP, but it should be fairly obvious that a move is nothing more than copying messages to a new mailbox and setting the \DELETED flag on the original messages. After the next mailbox checkpoint occurs, the original messages will be deleted and the new messages will be present.

UID

The UID command is used in conjunction with the FETCH, COPY, STORE, or SEARCH commands. It allows these commands to use actual UID numbers instead of sequence numbers in their message sets. The UID number is a 32-bit integer that uniquely identifies the mailbox messages within the mail system. Normally these functions will use the sequence number to identify the messages in the mailbox. Using the UID number allows the IMAP client to remember messages between IMAP sessions.

CAPABILITY

The CAPABILITY command requests a list of capabilities that the IMAP server supports. Listing 7.14 shows a sample CAPABILITY command session.

LISTING 7.14 Sample CAPABILITY Command Session

```
1  [riley@shadrach riley]$ telnet localhost 143
2  Trying 127.0.0.1...
3  Connected to localhost.
4  Escape character is '^]'.
5  * OK localhost IMAP4rev1 v12.250 server ready
6  a1 login riley firetruck
7  a1 OK LOGIN completed
8  a2 capability
9  * CAPABILITY IMAP4 IMAP4REV1 NAMESPACE IDLE SCAN SORT MAILBOX-REFERRALS
   ➥ LOGIN-RE
10 FERRALS AUTH=LOGIN THREAD=ORDEREDSUBJECT
11 a2 OK CAPABILITY completed
12 a3 logout
13 * BYE shadrach.smallorg.org IMAP4rev1 server terminating connection
14 a3 OK LOGOUT completed
15 Connection closed by foreign host.
16 [riley@shadrach riley]$
```

Line 8 shows the client issuing the CAPABILITY command, and lines 9 through 11 show the server's response, listing the capabilities that this particular IMAP server software supports.

NOOP

The NOOP command does what it says—nothing. It can be used to send automatic commands to the server to prevent an inactivity logout timer from expiring. The server response to the NOOP command should always be positive. Because the server is allowed to return status update information from any command, the NOOP command can often trigger a status report from the server. If something happened to the mailbox during the period of inactivity with the client, such as if the server deleted messages because of a mailbox rule set by the mail administrator, the new status can be returned as a response to the NOOP command.

LOGOUT

The LOGOUT command is used to log the current user ID out of the mail server and close any open mailboxes. If any messages were flagged \DELETED, they will be removed from the mailbox at this time.

Linux IMAP Implementation

A few IMAP software packages have been written for the Linux platform, both for IMAP clients and IMAP servers. With the growing popularity of IMAP4, we should expect to see more activity in this area of software development in the Linux world. This section looks at the most popular Linux packages for the IMAP server software and IMAP client software.

Linux as an IMAP Server

The imapd software package is a popular IMAP4 server implementation developed at the University of Washington. It is included in many Linux distributions as a binary package. If you do not have a binary distribution or want to install the latest version, you can obtain the source code from the University of Washington's FTP site at ftp.cac.washinton.edu. The most recent version is named imap.tar.Z. At the time of this writing, the version is imap-4.6.BETA.

The imapd program is invoked by the Internet server inetd and, by default, listens for connection requests on the standard IMAP TCP port 143. The configuration line in the /etc/inetd.conf file necessary for inetd to run imapd is

```
imap    stream  tcp     nowait  root    /usr/sbin/tcpd  imapd
```

The default mail directory for an IMAP client is the Linux $HOME directory specified in the /etc/passwd file for the user ID. See Chapter 12, "Installing and Configuring POP3 and IMAP," for detailed information on how to install the IMAP server software.

Linux as an IMAP Client

The fetchmail program can be configured to use the IMAP protocol to retrieve mail from multiple mailboxes on an IMAP server for a user. You can use the fetchmailconf program to configure the basic settings for the IMAP server, specifying IMAP as the mail transport protocol (see Chapter 6, "POP3 Protocol"). The fetchmailconf program will create a `.fetchmailrc` configuration file for the default mailbox for the user. This is usually the special INBOX mailbox. If you want to check other mailboxes that have been configured on the IMAP server, you can use the `-r` option in fetchmail:

```
fetchmail -r mailbox
```

where `mailbox` is the name of the mailbox (or folder) that will be checked instead of the default INBOX mailbox.

> **CAUTION**
>
> Care should be taken when using this option because fetchmail will forward any messages that it retrieves to your normal local mailbox on your Linux PC. Messages that were once separated into different mailboxes will now be combined into a single place.

Using IMAP on Network Clients

Many email clients offer a graphical interface for IMAP mailboxes. The Netscape Mail program, part of the Netscape Communicator suite, is a graphical program that can be configured to work with IMAP servers. Figure 7.1 shows the main mail server configuration screen used to configure the Netscape mail program.

The Incoming Mail Servers section allows you to configure one or more mail servers that the mail program will retrieve messages from. By clicking the Add button, a new mail server can be defined. Figure 7.2 shows the configuration screen for adding a new mail server.

The Server Type button allows you to select either a POP or IMAP server. If you select an IMAP type server, two additional tabs appear on the configuration screen. Figure 7.3 shows the IMAP tab configuration screen.

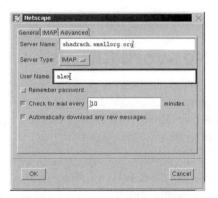

FIGURE 7.1
The Netscape Mail mail server configuration screen.

FIGURE 7.2
The Netscape Mail new incoming mail server configuration screen.

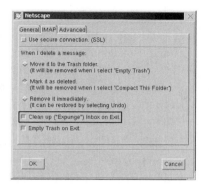

FIGURE 7.3
The Netscape Mail IMAP server configuration screen.

The IMAP configuration allows the user to select whether he is connecting to an IMAP server using the secure socket layer protocol. Because this is not our case, we will not select this option. Next the IMAP configuration asks how we want our deleted messages handled. After the discussions about what happens with messages that are flagged as deleted, these options should make some sense to you. By marking the message as deleted, we should decrease the network traffic some by saving the checkpoint housekeeping until we are ready to exit the mailbox, instead of performing a checkpoint after every message is marked as deleted. The Trash folder is Netscape's cute way of marking messages as deleted and then performing the checkpoint when you decide to empty the trash folder. It is also a good idea to perform an EXPUNGE command when exiting the INBOX to ensure that messages flagged as \DELETED actually are deleted. Figure 7.4 shows the Advanced IMAP options that can be set.

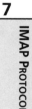

FIGURE 7.4
The Netscape mail Advanced IMAP configuration options.

The Advanced tab allows the user to select an IMAP server directory other than the default directory to use. Also, a nice feature is the ability to select only folders that have been subscribed to. Remember how the LIST and LSUB commands differed? The LIST command listed every file and directory in the user's $HOME directory. Without this option selected, Netscape will perform a LIST command and show everything in the $HOME directory as a possible mailbox or folder. If the user's Linux account is only used for mail, this might not be a problem. If the user also logs in to the server for other things, this can be an *extremely* long list of items.

After all the IMAP configuration parameters are set, you can use the graphical Netscape tool to traverse the various mailboxes configured on the Linux mail server. Messages can be read, moved, or deleted as necessary, all with the ease of a GUI interface. For more information on how to use Netscape Mail, see Chapter 15 "Configuring LAN Clients."

Summary

The Internet Mail Access Protocol (IMAP) was developed to retrieve mail that remains on remote mail servers. This method of mail retrieval has the advantage that a user's mail always stays in one place, and it can't get scattered among different client PCs. The IMAP protocol provides for multiple mailboxes, or folders, that reside on the server. The client can move messages around to different folders on the server. This type of client mail retrieval requires close administration because all mail messages and mailboxes reside on the server. If the server crashes, loses connectivity, or the disk space fills up, all users lose their capability of retrieving mail. The mail administrator responsible for an IMAP server must pay close attention to details on the mail server. Linux uses the imapd software program to implement IMAP server functions. Also, the standard fetchmail mail client program can be configured to use the IMAP protocol to retrieve mail from a remote IMAP server.

PPP Protocol

IN THIS CHAPTER

The previous chapters discussed common network protocols used to send and retrieve mail messages. Those protocols are all fine and good, as long as you have a network connection to use them on. Unfortunately, many small businesses do not have an Internet node at their sites.

To connect the Linux mailserver to the Internet requires a middleman. That middleman is most often an Internet service provider (ISP). An ISP can provide several different options to connect a small business network to the Internet. One method is to use a standalone router connected to the network that can dial into the ISP when connectivity is required. This option is good if the small business can afford the separate router and the ISP connection necessary to support the connectivity requirements. Another method is to allow the Linux server to dial directly into the ISP network using a standard modem and establish a method of transferring Internet Protocol (IP) packets across the modem line. The Linux mailserver can then treat the serial modem connection as if it were directly connected to a network and transfer mail or other IP traffic. After the IP traffic is finished, the Linux mailserver can drop the ISP connection, saving connection time.

A protocol that allows the Linux mailserver to use a modem to transfer IP packets is the Point-to-Point Protocol (PPP). PPP is defined in RFC 1661 as a method for two peers to transfer network packets across a full-duplex simultaneous bi-directional connection. After your network packets are passed to the ISP, it is the job of the ISP's PPP server to forward them to the appropriate place on the Internet.

PPP Protocol Overview

A normal PPP session consists of four phases:

1. Link establishment
2. Authentication (optional)
3. Protocol negotiation
4. Link termination

The PPP protocol uses several different protocols during each of the four phases. At the core of PPP is a framing protocol that encapsulates the PPP frames for transmission across a serial modem link—the High-Level Data Link Control (HDLC) protocol.

Before any data can be sent across the line, the link between the two peer devices must be established. PPP employs a special protocol for negotiating the link—the Link Control Protocol (LCP). LCP's main purpose is to negotiate options that the two devices must use to successfully transfer packets between themselves. Items such as packet size must be determined before the two devices can transfer data successfully. After the link is in an established state, the next phase of PPP can begin.

The authentication phase is officially listed in the RFC as optional, but in these days of network security, it is almost always required to establish a PPP connection. Currently, PPP supports two different types of userid authentication—the Challenge-Handshake Authentication Protocol (CHAP) and the Password Authentication Protocol (PAP). CHAP is the more secure of the two protocols, but PAP is easier to implement and, thus, the more popular of the two. After the remote host has successfully authenticated the connection, the next phase of the PPP cycle can begin.

The protocol negotiation phase of the PPP connection is what makes PPP unique among other serial network connections. Its predecessor, the Serial Line Internet Protocol (SLIP), supported only one protocol type (IP) to transmit across the serial line. PPP allows virtually any network protocol to be transmitted across the modem connection, as long as both peer devices support the protocol. After the connection is authenticated, the client PPP device must establish which protocols it wants to use over the connection. It is the PPP host's responsibility to refuse protocol requests for protocols that it does not support. The Network Control Protocol (NCP) is used to allow the two devices to negotiate which protocols will be supported on the connection. During the protocol negotiation, the host and client can determine options for each individual protocol. For example, during an IP protocol negotiation, the host can supply the client's IP address and the DNS server required for the client to properly talk on the host's network. After a protocol has been successfully negotiated, data packets can be transferred between the host and the client.

When the client wants to disconnect the PPP session, another LCP session is started to properly terminate the session. The host PPP server must recognize this request and drop the modem connection with the client.

PPP Protocol Frames

PPP can use modem connections to transfer network packets to another host that is connected to the Internet. A specific protocol is used to establish the connection between the modem on the Linux server and the modem on the ISP's host computer. A standard method of transferring frames across a serial connection is the HDLC protocol. This protocol can be used in several different modem environments using several different types of modems. The PPP protocol also has a specific frame format for transferring the packet information to the host computer. This section discusses the HDLC and PPP frame specifications and how they are used to transfer information between the client and host computer systems.

HDLC Frame

HDLC has been in use for many years in the mainframe computer environment. It has proven to be a stable method of transferring data between two devices connected together with

8

PPP PROTOCOL

modems. RFC 1662 defines the method used to encapsulate the PPP protocol in an HLDC frame. Figure 8.1 shows the basic frame format for an HDLC frame.

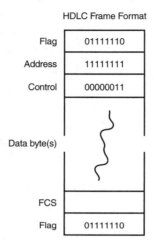

FIGURE 8.1
The HDLC frame format.

The HDLC frame format consists of five separate fields that encapsulate the PPP data sent on the modem line.

The Flag field is used to identify the start of an HDLC frame. It is defined as the binary value 01111110, or 0x7e in hex. The HDLC software should be able to detect this field and recognize it as the start of a new frame.

The Address field is always set to binary 11111111, or 0xff in hex. This is the broadcast address. Each station should recognize data sent to this address. Because there are only two devices in an HDLC "network," it is obvious that any data received with the broadcast address is intended for the device.

The HDLC Control field for PPP packets is always set to binary 00000011, or 0x03 in hex. The receiving device should discard frames with any other Control field values.

Because the Address and Control fields always contain the same values, they are often omitted from the frame to conserve bandwidth. Thus, the first value after the Flag field could be the start of the PPP packet, or the Protocol field (see the following PPP frame description). Because of this situation, the PPP Protocol field does not use the values 0xff and 0x03 because the receiver could confuse the PPP Protocol field with the HDLC Address and Control fields. This method of omitting HDLC fields is called *frame compression*.

The Frame Check Sequence (FCS) field is used for error detection during the transmission. The FCS is calculated using the Address, Control, and data fields of the HDLC packet. The Flag field and any start and stop bits or transparency bits inserted for various modem configurations are not included in this calculation.

The last Flag field identifies the end of the transmitted frame. If another frame follows, the closing Flag field must be omitted. The single Flag field identifies both the end of one frame and the start of a new frame until it is the last Flag field received, indicating the end of the transmission.

It is possible to have situations in which PPP data might have the same value as the HDLC Flag field and confuse the receiving device into thinking the frame has ended. To avoid this, a method called *frame transparency* is used. After the FCS computation, the sending device examines the fields between the two proper Flag fields and inserts a Control-Escape octet (binary 01111101 or hex 0x7d) in front of any data values that match the Flag value. The sending device then performs an Exclusive-OR of the data value with the value 0x20 to make it not equal to the Flag value. Of course, if a data value is equal to the Control-Escape data value, it also must be replaced by putting a Control-Escape value inserted before it, and Exclusive-ORing the value with 0x20. When the receiving device sees the Control-Escape octet, it knows that the next data value should be converted back to its original value.

It is possible for a PPP host to auto-detect a PPP connection request from a remote modem by examining the first group of octets transmitted from the client. A PPP connection can be identified by one of the three octet groups shown in Listing 8.1.

LISTING 8.1   PPP Starting Frames

```
1: 7e ff 03 c0 21
2: 7e ff 7d 23 c0 21
3: 7e 7d df 7d 23 c0 21
```

In Listing 8.1, line 1 shows a standard HDLC frame (7e ff 03) with a standard PPP LCP protocol field (c0 21). Lines 2 and 3 show methods of frame transparency that create the same frames. When any one of these three frame sequences is received on the modem line, the Linux server can assume that the client is attempting to initiate a PPP connection and can act accordingly. The mgetty+sendfax program uses this technique to auto-detect a PPP session on a standard dial-in modem line. If one of the three frame sequences is not received, the Linux server can assume that the data is not a PPP session. The data could be a user typing in his or her userid for a normal terminal session across the modem connection, or a fax connection being attempted on the modem. This allows sharing the same modem line for terminal, fax, and PPP sessions without forcing the individual user to dial in to a special phone number that supports their type of connection.

8

PPP PROTOCOL

PPP Frame

The PPP frames are placed within the data fields of the HDLC frame. The basic PPP frame is shown in Figure 8.2.

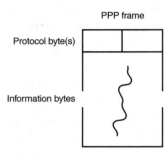

Figure 8.2

The PPP protocol frame format.

The Protocol field may be either one or two octets in length, and identifies the protocol used in the Information field. Table 8.1 shows some of the currently supported Protocol field values in PPP.

Table 8.1   PPP Protocol Field Values

Value	Description
0001	Padding Protocol
0021	Internet Protocol (IP)
002b	Novell IPX
002d	Van Jacobson Compressed TCP/IP
002f	Uncompressed Transmission Control Protocol (TCP)
8021	IP Control Protocol (IPCP)
802b	Novell IPX Control Protocol
c021	Link Control Protocol (LCP)
c023	Password Authentication Protocol (PAP)
c223	Challenge Handshake Authentication Protocol (CHAP)

The Information field is used to hold the next layer protocol data. Notice that there is no field indicating the length of the PPP packet. It is the responsibility of the next layer protocol to provide this information to the remote device.

PPP Negotiation Phases

Several protocols must be established for the PPP connection to pass data across the serial line. Each protocol is identified as a different phase of the complete PPP protocol. The Link Establishment phase negotiates values for the low-level protocol used for PPP. After the link is established, the client can authenticate himself to the server using the PPP Authentication phase. After authentication, each of the higher-level protocols that will be used on the link must be established in the Network Protocol Establishment phase. The following sections describe these phases in more detail.

Link Establishment Phase

After an HDLC modem connection is made between the two peer devices, the initiating device must attempt to negotiate the parameters necessary for the link to transfer data between the devices. Much like a TCP connection, several connection states are used to identify the connectivity status of the devices. The Link Control Protocol (LCP) is used to accomplish this task. These connection states are shown in Figure 8.3 and described in the following sections.

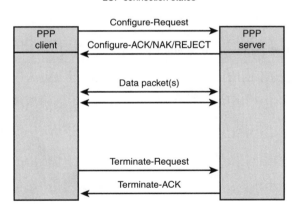

FIGURE 8.3
The LCP connection states.

LCP Protocol

The LCP protocol consists of formatted packets that transfer information between the two peers to negotiate connection parameters. Figure 8.4 shows the basic format of an LCP packet.

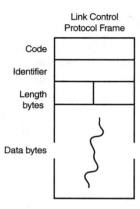

FIGURE 8.4

The Link Control Protocol packet format.

The Code LCP field is one byte in length and is used to identify the LCP packet type. LCP packets are mainly used for negotiating parameters of the link, but can also change the current state of the link (such as link termination, described later). Eleven different LCP packet types are defined in RFC 1661 and shown in Table 8.2.

TABLE 8.2   Link Control Protocol Code Field Values

Code	Description
1	Configure-Request
2	Configure-Ack
3	Configure-Nak
4	Configure-Reject
5	Terminate-Request
6	Terminate-Ack
7	Code-Reject
8	Protocol-Reject
9	Echo-Request
10	Echo-Reply
11	Discard-Request

The Identifier field is one octet in length and is used to uniquely identify the LCP packet so that the sending and receiving devices can match the proper reply to the proper request.

The Length field is two octets in length and is used to indicate the entire length of the LCP packet (including the Code, Identifier, Length, and Data fields). The total length of the LCP packet must not exceed the maximum receive unit (MRU) of the link.

The Data fields are multiple octets in length as specified in the Length field, and contain data as specified by the Code field.

The Code field controls the purpose of the LCP packet. As shown in Table 8.2, there are many different types of LCP packets. The following sections describe the purposes of some of the LCP packet types.

Configure-Request LCP Packet

The Configure-Request LCP packet is used to establish the link between two peer devices using PPP. Configuration options that the client wants to negotiate from the default values are listed in the Data fields of the packet. All options for which the client is requesting nondefault values should be included in this packet. Any options that use the default value are not included in the Configure-Request packet. Some Configure-Request options are defined in Table 8.3.

Configure-Ack LCP Packet

The Configure-Ack LCP packet is sent by the PPP host if it agrees with all of the option requests made in the associated Configure-Request packet. The options listed in this packet must match exactly the options in the Configure-Request packet. If any one of the option change requests is not acceptable to the server, it must not issue a Configure-Ack packet.

Configure-Nak LCP Packet

The Configure-Nak packet is used to indicate that at least one of the options in the Configure-Request packet was not acceptable to the PPP server. The server should indicate which option is not acceptable, and offer a value that would make the option acceptable in the Options fields of this packet.

Configure-Reject LCP Packet

The Configure-Reject LCP packet is used to indicate options from the Configure-Request packet that are either not recognized or are not acceptable for negotiation. When the client receives a Configure-Reject packet, it should recognize that none of the options listed in the packet is available for negotiation on the PPP server.

Terminate-Request LCP Packet

The Terminate-Request LCP packet is used to indicate that the client wants to terminate the current PPP session. The Data field of this packet can be zero bytes or can be filled with insignificant data. The PPP host must be able to recognize and act on this LCP packet at any time during the PPP session.

8

PPP PROTOCOL

Terminate-Ack LCP Packet

The Terminate-Ack LCP packet is used by the PPP server to acknowledge the client's request to close the PPP session. The Data fields can be zero bytes or can be filled with insignificant data. When a PPP server receives a Terminate-Request LCP packet, it *must* send a Terminate-Ack response and initiate closing the PPP session.

Code-Reject LCP Packet

The Code-Reject LCP packet is used if the PPP server receives an LCP packet with an invalid code from the client. This could indicate that the client is using a different version of PPP or has some PPP implementation problems. The PPP server should drop the PPP connection immediately after sending this packet.

Protocol-Reject LCP Packet

The Protocol-Reject LCP packet is used when the PPP server receives a PPP packet with either an invalid Protocol field or a protocol that it does not support. The Data field should contain a copy of the packet that was rejected. The PPP client should recognize that the PPP server does not support the requested protocol and should indicate that to the user.

Echo-Request LCP Packet

The Echo-Request LCP packet is used to provide a loopback method for the PPP connection. After receiving an Echo-Request LCP packet, the PPP device must issue an Echo-Reply packet. This is often used to keep data flowing across a connection that is susceptible to being closed due to inactivity. This can also be used for diagnostic purposes. A Magic-Number can be negotiated during the Configure-Request phase and be used in this packet to identify the connection.

Echo-Reply LCP Packet

The Echo-Reply LCP packet is used to respond to an LCP Echo-Request packet. If a Magic-Number has been negotiated for the connection, it must be included in this packet.

Discard-Request LCP Packet

The Discard-Request LCP packet is used to provide a mechanism to test the link. The receiving device will immediately discard the Discard-Request packet. No response to the Discard-Request packet is made. The Discard-Request packet should contain the Magic-Number negotiated by LCP.

LCP Negotiated Options

During the Configure-Request phase of the link negotiation, the client PPP device can request parameter changes for the link. If an option is not included in the Configure-Request packet, the default value for it is assumed. Figure 8.5 shows the format of the LCP Option portion of the Configure-Request packet.

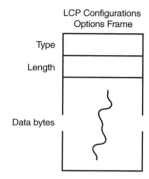

FIGURE 8.5
The LCP Configure-Request Option fields.

The Type field is used to identify the option being negotiated. Table 8.3 shows the available options.

TABLE 8.3   LCP Configure-Request Options

Type	Description
0	Reserved
1	Maximum Receive Unit
3	Authentication Protocol
4	Quality-Control
5	Magic-Number
7	Protocol Field Compression
8	Address and Control Field Compression

The Length field is one octet in length and indicates the length of the Option fields. This value includes the Type, Length, and Data fields.

Maximum Receive Unit Option

The most common LCP option that is negotiated is the Maximum Receive Unit, or MRU. This value determines the packet size that will be used on the link. The larger the packet size, the more data that can be transmitted with less overhead. However, too large a packet size can hinder the performance of error-prone connections because the entire packet must be retransmitted if an error does occur. When possible, a value of 1500 is used to simulate the packet size that is available on an Ethernet network. However, when using slower links, an MRU of 296 is used to decrease the chance of packet errors and retransmission times.

Quality Control Option

The Quality Control option is used when the devices want to determine the line quality of the connection. Often, if excessive errors are detected, it is desirable to detect the quality of the connection and terminate the connection if the quality is below a particular level. By default, no quality control method is used. The RFC specifies one type of quality control protocol: the Link Quality Report, type c025. Both devices must agree to implement quality control and agree to the same quality control type before line monitoring can begin.

Magic-Number Option

The Magic-Number option is used to detect a loopback situation in which the PPP connection is talking to itself. When the Configure-Request packet is sent with a Magic-Number, the PPP host compares this number to the Magic-Number sent in the last received Configure-Request packet. If the numbers match, it is most likely a loopback connection. After a Magic-Number is determined for a PPP session, that number can be used with the Echo-Request and Echo-Reply LCP packets to check the connection during the session to determine whether the loop-back condition exists.

Protocol Field Compression Option

The Protocol Field Compression option is used to identify a compression method that both devices can use to help conserve bandwidth. By default, the PPP Protocol field is set to two octets. If both devices agree to use Protocol Field Compression, the Protocol field can be reduced to just one octet. If several thousand frames are sent during the duration of the PPP session, significant data bandwidth can be saved. LCP packets cannot use Protocol Field Compression. Also, the FCS must be computed using the compressed frame, not the original.

Address and Control Field Compression Option

The Address and Control Field Compression option allows the PPP frame to compress the HLDC Address and Control fields. This saves even more bandwidth for slow-speed links. As with the Protocol Field Compression Option, LCP packets cannot use Address and Control Field Compression and the HLDC FCS must be computed using the compressed frame, not the original.

Authentication Protocol Option

The Authentication Protocol option allows the devices to negotiate which method will be used to authenticate the client to the host. In these days of network security, it is almost always required for a client to log in to a host before the PPP session will be established. Currently, two different values can be negotiated for authentication methods: type c223, the Challenge-Handshake Authentication Protocol (CHAP); and type c023, the Password Authentication Protocol (PAP). These two authentication protocols are discussed in further detail in the following section.

PPP Authentication Phase

In an attempt to improve on a plain text userid/password authentication system, two different authentication methods have been devised. PAP has been more popular in PPP implementations, but the CHAP method is more secure and is gaining in popularity. The PPP implementation for Linux supports both authentication methods.

CHAP

The Challenge-Handshake Authentication Protocol is used to implement a level of security in PPP authentication. The CHAP protocol uses a three-way handshake method to authenticate the client to the host. RFC 1994 describes the method used to implement the CHAP protocol. The basic CHAP packet format is shown in Figure 8.6.

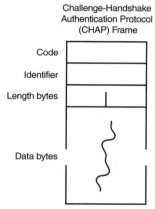

FIGURE 8.6
The CHAP packet format.

The Code field is one octet in length and identifies the type of the CHAP packet. Table 8.4 shows the possible values for this field.

TABLE 8.4   CHAP Code Field Values

Code	Description
1	Challenge
2	Response
3	Success
4	Failure

8

PPP PROTOCOL

The Identifier field is one octet in length and identifies the CHAP packet to help the client and host match the reply and requests together.

The Length field is two octets in length and indicates the length of the CHAP packet. The Length value should include the octet count from the Code, Identifier, Length, and Data fields.

The Data fields can be zero or more octets in length, and are used to support the functions identified by the Code value of the CHAP packet.

Figure 8.7 demonstrates the handshake protocol that CHAP uses to authenticate a client. The CHAP three-way handshake uses the following system:

- The host sends a Challenge CHAP packet to the client based on a random value.
- The client responds with a Response CHAP packet indicating a value calculated using the challenge value and a secret word combined using a one-way hash function.
- The host checks the client's response value with the value that it calculates itself for the challenge value and secret word. If they match, the host sends a Success CHAP packet and the PPP session is continued. If not, the host sends a Failure CHAP packet and the PPP session is terminated with a Terminate-Request LCP packet.

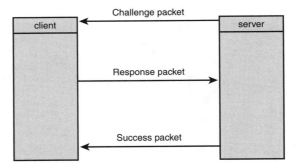

FIGURE 8.7
The CHAP handshake phases.

Another feature of the CHAP protocol is that the PPP host can reissue a request for the client to authenticate at any time during the PPP session. This feature can be used to prevent session hijacking by another device.

PAP

The Password Authentication Protocol is not as sophisticated as the CHAP protocol. It uses a simple userid/password mechanism to authenticate the user. The userid is sent as plain ASCII text. The password may or may not be encrypted, depending on the capability of the client.

After the client is authenticated, the PPP session is continued, and is not reauthenticated for the duration of the session. If the client does not authenticate properly, the PPP session may or may not be terminated by the PPP host.

The PAP authentication method is the easier of the two methods to implement, but it is the least secure. One reason why it has become so popular with ISPs is that even though it does not have the highest level of security, security on a dial-up connection is not often a determining factor. Tapping a phone connection to intercept a PPP session is much more difficult than observing a password sent in text mode across an Ethernet network. Thus, ease of configuration and use overrule level of security.

Network Protocol Establishment Phase

After the link layer has been established through the LCP negotiation phase, individual network layer sessions can be initiated. The PPP protocol allows for multiple network protocols to be transported across the connection simultaneously. To negotiate the network layer parameters, PPP uses a Network Connection Protocol for each individual protocol that can be transmitted during the PPP session. For the Linux mailserver, only one protocol is necessary: IP. The NCP used to negotiate an IP connection in a PPP session is called the IP Control Protocol, or IPCP.

IPCP Protocol

To support an IP network across a PPP session, both PPP devices must support the IP Control Protocol. IPCP is used to negotiate the IP connection parameters for both sides of the connection. The PPP Protocol field will have a value of 8021 when it contains an IPCP packet (as shown in Table 8.1).

IPCP uses the same frame format as LCP (shown in Figure 8.4). The IPCP Code field also uses the same codes as the LCP packet, but recognizes only codes 1 through 7 (refer to Table 8.2). The negotiation method is just like the LCP negotiation. A Configure-Request packet is sent with any options that the client wants to negotiate with the host. The host can respond with a Configure-Ack if it agrees with the options or a Configure-Nak if it does not agree with any of the options.

IPCP Options

The IPCP protocol allows the two PPP devices to negotiate IP parameters before the IP connection is established. IPCP options are sent in the Configure-Request packet, similar to the LCP protocol. Table 8.5 shows the IPCP options listed in the RFC.

TABLE 8.5 IP Control Protocol Options

Option	Description
1	IP Addresses
2	IP Compression Protocol
3	Remote IP Address

Option 1 has been deprecated from the RFC and is no longer in use. Its purpose was to allow the PPP devices to negotiate the IP addresses used on the link. It was found through experimentation that it was often difficult for the devices to converge on a mutually agreeable set of IP addresses. Option 3 has been added to replace the functionality of this option.

Option 2 is used to negotiate a method of IP packet compression to conserve bandwidth on the PPP session. Currently, the Van Jacobson method of TCP/IP header compression is supported by PPP. This method allows the device to reduce the TCP/IP header to as few as three octets. The Configure-Request value for requesting IP compression is 002d.

Option 3 is used to negotiate an IP address for the client device. This option allows the client to specify a desired IP address. If the PPP host is unable to support that address for some reason, it can return an alternative address for the client to use in the Configure-Nak packet. The client and host can negotiate a proper IP address for the client to use. The default address is no address.

After a successful IPCP negotiation, IP packets can be passed in the PPP session using one of three PPP Protocol field values: 0021 for normal uncompressed IP, 002b for compressed TCP/IP using Van Jacobson compression, or 002f for uncompressed TCP with compressed IP headers (also called Van Jacobson uncompressed).

Link Termination Phase

When the client wants to drop the PPP session, it can issue the Terminate-Request LCP packet (refer to the earlier discussion). When the PPP server sees a Terminate-Request LCP packet, it must reply with a Terminate-Ack LCP packet and drop the connection. This is not dependent on the current state of any IP connections active at the time the Terminate-Request command is issued. A client can terminate a PPP session with IP sessions still active. The PPP server cannot keep the PPP session active until the IP sessions are closed. After the PPP session is closed, to restart a new session the client must reissue the proper LCP connection request packets even if the physical layer did not disconnect.

Linux PPP Implementations

The Linux operating system supports PPP by splitting the function into two parts. The first part is internal to the Linux kernel, whereas the second part resides in a Linux application program.

The PPP functions required to send HDLC packets across the serial line are included as part of the Linux kernel so that they can access the serial lines more efficiently. Starting with the 2.0 versions of the Linux kernel, kernel modules can load and unload features to the kernel without recompiling the kernel. Older versions of the Linux kernel needed to recompile the kernel to add new features. Either way, your Linux kernel must be configured to support PPP. Many Linux kernels will default to include PPP support because it has become so popular.

You can determine whether your Linux kernel is configured to support PPP by watching the messages at boot-up. If you see a status line regarding PPP support go by (or see it in the messages log file), your kernel has PPP support configured. If not, refer to your Linux distribution documentation or the Linux PPP-HOWTO document for information on how to add PPP support to your specific Linux distribution.

The second part of Linux PPP support is a program used to control the PPP connection to the server. The de facto standard PPP software package in the Linux environment has become the pppd package written by Al Longyear, Paul Mackerras, and Michael Callahan. Most Linux distributions include a binary distribution of this program. The version included with Red Hat 6.0 is ppp-2.3.7, whereas the version included with Caldera OpenLinux 2.2 is ppp-2.3.5. The FTP site for the pppd package is located at cs.anu.edu.au in the /pub/software/ppp directory. The current version available for download at the time of this writing is ppp-2.3.10. Because this package is highly dependent on kernel configurations, I strongly suggest using the version that comes with your particular Linux distribution. That version has been fine-tuned to work with your particular Linux kernel version. However, if you are adventurous or for some (hopefully serious) reason you need to use the latest version, you can download the source for this package and compile and install it yourself. At the time of this writing the current version of pppd could be found at ftp://cs.anu.edu.au/pub/software/ppp/ppp-2.3.10.tar.gz. After downloading the file and untarring it, use the following steps to install the software:

1. Run the ./configure program from the ppp-2.3.10 directory. This configures the Makefile to your specific OS (Linux).

2. Run the GNU make program with the kernel option (make kernel). This creates the include files for your version of Linux with the new kernel pieces for pppd.

3. Recompile and install your new kernel with the new pppd support (refer to your Linux distribution documentation for specific details on how to do this).

4. Run the GNU make program to compile the pppd program.

5. As the root user, run the GNU make program with the install option (make install) to place the new executables in their proper places.

After you have installed pppd, either by your Linux distribution's binary distribution file or by compiling the source code, you can configure pppd to work as either a PPP client or a PPP server.

8

PPP PROTOCOL

Linux Client PPP Implementation

The pppd program can be configured as a PPP client, allowing your Linux mailserver to connect to an ISP PPP host and establish an IP network connection to pass mail and other IP traffic. Other Linux programs are available to assist the PPP client process. The following sections describe some of them.

pppd Client Parameters

To use pppd in client mode, you must supply some options that help it connect to the PPP server and establish the PPP session properly. The basic format for the pppd command is

```
pppd <tty line> <speed> [options]
```

where `<tty line>` is the Linux COM port where your modem is connected (refer to Chapter 3, "Installing Communication Devices in Linux") and `<speed>` is the speed at which you want to connect to the modem. The art of using the pppd program comes in choosing the proper options for the client and server commands. The rest of this section describes some of the options available to pppd as a client.

The connect option allows the pppd program to use an executable or shell script to set up the serial link before the pppd program attempts to connect.

The crtscts option uses RTS/CTS hardware flow control on the serial line.

The defaultroute option adds a default route to the kernel routing table pointing to the remote IP address of the PPP server. The route table entry is deleted when the PPP session is terminated. This allows your Linux server to know to send IP traffic destined for other network devices through the PPP connection.

The lock option is used to create a UUCP-style lock file to indicate that the modem is in use.

The mru and mtu options allow the client to attempt to set the Maximum Receive Unit (mru) and Maximum Transmit Unit (mtu) sizes during the LCP negotiation phase. Remember that it is still up to the PPP server to agree to the new sizes. Often this is used on slower modem connections to reduce the PPP packet size.

The modem option allows Linux to use the modem control lines. With this option, the pppd program will wait for the CD (carrier detect) modem signal when opening the modem line, and will drop DTR (data terminal ready) briefly when the PPP connection is terminated.

chat Program

The chat program is a part of the pppd distribution, and is used to simplify the connect string for pppd. The chat program can use a simple script file and communicate with the modem to initiate the connection with the PPP server. The chat script uses text strings that it can send to the remote server in response to text strings received. It tries to match the text strings in a chat session—one response for each string received. Listing 8.2 shows an example of a sample chat script used for pppd.

LISTING 8.2   Sample Chat Script `isp.chat`

```
1   ""
2   ATDT5551234
3   CONNECT
4   ""
5   "ogin:"
6   rich
7   "word:"
8   guitar
9   "rich]$"
10  "exec /usr/sbin/pppd silent modem crtscts proxyarp 10.0.0.100:10.0.0.2"
```

In Listing 8.2, line 2 shows the command that pppd sends to the modem to dial the ISP phone number. Line 3 shows what text string pppd should wait for to establish that a connection has been made to the PPP server. Line 4 indicates that when the chat program receives a connection notice from the modem, it should send a single carriage return. Line 5 shows what text string to wait for from the server. If the server is allowing terminal logins from this modem line, it should issue a welcome banner with a login prompt. In line 6, pppd sends the userid to the PPP server; in line 8, it sends the password. When pppd gets a command prompt from the PPP server (as shown in line 9), it then issues the host pppd command on the PPP server. The parameters used in this pppd command will be discussed in detail in "Linux Server PPP Implementation," later in this chapter.

After a successful chat script is created, it can be used in the client's pppd configuration to dial the PPP server when the pppd program is executed. The connect pppd option calls the chat script using the following format:

```
pppd ttyS1 38400 connect '/usr/sbin/chat -v -f /home/rich/isp.chat' \
    modem crtscts defaultroute
```

The connect option uses the chat program in its script to connect to the PPP server. The preceding command line will automatically call the PPP server and start the pppd program on the server. The -v option used in the chat program allows for extremely verbose output to the /var/log/messages file. Use this for testing purposes, and then remove it when you have all the bugs worked out. Listing 8.3 shows the lines that the pppd and chat programs place in the message log during a client PPP session.

8

PPP PROTOCOL

LISTING 8.3 Lines from `/var/log/messages` for pppd and chat

```
Sep 22 06:56:56 shadrach pppd[663]: pppd 2.3.5 started by root, uid 0
Sep 22 06:56:56 shadrach kernel: registered device ppp0
Sep 22 06:56:57 shadrach chat[664]: send (ATZS7=100^M)
Sep 22 06:56:57 shadrach chat[664]: expect (OK)
Sep 22 06:56:57 shadrach chat[664]: ATZS7=100^M^M
Sep 22 06:56:57 shadrach chat[664]: OK
Sep 22 06:56:57 shadrach chat[664]:  -- got it
Sep 22 06:56:57 shadrach chat[664]: send (ATDT5551234^M)
Sep 22 06:56:58 shadrach chat[664]: expect (CONNECT)
Sep 22 06:56:58 shadrach chat[664]: ^M
Sep 22 06:57:18 shadrach chat[664]: ATDT5551234^M^M
Sep 22 06:57:18 shadrach chat[664]: CONNECT
Sep 22 06:57:18 shadrach chat[664]:  -- got it
Sep 22 06:57:18 shadrach chat[664]: send (^M)
Sep 22 06:57:18 shadrach chat[664]: expect (ogin:)
Sep 22 06:57:18 shadrach chat[664]:  28800/V42BIS^M
Sep 22 06:57:19 shadrach chat[664]: ^M
Sep 22 06:57:19 shadrach chat[664]: ^MRed Hat Linux release 5.2 (Apollo)
Sep 22 06:57:19 shadrach chat[664]: ^MKernel 2.0.36 on an i486
Sep 22 06:57:19 shadrach chat[664]: ^M
Sep 22 06:57:19 shadrach chat[664]: ^M^M
Sep 22 06:57:19 shadrach chat[664]: mail1.isp.net login:
Sep 22 06:57:19 shadrach chat[664]:  -- got it
Sep 22 06:57:19 shadrach chat[664]: send (rich^M)
Sep 22 06:57:19 shadrach chat[664]: expect (word:)
Sep 22 06:57:19 shadrach chat[664]:  rich^M
Sep 22 06:57:19 shadrach chat[664]: Password:
Sep 22 06:57:19 shadrach chat[664]:  -- got it
Sep 22 06:57:19 shadrach chat[664]: send (guitar^M)
Sep 22 06:57:20 shadrach chat[664]: expect (rich]$)
Sep 22 06:57:20 shadrach chat[664]:  ^M
Sep 22 06:57:20 shadrach chat[664]: Last login: Tue Sep 21 20:45:47^M
Sep 22 06:57:21 shadrach chat[664]: [rich@mail1 rich]$
Sep 22 06:57:21 shadrach chat[664]:  -- got it
Sep 22 06:57:21 shadrach chat[664]: send (exec /usr/sbin/pppd passive
➥ silent modem crtscts^M)
Sep 22 06:57:22 shadrach pppd[663]: Serial connection established.
Sep 22 06:57:23 shadrach pppd[663]: Using interface ppp0
Sep 22 06:57:23 shadrach pppd[663]: Connect: ppp0 <--> /dev/ttyS1
Sep 22 06:57:27 shadrach pppd[663]: local  IP address 10.0.0.100
Sep 22 06:57:27 shadrach pppd[663]: remote IP address 10.0.0.2
```

Using the chat script and the pppd client commands establishes a PPP session with the PPP server. This can be placed in a script file to create a method to start the PPP session when needed. However, this method still needs some external event to trigger it to start—an event such as the cron process running the PPP script whenever mail needs to be checked. The next program allows the PPP client to start automatically when it is needed.

diald Program

Now that you have your chat script perfected and can dial into the PPP server and establish a connection, you might want to automate things a little more. If you decide to connect your Linux mailserver directly to the ISP, you must implement a policy on how often your server will connect to the ISP to transfer mail (see Chapter 13, "Connecting the Mailserver to an ISP"). One method is to use dial-on-demand IP routing. This feature automatically starts the PPP connection whenever it detects data that needs to use the ISP network.

A great program for implementing dial-on-demand routing is the diald program written by Eric Schenk. Some Linux distributions include a binary package for diald. If your Linux distribution doesn't, you can download a version from the new diald Web site at `http://diald.unix.ch`.

The format of the diald program is

`/usr/sbin/diald [device1....] [options...] [-- [pppd options]]`

where *device1* is the Linux tty line your modem is connected to, *options* are diald options, and *pppd options* are the options that diald will pass to the pppd program when diald calls it. It is also possible to set the parameters by using a configuration file for diald.

The diald program's configuration file is used to set parameters for it to call the chat and pppd programs as required, as well as list scenarios in which you want diald to start and stop pppd. The configuration file is located at `/etc/diald.conf`. Listing 8.4 is a sample `diald.conf` file that replaces the pppd options used in the pppd example shown earlier.

LISTING 8.4   Sample `/etc/diald.conf` Configuration File

```
1  ###
2  # /etc/diald.conf - diald configuration
3  #
4  # see /usr/lib/diald for sample config files
5  #
6  mode ppp
7  connect '/usr/sbin/chat -f /home/rich/isp.chat -t 35000'
8  connect-timeout 180
9  device /dev/ttyS1
10 speed 115200
11 modem
12 lock
```

continues

8

PPP PROTOCOL

LISTING 8.4   continued

```
13 crtscts
14 local 10.0.0.100
15 remote 10.0.0.2
16 defaultroute
17 include /usr/lib/diald/standard.filter
18 fifo /etc/diald/diald.ctl
```

In Listing 8.4, line 7 shows the diald connect parameter that calls the chat program using the same chat script that was used in the pppd example. Line 8 was added to compensate for the fact that the PPP host modem is set to answer after four rings (so as not to annoy friends and family who would call the same line using voice). It allows the chat script up to three minutes to complete. Line 17 includes a file `standard.filter` that diald uses to specify the conditions under which it will start the PPP session and when it will stop the session. Line 18 is used to specify a special file that a companion program, dctrl, uses to monitor the PPP session. dctrl is a graphical program that can monitor the PPP link and report any error conditions as well as the throughput of the connection.

After the diald configurations are set, you can test them. diald runs in background mode. You must start it as the root userid. When diald detects a network condition that warrants a connection to the PPP server, it starts the chat program that creates the PPP session with the server, and then starts the pppd program on the local host. When you are satisfied with the performance of diald, you can create a startup script for it and put it in the `/etc/rc.d` area on your Linux distribution so that it starts automatically at boot time. Then, every time a program needs to access a remote host via IP (such as fetchmail), diald will kick in and start the PPP session. Nice.

kppp Program

If you are using a Linux distribution that has the K Desktop Environment (KDE) window manager, you can use another option to simplify your PPP connection. The kppp program is a graphical interface that helps you configure and start the pppd program. Figure 8.8 shows the main screen that appears when you start the program.

FIGURE 8.8
The kppp program main screen.

From the main screen, you can select a configured PPP host and start the pppd connection simply by entering your password and clicking the Connect button. Clicking the Setup button on the main screen starts the kppp Configuration screen. Multiple accounts can be preconfigured by using the Accounts tab on the Configuration screen. Figure 8.9 shows the Accounts tab.

FIGURE 8.9

The kppp Accounts configuration tab.

Individual accounts can be configured by clicking the New button, as shown in Figure 8.10.

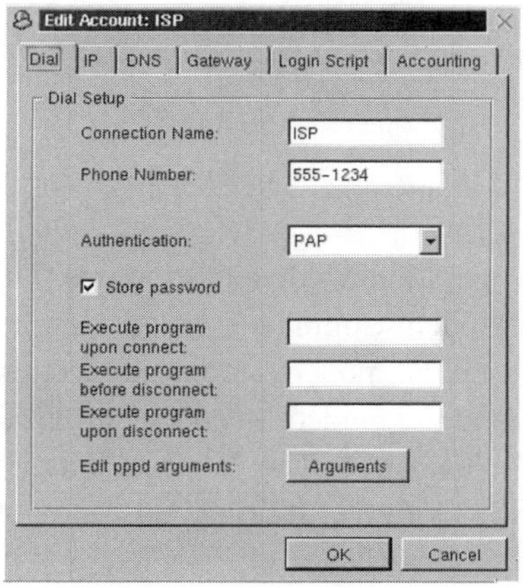

FIGURE 8.10

The kppp account setup screen.

Each property for the new account can be configured on the Edit Account screen. You can input the phone number and authentication method required to initiate the PPP session.

Authentication methods available include PAP, CHAP, a chat script, and a pop-up terminal session that enables you to manually log in and issue the `pppd` command on the remote PPP server. The IP tab enables you to determine how your local IP address will be configured—either dynamically by the PPP host or statically by you. You can use the DNS and Gateway tabs to select how the PPP client will obtain the DNS server and IP router addresses—either dynamically from the PPP host or statically by you.

Figure 8.11 shows the kppp configuration Device tab settings. This enables you to configure the modem that will be used for dialing the ISP and various settings that will affect the modem, such as the flow control method and the line termination method. The Use Lock File checkbox allows you to utilize the `pppd lock` option to create UUCP-style modem lock files so that another process won't try to use the modem at the same time.

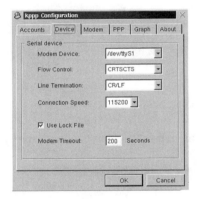

FIGURE 8.11
The kppp Device configuration tab.

Figure 8.12 shows the kppp configuration Modem tab settings. These settings allow you to set parameters for the modem. The Modem Commands button enables you to add initialization parameters to your modem to set up the modem for the connection. The Query Modem button enables you to send query strings to the modem to check current configuration settings. Up to eight settings can be shown with this option. The Terminal button is definitely handy when trying to create dial-up scripts for the first time. It brings up a mini-terminal that enables you to talk with the modem and dial in to the PPP server. This feature is great for dialing in to the server to observe return strings required to set the dial-up script settings properly.

After all the account parameters are configured, connecting is just a matter of selecting the account you want to dial in to, supplying the proper userid and password, and clicking the Connect button. The kppp program will automatically start pppd using the parameters that you had configured for the account. Speaking of accounts, there is also a handy accounting feature that will log your total session times and produce a nicely formatted report showing all your connection times for a given month.

FIGURE 8.12
The kppp Modem configuration tab.

Linux Server PPP Implementation

The same pppd program used to connect as a client to a PPP server can also be used as the pppd server. Refer to line 10 in Listing 8.2; the client ran the pppd command on the PPP server to start the PPP session. Besides running pppd manually, programs have been created that allow the Linux server to run pppd automatically when a PPP request is detected on a dial-in line. This section also discusses the benefits of using the mgetty+sendfax program with pppd.

pppd Server Parameters

Some pppd options are used to allow the pppd program to behave in a server mode. Although PPP is a peer-to-peer protocol, one side of the connection acts as a server waiting to establish PPP connections from client computers. Some of the options used on the server side are discussed in the following paragraphs.

The passive and silent options are used to allow the pppd program to wait for an LCP Configure-Request packet to initiate the PPP session.

The proxyarp option is used to allow the PPP host computer to respond to arp requests on the local network on behalf of the PPP client. This allows other computers to connect to the PPP client.

> **CAUTION**
>
> The proxyarp option allows other computers to connect to the PPP client. When you establish a PPP connection to the ISP, your Linux server becomes a network device on your ISP's network and is susceptible to the same network hacks as any other device directly connected to the network. I strongly recommended using firewall software to control access to the Linux server by external clients. Extreme care should be taken if no firewall software is being used on the PPP connection. Please watch the system logs for invalid access attempts.

The Local_IP:Remote_IP option allows pppd to assign IP addresses to remote devices. The Local_IP address is the address of the PPP host, whereas the Remote_IP address is the address that will be assigned to the remote PPP client.

Instead of using command-line options for pppd, you can place options in configuration files. By default, pppd will check the /etc/ppp/options file for a list of options to use. Another handy feature is that the pppd program also checks another options file depending on the tty line that it is initialized from. This enables you to specify specific options for each tty line, such as the remote IP address. If you have three modems on tty lines ttyS0, ttyS1, and ttyS2, you can have three separate pppd options files: /etc/ppp/options.ttyS0, /etc/ppp/options.ttyS1, and /etc/ppp/options.ttyS2. Each option file will have a different Local_IP:Remote_IP pair specified. That way, multiple PPP clients will not accidentally have duplicate IP addresses assigned to them.

mgetty+sendfax Program

If you want your Linux server to act as a PPP server and be able to listen for clients to connect, the mgetty+sendfax program is a great utility to have around. Most Linux distributions come with a binary package for this. If your Linux distribution did not include it, you can find it at sunsite.unc.edu in the /pub/Linux/system/serial directory. mgetty+sendfax was written by Gert Doering.

Normally, Linux uses the getty program to monitor serial lines for incoming logon attempts. When the serial line detects a connection, it uses the login program to authenticate the userid that is entered. The mgetty+sendfax program includes a new program, mgetty, that replaces the standard getty program for the serial line. mgetty allows more flexibility than getty by automatically detecting the type of incoming call and by using lock files.

The mgetty program uses both command-line options and a configuration file to control how it operates. The Linux file that controls what programs interact with what serial lines is the

/etc/inittab file. Each tty line for the Linux server has its own terminal line in the /etc/inittab file. The entry for the inittab file that allows mgetty to monitor a serial line looks like this:

```
# Set serial line for modem
s1:12345:respawn:/sbin/mgetty -D -s 38400 -n 4 ttyS0
```

Colons are used to separate the different parameters. The first parameter is a unique identifier for the terminal line. The second parameter indicates what init level the terminal will be active for. This line allows the terminal to be active for init levels 1 through 5. The third parameter is used to indicate how the init program will treat the line. The respawn keyword tells init to start the program at the indicated run level, and then restart it every time it terminates. This allows the modem line to recycle after a client disconnects from the modem. The fourth parameter is the program that init will spawn to monitor the terminal line. The format for the mgetty command is

```
mgetty [options] ttydevice
```

where [options] are mgetty options that control the behavior of the modem line and ttydevice is the Linux tty line that mgetty will monitor. Table 8.6 shows the options available for mgetty.

TABLE 8.6 mgetty Command-Line Options

Option	Description
-x LEVEL	Sets the debugging level to LEVEL
-s SPEED	Sets the line speed to SPEED
-a	Tries to autodetect the modem connection speed
-k SPACE	Sets the number of kilobytes required in the incoming fax spool directory to SPACE
-m 'EXPECT SEND'	Sets a modem initialization chat script
-r	Used to indicate a direct line
-p LOGIN_PROMPT	Sets the login prompt for the modem line
-n RINGS	Sets the number of rings before mgetty answers the modem
-D	Locks the modem to data mode
-F	Locks the modem to fax mode
-R SEC	Enables ring-back mode—callers must call twice
-i 'issue'	Specifies an issue file to display on a connection
-S 'FAX DOC'	Specifies a default fax document to send to polling fax machines

8

PPP PROTOCOL

As shown in the `inittab` example, the modem is locked in data mode at a speed of 38,400 bps. Also, the modem will not answer the phone until after the fourth ring (as noted, so as to keep my friends and family from hearing my modem when they call). One thing that might trick you is that mgetty does not place the modem in auto-answer mode. It listens for the modem to issue `RING` messages, and performs an `ATA` to pick up the line after the set number of `RING`s is found. Using this method, the modem should never answer the phone if the mgetty program locks up—a nice feature for those of us who have had servers answer the modem connection and not been able to issue a logon prompt.

Besides the command-line options, mgetty also uses configuration files to define its operation. The `/etc/mgetty+sendfax/login.conf` file is used to define the programs to which mgetty will pass the established connection. As mentioned earlier, a normal terminal session will be passed to the login program to process the userid. mgetty has the capability to autodetect an incoming PPP connection, and automatically pass it to the pppd program. The line in the `/etc/mgetty+sendfax/login.conf` file that does this is

```
/AutoPPP/ -     ppp    /usr/sbin/pppd auth -chap +pap login modem \
➥crtscts lock proxyarp
```

The `AutoPPP` part is case sensitive, so be careful. mgetty will pass the PPP connection to the pppd program using the parameters specified on the `AutoPPP` line. These parameters will be added to any parameters in the pppd options files. The `+pap` parameter is especially important for dial-in Windows clients. Chapter 16, "Supporting Dial-In Clients," describes the `AutoPPP` configuration in more detail.

After adding the mgetty information to the `/etc/inittab` file, you must use the Linux `telinit Q` command (or issue a `KILL HUP 1`) to have the init program reread the `inittab` file.

mgetty produces its own log files in the `/var/log` directory. Each modem line has its own log file by appending the tty line name to the `mgetty.log` filename. Listing 8.5 shows a sample mgetty session in the mgetty log file.

LISTING 8.5   mgetty Log File Output

```
1  09/19 06:43:56 yS0   mgetty: experimental test release 1.1.14-Apr02
2  09/19 06:43:56 yS0   check for lockfiles
3  09/19 06:43:56 yS0   locking the line
4  09/19 06:43:56 yS0   lowering DTR to reset Modem
5  09/19 06:43:57 yS0   send: \dATQ0V1H0[0d]
6  09/19 06:43:57 yS0   waiting for ``OK'' ** found **
7  09/19 06:43:58 yS0   send: ATS0=0Q0&D3&C1[0d]
8  09/19 06:43:58 yS0   waiting for ``OK'' ** found **
9  09/19 06:43:58 yS0   waiting...
10 09/19 06:45:23 yS0   waiting for ``RING'' ** found **
```

```
11 09/19 06:45:23 yS0   waiting for ``RING'' ** found **
12 09/19 06:45:29 yS0   waiting for ``RING'' ** found **
13 09/19 06:45:35 yS0   waiting for ``RING'' ** found **
14 09/19 06:45:59 yS0   send: ATA[0d]
15 09/19 06:45:59 yS0   waiting for ``CONNECT'' ** found **
16 09/19 06:46:13 yS0   send:
17 09/19 06:46:13 yS0   waiting for ``_'' ** found **
18 09/19 06:46:16 ##### data dev=ttyS0, pid=2766, caller='none',
➥ conn='38400/ARQ/28800 LAP-M', name='', cmd='/usr/sbin/pppd', user='/AutoPPP/'
```

In Listing 8.5, lines 1 through 9 show mgetty initializing the modem on ttyS0. Lines 10 through 14 show mgetty receiving the RING string from the modem, indicating an incoming call. After the fourth RING, mgetty issues an ATA command to pick up the line. Line 18 shows that mgetty autodetected a PPP connection and issued the /usr/sbin/pppd command for the line.

Summary

The Point-to-Point Protocol (PPP) is used for passing network protocols between two devices using a modem connection. For the Linux mailserver, this means is that you can use a standard asynchronous modem connected to a COM port on the PC to dial into an Internet service provider (ISP) to establish an IP connection to the Internet. This allows the mailserver to send and receive mail messages from other mail hosts on the Internet. Linux supports the PPP protocol with the pppd program. It is designed to work both on either end of a PPP connection. It can behave as a server by waiting for other PPP devices to dial in to it and establish a PPP session, or it can be used to dial in to an ISP and establish a session. A companion program to pppd is the Linux chat program. This allows the Linux server to converse with the modem to dial into the ISP and start the remote PPP session. Another Linux program, diald, can be used to automate the PPP process even further. diald will monitor the network watching for IP traffic waiting to use the PPP connection. It then automatically starts the chat script to contact the ISP and start the PPP session. To create a PPP server, you can use the mgetty+sendfax program that autodetects an incoming PPP connection and automatically starts the pppd program on the server. This works very well when supporting Windows 95, 98, and NT PPP clients.

8

PPP PROTOCOL

UUCP Protocol

IN THIS CHAPTER

The previous chapters described methods of transferring mail from the Linux mailserver across a network connection to the Internet. In some instances—either for security reasons or expense—it is not possible to connect the mailserver to the Internet via an IP network. There is another method of establishing a mailserver without the risk or expense of a dedicated or dial-up IP network.

The Unix-to-Unix CoPy (UUCP) protocol was used in the early days of UNIX to transfer messages and files between remote UNIX computers via phone lines and modems. An entire suite of protocols and programs was written to create a point-to-point mesh network of UNIX computers across the country. When the Internet became available, the popularity of UUCP faded almost to extinction. Now UUCP is making a comeback because many businesses and ISPs are looking for more secure and cost-efficient methods to transfer email.

Using a UUCP connection, the mailserver is never connected to the Internet. It is not possible for intruders to TELNET to the server via the UUCP connection or to perform any kind of network denial-of-service attack. No programs can be executed unless you specifically give your ISP permission to do so. The UUCP software allows tight control of the connectivity between the two computers that are using it.

Many businesses opt to use a UUCP mail connection to augment their normal PPP network connection. If a business has a lot of interactive IP traffic, such as Web and FTP clients, it does not want to bog down the PPP line with extra traffic for transferring mail. Instead of buying larger PPP bandwidth, it is possible to purchase a cheaper dial-up UUCP connection to the ISP that is responsible for just handling mail transfers—leaving the PPP connection for the interactive traffic.

This chapter discusses the protocols used in a UUCP connection. When connecting to an ISP via UUCP, it helps to know what protocols you are talking about. This chapter also discusses the most popular Linux UUCP distribution (Taylor UUCP), and provides sample configuration files for implementing UUCP on a Linux mailserver as either a client or as a server for other UUCP computers to connect to.

UUCP Protocol Description

The UUCP protocol was developed at AT&T Bell Labs by Mike Lesk in the late 1970s. It's purpose was simple: to implement a file- and mail-transfer protocol between two UNIX computers. There are three phases to a UUCP connection:

- Initial handshake
- Data transfer
- Closing handshake

Because UUCP was invented long before the client/server paradigm was devised, its terminology is a little different. What would now be called the server is actually called the UUCP *slave*, and the client computer is called the *master* because it controls the UUCP connection (see Figure 9.1). Either computer can initiate a connection; the initial handshake determines which host plays which role. Of course, just to confuse things, the computers are allowed to switch roles during the UUCP session if they want to.

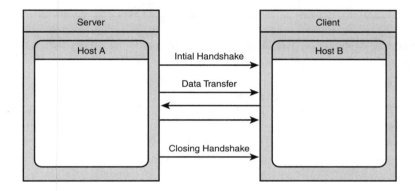

FIGURE 9.1
The UUCP session phases.

Initial Handshake

During the initial handshake, the two computers lay down the ground rules for the UUCP communication. During the initial handshake, a packet is defined by a starting character (`0x10` hex) and an ending character (`0x00` hex). When the master computer places a call to the slave, the slave should respond with the following packet:

`Shere=hostname`

where `hostname` is the UUCP name of the slave computer. A UUCP name has nothing to do with the DNS name of a computer, although attempts are being made to reconcile the two systems by offering a uucp domain in the Internet community. If the master receives the slave's hostname, it can respond with the following:

`Shostname options`

where `hostname` is the UUCP name of the master and `options` are items negotiated by the two hosts. Table 9.1 shows the options available for negotiation.

TABLE 9.1   UUCP Initial Handshake Options

Option	Description
-Qseq	Matches a calling sequence number `seq`
-xlevel	Requests that the slave set its debugging mode to the value of `level`
-pgrade	Requests that the slave transfer only files of priority `grade` or higher
-N	Indicates that the master understands Taylor size limit extensions

The slave computer should respond to any options selected by the master by sending one of the return codes specified in Table 9.2.

TABLE 9.2   UUCP Slave Return Codes

Code	Description
ROK	The options are acceptable
ROKN	Same as `ROK` but also understands the Taylor size limit extensions
RLCK	The slave computer has a UUCP lock for the master hostname and can't continue
RCB	The slave will hang up and initiate a callback to the master
RBADSEQ	The sequence number in the –Q option did not match; thus, the connection might be an imposter
RLOGIN	The master computer logged in with a wrong login ID to establish the UUCP connection
RYou are unknown to me	The slave computer does not have an entry for the master computer in its `config` files

If the slave's response is ROK or ROKN, the next part of the initial handshake phase is started. If any other return code is returned, the master computer drops the connection.

The next part of the handshake is for the two computers to decide on a UUCP protocol. Over the years, various methods of encapsulating the core UUCP protocol have been designed. Each protocol has been assigned a letter from a to z. The original UUCP protocol has been assigned the letter g. The Taylor UUCP distribution normally uses the i protocol when communicating with another Taylor UUCP computer. The slave computer will initiate the exchange with the packet

Pprotocollist

where `protocollist` is a list of letters of the protocols that the slave supports. If the master computer can match a supported protocol, it returns

`Uprotocol`

where `protocol` is the letter of the matching protocol that the master will use. If there are no matching protocols, the master computer should return

`UN`

and drop the connection. After a protocol has been decided, the two computers can perform any negotiations necessary for the individual protocol (see "UUCP Protocol Types," later in this chapter). After the negotiations are complete, the initial handshake phase is over and the data transfer phase can begin.

Data Transfer

As mentioned earlier, the master computer controls the flow of data across the UUCP connection. After the initial handshake is complete, the master computer takes control of the session and can issue commands to the slave. There are five data transfer commands that can be used by the master. Figure 9.2 shows the five commands and the direction of action that each command uses.

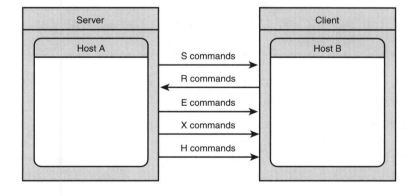

FIGURE 9.2
The UUCP data transfer commands.

Send a File Command

The `S` command is used to send a file from the master computer to the slave computer. The slave computer can either accept or reject the file transfer request. The format of the `S` command is

`S fileout filein user -options temp mode notify size`

`fileout` is the name of the file that the master computer wants to transfer. Files located in a user's directory are preceded by ~USER/ and files located in the UUCP public area are preceded by ~/.

`filein` is the filename that the slave computer should try to use when saving the file. If `filein` begins with an X., it represents an execution file that will be run by the slave using the uux Linux command. If `filein` begins with D., it represents a data file that will be used by an execution file.

`user` is the username of the user who requested the file transfer.

`-options` are additional options that control the action of the file transfer. Table 9.3 lists the available options.

TABLE 9.3   s Command Options

Option	Description
C	The file should be saved in the slave's UUCP spool directory
c	The file should be saved as specified in `filein`
d	The slave should create directories as needed to match the `filein` filename
f	The slave not create any needed directories, but should fail the transfer
m	The master should send mail to the user when the transfer is complete
n	The slave should send mail to the address specified by notify when the transfer is complete

`temp` is the name of the file in the UUCP spool directory to transfer if the C option is used. If not, `temp` is a dummy value that will be deleted if the transfer is successful.

`mode` is an octal number that indicates the UNIX mode of the file. Generally, the mode 0666 is used to represent read/write privileges for the user, his group, and all other users on the system. If the file is in the UUCP spool area, it may be set with a mode of 0600 to prevent reading and writing from other users.

`notify` is the mail address of the user to send notification messages to. If there is no user to notify, but the size option is used, the notify option should be set to the dummy value of either " " or dummy.

`size` is used for Taylor UUCP implementations to indicate the size of the data file transferred in decimal bytes.

After the s command is sent, the slave must send a return command to indicate the status of the transfer. All s command return values begin with s. Table 9.4 shows the possible return codes by the slave.

TABLE 9.4 s Command Return Codes

Code	Description
SY	All options are accepted; begin the file transfer
SN2	The file transfer will not succeed as requested
SN4	The slave cannot create the temporary file at this time
SN6	Used by Taylor UUCP; the slave indicates that the file is too large to save at this time
SN7	Used by Taylor UUCP; the slave indicates that the file is too large to transfer at any time

If the s command return code is SY, the master starts the file transfer using the appropriate protocol negotiated by the initial handshake. At the end of the file transfer, the slave must send a return code indicating the status of the transfer. Table 9.5 shows the possible s command completion codes.

TABLE 9.5 s Command Completion Codes

Code	Description
CY	The file transfer was successful
CN5	The temporary file could not be moved to the file location specified by `filein`

After the master receives the completion code from the slave, the data transfer is finished and the master is free to initiate another data transfer or close the UUCP session.

Receive a File command

The R command is used for the master to receive a file from the slave. The format for the R command is

```
R fileout filein user -options size
```

`fileout` is the filename of the file on the slave computer. This file must not reside in the UUCP `spool` directory, and it can not use any wildcard characters to indicate multiple files.

`filein` is the filename used on the master computer to save the file.

`user` is the username of the user requesting the file transfer.

`-options` are additional options that control the action of the file transfer. Table 9.6 shows the options that are available for the R command.

TABLE 9.6   R Command Options

Option	Description
d	The master should create directories as needed by `filein`.
f	The master should not create directories as needed by `filein`, and the transfer should fail.
m	The master should send mail to the user to notify him when the transfer is complete.

`size` indicates the largest file size that the master computer is able to accept from the slave.

After the R command is sent, the slave computer should send a return code indicating the status of the file transfer. Table 9.7 shows the possible return codes.

TABLE 9.7   R Command Return Codes

Code	Description
RY mode	The slave is able to transfer the file. `mode` indicates the UNIX permissions of `fileout`, and should be used for `filein`.
RN2	The slave is unable to transfer the file because either it does not exist or it has permissions that prevent the transfer.
RN6	Used by Taylor UUCP; indicates that the file is too large for the indicated size limit.

If the R command return code is RY, the slave initiates the file transfer using the appropriate UUCP protocol. When the file transfer is complete, the master will send a completion code to the slave. Table 9.8 shows the possible completion codes used.

TABLE 9.8   R Command Completion Codes

Code	Description
CY	File transfer successful.
CN5	The temporary file could not be moved to the file location specified by `filein`.

After the master sends the completion code, the file transfer is complete. The master is then free to initiate another data transfer or close the session.

Execute a Command

The E command is used by Taylor UUCP implementations to execute a command on the slave computer. As mentioned earlier, the original method used by UUCP to execute commands on the slave computer was to place the commands in a file beginning with an X. and transfer the file using the S command. When the slave noticed the X. file, it used the uux command to execute the commands in the file. Taylor UUCP attempts to improve on this method by implementing the E command. The format of the E command is

```
E fileout filein user -options temp mode notify size command
```

The fileout, filein, user, temp, mode, notify, and size parameters behave the same way as for the S command. The —options recognized by the E command are shown in Table 9.9.

TABLE 9.9   E Command Options

Option	Description
C	filein has been copied to the UUCP spool directory.
c	filein has not been copied to the UUCP spool directory.
N	No mail message should be sent indicating the status of the command.
Z	A mail message should be sent to the user indicating the status of the command.
R	A mail message should be sent to the address specified in notify indicating the status of the command.
e	The command should be executed using /bin/sh instead of uux.

command is the Linux command to be executed by the slave.

After the E command is sent, the slave responds with a return code. The E return codes are the same as the S return codes, with the exception that the first letter is E instead of S. After the master receives an EY return code, the data transfer is considered complete and the master is free to initiate another transfer or close the session.

Remote Host Transfer Command

The X command is used as a way to get the slave to send a file to somewhere else. The X command causes the slave to execute the uucp command (see "UUCP Commands," later in this chapter) using the parameters passed by the X command. The format for the X command is

```
X fileout filein user
```

fileout indicates the filename of the file that the slave should transfer using the uucp command.

`filein` is the filename and path to which the slave should transfer the file. This uses standard UUCP transfer conventions, such as `hostname!filename`, where `hostname` is the UUCP name of a remote host. This allows the master to initiate a file transfer from the slave computer to another remote computer on the UUCP network.

There are only two return codes that the slave can issue. An `XY` return code indicates that the slave accepts the command and will queue a job to perform the requested file transfer. An `XN` command indicates that the slave will not process the command.

After receiving the return code, the data transfer is complete (no data is transferred in this command) and the master is free to initiate another command or close the UUCP session.

Halt Command

The `H` command is used to close the UUCP session by the master computer. It is sent by itself with no options or parameters. The slave computer responds with one of two possible return codes.

The `HY` return code indicates that the slave agrees that the session is done, and allows the connection to terminate. The master then responds with another HY return code and drops the connection.

The `HN` command indicates that the slave agrees to terminate the session, but wants to start another UUCP session with the roles reversed. The slave computer then assumes the role of the master and issues new commands to transfer files to the old master, which has now assumed the slave role. When finished, the new master can send an H command and the new slave can either allow the connection to be closed or reverse the roles again and begin a new session as the new master (how's that for client/server bashing?).

Closing Handshake

The closing UUCP handshake is nothing more than a protocol formality. It indicates that both sides of the UUCP connection agree to drop the connection (as was already established in the `H` command communications). As in the initial handshake protocol, packets start with a `0x10` hex value and end with a `0x00` hex value. The master initiates the closing by sending a packet with six Os (000000). If the slave agrees to close the UUCP connection, it responds with a packet of seven Os (0000000). At that point, the UUCP connection is officially over and the modem line should be dropped.

Sample UUCP Session

To help clarify the complex UUCP command structure, Listing 9.1 shows a sample UUCP session between a master and a slave.

LISTING 9.1 Sample UUCP Session

```
1   SLAVE:  Shere=ispmail
2   MASTER: Sshadrach
3   SLAVE:  ROK
4   SLAVE:  Pgi
5   MASTER: Ui
6   MASTER: S test1.txt /home/rich/test1.txt rich x 066 dummy 1000
7   SLAVE:  SY
8   -- data transfer begins --
9   SLAVE:  CY
10  MASTER: R /home/rich/test2.txt test2.txt rich 1500
11  SLAVE:  RY 0666
12  -- data transfer begins --
13  SLAVE:  CY
14  MASTER: H
15  SLAVE:  HY
16  MASTER: 000000
17  SLAVE:  0000000
```

After the master host initiates the UUCP connection, the slave issues the initial handshake banner, shown in line 1. The master host responds with its handshake banner shown in line 2. In line 4, the slave host queries the master as to which UUCP protocol type it wants to use by listing the protocols that the slave supports. Line 5 shows the mater host's choice of protocol to use.

Line 6 shows the master host using the send file command to send a file to the slave computer. In line 7, the slave computer accepts the file transfer; and in line 8, the data transfer of the file occurs. When the transfer is complete, the slave responds with the CY command in line 9.

Line 10 shows another file transfer initiated by the master host. This time, it requests to receive a file from the slave host. The slave host accepts the file transfer request in line 11; in line 12, the data transfer of the file occurs. When the transfer is complete, the slave responds with the CY command shown in line 13.

Line 14 shows the master host requesting that the UUCP connection be terminated. The slave agrees in line 15, and lines 16 and 17 show the standard closing handshake packets being traded. At this point, the UUCP protocol is complete, and the modem connection is dropped.

UUCP Protocol Types

During the initial handshake, the two UUCP computers negotiate a UUCP protocol to use. The core UUCP description earlier can be encapsulated in another protocol to preserve data integrity on various types of data connections. A noisy phone line requires a higher degree of

9

UUCP PROTOCOL

error checking than an error-correcting TCP/IP connection. To compensate for this, several flavors of UUCP protocols have been written. Table 9.10 shows some of the more popular UUCP protocols. This section discusses these protocols in more detail.

TABLE 9.10   UUCP protocols

Protocol	Description
g	Earliest protocol used, provides large degree of error correction.
i	Can transfer data in both directions simultaneously with higher data rates.
t	Used for UUCP over TCP/IP, no error correction provided.
e	Another TCP/IP implementation, using ASCII control packets.

g Protocol

The g protocol was the first protocol written for UUCP. It was created to help pass UUCP packets across noisy, error-prone phone lines using low-speed modems. It has the largest packet overhead of any protocol. Often it is used as a least common denominator when computers are negotiating UUCP protocols because every UUCP implementation must support it.

The g protocol uses a six-byte header attached to each UUCP packet. Besides the normal data packets for UUCP, the g protocol introduces control packets to further control the UUCP connection above the initial handshake parameters. Figure 9.3 shows the layout of a g protocol packet header.

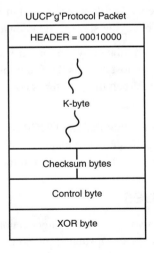

UUCP 'g' Protocol Packet

HEADER = 00010000
K-byte
Checksum bytes
Control byte
XOR byte

FIGURE 9.3
The UUCP g protocol packet header layout.

The g protocol uses the 0x10 hex start value from the core UUCP protocol. The next value in the header packet is the K-byte. The K-byte value represents the length of the data portion of the packet. The data portion of the g protocol packet contains the core UUCP packet as discussed earlier. Table 9.11 shows the possible values for the K-byte.

TABLE 9.11   g Protocol K-byte Values

K-byte Value	Data Length (Bytes)
1	32
2	64
3	128
4	256
5	512
6	1024
7	2048
8	4096
9	0

A K-byte value of 9 represents a special case; the g protocol packet does not contain data, but is a control packet. Control packets help the UUCP computers establish the communication channel and perform error correction for the core UUCP packets.

The checksum bytes are used to detect errors in the transmission of the packet. An algorithm is used to calculate the checksum of the entire data packet. The receiving computer recalculates the checksum and compares the values.

The control byte is used in conjunction with the K-byte value to determine the use of the control packet. The format of the control byte is shown in Figure 9.4. The parameters in the control byte take different meanings depending on the K-byte value.

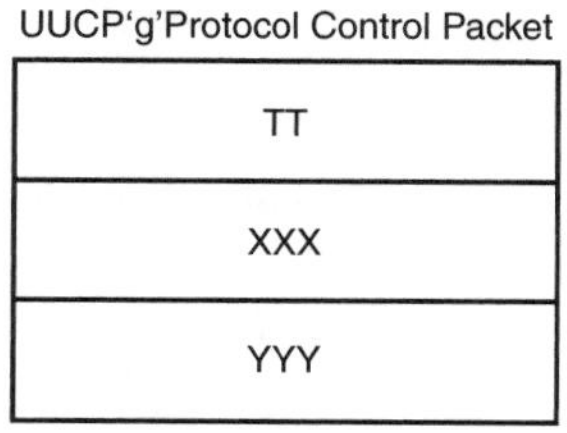

UUCP'g'Protocol Control Packet

TT
XXX
YYY

FIGURE 9.4
The UUCP g protocol control byte format.

If the K-byte value is 9, the control byte does what its name implies—it is a control byte that identifies a control action that must be taken by one of the two computers. The TT bits will have a value of 0, and the XXX bits represent a code for the control action. The YYY bits represent a value for the control action. Table 9.12 shows the possible values of the XXX bits.

TABLE 9.12   g Protocol Control Byte XXX Bits

Value	Mnemonic	Description
1	CLOSE	Indicates to the remote computer that the sending computer wants to close the UUCP connection. Note that this means that only the g protocol portion will be closed, not the actual UUCP connection; although normally, it triggers the UUCP connection to enter the closing handshake phase.
2	RJ	Indicates the last packet sent by the remote computer was not received properly. The YYY bits represent the packet sequence number of the last received packet.
3	SRJ	Indicates a particular packet sequence number was not received properly and should be resent. The YYY bits represent the sequence number of the bad packet. UUCP does not use this control code.
4	RR	Indicates a packet sequence has been received correctly. The YYY bits represent the sequence number of the last received packet.
5	INITC	Identifies the last handshake control packet. Both slave and master computers will send an INITC control packet. The YYY bits represent the maximum window size the computer will use in packets. After each computer receives the other's INITC packet, the g protocol handshake is complete.
6	INITB	Identifies the second handshake control packet. Both slave and master computers will send an INITB control packet. The YYY bits represent the largest packet size that the computer can accept. The value format is similar to the K-byte value, but is one number less. Thus, an INITB value of 1 represents 64 bytes, 2 represents 128 bytes, and so on.
7	INITA	Identifies the starting g protocol handshake. Both slave and master computers send an INITA control packet. The YYY bits represent the maximum window size the computer can receive in packets.

If the K-byte value is less than 9, the control byte serves a different purpose. The control byte identifies the type of data packet that the packet is. If the TT bits value is 2, the packet is a long data packet. If the TT bits value is 3, the packet is a short data packet.

In a long data packet, the XXX and YYY bits of the control byte are used to represent the sequence number (XXX) and the acknowledgement number (YYY). Each packet is sequenced and acknowledged to trace missing packets. Missing packets are retransmitted. All bytes following the control byte (up the K-byte value of bytes) are considered data. The core UUCP packet will be in these bytes.

A short data packet is a little different. The XXX and YYY bits still represent the sequence and acknowledge numbers, but the first two bytes of the data are used to represent the difference between the physical and logical packet sizes. As shown in Table 9.11, a K-byte value of 1 indicates that a 32-byte data packet will be sent. If the sender has fewer than 32 bytes of data to transmit, it must use a short data packet format. The first two bytes represent the difference between the logical data size (32) and the actual physical size of the data.

If the difference value is less than 128, one data byte is used. If the difference value is 128 or larger, two data bytes are used. The high bit of the first byte indicates how many bytes are used: a 0 indicates one byte and a 1 indicates two bytes.

The last byte of the g protocol control header is used for error detection. The XOR byte is used as an error check for the header. It is an Exclusive OR of the K-byte, the checksum bytes, and the control byte. It is used as a final double-check to ensure that the g packet is error-free. The g protocol uses the XOR byte because the g protocol was originally designed for error-prone phone lines.

i Protocol

The i protocol was written by Ian Taylor, of Taylor UUCP fame. It is similar in operation to the g protocol, but has the capability to transfer data in both directions simultaneously. It attempts to use a large window value whenever possible to increase the throughput of the data transmission. The i protocol uses five different packet types to identify control packets and data. Table 9.13 shows the packet types used by the i protocol.

TABLE 9.13   The UUCP i Protocol Packet Types

Packet Type	Description
Data	Data packet
SYNC	Protocol initialization packet
ACK	Acknowledgment packet
NAK	Negative acknowledgment
SPOS	Change of file position
CLOSE	Closes the UUCP session

t Protocol

The t protocol is used for transmitting UUCP packets across a TCP/IP connection. The TCP/IP connection provides a method for packet sequencing and error correction, so those features are not used in the t UUCP protocol. The t protocol uses large blocks to transfer packets. Control packets are sent in multiples of 512 bytes, whereas data packets are sent in blocks that are multiples of 1,024 bytes.

e Protocol

Similar to the t protocol, the e protocol was designed to work on TCP/IP networks. It does not perform any error correction or packet sequencing. It uses plain ASCII text to transfer the control packets. File sizes are sent as decimal ASCII numbers to the receiving computer before the transfer begins.

Taylor UUCP

The most popular Linux implementation of UUCP was developed by Ian Taylor and is called Taylor UUCP. Taylor UUCP uses a set of configuration files to define the UUCP hosts, permissions, modems, chat scripts, and communication settings. Red Hat, Caldera, and Mandrake Linux all place the configuration files in the `/etc/uucp` directory. Figure 9.5 shows the relationship between the configuration files. The configuration files use plain ASCII text to define the parameters used for the UUCP connections.

For the Linux server to communicate as either a master or as a slave with another UUCP host, the remote host must be configured in the configuration files. There is also a configuration for an "unknown" host that allows any UUCP host to connect to the server and transmit or receive files from a public directory. The following sections look at the configuration files needed by Taylor UUCP.

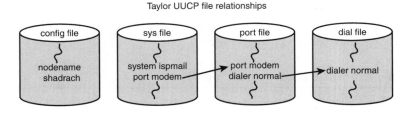

FIGURE 9.5

The Taylor UUCP configuration file relationships.

config File

The config file defines the local UUCP host. All the items in the config file will take on default values if not specifically defined in the file. Table 9.14 lists the properties that are valid in the config file.

TABLE 9.14 Taylor UUCP config File Properties

Property	*Description*
hostname	Defines the UUCP name of the node
nodename	Same as hostname
uuname	Same as hostname
spool	Location of the UUCP spool directory
pubdir	Location of the UUCP public directory
lockdir	Location of the UUCP lock directory
unknown	sys file commands allowed for anonymous UUCP hosts
max-uuxqts	Maximum concurrent uuxqt processes that can be running
run-uuxqt	When the uuxqt program will run relative to uucico
timetable	Defines a text definition of times
v2-files	Process UUCP Version 2 type configuration files
hdb-files	Process UUCP Honeydanber type configuration files
sysfile	Location of the sys file(s)
portfile	Location of the port file(s)
dialfile	Location of the dial file(s)
dialcodefile	Location of the dialcode file(s)
callfile	Location of the call file(s)
passwdfile	Location of the passwd file(s)
logfile	Location of the UUCP log file
statfile	Location of the UUCP stat file
debugfile	Location of the UUCP debug file
debug	Set debug level

9

UUCP PROTOCOL

The hostname, nodename, and uuname properties are synonyms—only one is used. They allow the UUCP config to specify the UUCP node name of the Linux server.

The `spool`, `pubdir`, and `lockdir` properties are used to override the default locations of the spool files, `public` directory, and `lock` directory. The `spool` directory is where temporary UUCP files are placed before they are transmitted and received files are placed before they are copied to their final destination. The `public` UUCP directory is a place where remote hosts can send and receive files without special host file permissions. The `lock` directory is where UUCP places its lock files. When UUCP calls a host, it creates a lock file so that no other process can call the same host at the same time.

The `unknown` property is used to define allowed behavior for anonymous UUCP hosts. If no unknown commands are listed, no anonymous UUCP connections are allowed. Normal `sys` file properties can be placed after the `unknown` command to define the behavior, similar to defining behavior for a known host. Multiple `unknown` properties can be included in the `config` file. This property is not normally needed for processing mail across a UUCP connection. The `unknown` property can be used to allow anonymous UUCP hosts access to the UUCP `public` directory area.

The `timetable` property enables you to define special times that can then be used in other configuration files. Normally, times are defined by the day and hour access is allowed. For example, `Tu0800-2000` means Tuesdays from 8 a.m. to 8 p.m.. You can use the `timetable` command to set a name for a particular time range, such as

```
timetable WorkHours Wk0800-1730
```

This creates a time named `WorkHours` that represents the times from 8:00 a.m. to 5:30 p.m. Monday through Friday. This time tag can then be used in other configuration files as a normal time definition. Listing 9.2 shows a sample config file.

LISTING 9.2   Sample Taylor UUCP `config` File

```
nodename    shadrach
logfile     /var/log/uucp
```

Line 1 shows the UUCP hostname of the local system, and line 2 shows an alternate location for the UUCP log files. This is usually all that is needed in a `config` file; it is not too complicated.

sys File

The `sys` file defines other UUCP hosts to the Linux server. Each remote host has its own section in the `sys` file. Each section defines specific parameters for communicating with the remote host. Table 9.15 shows the properties available in the `sys` file.

TABLE 9.15 Taylor UUCP sys File Properties

Property	Description
system	Defines the UUCP name of a remote site
alternate	Define alternate properties
default-alternates	If set to false, don't use any alternates
alias	Specifies an alias used for the remote system
myname	Specifies a different hostname used when calling the specific remote host
time	Specifies when the system can be called
timegrade	Specifies the times that specific grades of jobs can be run
max-retries	Specifies the maximum times the system can be tried after a failure
success-wait	Specifies how long to wait after a successful connection
call-timegrade	Specifies grades of jobs that will be processed if called at the specified time
speed	Specifies the speed of the connection
port	Specifies the type of port used from the port file
phone	Specifies the phone number used to contact the system
chat	Specifies a chat script to use to contact the remote system
chat-timeout	Specifies the time to wait for the chat script to succeed
chat-fail	Specifies text strings to indicate the chat script failed
call-login	Specifies a login userid to use for the chat script
call-password	Specifies a login password to use for the chat script
callback	Specifies that the remote system should call the local system back
protocol	Specifies the UUCP protocols that can be used with the system
send-request	Specifies that the remote system is allowed to request files from the local system
receive-request	Specifies that the remote system is allowed to send files to the local system
local-send	Specifies that files in the directories listed can be sent to the remote system by a local user
remote-send	Specifies that files in the directories listed can be sent to the remote system by a remote user
local-receive	Specifies that files in the directories listed can be received by a local user

9

UUCP PROTOCOL

continues

TABLE 9.15   continued

Property	Description
remote-receive	Specifies that files in the directories listed can be received when requested by a remote user
forward-to	Specifies systems to which files can be forwarded
forward-from	Specifies systems from which files can be forwarded
forward	Specifies systems that can be both forwarded to and forwarded from
commands	Specifies a list of commands that the remote system can execute on the local system

The system property starts the section for a remote site. Each property needed for the site is listed afterward. The port property identifies the section of the port file that is used to call the remote system. For just transferring email, none of the file permission properties needs to be defined in the sys file. If no protocol property list is specified, the two UUCP hosts attempt to auto-negotiate a common protocol to use. If both hosts are using Taylor UUCP, they will most likely default to the i protocol. Individual protocols also have properties available to fine-tune parameters.

The commands property is particularly useful as a security check. When a remote site transfers mail via UUCP, it implements the rmail command on the remote computer. To restrict UUCP access to mail processing only, you can only allow the rmail command to be executed from the remote system. Listing 9.3 shows a sample sys file.

LISTING 9.3   Sample Taylor UUCP sys File

```
system    ispmail
time      Wk0800-1730
phone     555-1234
port      modem1
speed     38400
chat      ogin: shadrach word: guitar

system    isp2mail
time      Wk0800-1730
phone     555-4321
port      modem2
speed     38400
chat      ogin: backup word: bass
```

Listing 9.3 shows two UUCP hosts defined for the local host to communicate with. Each UUCP host has its own section in the sys file. Each section defines the parameters necessary to connect with the remote UUCP host.

port File

The `port` file is used to define methods of connecting the UUCP session. Multiple ports may be defined in a single `port` file. Each new section starts with a `port` property. Properties that can be common to all the ports can be listed before the first `port` property. Table 9.16 shows the properties available in the `port` file.

Table 9.16 Taylor UUCP `port` File Properties

Property	Description
port	Defines a new connection name
type	Defines the type of connection
protocol	Defines a list of protocols that the port can use
reliable	Boolean variable used to help protocol negotiation across an unreliable connection
half-duplex	Boolean variable used to help protocols identify half-duplex connection
device	Defines a Linux device that supports this port
speed	Speed at which the port runs
carrier	Boolean variable that defines whether the port supports carrier detection
hardflow	Boolean variable the defines whether the port supports hardware flow control
dialer	Defines the dialer to use from the dialer file
service	If a TCP connection, defines the TCP port number to use
command	Defines the command to use when using a pipe-type of port

Each port definition starts with a `port` property, specifying the port name as defined in the `sys` file for the remote host. The `type` property defines the type of port to use for the connection. Table 9.17 shows the available port types.

Table 9.17 Taylor UUCP Port Types

Type	Description
modem	A modem connection
stdin	Uses standard input and output
direct	A direct connection to the remote system
tcp	A TCP/IP connection
tli	A TLI connection
pipe	A connection using a pipe to another program

9

UUCP Protocol

The modem type is used to define a modem connection to the remote host. The stdin type is often used to support a connection that uses uucico as the login shell on a Linux server (see the "Linux UUCP Implementation" section later in this chapter). The tcp type allows a Linux server to connect to the UUCP host via a TCP/IP connection. There are several different possibilities to this scenario. If the Linux mailserver shares a modem connection with a PPP link, the UUCP connection can use an established PPP link to initiate the UUCP session to the mail host. The pipe type can forward the UUCP connection to another program, specified by the command property. Listing 9.4 shows a sample port file.

LISTING 9.4   Sample Taylor UUCP port File

```
port      modem1
type      modem
device    /dev/ttyS0
speed     38400
dialer    normal

port      modem2
type      modem
device    /dev/ttyS1
speed     38400
dialer     normal
```

Each port that can be available for UUCP to use is listed in the port file. Listing 9.4 shows how two modems can be configured, each using a different connection name.

dial File

The dial file defines how a remote host will be called via the modem. The dialer property defines the start of a dial section. Multiple dialer sections can be included in the dial file, each separated by the dialer command. Any properties common to all the dialer sections can be listed at the top of the file before any dialers are defined. Table 9.18 shows the properties available for the dial file.

TABLE 9.18   Taylor UUCP Dialer Properties

Property	Description
dialer	Defines a dialer to use
chat	Specifies a chat script to use to call the remote host
chat-timeout	Specifies a timeout value to wait for a successful chat script
chat-fail	Specifies a string to watch for to indicate a failed chat script
dialtone	The string to send to the modem to wait for a secondary dial tone

Property	Description
carrier	Boolean variable that defines whether the modem supports carrier detection
carrier-wait	Specifies how long to wait for a carrier
dtr-toggle	Boolean variable that defines whether the host will toggle the DTR line before using the modem
complete-chat	Specifies a chat sequence to send after a UUCP session completes

The chat script has variables that can be used to extract values from other configuration files without repeating them in the dial file. Table 9.19 shows a list of variables that can be used with the chat script.

TABLE 9.19 Taylor UUCP Chat Script Variables

Variable	Description
\T	Phone number with dial code translation
\D	Phone number without dial code translation
\M	Do not require carrier
\m	Require carrier

Listing 9.5 shows a sample dial file that can be used in a Taylor UUCP configuration.

Listing 9.5 Sample Taylor UUCP dial File

```
dialer     normal
chat       "" ATZ OK ATDT\T CONNECT
```

Line 1 defines the dialer name that the port file will use. Line 2 defines the chat script necessary to dial the modem to connect to the remote UUCP host. The \T variable is used in the chat script to insert the phone number listed in the port file in the modem dial string.

UUCP Commands

After the UUCP configuration files are created, the Linux system is ready to communicate via UUCP to a remote host. To do this, additional Linux commands are necessary to start the connection and transfer data. The standard UUCP package for Linux is the Taylor UUCP package. It comes complete with executable commands that control the use of UUCP on the server. Some commands are reserved for system use, whereas other commands enable the administrator to control the UUCP connections. If you allow users to transfer files to and from your

9

UUCP PROTOCOL

Linux server via UUCP, the Taylor UUCP package has executables that have the ability to do that also.

uucico

The `uucico` command is used to process UUCP requests. The requests are normally queued by users, but could also be generated by the system. The job of the `uucico` command is to call the remote sites specified by the job and establish the UUCP transfer of the data. The format of the `uucico` command is

`uucico [options]`

When called with no options, the process starts in slave mode and waits for a request from a remote device. It is common to create a special Linux userid that uses the uucico program as the default shell. This allows a remote site to log in to the server and UUCP to start automatically. The options available for `uucico` are shown in Table 9.20.

TABLE 9.20   `uucico` Options

Option	Description
`-r1`	Starts in master mode
`-r0`	Starts in slave mode
`-s nodename`	Calls system `nodename`
`-S nodename`	Calls system `nodename` immediately, ignoring any required wait period
`-f`	Ignores any required waiting periods to call
`-l`	Prompts for login name and password
`-p port`	Specifies a port to use to call
`-e`	Enters endless loop of login prompts in slave mode
`-w`	After calling out to a system, enters the –e loop
`-q`	Does not start uuxqt when finished
`-c`	If no calls are allowed at the time, does not call and does not generate an error in the log
`-C`	Only calls the system specified by –s or –S if there are jobs to be sent.
`-D`	Does not detach from the terminal when finished
`-u name`	Sets the login name to `name`
`-z`	If the call fails, tries any alternates listed in the `sys` file
`-i type`	Sets the type of port used to `type`
`-x type`	Turns on debugging type specified by `type`
`-I file`	Sets `config` file to file

Option	Description
-v	Reports the version
--help	Prints a help message

To start a UUCP session with a particular remote host, enter

uucico -s nodename

where nodename is the UUCP name of the remote system. When the uucico program is run in host mode, the Taylor UUCP system uses the information available in the configuration files to establish the UUCP connection with the remote host. After the UUCP connection is established, all UUCP jobs waiting to be transferred to the remote site are processed.

uuxqt

The uuxqt command is normally called by uucico after a successful UUCP session to process any commands that were transferred using uux. To differentiate, the uux program places jobs in the UUCP job queues to be executed. The uuxqt program is the program that actually processes the jobs. Normally, this happens automatically if you use uucico to connect to the remote host.

Sometimes, if there are a lot of jobs in the queue, you might need to individually process the important jobs. You can manually execute the command to process individual jobs if you used the –q option for uucico. The format for the uuxqt command is

uuxqt [options]

When no options are specified, uuxqt processes jobs in the UUCP spool that have been placed there by either local or remote users. Table 9.21 lists options that can be used with uuxqt.

TABLE 9.21   uuxqt Options

Option	Description
-c command	Executes requests only for the specified command
-s system	Executes requests only for the specified system
-x type	Turns on debugging type specified by type

The –c option is particularly useful for mail servers. By specifying the –c rmail option, UUCP processes only mail requests. Thus, no files can enter or leave your mailserver via UUCP. The rmail executable is restricted to passing messages to the local mail transport agent on the Linux server; that agent is often sendmail (see Chapter 11, "Installing and Configuring sendmail").

uustat

The uustat command is an extremely powerful UUCP command. It can be used by the root user to examine the UUCP spool file and report on jobs waiting to be processed or jobs being processed, as well as delete or start UUCP jobs in the queue. The uustat command has many different formats depending on the function you want to perform.

The –a option is used to display all the queued file transfer jobs. The –K option can be used to kill UUCP jobs. The killed jobs can be selected by job ID, by remote system name, by username, or by many other parameters. Listing 9.6 shows a sample uustat output.

LISTING 9.6 Sample uustat Output

```
1  [rich@shadrach rich]$ uustat -a
2  ispmail.CLMcwusAADmB ispmail rich 10-02 06:57 Executing rmail
➥  Rich.Blum@isp.net (sending 387 bytes)
3  ispmail.CLNXU37AADmN ispmail rich 10-02 06:58 Executing rmail
➥  rich@smallorg.org (sending 390 bytes)
4  ispmail.CLOJEcNAADmT ispmail rich 10-02 06:59 Executing rmail
➥  prez@microsoft.com (sending 456 bytes)
5  ispmail.CLOpGOZAADmZ ispmail rich 10-02 06:59 Executing rmail
➥  postmaster@linux.org (sending 449 bytes)
6  [rich@shadrach rich]$
```

In Listing 9.6, lines 2 through 5 show mail jobs queued to be sent via UUCP. The first field is the job ID. The second field is the remote UUCP hostname, and the third field is the username of the person who initiated the job.

uucp

The uucp command is used to allow users to transfer files to users on remote UUCP computers. The format of the uucp command is

```
uucp [options] source destination
```

The source file can be specified as either a local or remote filename. A remote filename is specified in the format

```
remotehost!filepath
```

where remotehost is the UUCP name of the computer where the file is located. If the file is on the local computer, no remotehost name is required. The destination file can be either a filename or a directory name on either the local computer or a remote computer.

The success of the uucp command depends on the specified permissions in the UUCP configuration files for the location of the file being transferred and the username of the person performing the transfer.

uux

The uux command is used to execute commands on a remote computer. The requested command is queued in the UUCP spool directory as a job, and is processed the next time UUCP calls the remote computer by the uucico program. The uux command is processed as a normal file transfer, except that it is flagged as an executable file. When the command is sent to the remote computer, it is executed by the uuxqt command on the remote computer.

Linux UUCP Implementation

As mentioned in the previous section, the Taylor UUCP package written by Ian Taylor has become the standard UUCP package for Linux systems. Most Linux distributions include a binary package for it. The Mandrake system included in this book's CD includes it in file uucp-1.05.i586.rpm. You can use the RPM installer program as root to install the UUCP functions.

If your Linux does not include a UUCP distribution, there is a source code package available that can be compiled for Linux. I found one at the common Linux site sunsite.unc.edu in the /pub/Linux/systems/network/uucp directory as file uucp-1.05.tar.gz. If you have been reading along in the book, you should know the standard drill for installing and compiling Linux source code. If not, here are the basic steps:

1. Unpack the source files into a work directory:
   tar —zxvf uuco-1.05.tar.gz
2. Change to the newly created uucp-1.05 subdirectory.
3. Run the configure command to create a Makefile specific to your system. You may add parameters to configure if you want to change the default location of the UUCP configuration or log files. Type **configure —help** for instructions on how to do that.
4. Run the GNU make utility to compile the source code.
5. As the root user, run the make install option to install the binary files into their proper directories.

After the binary files are installed, you are ready to start configuring UUCP. The use of UUCP on a Linux mailserver requires knowledge of how the server will connect to the UUCP slave as well as what calling method and times will be used. The following sections show an example of configuring a Linux server both as a UUCP master and as a UUCP slave. The UUCP master will call a host UUCP site (an ISP) to deliver and check for mail. The UUCP slave will be configured to accept UUCP connections from a remote master UUCP computer. This technique can be used to move mail from a remote site Linux mailserver to the main office Linux mailserver. Figure 9.6 shows the relationship between UUCP master and slave hosts.

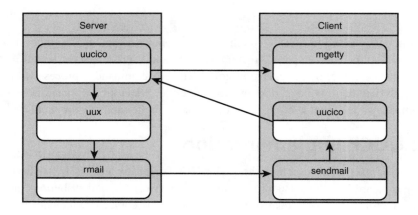

FIGURE 9.6
The UUCP SOHO master and ISP slave hosts.

Linux UUCP Master

The first UUCP file to configure is the `config` file. This is a simple task because no parameters need to be changed. Listing 9.7 shows a sample `config` file for the client.

LISTING 9.7   Sample Taylor UUCP Master `config` File

```
nodename    shadrach
```

The next file to configure is the `sys` file that defines the remote host we will call. Listing 9.8 shows a sample `sys` file set to call the ISP UUCP host during normal working hours to check for mail.

LISTING 9.8   Sample Taylor UUCP Master `sys` File

```
system    ispmail
time      Wk0800-1730
phone     555-1234
port      modem
speed     38400
chat      ogin: shadrach word: guitar
```

The chat script defines what text strings to look for and what text strings to send. This allows uucico to log in to the remote server. This sample chat script assumes that the remote UUCP host will automatically run uucico as the default shell. If that is not the case, it could be extended to look for a user prompt and then send the `uucico` command.

Next is the `port` file. Listing 9.9 shows the sample `port` file used to define the modem.

LISTING 9.9 Sample Taylor UUCP Master `port` File

```
port      modem
type      modem
device    /dev/ttyS0
speed     38400
dialer    normal
```

The last file needed is the `dial` file. This file tells uucico how to communicate with the selected port. Listing 9.10 shows a client `dial` file.

LISTING 9.10 Sample Taylor UUCP Master `dial` File

```
dialer    normal
chat      "" ATZ OK ATDT\T CONNECT
```

To test the configuration, type the following command as the root user:

```
uucico -f -x chat -s ispmail
```

This command tells uucico to dial the `ispmail` UUCP system ignoring the time restrictions, and to log the chat process. After a few seconds, you should hear the modem dialing the remote site. You should be able to look at the UUCP log file (`/var/log/uucp/Log`) to see whether the sites connected properly. The debug lines should be in the file `/var/log/uucp/Debug`.

Now that the UUCP connection is working, the next step is to make it run automatically. The best tool to use for this is the Linux cron program. The cron program runs in the background and reads a set file looking for programs to execute at set times. By logging in as the root user, type the following to edit the `cron` file:

```
crontab -e
```

Add the lines shown in Listing 9.11 to the `cron` file for the root user.

LISTING 9.11 `cron` Lines to Execute UUCP Automatically

```
4,9,14,19,24,29,34,39,44,49,54,59 * * * * /usr/sbin/touch
➥ /var/spool/uucp/ispmail/C./C.ispmailA0000
5,10,15,20,25,30,35,40,45,50,55 * * * * /usr/sbin/uucico -s ispmail
```

9

UUCP PROTOCOL

The first line creates a file every five minutes that tells uucico to poll the remote site. The second line executes the uucico program to process the queued UUCP jobs.

See Chapter 13, "Connecting the Mailserver to an ISP," for details on how to redirect mail through the UUCP connection to an ISP mail host.

Linux UUCP Slave

The UUCP slave computer will quietly wait for connections from master UUCP computers. Again, the first file needed is the `config` file. Listing 9.12 shows this.

LISTING 9.12   Sample Taylor UUCP Slave `config` File

```
nodename    ispmail
```

Next is the `sys` file. Because the slave computer will not call any remote systems and no remote systems need access to any file areas, this file becomes trivial. Listing 9.13 shows the `sys` file.

LISTING 9.13   Sample Taylor UUCP Slave `sys` File

```
system      shadrach
port        dialin
time        Never
commands    rmail
```

The `port` file to support the dial-in clients is also very simple. As the clients connect and run uucico themselves, the `port` file just needs to indicate the type of connection that will be used. Listing 9.14 shows the `port` file.

LISTING 9.14   Sample Taylor UUCP Slave `port` File

```
port        dialin
type        stdin
```

Because the slave computer does not call any remote computers, it does not need any `dial` files. The next step is to create a login ID for the remote system to log in as. Userids are kept in the `/etc/passwd` file. To allow UUCP to start automatically when the system calls in, you can specify uucico as the default shell. The line in the `/etc/passwd` file should look similar to this:

```
shadrach:x:510:510:Remote UUCP host:/home/shadrach:/usr/sbin/uucico
```

This allows the remote system shadrach to log in as userid shadrach and start the uucico program in slave mode automatically. The root user must assign a password for the shadrach userid to use, the remote host will not be able to change this password.

Summary

A relatively simple and secure way to connect the Linux mailserver to an ISP mail host is by using the UNIX to UNIX CoPy (UUCP) protocol. Although UUCP is an old protocol, it is extremely efficient in transferring mail across a modem line to a remote computer without establishing a network connection. Many ISPs support UUCP connections for mail purposes. Linux implements UUCP using the Taylor UUCP package created by Ian Taylor. It consists of configuration files and executables to configure and run a full-featured UUCP master or slave computer on the Linux server. After a UUCP connection is established, the Linux mail software can be configured to route all mail through the UUCP connection.

The sendmail Program

IN THIS CHAPTER

To properly send mail to and receive mail from other systems, the Linux mailserver must have a Mail Transport Agent (MTA) installed. The MTA's job is not to deliver mail to local users, but rather to process remote mail messages. If the MTA receives a message destined for a local user, it will pass the message off to another program that can properly deliver it. Messages destined for users on remote hosts will be sent off either to the destination host or to another system that can forward the message to the final destination. After the message is passed off, the MTA's job is done.

Many different MTA programs are available for Linux. Some were written to be more functional, whereas others were written to be more administrator friendly. The granddaddy of all MTA software on the UNIX platform, the sendmail program, is often described as the most versatile but also the most complicated MTA program available. This chapter describes the components of the sendmail program. Chapter 11, "Installing and Configuring sendmail," shows how to configure sendmail to be the workhorse of your Linux mailserver.

---

sendmail and Security

The sendmail program has been in use on the Internet for many years on a wide variety of platforms. In its infancy, it was notorious for having back doors and programming flaws that could allow hackers access to the host server. Two examples of this were the not-so-secret `debug` and `wiz` SMTP commands that sendmail recognized. Using these two commands via an anonymous SMTP session, a hacker could gain access to the host computer and use other programs to gain root access. When sendmail became popular as a production-quality MTA, the back doors were removed; subsequently, many of the programming flaws have been fixed.

Unfortunately, many mail administrators refuse to use sendmail, citing old security flaws that have long since been fixed. Yes, new flaws still pop up on occasion, but that has become common with all mail packages. The sophistication of hackers on the Internet has increased, so the sophistication of software on the Internet must also increase. One thing that sendmail has going for it is that a large base of dedicated software professionals exists. They are willing and able to correct and improve the sendmail code to increase its stability and security. There aren't too many mail packages around that can boast that.

It would be a shame to discount using the sendmail program, with all its advanced capabilities, simply because of rumors and misinformation.

---

sendmail Files and Directories

The sendmail program does not work alone. It requires a host of files and directories to properly do its job. This section lists and describes the files and directories needed by a default installation of sendmail. Often other files are required based on configuration options. Chapter 11 describes some of the alternative files used by sendmail.

sendmail Program

Name: `/usr/sbin/sendmail`

The sendmail program is the mail engine for sendmail. It is normally run as a daemon waiting for connections for incoming mail, and checking the mail queue at set intervals for outgoing mail. Alternatively, the `inetd` TCP wrapper program can configure sendmail to run on demand. This saves some server memory by not having the sendmail program in background all the time, but does decrease performance because sendmail must read its configuration file every time it starts. The sendmail program is `setuid` to the root user, so it can access directories owned by root. Non-root users can run sendmail, but will not have access to many of the default file locations, such as the default mail queue.

Primary Configuration File

Name: `/etc/sendmail.cf`

For sendmail to operate properly in your environment, you must configure it for your specific server implementation. All definitions of how sendmail processes mail are stored in the configuration file `/etc/sendmail.cf`. These definitions are called *rule sets*. sendmail uses the rule sets to parse the sender and recipient addresses in messages, and determines how to deliver the messages to intended recipients. sendmail reads the configuration file when it starts up. Any changes to the configuration file require the sendmail program to be restarted to take effect.

Message Queue File

Name: `/var/spool/mqueue`

The `mqueue` directory is created to hold the queued mail messages waiting to be processed. The owner of this directory will be the root user. sendmail ensures that all queue files stored in `mqueue` have the proper permissions that prevent users from reading mail queues. The location of the mail queue directory can be changed. It can be set by either an entry in the `sendmail.cf` file or by an option on the sendmail command line.

Queue Status Program

Name: `/usr/sbin/mailq`

The `mailq` executable file is a symbolic link to the sendmail program. When executed as `mailq`, sendmail prints a summary of the contents of the mail queue.

Create Alias Database

Name: `/usr/sbin/newaliases`

The `newaliases` executable file is also a link to the sendmail program. When sendmail runs as the newaliases program, it reads the text aliases file and creates an aliases database using an installed Linux database package. On Linux systems, it's common to create a hash database file.

Alias Text File

Name: `/etc/aliases`

The `/etc/aliases` file lets the mail administrator define mail aliases for users. The `/etc/aliases` file is the text version of the aliases hash database that the sendmail program uses. Each alias will be on a separate line, and be in the format

```
alias:    userid
```

where *alias* is the desired alias name and *userid* is the name of a valid local user on the Linux host.

After the aliases file is created or modified, the mail administrator will run the newaliases program to create the hash aliases database, often called `/etc/aliases.db`. The sendmail program reads the hash database when processing messages. If a recipient field matches a value in the aliases database, the message is forwarded to the local address specified.

Often it is advantageous to alias unused usernames to a common username to help monitor strange behavior. Normally, the Linux distribution will install many unused usernames by default. You can alias those usernames to a common username that you can log in as to check for bogus mail messages or even illegal attempts at your Linux system. Listing 10.1 shows a sample aliases file that uses this technique.

LISTING 10.1 Sample `/etc/aliases` File

```
1  #
2  #   @(#)aliases 8.2 (Berkeley) 3/5/94
3  #
4  #  Aliases in this file will NOT be expanded in the header from
5  #  Mail, but WILL be visible over networks or from /bin/mail.
6  #
7  #  >>>>>>>>>  The program "newaliases" must be run after
8  #  >> NOTE >>  this file is updated for any changes to
9  #  >>>>>>>>>>  show through to sendmail.
10 #
11
12 # Basic system aliases -- these MUST be present.
13 MAILER-DAEMON:  postmaster
14 postmaster: root
15
```

```
16 # General redirections for pseudo accounts.
17 bin:          root
18 daemon:       root
19 games:        root
20 ingres:       root
21 nobody:       root
22 system:       root
23 toor:         root
24 uucp:         root
25
26 # Well-known aliases.
27 manager:      root
28 dumper:       root
29 operator:     root
30
31 # trap decode to catch security attacks
32 decode:       root
33
34 # Person who should get root's mail
35 root:         rich
```

In Listing 10.1, lines 13 and 14 define standard email error usernames (how often have you seen the message "send all complaints to postmaster" at the bottom of Web sites?), pointing them to the root user. Lines 17 through 24 point standard default usernames that would not normally log in to the system to the root username. Lines 27 through 32 point some standard alias names also to the root username. Finally, because most good mail administrators hardly ever log in as the root user, line 35 points any mail going to the root user to the username of the administrator who logs in daily and faithfully checks his or her mail.

The Postmaster Account

With the popularity of the Web and Web servers, the postmaster account has become an important generic account. Most Web sites include it as a way for people to contact the administrator of the Web site. For busy sites, it is often beneficial to create a special mail administrator account and point the postmaster alias to that account rather than using a normal user account. Just remember to log in as the mail administrator account daily to check for messages.

Report Host Status
Name: `/usr/sbin/hoststat`

The `hoststat` executable is another link to the sendmail program. When executed as `hoststat`, sendmail will attempt to read the host statistics file and display the status of the last mail transaction to all the remote hosts where it has sent mail.

Clear Host Status

Name: `/usr/sbin/purgestat`

The purgestat executable is also a link to the sendmail program. When executed as purgestat, sendmail will delete all the information in the host statistics file.

Host Status File

Name: `/var/spool/mqueue/.hoststat`

The directory `/var/spool/mqueue/.hoststat` holds files that contain statistics for each accessed remote host. The hoststat program uses these files to show the status of remote host transactions.

Statistics Collection Switch File

Name: `/etc/sendmail.st`

The presence of the sendmail.st file indicates that the mail administrator wants to collect statistics about the outgoing mail traffic. This is initially created as a null file. Although the /etc directory is the default location, many Linux distributions, including Red Hat, Caldera, and Mandrake, change the default location to `/var/log/sendmail.st`.

Personal Mail Forwarding File

Name: `$HOME/.forward`

Each local user on the system can create a .forward file in his $HOME directory. Before sendmail attempts to pass mail for the local user to the local mail processor, it will check for this file. If the file exists and contains valid email addresses, sendmail will instead forward the message to the indicated email addresses. The email addresses will be in standard format (*username@hostname*) with one email address per line.

CAUTION

Beware of forwarding loops. If user katie has her mail forwarded to user jessica, and jessica has her mail forwarded to katie, sendmail will endlessly loop trying to forward the messages. This is often a difficult problem to troubleshoot because no messages are ever generated.

Help File Format

Name: `/usr/lib/sendmail.hf`

The sendmail.hf file produces a help file for the SMTP HELP command. The help file is in a special format that sendmail can parse while remote SMTP hosts request information using the

SMTP HELP command. As shown in Chapter 5, "SMTP Protocol," remote clients can issue either a general SMTP HELP command or specific HELP commands along with the command that they want help on. To parse the information in the help file, sendmail uses tags at the start of each line. Listing 10.2 shows a partial sendmail.hf file.

LISTING 10.2   Partial /usr/lib/sendmail.hf File

```
1  cpyr
2  cpyr     Copyright (c) 1998 sendmail, Inc.  All rights reserved.
3  cpyr     Copyright (c) 1983, 1995-1997 Eric P. Allman.  All rights reserved.
4  cpyr     Copyright (c) 1988, 1993
5  cpyr        The Regents of the University of California.  All rights
➥reserved.
6  cpyr
7  cpyr
8  cpyr     By using this file, you agree to the terms and conditions set
9  cpyr     forth in the LICENSE file which can be found at the top level of
10 cpyr     the sendmail distribution.
11 cpyr
12 cpyr     @(#)sendmail.hf 8.18 (Berkeley) 11/19/1998
13 cpyr
14 smtp     Topics:
15 smtp        HELO    EHLO    MAIL    RCPT    DATA
16 smtp        RSET    NOOP    QUIT    HELP    VRFY
17 smtp        EXPN    VERB    ETRN    DSN
18 smtp     For more info use "HELP <topic>".
19 smtp     To report bugs in the implementation send email to
20 smtp        sendmail-bugs@sendmail.org.
21 smtp     For local information send email to Postmaster at your site.
22 help     HELP [ <topic> ]
23 help        The HELP command gives help info.
24 helo     HELO <hostname>
25 helo        Introduce yourself.
26 ehlo     EHLO <hostname>
27 ehlo        Introduce yourself, and request extended SMTP mode.
28 ehlo     Possible replies include:
29 ehlo        SEND       Send as mail           [RFC821]
30 ehlo        SOML       Send as mail or terminal    [RFC821]
31 ehlo        SAML       Send as mail and terminal   [RFC821]
32 ehlo        EXPN       Expand the mailing list     [RFC821]
33 ehlo        HELP       Supply helpful information   [RFC821]
34 ehlo        TURN       Turn the operation around    [RFC821]
35 ehlo        8BITMIME   Use 8-bit data         [RFC1652]
36 ehlo        SIZE       Message size declaration    [RFC1870]
```

continues

10

THE SENDMAIL
PROGRAM

LISTING 10.2   continued

```
37 ehlo        VERB        Verbose              [Allman]
38 ehlo        ONEX        One message transaction only    [Allman]
39 ehlo        CHUNKING    Chunking             [RFC1830]
40 ehlo        BINARYMIME  Binary MIME          [RFC1830]
41 ehlo        PIPELINING  Command Pipelining       [RFC1854]
42 ehlo        DSN     Delivery Status Notification    [RFC1891]
43 ehlo        ETRN        Remote Message Queue Starting   [RFC1985]
44 ehlo        XUSR        Initial (user) submission    [Allman]
45 mail    MAIL FROM: <sender> [ <parameters> ]
46 mail        Specifies the sender.  Parameters are ESMTP extensions.
47 mail        See "HELP DSN" for details.
48 rcpt    RCPT TO: <recipient> [ <parameters> ]
49 rcpt        Specifies the recipient.  Can be used any number of times.
50 rcpt        Parameters are ESMTP extensions.  See "HELP DSN" for details.
51 data    DATA
52 data        Following text is collected as the message.
53 data        End with a single dot.
54 rset    RSET
55 rset        Resets the system.
56 quit    QUIT
57 quit        Exit sendmail (SMTP).
```

In Listing 10.2, lines 14 through 21 show the standard help message that will be returned in response to an SMTP HELP command. After that, each individual command is listed with the command on the left side and the HELP message displayed. For example, the SMTP command 'HELP MAIL' will result in lines 45, 46, and 47 being sent to the client. To test this we can log in to the sendmail TCP port and issue the SMTP command ourselves, as demonstrated in Chapter 5 and shown again in Listing 10.3.

LISTING 10.3   Sample SMTP HELP Command

```
1  [kevin@shadrach kevin]$ telnet localhost 25
2  Trying 127.0.0.1...
3  Connected to localhost.
4  Escape character is '^]'.
5  220 shadrach.smallorg.org ESMTP sendmail 8.9.3/8.9.3; Tue, 5 Oct 1999
➥19:19:39 -0500
6  HELP MAIL
7  214-MAIL FROM: <sender> [ <parameters> ]
8  214-    Specifies the sender.  Parameters are ESMTP extensions.
9  214-    See "HELP DSN" for details.
10 214 End of HELP info
11 QUIT
12 221 shadrach.smallorg.org closing connection
13 Connection closed by foreign host.
14 [kevin@shadrach kevin]$
```

The sendmail Command Syntax

The sendmail program's command syntax can often become as complicated as its configuration file. This section will describe the parameters and options that modify the behavior of the sendmail program.

The format of the `sendmail` command is

```
sendmail [flags] [address ...]
```

By default with no flags specified, `sendmail` will read the standard input until it reaches an end-of-file marker or a line with a single period (.). It will then consider that text a message and attempt to mail it to the addresses listed in the command line. This behavior mimics the normal behavior present in the Linux `mail` command. This is not the normal way to use the sendmail program. It does, however, demonstrate the versatility of the sendmail program. For the purposes of the Linux mailserver, we will use the sendmail program running as a background daemon process using command-line flags.

Flags can be added to the command line to control the behavior of `sendmail`. Flags are separated into two groups. The first group is considered parameters that can modify the sendmail actions taken, whereas the second group is considered options that override the default values of items in the configuration file. At no time are the configuration file values changed.

sendmail Command-Line Parameters

The sendmail program controls its behaviors with command line parameters. The functionality of sendmail vastly changes depending on what command-line parameters are used when it is run. By default, the sendmail program reads a configuration file when it is launched to set operating values. Command-line parameters can also be used to modify these values on the fly instead of creating a new configuration file. This section describes the parameters used and how they change the default sendmail behavior.

Message Body Format

Parameter: **-B**

The `-B` parameter tells sendmail the format of the message body. Values can be either 7BIT or 8BITMIME.

sendmail Operational Mode

Parameter: **-b**

The `-b` parameter sets sendmail's mode of operation. Table 10.1 shows the values available for this parameter.

10

Table 10.1   sendmail `-b` Modes

Mode	Description
a	ARPANET mode
d	Runs as a background daemon
D	Runs as a foreground daemon
h	Prints the persistent host database (same as `hoststat`)
H	Purges the persistent host database (same as `purgestat`)
i	Initializes the alias database
m	Delivers mail (default)
p	Prints a listing of the mail queue (same as `mailq`)
s	Uses the SMTP protocol on the input and output
t	Runs in test mode
v	Verifies names only; doesn't deliver messages

Many of the parameters require root privileges to use. sendmail prevents unauthorized users from using these parameters. For normal operation the `-bd` parameter lets sendmail work in the background as a daemon process. When testing new configuration files, the `-bt` parameter is used. The `-bt` parameter places sendmail in testing mode. This mode allows sendmail to process a rule set and produce the results of the rule set without responding to normal mail traffic on the server. This allows any user to run sendmail with the `-bt` parameter, as well as allowing users to run sendmail without conflicting, even when an existing sendmail daemon is running in background.

Alternate Configuration Setup

Parameter: `-C`

The `-C` parameter specifies a different configuration file from the default (`/etc/sendmail.cf`). When this parameter is present, sendmail will not run as the root user and will instead run as the user executing sendmail. This parameter is normally used to test new configuration files, although it can be used to specify an alternative configuration file. When testing a new configuration file with the `-bt` parameter, the `-C` parameter is normally used so that the original configuration file does not need to be changed.

Turn On Debugging Mode

Parameter: `-d`

The `-d` parameter activates debugging flags in sendmail. The multiple debugging flags each have multiple debugging levels. Multiple flags can be specified in the `-d` parameter.

The debugging flags allow for more verbose output in the normal mail logging files. Each debug flag produces more verbose logging for a particular mail function. Table 10.2 shows some examples of using the debug parameter.

TABLE 10.2 Sample sendmail -d Parameters

Parameter	Description
-d1	Sets debug flag 1 to level 1
-d1.4	Sets debug flag 1 to level 4
-d2-5.2	Sets debug flags 2 through 5 to level 2
-d12.9,15.9	Sets debug flags 12 and 15 to level 9

CAUTION

Be careful when using additional debugging modes. By adding higher debugging modes, additional logging lines are added to the log files. Debug levels that are too high can create huge log files and fill up disk space.

Set Sender Name

Parameter: **-F**

The -F parameter sets the full name of the message sender. When sendmail delivers the message to the remote site, this value will be used as the "From:" parameter in the message.

Set Sender Username

Parameter: **-f**

The -f parameter lets users set the "From:" username to a different username from what they are logged in as. Only a "trusted" user such as root or daemon can use this.

Set Hop Count

Parameter: **-h**

The -h parameter sets the total hop count allowed for the sent message. As a mail router forwards a message, the message's hop count is incremented. If the hop count is incremented past the set value, sendmail will discard the message. This option can be used to help stop mail routing loops.

Change End of Message Indicator

Parameter: **-i**

The -i parameter tells sendmail to ignore periods that are alone on a line. By default, a single period on a line indicates the end of the message. This parameter is often used when reading

10

THE SENDMAIL
PROGRAM

data from a file where it is possible to have a period on a line by itself without indicating the end of the message. When this parameter is used, the end of message is denoted by a Control+D character (ASCII 0x04).

Set Notification Option

Parameter: `-N`

The `-N` parameter sets the delivery status notification of the message. Possible values are NEVER for no notification, FAILURE if sendmail wants to be notified of a failure to deliver the message, DELAY if sendmail wants to be notified of a delay in delivering the message, and SUCCESS if sendmail wants to be notified when the message is successfully delivered.

Set No Forwarding Option

Parameter: `-n`

The `-n` parameter tells sendmail not to do address aliasing or forwarding of the messages.

Set Mail Transport Protocol

Parameter: `-p`

The `-p` parameter defines a protocol for transferring the message. Protocol values can be set as just the protocol name, such as SMTP or UUCP, or can be set as a protocol name and a relay host separated by a colon, such as `smtp:mail.isp.net` or `uucp-dom:ispmail`. When the `-p` parameter is present, sendmail will attempt to use the protocol and optional host specified to deliver the message; otherwise it follows the normal settings from the configuration file. Use this to temporarily redirect mail to another host if your primary relay host is down.

Set Queue Processing Option

Parameter: `-q`

The `-q` parameter defines methods for processing the mail queue. When the `-q` parameter is used alone, sendmail will process the mail queue once and exit.

Alternatively, a time can be specified after the `-q` parameter to indicate an interval at which sendmail will repeat mail queue processing. Times are indicated by seconds "(s)", minutes "(m)", hours "(h)", days "(d)", and weeks "(w)". For example, `-q30m` sets sendmail to check the mail queue every 30 minutes and to process any mail that needs to be sent. This format is often used with the `-bd` parameter, to enable sendmail to run in the background and process the mail queue at a regular interval.

Still another format of the `-q` parameter uses a substring match to process messages in the mail queue. These formats search in specific mail header locations for messages containing the string *string* and processes any messages found. Types of formats include

- -qIstring—Searches for string in queue identifier
- -qRstring—Searches for string in recipient's field
- -qSstring—Searches for string in the sender field

Multiple -q parameters of this type are allowed on the command line. This feature enables a mail administrator to process only certain types of mail from a mail queue without sending all the messages out. This technique is often used when a mail system has been down and lots of mail has backed up in the mail queue. Often in this case, it is advantageous to process certain mail messages before others.

Undeliverable Message Response Option

Parameter: **-R**

The -R parameter specifies what information sendmail will return if the message is undeliverable. The value for this parameter can be either "full" to return the entire message or "hdrs" to return just the RFC822 header.

Extract Recipients from Message Header

Parameter: **-t**

The -t parameter extracts addresses to send the message from the RFC822 header of the message. All To:, CC:, and BCC: lines are scanned, and receiving addresses are processed. The message is then sent.

Blind Carbon Copies

The purpose of BCC: is to forward a message to other recipients without the main recipients knowing. That is why the BCC: lines should be deleted from the message before it is sent.

Identify Message Source

Parameter: **-U**

The -U parameter indicates that the message has been sent from a Mail User Agent (MUA), and not passed from another MTA. This allows sendmail the option to handle the mail message differently depending on where it originated. Currently sendmail does not implement any message-handling capabilities based on this parameter.

Set Envelope ID

Parameter: **-V**

The -V parameter sets an envelope ID to the value provided. The envelope ID is used in an RFC 822–formatted message header to identify the message. By setting the envelope ID value from sendmail, the mailer can identify the specific messages from this host. This parameter can be used along with the –N parameter to identify messages that are undeliverable by the remote MTA.

Verbose Option
Parameter: **-v**

The -v parameter specifies that sendmail will use verbose mode. All tasks that sendmail performs will be displayed to the standard output. This parameter is used for debugging problems in mail transport, and should not be used in a normal production environment.

Set Logging Option
Parameter: **-X**

The -X parameter specifies a logfile to which sendmail can log all incoming and outgoing messages. An extremely large log file results, hence the -X parameter should only be used for debugging purposes.

End of Parameters
Parameter: **--**

The -- parameter indicates that the parameter section is finished and that any further data on the command line will be considered as addresses.

Change Option Configuration File
Parameter: **-O**

-o

The -O and -o parameters are used to replace option values specified in the configuration file. Options define characteristics of how sendmail interacts with remote sites and how it behaves on the local computer. Previously, sendmail used single-character option names. As single characters quickly ran out, new option names were created that used longer text strings to describe the option.

The -o parameter sets the value of any short (single character) format options. The format of the -o parameter is

`-ox value`

where *x* is the single character option name and *value* is the desired new value of the option.

The -O parameter replaces the value of options that use the long name format. The format of the -O parameter is

`-O option=value`

where *option* is the name of the option and *value* is the desired new value of the option. The next section, "sendmail Configuration File," describes sendmail options and how they can be used to control the behavior of the sendmail program.

sendmail Configuration File

The sendmail program needs to be told how to handle messages as they come into the server. As an MTA, sendmail processes incoming mail and redirects it to another mail package, either on a remote system or on the local system. The configuration file tells sendmail how to manipulate the destination mail addresses to determine where and how to forward the message. The default location for the configuration file is /etc/sendmail.cf.

The /etc/sendmail.cf file consists of rule sets that parse the incoming mail message and determine what actions to take. Each rule identifies certain mail formats and instructs sendmail on how to handle that message. As a message is received, its header is parsed and passed through the various rule sets to determine what action to take on the message. Rules are created to let sendmail to handle mail in many different formats. Mail received from an SMTP host has different header fields than mail received from a UUCP host. sendmail must know how to handle any mail situation.

Rules also have helper functions defined in the configuration file. *Classes* define common phrases that help the rule sets identify certain types of messages. *Macros* are values set to simplify the typing of long strings in the configuration file. *Options* are defined to set parameters for the sendmail program's operation (see the sendmail command in the previous section).

The configuration file is made up of a series of text lines. Each line begins with a single character that defines the action for that line. Lines that begin with a space or a tab are continuation lines from a previous action line. Lines that begin with a pound sign (#) indicate comments and are not processed by sendmail. Table 10.3 shows the standard sendmail configuration file lines and what they represent.

TABLE 10.3　sendmail Configuration File Lines

Configuration Line	Description
C	Defines classes of text
D	Defines a macro
F	Defines files containing classes of text
H	Defines header fields and actions
K	Defines databases that contain text to search
M	Defines mailers
O	Defines sendmail options
P	Defines sendmail precedence values
R	Defines rule sets to parse addresses
S	Defines rule set groups

10

THE SENDMAIL
PROGRAM

> **CAUTION**
>
> The sendmail configuration file is case sensitive. All lines must begin with an upper-case configuration line character or sendmail will not recognize them.

Configuration File Contents

The configuration file's main job is to support the rule sets used to process mail messages. Macros, classes, files, and databases are all used to simplify the rule writing process. After a macro, class, file, or database is defined, it is used to represent the data in a rule. This greatly reduces the amount of code required to create a rule. This section describes the format of the configuration file lines and what actions they represent to the sendmail program.

Macro D Lines

Configuration lines that start with a D define macros used in the rule sets. A macro is a long word or phrase that is represented by a single macro name, similar to environment variables. A macro name is defined as a single character, or as a word enclosed in braces ({}). sendmail uses lowercase letters and special symbols internally to predefine some macros. The mail administrator can use uppercase letters to define site-specific values. The format of the D line is

```
Dx value
```

where *x* is the macro name and *value* is the value of the macro. After the macro is defined, it can be expanded by the command $*x*, where *x* is the macro name.

Conditional macros can be created that test whether a macro has been previously defined. The format for a conditional macro is

```
$?x value1 $| value2 $
```

where *x* is the macro name to test, *value1* is the value that the macro will take if the macro name has been set, and *value2* is the value that the macro will take if the macro name has not been set. The '$|' does not have to be included in the command.

As stated previously, sendmail uses some predefined macros to substitute for commonly used phrases. Table 10.4 shows some of the predefined macro names used in sendmail.

TABLE 10.4   sendmail D Macros

Macro	Description
$a	The date of the message from the 'Date:' field
$b	The current date in RFC822 format
$c	The hop count of the message
$d	The current date in UNIX format
$f	The sender address
$g	The sender address relative to the recipient (includes hostname)
$h	The recipient host
$i	The queue ID
$j	The full domain name for the site
$k	The UUCP node name for the site
$m	The domain part of the gethostname value
$n	The name of the sendmail daemon
$p	sendmail's process ID
$q	Default format of sender address
$r	Protocol used to receive the message
$s	Sender's hostname
$t	A numeric representation of the current time
$u	The recipient user
$v	The version number of sendmail
$w	The hostname of the site
$x	The full name of the sender
$z	The home directory of the recipient
$_	The validated sender address
${bodytype}	The message body type
${client_addr}	The IP address of the SMTP client
${client_name}	The hostname of the SMTP client
${client_port}	The TCP port number of the SMTP client
${envid}	The envelope ID passed to sendmail
${opMode}	The current operation mode (using the -b parameter)
${deliveryMode}	The current delivery mode (from the DeliveryMode option)

10

THE SENDMAIL
PROGRAM

Categorize Phrases with C Lines

Configuration lines that begin with a C define classes of phrases that can be used in the rules. Classes group phrases that have something in common so that the rule sets can scan the class for matches. The format of a C line is

```
Ccphrase1 phrase2 ...
```

where *c* is the name of the class, and *phrase1*, *phrase2*, and so on are phrases that will be grouped together in the class. Similar to the D line command, class names must be either a single character or a word enclosed in braces ({}). Class names that are a lowercase letter or a special character are reserved for internal sendmail use. Mail administrators can use uppercase letters to define site-specific classes. Table 10.5 shows a list of some predefined class names used internally in sendmail.

TABLE 10.5   sendmail C Classes

Class	Description
e	Content-Transfer-Encodings (can be 7-bit, 8-bit, or binary)
k	The UUCP node name
m	The domain name
n	Set of MIME body types that cannot be encoded as 7-bit
q	Set of Content-Types that cannot not be encoded as base64
s	Set of subtypes of messages that can be treated recursively
t	Set of trusted users
w	Set of all names this host is known by

Identify Classes Within Files with F Lines

Configuration lines that begin with an "F" also define classes that can be used by the rule sets, but a little differently than the C lines. F lines point to filenames that contain the list of phrases to use in the class. The format of an F line is

```
Fc filename
```

where *c* is the single character class name, and *filename* is the full pathname of the file containing the phrases. Each phrase will be on a separate line in the file.

As with C lines, sendmail uses lowercase letters and special characters as internal class names. Mail administrators can use uppercase letters to define site-specific class names.

Define Database Class with K Lines

Like the F lines, K lines are used to define a file that contains multiple phrases used in a rule. However, K lines define a special type of file. Configuration lines that begin with a "K" define special mapped databases that sendmail uses to look up different types of information. By using a database, sendmail can access the information in the file quicker and more efficiently than the F-type files. The format of the K line is

```
Kmapname mapclass arguments
```

where *mapname* is the name of the database as used in the configuration file, *mapclass* is the type of database generated, and *arguments* are passed to sendmail to help create the database. Often *arguments* include the location of the database and flags used to help in processing the database.

Maps are referenced by the rule sets using the following syntax:

```
$(map key $@ arguments $: default $)
```

where *map* is the mapname, *key* and *arguments* are passed to the mapping function to obtain the return record, and *default* is a value to use if no record is returned.

The mapclass is the type of database that sendmail uses to access the data. Each database type has its own specific methods of indexing and accessing data. There are many different types of mapclasses that sendmail can use. Table 10.6 lists some of the more common classes available.

TABLE 10.6   sendmail K Mapclasses

Mapclass	Description
dbm	Uses the ndbm(3) library
btree	Uses the btree interface to the Berkeley DB library
hash	Uses the hash interface to the Berkeley DB library
nis	Uses NIS lookups
ldapx	Uses LDAP x.500 directory lookups
text	Uses text file lookups
implicit	Used to get default lookups for alias files
user	Uses the getpwnam() function to look up usernames
host	Uses DNS to find hostnames
bestmx	Uses DNS to find the best MX record for a host
sequence	Uses a list of multiple maps for lookups
program	Uses an external program for lookups

10

THE SENDMAIL
PROGRAM

Currently Linux supports only the `btree` and `hash` types of mapclasses. Of those two, hash database maps are the more commonly used for sendmail database maps.

Mapped databases can be created from text files by using the `makemap` command. The format used for the `makemap` command is

```
makemap mapclass outputfile < textfile
```

where *mapclass* is the type of database map to use, *textfile* is the text database file used for input, and *outputfile* is the converted database.

Header Definition with H Lines

Configuration lines that begin with an "H" define the format of header lines that sendmail inserts into the message. The header lines make use of macros and macro flags to determine the proper syntax for a mail message header, depending on the protocol used to transfer the message. SMTP hosts expect mail headers to be in a different format than UUCP hosts. The format of the H line is

```
H[?mflags?]hname:htemplate
```

where *mflags* are the macro flags that must be specified if this is present, *hname* is the name of the header line, and *htemplate* is the format of the header line using macros. The macros are expanded to their normal names before being placed in the outgoing message.

Another format of the H line will pass the message to a particular rule set if a specific header is present. The format for this is

```
Hheader:$>Ruleset
```

where *header* is the header field that will be present, and *Ruleset* is the rule set number (see the "Rule Sets" section later in the chapter). A sample of H lines is shown in Listing 10.4.

LISTING 10.4   Sample sendmail H Lines

```
1   H?P?Return-Path: <$g>
2   HReceived: $?sfrom $s $.$?_($?s$|from $.$_)
3       $.by $j ($v/$Z)$?r with $r$. id $i$?u
4       for $u; $|;
5       $.$b
6   H?D?Resent-Date: $a
7   H?D?Date: $a
8   H?F?Resent-From: $?x$x <$g>$|$g$.
9   H?F?From: $?x$x <$g>$|$g$.
10  H?x?Full-Name: $x
11  # HPosted-Date: $a
12  # H?l?Received-Date: $b
```

```
13 H?M?Resent-Message-Id: <$t.$i@$j>
14 H?M?Message-Id: <$t.$i@$j>
```

In Listing 10.4, line 1 shows a simple H line that is conditional upon a macro being defined. If the P macro is defined, which was defined earlier in this sendmail.cf as a period (.), sendmail will add a Return-Path header field using the $g macro as the data value. As you remember from Table 10.4, the $g macro will expand to the sender's address relative to the receiver. Thus this H line will cause sendmail to add the fully qualified username and hostname in the Return-Path header field of the message if the P macro flag is specified.

Mailer Forwarding with M Lines

Configuration lines that begin with an "M" define a mailer that sendmail uses to forward messages. Each different type of mailer sendmail uses must have an M line definition for sendmail to know how to use the mailer. The format for the M line is

```
Mprog,[field=value]...
```

where *prog* is the name of the mailer program, and each *field=value* pair defines attributes required for sendmail to use the mailer. Field names can use the whole field name, but sendmail uses only the first character of the field name. Table 10.7 shows the M line fields that can be used.

TABLE 10.7   sendmail M Line Fields

Field	Description
Path	The pathname of the mailer
Flags	Flags used for the mailer
Sender	Rule sets used for the sender address
Recipient	Rule sets used for the recipient address
Argv	Any arguments passed to the mailer
Eol	The end-of-line string used by the mailer
Maxsize	The maximum message length used by the mailer
Linelimit	The maximum line length used by the mailer
Directory	The working directory of the mailer
Userid	The default userid and groupid to use when running the mailer
Nice	The UNIX nice() value for the mailer
Charset	The default character set for 8-bit characters
Type	The MTS-type information used by error messages

The `Flags` field is used to identify how sendmail will use the mailer. Flags define actions that sendmail might use when calling the mailer program. Multiple values can be used in the `Flags` field. Multiple flags are written as a string with no spaces between flag values. Table 10.8 shows sample flags.

TABLE 10.8   sendmail *M* Line Flags

Flag	Description
a	Use ESMTP.
A	Use the aliases database.
b	Force a blank line at the end of the message.
c	Do not include comments in addresses.
C	Add the local domain name to received addresses without an @ sign.
d	Do not include angle brackets around route-address syntax addresses.
D	Include a "Date:" header field.
F	Include a "From:" header field.
h	Preserve uppercase in hostnames.
l	The mailer is local.
m	The mailer can send to multiple users in one transaction.
M	Include a "Message-Id:" header field.
n	Do not insert a UNIX-style "From" line.
S	Do not reset the userid before calling the mailer.
u	Preserve uppercase usernames.
U	Use UUCP-type "From" lines.
5	If no aliases are found, use rule set 5 to find an alternative resolution.
9	Do limited 7 to 8-bit MIME conversion.

Listing 10.5 shows some `M` configuration lines from a sample `sendmail.cf` file.

LISTING 10.5   Sample *M* Configuration Lines

```
1  ###   SMTP Mailer specification   ###
2  Msmtp,        P=[IPC], F=mDFMuX, S=11/31, R=21, E=\r\n, L=990,
➡T=DNS/RFC822/SMTP,
3  Mesmtp,       P=[IPC], F=mDFMuXa, S=11/31, R=21, E=\r\n, L=990,
➡T=DNS/RFC822/SMTP,
4  Msmtp8,       P=[IPC], F=mDFMuX8, S=11/31, R=21, E=\r\n, L=990,
➡T=DNS/RFC822/SMTP,
```

```
5  Mrelay,          P=[IPC], F=mDFMuXa8, S=11/31, R=61, E=\r\n, L=2040,
➥T=DNS/RFC822/SMTP,
6  ###   UUCP Mailer specification   ###
7  Muucp,           P=/usr/bin/uux, F=DFMhuUd, S=12, R=22/42, M=100000,
8  Muucp-old,       P=/usr/bin/uux, F=DFMhuUd, S=12, R=22/42, M=100000,
9  Msuucp,          P=/usr/bin/uux, F=mDFMhuUd, S=12, R=22/42, M=100000,
10 Muucp-new,       P=/usr/bin/uux, F=mDFMhuUd, S=12, R=22/42, M=100000,
11 Muucp-dom,       P=/usr/bin/uux, F=mDFMhud, S=52/31, R=21, M=100000,
12 Muucp-uudom,     P=/usr/bin/uux, F=mDFMhud, S=72/31, R=21, M=100000,
13 ###   PROCMAIL Mailer specification   ###
14 Mprocmail,       P=/usr/local/bin/procmail, F=DFMSPhnu9, S=11/31, R=21/31,
➥T=DNS/RFC822/X-Unix,
15 ###   Local and Program Mailer specification   ###
16 Mlocal,          P=/usr/local/bin/procmail, F=lsDFMAw5:/|@qSPfhn9, S=10/30,
➥R=20/40,
17 Mprog,           P=/bin/sh, F=lsDFMoqeu9, S=10/30, R=20/40, D=$z:/,
```

In Listing 10.5, lines 2 through 5 define SMTP mailers, lines 7 through 12 define UUCP mailers, line 14 defines the procmail mailer, and lines 16 and 17 define mailers used on the local host. The mailer path is defined to point sendmail to the executable file that executes the mailer. For SMTP type connections, sendmail can use an internal IPC connection to forward the mail using its own SMTP software.

Line 11 shows a special mailer that is often used for offices using UUCP connections to the Internet. The uucp-dom mailer is special in that it uses the UUCP protocol to transfer the mail message, but retains the original RFC822 message headers. We can decode how sendmail forwards messages to this mailer by reading the M line flags:

- The path (P) for the executable is /usr/bin/uux.
- The flags (F) sent to the executable are
    1. m—sendmail can send message to multiple users in one transaction.
    2. D—sendmail forwards the original RFC822 Date field.
    3. F—sendmail forwards the original RFC822 From field.
    4. M—sendmail forwards the original RFC822 Message ID field.
    5. h—sendmail preserves uppercases and lowercases in hostnames.
    6. u—sendmail preserves uppercase usernames.
    7. d—sendmail does not include any special angle brackets in the routing information.
- The Sender rule sets are rules 52 and 31.
- The Recipient rule set is 21.
- The maximum message size forwarded is 100,000 bytes.

One thing that is interesting about line 11 is what flag is not present. Notice in lines 7 through 10 that the U flag is present. This instructs sendmail to forward the message using UUCP-style From fields. Because the uucp-dom protocol does not change the format of the message, this flag must be left off.

Precedence Priority with P Lines

Configuration lines that begin with a "P" define precedence values. Each RFC822-formatted message can use the Precedence: header field to define the urgency of the message. The purpose of the Precedence field is to allow for special handling of important messages. The P configuration lines help sendmail assign a numeric priority value based on the Precedence: field text string. Mail forwarding is based on the Precedence field. The format of the P line is

```
Ptext=value
```

where *text* is the Precedence: field string, and *value* is a numeric value that sendmail uses to rank messages. Higher values indicate higher priority messages than lower values do. Some sendmail configuration implementations assign negative values to the Precedence: field values of "bulk" and "junk" to ensure that those classes of mail get lowest priority when transferring mail to remote hosts. A common message ranking in a configuration file is

```
Pfirst-class=0
Pspecial-delivery=100
Plist=-30
Pbulk=-60
Pjunk=-100
```

This configuration allows mail set to first-class to have higher priority, whereas spam messages (labeled as junk) get lowest priority.

Defining Options with O Lines

Configuration lines that begin with an "O" define options that control the behavior of the sendmail program. A large number of global options can be set. Besides specifying options in the configuration file, you can also specify them from the command line using the -o or -O parameters.

Older versions of sendmail used single-character option names. The format of the O lines using these options is

```
Oo value
```

where o is the single-character option name, and *value* is the value for the option. Currently sendmail recognizes long option names. The format for the O lines using long option names is

```
O option=value
```

where *option* is the long option name, and *value* is the value for the option. Depending on the option, *value* can be a string, an integer, a Boolean, or a time interval.

Lots of options are available to control the behavior of sendmail—too many to cover in this chapter. Table 10.9 shows some of the more common options for configuring sendmail on a standard mailserver.

TABLE 10.9 sendmail Options

Option	Description
AliasFile	File to specify mail aliases.
DefaultUser	Sets the userid and groupid for sendmail to run under.
DontBlamesendmail	Allows world-writable files and directories—very dangerous.
HoldExpensive	Allows sendmail to queue mail for expensive mailers to process when desired.
CheckpointInterval	Performs a checkpoint on the mail queue as specified.
DeliveryMode	Sets delivery mode of sendmail to interactive, background, queued, or deferred.
ErrorMode	Sets method to report errors via print or mail, or to not report them.
SaveFromLine	Keeps all UNIX-style "From:" header lines, even if redundant.
MaxHopCount	Sets number of times messages can be processed by an MTA. Discards message if number is exceeded.
IgnoreDots	Ignores dots in incoming messages. Always disabled for SMTP.
SendMimeErrors	Sends error messages in MIME format.
ConnectionCacheTimeout	Sets the maximum amount of time a cache connection can be idle.
LogLevel	Sets the log level. Default is 9.
MeToo	Sends message to username even if it is in an alias expansion.
CheckAliases	Validates aliases when rebuilding the alias database.
OldStyleHeaders	Assumes headers might be in old format using spaces to delimit names.
QueueDirectory	Specifies the mail queue directory.
StatusFile	Logs summary statistics in a file for mail status.
Timeout.queuereturn	Sets how long to wait for a message.
UserDatabaseSpec	Sets the user database specification.
ForkEachJob	Uses a separate process to deliver each job in the queue.
SevenBitInput	Strips input to seven bits.

continues

10

THE SENDMAIL PROGRAM

TABLE 10.9 continued

Option	Description
EightBitMode	Sets method of handling 8-bit data.
MinQueueAge	Only processes jobs that have been in the queue longer than a set time.
DefaultCharSet	Sets character set to convert non-MIME data to MIME.
DialDelay	Allows a delay time for dial-on-demand networks to establish the connection.
NoRecipientAction	Sets action to take for messages that have no valid recipients.
MaxDaemonChildren	Sets number of sendmail children that can process incoming mail simultaneously.
ConnectionRateThrottle	Sets number of incoming daemon connections enabled concurrently.

Some examples of options used in a standard configuration file are

```
O AliasFile=/etc/aliases
O DefaultUser=8:12
O DeliveryMode=background
O HelpFile=/usr/lib/sendmail.hf
```

This group of O lines sets specific values to commonly used sendmail options.

Rule Sets

The core of the configuration file is the rule set. *Rule sets* instruct sendmail on how to parse the incoming messages and determine how to deliver a message to the intended recipients. Rule sets use the R and S configuration lines. R configuration lines define the actual processes to perform on the message, whereas S configuration lines are used to define groups of rule sets. The following sections describe the R and S configuration lines.

Identifying Actions for Received Messages with (R) Lines

The R lines use tokens and parsing to process an incoming message to determine the proper recipient(s) and the method(s)used to send the message to the recipient(s). Each R line represents a separate rule. A rule has two parts—the left-hand side (LHS) and the right-hand side (RHS). The LHS defines what tokens to look for in the incoming message. The RHS defines how to rewrite the address based on tokens found in the LHS. The format of an R line is

```
Rlhs     rhs      comments
```

Each field must be separated by at least one tab character. Any macros and classes used in the rule set are expanded to match the parsed information. The LHS defines new metasymbols to use to parse the messages. Table 10.10 shows the metasymbols used in the LHS macros.

TABLE 10.10   sendmail Rule Set LHS Metasymbols

Symbol	Description
$*	Matches zero or more tokens
$+	Matches one or more tokens
$-	Matches exactly one token
$@	Matches zero tokens
$=x	Matches any item in class x
$~x	Matches any item not in class x

When tokens match a metasymbol in the LHS, they are assigned as macro values to the RHS part. Each new macro name has the form $n, wherein n is the numeric index of the token in the message. For example, if the LHS "$-:$+" is applied to an input of uucp-dom:ispmail, the values passed to the RHS are $1 equal to "uucp-dom" and $2 equal to "ispmail".

If the LHS metasymbols do not match the message, nothing is done with the rule set. If the LHS metasymbols do match an incoming message, the input is rewritten using the format of the RHS. The RHS also uses metasymbols as it rewrites the message. Table 10.11 shows the metasymbols used for the RHS.

TABLE 10.11   sendmail Rule Set RHS Metasymbols

Symbol	Description
$n	Substitutes token n from LHS
$[name$]	Canonicalizes a name
$(map key $@ arguments $:Default $)	Generalized key mapping function
$>n	"Calls" rule set n
$#mailer	Resolves to mailer
$@host	Specifies host
$:user	Specifies user

As shown in Table 10.9, any hostnames that are passed to the RHS enclosed with $[and $] are expanded to their full hostname to include the domain name. Also as shown in Table 10.9, one rule set can directly pass off to another rule set using the $>n metasymbol, where n is the S line identifier of the next rule set to process the tokens.

> **CAUTION**
>
> Rule sets are not for the faint-of-heart. In almost all situations, the default rule sets are sufficient to handle all the normal email requirements of a small business. New rule sets are sometimes implemented to ward off possible email problems by filtering out certain types of messages.

Forming a Rule Set with S lines

Configuration lines that begin with an "S" identify a group of rules that form a rule set. sendmail rule sets are normally identified by a numerical value. The sendmail program uses rule sets to parse the mail messages and find the recipients to forward the message to. There are six standard rule sets that sendmail uses for messages, shown in Table 10.12.

TABLE 10.12   sendmail S Rule Set Numbers

Rule Set	Description
0	Resolves a mailer, host, and user
1	Applied to all sender addresses
2	Applied to all recipient addresses
3	Turns addresses into canonical form
4	Translates internal addresses to external addresses
kj	Applied to local addresses that do not have aliases

As shown previously in the R line section, there can also be special rule sets that begin with the string check. These rule sets identify messages that will be forwarded to the error or discard mailers. Figure 10.1 shows the typical path that a message takes through the standard rule sets.

As shown in Figure 10.1, all messages are first passed through rule set 3. This rule set "cleans up" the addresses by turning hostnames into the proper canonical format. After rule set 3 is finished, rule set 0 extracts the mailer, hostname, and username from the address. It then passes the message off to the appropriate mailer system.

Likewise, rule set 1 rewrites any sender addresses, and rule set 2 rewrites any recipient addresses. That information is then passed to rule set 4 to resolve the addresses to an external format.

You can watch the various rule sets in action by using the sendmail program with the -bt option. This option tests an intended address and shows how rule sets act given the configuration file and the address that was input. Often this option is used with the -C option to test a new configuration file. Listing 10.6 shows a sample sendmail session that uses the -bt and -C options.

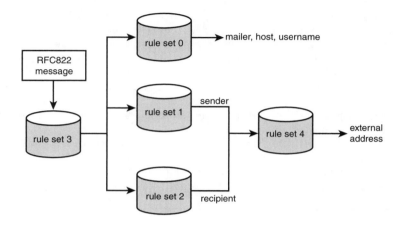

FIGURE 10.1

sendmail rule set paths.

LISTING 10.6   Sample sendmail -bt Session

```
1  [rich@shadrach rich]$ /usr/sbin/sendmail -bt -C test.cf
2  ADDRESS TEST MODE (ruleset 3 NOT automatically invoked)
3  Enter <ruleset> <address>
4  > 3,0 rich
5  rewrite: ruleset   3  input: rich
6  rewrite: ruleset  96  input: rich
7  rewrite: ruleset  96 returns: rich
8  rewrite: ruleset   3 returns: rich
9  rewrite: ruleset   0  input: rich
10 rewrite: ruleset 199  input: rich
11 rewrite: ruleset 199 returns: rich
12 rewrite: ruleset  98  input: rich
13 rewrite: ruleset  98 returns: rich
14 rewrite: ruleset 198  input: rich
15 rewrite: ruleset 198 returns: $# local $: rich
16 rewrite: ruleset   0 returns: $# local $: rich
17 > 3,0 president@whitehouse.gov
18 rewrite: ruleset   3  input: president @ whitehouse . gov
19 rewrite: ruleset  96  input: president < @ whitehouse . gov >
```

continues

10

LISTING 10.6 continued

```
20 rewrite: ruleset  96 returns: president < @ whitehouse . gov >
21 rewrite: ruleset   3 returns: president < @ whitehouse . gov >
22 rewrite: ruleset   0   input: president < @ whitehouse . gov >
23 rewrite: ruleset 199   input: president < @ whitehouse . gov >
24 rewrite: ruleset 199 returns: president < @ whitehouse . gov >
25 rewrite: ruleset  98   input: president < @ whitehouse . gov >
26 rewrite: ruleset  98 returns: president < @ whitehouse . gov >
27 rewrite: ruleset 198   input: president < @ whitehouse . gov >
28 rewrite: ruleset  95   input: < uucp-dom : ispmail > president < @
➥whitehouse . gov >
29 rewrite: ruleset  95 returns: $# uucp-dom $@ ispmail $: president < @
➥whitehouse . gov >
30 rewrite: ruleset 198 returns: $# uucp-dom $@ ispmail $: president < @
➥whitehouse . gov >
31 rewrite: ruleset   0 returns: $# uucp-dom $@ ispmail $: president < @
➥whitehouse . gov >
32 >
```

In Listing 10.6, line 1 shows using the sendmail program with the -bt option to test a configuration file, specified with the -C option. In line 4, the address 'rich' is tested using first rule set 3, then rule set 0. Lines 5 through 8 show that rule set 3 is called with 'rich' as the input. Rule set 3 calls rule set 96 to process the input, and then returns with 'rich' as its output. Lines 9 through 16 show rule set 0 in action. The input to rule set 0 is again 'rich'. Rule set 0 calls rule sets 199, 98, and 198, which are further rules used to parse the messages on the local sendmail configuration. The output of rule set 0 shown in line 16 is the mailer, local, and the address, rich. Not too exciting.

Lines 17 through 31 show a more interesting trial. Again rule sets 3 and 0 are tested using an external address—president@whitehouse.gov. Lines 18 through 21 show rule set 3 processing the input. This time the output of rule set 3 is different from the original input. Rule set 3 separated the username portion (president) from the hostname portion (whitehouse.gov) to pass on to rule set 0. Lines 22 through 31 show how rule set 0 processed the input. Many intermediate rules were called by rule set 0 before it came up with its return value. As stated earlier, rule set 0 produced the mailer that was required to send the message (uucp-dom), the hostname to forward the message to (ispmail), and the username of the recipient (president@whitehouse.gov). This shows that the sample configuration file is set to forward any external mail messages via UUCP to the host ispmail. To exit this mode, press the Ctrl-D keys.

Sample Rule Set

It might do some good to look at an example of a rule set to help understand how the configuration lines work together in sendmail. On March 26, 1999, the Melissa virus took the Internet by storm. Melissa was a Microsoft Word macro virus that used an unsuspecting victim's Microsoft Outlook directory to mail copies of itself to up to 50 other victims. A few hours after Melissa was identified, sendmail Inc., a company dedicated to the use and support of the sendmail program, released a new rule set that allowed sites using sendmail to block any suspected Melissa virus messages from entering the mailserver.

Remember that sendmail is an MTA; its job is just to forward mail. By using a rule set that did not forward a suspected virus message, mailservers using sendmail were able to stem the spread of Melissa. Listing 10.7 shows the configuration file update that was released by sendmail, Inc.

LISTING 10.7   sendmail Melissa Virus Update

```
1   HSubject: $>Check_Subject
2   D{MPat}Important Message From
3   D{MMsg}This message may contain the Melissa virus.
4
5   SCheck_Subject
6   R${MPat} $* $#error $: 553 ${MMsg}
7   RRe: ${MPat} $*     $#error $: 553 ${MMsg}
```

In Listing 10.7, lines 1 through 3 define some macros that should look familiar by now. Line 1 defines an H line that forwards any message with a Subject header to the rule set labeled Check_Subject. Line 2 defines a macro with text that was commonly found in messages infected by the Melissa virus. With the newer advent of Melissa variants, you can easily expand this to be an F line that defines a separate file containing multiple lines that can be checked. Line 3 defines another macro that is used as a return message when an infected message is detected.

Line 5 defines the start of the new rule set, called Check Subject. As defined in the H line, any message that has an RFC822 Subject field will be passed to this rule during processing. Lines 6 and 7 define the new rules to stop Melissa.

The Melissa virus was known to create bogus mail messages that included the subject field "Important Message From" and the name of the victim who sent the messages. The rule set in line 6 looks for subject lines that include that subject phrase along with zero or more other tokens (the $* metasymbol). It then forwards the message to the error mailer, with an appropriate rejection notice to the sender of the message.

Line 7 duplicates the process for messages where the subject had been mistakenly replied to and added the standard "Re:" to the subject line. Again, it forwards the message to the error mailer with a rejection notice sent to the sender of the message.

10

THE SENDMAIL PROGRAM

Although the Melissa virus did not affect the sendmail program, sendmail was able to effectively block infected messages from getting into the mailserver to infect users' Microsoft Outlook clients. This example demonstrates the flexibility of the sendmail program.

Summary

The Linux mailserver requires a Mail Transport Agent (MTA) to transfer mail to intended recipients. The sendmail program is one of the oldest and most advanced MTA packages available for the Linux platform. Configuring the sendmail program to process mail properly for your Linux environment is done with the `/etc/sendmail.cf` configuration file. The configuration file consists of rule sets that let sendmail parse incoming message headers and determine the proper recipients, and what mailers to use to transfer the message to them. Rule sets can also be used to configure mail filters to stop unwanted messages from being transferred. Concerns about sendmail's difficult and confusing configuration file should now be resolved because this chapter stepped through each configuration file process. The next chapter, "Installing and Configuring sendmail," shows an easier way to custom configure the sendmail configuration file.

Installing Email Services in Linux

IN THIS PART

Installing and Configuring sendmail

IN THIS CHAPTER

The previous chapter discussed the details of the sendmail program and its configuration file. This chapter explains how to download and install the sendmail program. Also explained in this chapter is the GNU m4 macro processor. sendmail uses the m4 macro processor to simplify the configuration file building process. Short, simple macro files can be created to incorporate the functions that the mail administrator wants to include in the configuration file. The m4 processor can parse the macro file and create a full-blown configuration file.

Installing sendmail

Over the years, the sendmail program has been through many different versions. The current version is 8.9.3. Because many upgrades to sendmail involve security fixes, it is often wise to install the latest version as it becomes available. Version 8.9.3 was released mainly to fix a TCP Denial of Service attack that sendmail was vulnerable to. After you determine your proper configuration file details, you can often upgrade the binary programs without having to re-create your configuration file. This section describes how to install the sendmail program by either the binary distribution packages included with most Linux distributions, or by downloading the sendmail source code from the sendmail Web site and compiling it.

Binary Distributions

Most Linux distributions come with sendmail binary packages. These packages contain the compiled sendmail programs and skeleton configuration files necessary to implement sendmail on the particular Linux distribution. Unfortunately, many Linux distributions do not include the latest version of sendmail. Although usually older versions of sendmail work fine for small internal mailservers, if you plan on putting your Linux mailserver on the Internet, it would be wise to download the most recent version. You can check the `sendmail.org` Web site (`http://www.sendmail.org`) to see the latest version of sendmail. If your Linux distribution comes with the latest version—great, use it! If not, you can download the latest version using the instructions detailed in the next section.

Most Linux distributions that use the RPM method of installing binary packages (Red Hat, Mandrake, and Caldera), split the sendmail package into three separate packages. The Mandrake Linux 6.0 distribution uses `sendmail-8.9.3-9mdk.i586.rpm`, `sendmail-cf-8.9.3-9mdk.i586.rpm`, and `sendmail-doc-8.9.3-9mdk.i586.rpm`. These distribution files use sendmail version 8.9.3. You can use an RPM package utility to see what files are contained in each sendmail distribution package. Figure 11.1 shows the X Window utility kpackage as it displays the information screen on the `sendmail-8.9.3-9mdk.i586.rpm` package.

Installing and Configuring sendmail

CHAPTER 11

301

11

INSTALLING AND
CONFIGURING
SENDMAIL

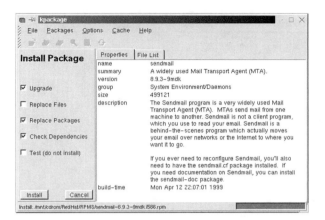

FIGURE 11.1

A kpackage display of `sendmail-8.9.3-9mdk.i586.rpm`.

Listing 11.1 shows the files included in the `sendmail-8.9.3-9mkd.i586.rpm` distribution package. This RPM package contains the main sendmail binaries and support files as configured for Mandrake Linux.

LISTING 11.1   `sendmail-8.9.3-9mdk.i586.rpm` Files

```
1   /etc/aliases
2   /etc/aliases.db
3   /etc/mail
4   /etc/mail/deny
5   /etc/mail/deny.db
6   /etc/mail/ip_allow
7   /etc/mail/name_allow
8   /etc/mail/relay_allow
9   /etc/rc.d/init.d/sendmail
10  /etc/rc.d/rc0.d/K30sendmail
11  /etc/rc.d/rc1.d/K30sendmail
12  /etc/rc.d/rc2.d/S80sendmail
13  /etc/rc.d/rc3.d/S80sendmail
14  /etc/rc.d/rc4.d/S80sendmail
15  /etc/rc.d/rc5.d/S80sendmail
16  /etc/rc.d/rc6.d/K30sendmail
17  /etc/sendmail.cf
18  /etc/sendmail.cw
19  /etc/smrsh
```

continues

LISTING 11.1   continued

```
20 /etc/sysconfig/sendmail
21 /usr/bin/hoststat
22 /usr/bin/mailq
23 /usr/bin/makemap
24 /usr/bin/newaliases
25 /usr/bin/purgestat
26 /usr/bin/rmail
27 /usr/lib/sendmail
28 /usr/lib/sendmail.hf
29 /usr/man/man1/mailq.1.bz2
30 /usr/man/man1/newaliases.1.bz2
31 /usr/man/man5/aliases.5.bz2
32 /usr/man/man8/mailstats.8.bz2
33 /usr/man/man8/makemap.8.bz2
34 /usr/man/man8/praliases.8.bz2
35 /usr/man/man8/rmail.8.bz2
36 /usr/man/man8/sendmail.8.bz2
37 /usr/sbin/mailstats
38 /usr/sbin/makemap
39 /usr/sbin/praliases
40 /usr/sbin/sendmail
41 /usr/sbin/smrsh
42 /var/log/sendmail.st
43 /var/spool/mqueue
```

In Listing 11.1, lines 21 through 26 show some of the sendmail executables located in the /usr/bin directory on Mandrake Linux. The actual sendmail program is located in the /usr/sbin directory. Lines 9 through 16 show the sendmail scripts used for starting and stopping sendmail automatically at different init levels. Lines 29 through 36 show the files necessary for the sendmail man pages. In line 43, the /var/spool/mqueue directory is created to store mail messages waiting for delivery. All the configuration, support, and manual files necessary for sendmail are included in this distribution.

To install the sendmail rpm distribution, you can use the automated kpackage installer from an X session. You can also use the rpm program from an X terminal window or the console screen. To do this enter the following as the root user:

```
rpm -Uvh sendmail-8.9.3-9mdk.i586.rpm
```

The second distribution file—sendmail-cf-8.9.3-9mdk.i586.rpm—includes the files necessary for rebuilding the configuration file using the GNU m4 macro processor (see the "Configuring sendmail" section later in this chapter). After it is installed, the necessary sendmail configuration files are located in the /usr/lib/sendmail-cf directory. You can install the rpm package using the rpm -Uvh command as shown previously.

The third distribution file—sendmail-doc-8.9.3-9mdk.i586.rpm—includes the documentation files for sendmail. The documentation files are located in the /usr/doc/sendmail directory. They include the "sendmail Installation and Operation Guide" and the "Introduction to sendmail" documents, both in PostScript format. You can also install the documentation files using the rpm –Uvh command shown previously.

Downloading from the Internet

It is always advisable to watch the sendmail.org Web site for new releases of sendmail. When there is a new release, you can download the source code from the ftp.sendmail.org FTP site. The sendmail distributions are located in the /pub/sendmail directory. Several different versions of sendmail are available for download, so be careful. The current version available at the time of this writing is sendmail.8.9.3.tar.gz. This is a UNIX tarred file that has been zipped with the GNU zip program. Alternatively, there is also another version named sendmail.8.9.3.tar.Z, which uses the UNIX compress method. Because that file is larger, most Linux users should opt to download the GNU zipped version.

Linux Compression Techniques

The Linux operating system supports multiple methods of file compression. The three most common methods are the UNIX compress utility (.Z files), the GNU gzip utility (.gz files), and the block-sorting file compression utility (.bz2 files). Often, distribution files are offered in all three methods. Linux users can download the smallest file to save download time. For .Z and .gz files, using the tar command with the –z option automatically decompresses the source code.

When the source code file has been downloaded to a working directory, the source code can be extracted using the Linux tar command:

```
tar –zxvf sendmail.8.9.3.tar.gz
```

This command extracts the source code files into a base subdirectory called sendmail-8.9.3 in the current working directory.

The next step is to compile the binary executables from the source code. You can change directories to the sendmail-8.9.3 subdirectory and type the make all command. The sendmail distribution includes a subdirectory called BuildTools that helps the compiling process. A script file named Build is used to step through the various Makefiles to create the binary distribution. The Build script determines the system it is running on by issuing a uname –a command and creates subdirectories based on the uname value that contain the built executables. On my Mandrake 6.0 system, it created directories named obj.Linux.2.2.9-19mdk.i586.

To install the newly created sendmail files, type `make install` from the `sendmail-8.9.3` subdirectory. Make sure that you are the root user when you do this, or you will not have permission to place the files in the proper directories on your Linux system.

Configuring sendmail

After sendmail has been properly installed, it must be configured to operate in the environment that your Linux mailserver must work in. Chapter 10, "The sendmail Program," described the sendmail configuration file and the vast quantity of configuration options available. If you are getting worried, don't. There is an easier way to configure sendmail than plugging through the entire configuration file line by line. sendmail uses the GNU m4 macro processor to enable a mail administrator to create a small and simple macro file that describes the sendmail features and settings desired. The macro file is combined with a sendmail skeleton macro file by the m4 processor to create a complete sendmail.cf configuration file. This section describes the GNU m4 macro processor and the format of the macro file used to create a sendmail configuration file.

The GNU m4 Macro Processor

The GNU m4 macro processor is used to create the sendmail configuration file from a set of macro files. As a macro file is read into the input, macros are expanded before being written to an output file.

Some macro definitions are built into the m4 processor program. Other macro definitions may be defined separately and included in the macro processor at run time. Besides expanding macros, the m4 macro processor can also contain built-in functions such as running shell commands, manipulating text, and performing integer arithmetic. The most current version of GNU m4 is version 1.4 and is available on most Linux distributions. Figure 11.2 demonstrates how the m4 processor reads the created macro file and parses it into the configuration file using the predefined sendmail macro files.

The sendmail configuration distribution includes m4 macro files that define commonly used configuration options and features. The location of the sendmail configuration distribution varies. The Mandrake Linux configuration distribution package is called `sendmail-cf-8.9.3-9mdk.i586.rpm`. When it is installed, it creates a subdirectory `/usr/lib/sendmail-cf` that includes the sendmail macro files. If you downloaded the sendmail distribution from `sendmail.org`, the configuration macro files are located in the `cf` subdirectory located in the source directory (`sendmail-8.9.3` for the most recent version).

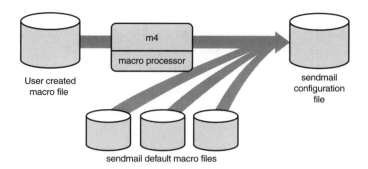

FIGURE 11.2

A GNU m4 macro processor operation.

---

sendmail and m4

Don't let this section confuse you, the sendmail program configuration file can be built entirely by hand without the help of m4. However, the sendmail developers have utilized the m4 macro processor to assist mail administrators in the configuration process. The m4 processor uses its own directives language to generate the appropriate sendmail configuration file lines. Learning the m4 sendmail directives in this section is an alternative to learning the sendmail configuration lines and creating the configuration file by hand. Generating a configuration file using the m4 macro processor is intended to be easier than creating one by hand. Often, only a short m4 macro file is necessary to create a fully functional sendmail configuration file. Knowing what features your sendmail environment requires helps to determine what m4 directives to include in your m4 macro file. If this section seems confusing, take a peek at the examples at the end of this chapter to see how the m4 directives fit together to produce a complete sendmail configuration file.

---

sendmail m4 Directives

m4 reads the input macro file and creates a configuration file based on predefined macro directives. Each m4 macro directive in the macro file expands to produce a section in the output sendmail configuration file. For example, the m4 directive

```
FEATURE(`virtusertable', `hash /etc/virtusertable')
```

produces the following K line in the generated sendmail configuration file:

```
# Virtual user table (maps incoming users)
Kvirtuser hash /etc/virtusertable
```

By knowing what sendmail features and options are required, a small m4 macro file with directives can be created. The m4 processor can then create a fully functional sendmail configuration file from the small m4 macro file. Although this example was trivial, often a single macro directive can expand to dozens of lines in the configuration file, saving time and effort.

This section describes the macro directives that are available to use when creating a macro file. The following section demonstrates how to combine the directives to produce a functional sendmail configuration file for specific sendmail environments.

> **CAUTION**
>
> The m4 macro processor is case sensitive. Make sure that all macro directives are entered into the macro file with the proper case, or they will not get processed into the output configuration file properly. Also, note that many directives use the backtick character (`) to start a parameter. This must be a backtick, it is not a normal single quote. The ending character for a parameter is a single quote ('). These items often result in errors in the sendmail configuration file.

Identify New Configuration File

Often, the first two directives used in macro files are

```
divert(-1)
divert(0)
```

The `divert(-1)` directive is used to clean out the macro buffer of any previous macro attempts. The `divert(0)` directive is used to identify the start of the new macro file.

Include Other Macro Files

Another necessary directive is the `include` directive. This directive includes lines from another macro file to be used in the current macro file. To properly process your macro file, you must include the `cf.m4` macro file usually located in the m4 subdirectory of the sendmail configuration file location. Depending on where your sendmail configuration files are located, the `include` directive should look something like this:

```
include(`/usr/lib/sendmail-cf/m4/cf.m4')dnl
```

The `dnl` at the end of the `include` directive is used to tell the m4 macro processor about line breaks. The m4 macro processor is stream based, and does not recognize end-of-line returns. Thus, to reduce blank lines in the output configuration file, the dnl tag is used to indicate the end of a directive.

Identify Operating System Parameters

Directive: **OSTYPE**

The OSTYPE directive must be defined in the macro file. It directs m4 to the proper location to find executables and configuration files dependent on the operating system. The format of the OSTYPE directive is

```
OSTYPE(`os')dnl
```

Where os is the name of the operating system on which you are running sendmail. Because this is a book on Linux mailservers, we should use the linux OSTYPE. The OSTYPE declared relates to a macro file of the same name that defines variables overridden by m4. Using an OSTYPE of linux includes a macro file called linux.m4. Listing 11.2 shows a linux.m4 file defined in the Mandrake Linux 6.0 distribution.

LISTING 11.2   linux.m4 Macro File

```
1  divert(-1)
2  #
3  # Copyright (c) 1998 sendmail, Inc.  All rights reserved.
4  # Copyright (c) 1983 Eric P. Allman.  All rights reserved.
5  # Copyright (c) 1988, 1993
6  #       The Regents of the University of California.  All rights reserved.
7  #
8  # By using this file, you agree to the terms and conditions set
9  # forth in the LICENSE file which can be found at the top level of
10 # the sendmail distribution.
11 #
12 #
13
14 divert(0)
15 VERSIONID(`@(#)linux.m4 8.7 (Berkeley) 5/19/1998')
16 define(`PROCMAIL_MAILER_PATH', `/usr/bin/procmail')dnl
17 # define(`LOCAL_MAILER_FLAGS', `ShPfn')dnl
18 # define(`LOCAL_MAILER_ARGS', `procmail -a $h -d $u')dnl
19 define(`STATUS_FILE', `/var/log/sendmail.st')dnl
```

In Listing 11.2, lines 16 and 19 redefine the locations of the procmail executable and the sendmail.st status file for this particular Linux distribution. These values will appear in the final sendmail.cf configuration file. The procmail path appears in the procmail mailer definition, and the status file path appears in the STATUSFILE option. The define directive will be discussed in more detail later in this section.

Specify Message Handling Methods

Directive: **DOMAIN**

The DOMAIN directive is used to identify special methods used to handle messages if required by the sendmail environment. Table 11.1 shows the available DOMAIN values that can be used.

TABLE 11.1   DOMAIN Values

Value	Description
BITNET_RELAY	The host that will accept BITNET addressed mail
DECNET_RELAY	The host that will accept DECNET address mail
FAX_RELAY	The host that will accept mail to the .FAX pseudo-domain
LUSER_RELAY	The host that will handle addresses that appear to be local users
UUCP_RELAY	The host that will accept UUCP addressed mail

The format of the DOMAIN directive is

DOMAIN(*relay*, `*mailer:hostname*')

where relay is the value identified in Table 11.1, mailer is the mailer type used to transport the messages, and hostname is the name of the remote host to transfer the messages to.

Identify sendmail Features

Directive: FEATURE

The FEATURE directive allows m4 to processes predefined features of sendmail into the configuration file with a minimum amount of work on the mail administrator's part. The format of the FEATURE directive is

FEATURE(`*value*', `[*options*]')

where value is the feature name included in the sendmail configuration file, and options are any options required to implement the feature. This section describes the features available as of sendmail version 8.9.3.

accept_unqualified_senders

The accept_unqualified_senders feature allows sendmail to accept mail where the FROM: header field addresses do not have fully qualified hostnames. This may be necessary if your local mailer sends messages without appending the local hostname in the FROM: field.

accept_unresolvable_domains

The accept_unresolved_domains feature allows sendmail to accept mail where the FROM: header field addresses do not have a valid domain name. In normal operation, sendmail attempts to verify the domain name of any addresses extracted from the FROM: RFC822 header field. If the domain name is not resolved, sendmail will not accept the message. If your mail gateway is unable to perform DNS name resolutions, you may have to include this feature to allow sendmail to accept messages.

access_db

The access_db feature enables the access database for sendmail. The access database allows the mail administrator to list domains and users that need special processing. This includes sites that are allowed to use the mailserver as a mail relay, or sites that need to be blocked from sending mail through the mailserver. This feature comes in handy if you identify mail spammers that need to have their messages blocked.

By default, access_db creates a database using the Berkeley hash database type, with the database located at /etc/mail/access. The default access_db values can be changed by using the options format:

```
FEATURE(`access_db', `db [options]')
```

where db is the database map type, and options are any options required to create the database. For example, the default database could be created using the following directive:

```
FEATURE(`access.db', `hash -o /etc/mail/access')
```

This directive creates a hash database at the default location of /etc/mail/access. Because the type of the database is 'hash', the Linux makemap function must be used to create the hash database from a text file. The text file contains a list of domain names or IP addresses and actions. Each specific location must be tagged as to the action that sendmail should take. Table 11.2 shows the tags that can be used in the access database.

TABLE 11.2   Access Database Tags

Tag	Description
OK	Accept mail even if other rules might reject it
RELAY	Accept mail from the specified domain or destined to the specified domain for relay
REJECT	Refuse any messages with the specified sender or recipient and send an error message
DISCARD	Refuse any messages with the specified sender or recipient without any error messages
nnn text	Refuse any messages with the specified sender or recipient and send a message with RFC821 error message number *nnn* and *text*

Listing 11.3 shows a sample access text database that can be used to block mail from specific locations.

LISTING 11.3 Sample Access Text Database

```
1  spammer@ispmail.net      REJECT
2  microsoft.com            DISCARD
3  linux.org                OK
4  smallorg.org             RELAY
5  198.162.10               550 Sorry, I can't relay mail for your domain
```

In Listing 11.3, line 1 shows that any mail message received from or destined to the address spammer@ispmail.net will be rejected. Line 2 indicates that any messages sent to or received from anyone at microsoft.com will be silently discarded. In line 3, any message from anyone at linux.org will be accepted. Line 4 shows an example of allowing the mailserver to relay messages from hosts in a subdomain. Line 5 shows an example of using the access_db to block mail coming from a specific IP subnet and return a specific SMTP error message.

To create the access database from the access.txt file, type the following command:

```
makemap hash /etc/mail/access < /etc/mail/access.txt
```

The Linux makemap utility will create a hash database from the text file for sendmail to use.

allmasquerade

The allmasquerade feature is used if masquerading is being used by the sendmail configuration (see the "MASQUERADE_AS" section later in the chapter). If masquerading is being used, the allmasquerade feature will cause recipient addresses to also show as being from the host defined in the MASQUERADE_AS directive. Be careful when using this feature because it can confuse sendmail if you are using local aliases. This feature is often used when the mailserver is masquerading multiple hosts.

always_add_domain

The always_add_domain feature is used to include the local host domain to all addresses even if the messages are just being delivered to local users. By default, messages sent to local users from other local users do not include the hostname in the message address fields.

bitdomain

The bitdomain feature allows sendmail to look up BITNET hosts in a lookup table defined in the directive. The format of this directive is

```
FEATURE(`bitdomain', `db [options]')
```

where *db* is the database map type used, and *options* are any options required to create and access the database. The default values are the hash map type and the filename `/etc/bitdomain.db`.

bestmx_is_local

The `bestmx_is_local` feature allows sendmail to accept mail as if it were locally addressed from hosts that use this mailserver as the best possible MX record. The format for this directive is

```
FEATURE(`bestmx_is_local', `domains ...')
```

If *domains* are listed, the feature will be limited to the listed domains.

blacklist_recipients

The `blacklist_recipients` feature allows sendmail to include lists of users who should not receive mail to the access database described previously in the `access_db` feature. This expands on the `access_db` feature because you may blacklist a single email address or hostnames as well as domains.

domaintable

The `domaintable` feature allows sendmail to create a domain name database to map domain names. This is not an ordinary function, although there may be instances where you want to change a domain name on-the-fly (such as if you recently changed domain names and your clients forget). This feature creates a database based on a map type and a default location, which by default are the hash map type and `/etc/domain`. The first field of the text database should be the old domain name, with the second field being the new domain name. As always, use the makemap program to create the mapped database.

genericstable

The `genericstable` feature allows sendmail to create a table of usernames and/or domain names that allow sendmail to change names on-the-fly. Again, this is also not an ordinary function, but may come in handy if an email system is in the process of changing either usernames or domain names. As in the other database features, a map type and options can be specified to create the database, and the makemap program needs to be used to convert a text database into the mapped database.

limited_masquerade

The `limited_masquerade` feature allows sendmail to selectively use the masquerade feature. Instead of using the masquerade feature on all hostnames listed in the Cw or Fw configuration lines, `limited_masquerade` only masquerades hostnames in the DM configuration lines.

local_lmtp

The `local_lmtp` feature allows sendmail to use an LMTP capable mailer when delivering local mail. Usually, this is not the case on Linux systems, so this feature is often not used.

local_procmail

The `local_procmail` feature tells sendmail to use the procmail program as the local mailer. This feature is often used on Linux mailservers because the procmail program is normally included in Linux distributions. The format of this directive is

```
FEATURE(`local_procmail', `pathname')
```

where *pathname* is the location of the procmail program. The default location is the `PROCMAIL_MAILER_PATH` variable as defined in the `OSTYPE` directive. By default, this is `/usr/local/bin/procmail`. As shown in Listing 11.2, Mandrake Linux changes this value to `/usr/bin/procmail`.

loose_relay_check

The `loose_relay_check` feature changes the method that sendmail uses when handling mail addresses that use the `%` symbol. This has become an obsolete method of addressing mail, so this feature is normally not necessary.

mailertable

The `mailertable` feature allows sendmail to create a database of hosts describing the methods required to transport mail to them. The format of the `mailertable` directive is

```
FEATURE(`mailertable', `db [options]')
```

where *db* is the database map type, and *options* are any options required to create and access the database. As in the other database features, `mailertable` uses the makemap program to create the mapped database from a text file. The format of the text file is

```
host     mailer:domain
```

where *host* is the destination host or domain name, *mailer* is the mailer type required to transport the message, and *domain* is the remote host to forward the message to. The `mailertable` database can forward messages destined for either a particular host or for an entire domain to a remote host. This feature is particularly useful in UUCP sites that need to create a database of where to forward messages to hosts that are not directly connected via the UUCP links.

masquerade_entire_domain

The `masquerade_entire_domain` feature allows sendmail to masquerade any messages coming from hosts within a domain rather than just messages coming from the mailserver host. If the mailserver is acting as a mail gateway for an entire domain of hosts, this feature allows all the users on all the hosts in the domain to use the masqueraded domain name.

For example, if there are three mail servers in a domain—`shadrach.smallorg.org`, `meshach.smallorg.org`, and `abednego.smallorg.org`—any mail messages sent through the mail gateway from a user on any of the three mail servers would not have the original host-name in the addresses part. Instead it would include the single masquerade name, which could be set to `smallorg.org`. This is a handy way to hide individual mailservers on a large network.

masquerade_envelope

The `masquerade_envelope` feature allows sendmail to use the masquerade domain name on the envelope sender and recipient as well as any header fields.

nocanonify

The `nocanonify` feature tells sendmail not to attempt to pass addresses to the rule sets to add the fully qualified host domain name to the address. This is a common feature for email gateways because the messages sent to them usually already have the full email address included. Further processing of the address is not necessary.

nodns

The `nodns` feature has been deprecated from sendmail 8.9.3. You may still encounter it in some older macro files, so it is still worth knowing about. The `nodns` feature indicates that the mailserver does not use DNS to look up hostnames. Now if you use this feature, the m4 processor reports the following error message:

```
FEATURE(nodns) is no-op.
Use ServiceSwitchFile (/etc/service.switch) if your OS does not provide its own
instead.
```

In sendmail version 8.9.3, hostname lookups attempt to follow the order set by the operating system's `/etc/service.switch` file. In Linux, this file is normally located at `/etc/nsswitch.conf`. The variable `host` lists the order in which both Linux and sendmail will attempt to resolve hostnames.

nouucp

The `nouucp` feature tells sendmail not to attempt to change UUCP-formatted addresses but to keep them "as-is."

nullclient

The `nullclient` feature is usually used alone in a macro file for a special case. This feature tells sendmail that the mailserver is really a workstation that does not do mail processing, but instead passes any mail (including mail to "local" users) to another mailserver. The only other feature that may be used with the `nullclient` feature is the `nocanonify` feature described previously.

If you use Linux or other UNIX workstations on your network, this is a great feature. If users are accustomed to moving around to different workstations throughout the day, it would be difficult to find a host and username to use to send messages to. By establishing a central mailserver and pointing each of the workstations to that mailserver, there becomes a common location to send messages to. Each user would then send messages to other users on the central mailserver, even if the recipient has an account on the same workstation. Users could then retrieve their mail from the central mailserver from whichever workstation they happened to be using.

The format of the `nullclient` directive is

```
FEATURE(`nullclient', `address')
```

where *address* is the hostname of the central mailserver. This address can be entered as a numeric IP address to avoid any DNS problems with the workstation. If a numeric IP address is used, it must be enclosed in square brackets (`[]`).

promiscuous_relay

The `promiscuous_relay` feature allows sendmail to accept messages from hosts outside your domain and forward them to other hosts outside your domain. By default, sendmail will not forward messages from one external domain to another external domain. Spammers rely on this feature to help hide their original location. Turning on `promiscuous_relay` is extremely dangerous if your Linux mailserver is constantly connected to the Internet. Eventually, someone will find you and exploit your mailserver for spamming purposes. A better method is to use one of the controlled relay features described later, or the `access_db` feature described earlier.

rbl

The `rbl` feature allows sendmail to reject messages based on an Internet-wide spammers list (how convenient). The Realtime Blackhole List is maintained on server `rbl.maps.vix.com`. sendmail will query this server to determine whether a username or hostname has been blacklisted on the Internet. You can find out more about the RBL by visiting the Web site `http://maps.vix.com/rbl/`.

redirect

The `redirect` feature allows sendmail to return an error message for users whose addresses have been identified as being redirected to another host using the `.REDIRECT` tag.

relay_based_on_MX

The `relay_based_on_MX` feature allows sendmail to accept an incoming message based on the DNS MX record for the hostname in the recipient header fields. This feature can be used to allow your mailserver to accept mail for other hosts as long as they point their MX records to your mailserver in the DNS configuration (see Chapter 4, "DNS and Domain Names").

relay_entire_domain

The `relay_entire_domain` feature allows sendmail to accept mail messages destined from any host in your domain. This feature can be used to create a central mail gateway where messages for any host in your domain will be relayed through a central mailserver.

relay_hosts_only

The `relay_hosts_only` feature allows sendmail to use hostnames in the `access_db` database and declare them with the `RELAY` tag. Normally, only domain names can be used in the `access_db` database (see the `access_db` feature described earlier).

relay_local_from

The `relay_local_from` feature allows sendmail to relay messages that appear to be coming from the local host. This feature can be handy for users using remote clients and forwarding mail using SMTP through your mailserver. By default, the clients can use the local host domain name as the sender address. Unfortunately, spammers can also use this feature to fake your local domain name on their emails and push them through your mailserver.

smrsh

The `smrsh` feature instructs sendmail to use the restricted `smrsh` shell instead of the normal `/bin/sh` shell on the mailserver. This helps the mail administrator control what programs can be run through email.

stickyhost

The `stickyhost` feature changes the way sendmail handles messages that use the local domain name in the address. Normally messages sent to a user at the local host are matched against the user database. By using the `stickyhost` feature, you can distinguish between the email addresses `user` and `user@localhost`.

use_ct_file

The `use_ct_file` feature allows sendmail to read a file of trusted users for the `-f` command-line parameter (see Chapter 10, "The sendmail Program"). By default, the filename is `/etc/sendmail.ct`. To change the default filename, you can redefine the `confCT_FILE` variable.

use_cw_file

The `use_cw_file` feature allows sendmail to read a file of alternate names for the mailserver. By default, the filename is `/etc/sendmail.cw`. If you want to change the location of the filename, you can redefine the `confCW_FILE` variable (see the "Specify sendmail Options" section below).

uucpdomain

The uucpdomain feature allows sendmail to create and use a mapped database of UUCP hosts. This feature uses the same techniques as the domaintable feature to map old UUCP hostnames to new UUCP hostnames. The default location of the mapped database is /etc/uucpdomain.db. As with the domaintable feature, this is not a frequently used sendmail feature unless you are changing UUCP hostnames.

virtusertable

The virtusertable feature allows sendmail to alias users from other domains and directs the mail messages to a specific location. The receiving location can be an individual or another mailserver. This feature is often used to virtually host multiple domains on the same mailserver. The format of the virtusertable directive is

```
FEATURE(`virtusertable', `db [options]')
```

where *db* is the database map type, and *options* are any options required to create and access the database. The default is the Berkeley hash database map type using the /etc/virtusertable database file. The format of the text virtusertable file is

```
alias     location
```

where *alias* is the virtual alias that will be hosted, and *location* is the hostname or email address sendmail will send messages to.

This feature can be used to redirect mail for an entire domain to a specific host or userid, as well as redirect mail for a single user to another userid. Listing 11.4 shows some examples of the virtusertable values.

Listing 11.4 Sample virtusertable Text File

```
1  @smallorg.org            mailbox@ispmail.net
2  @anotherorg.org          %1@smallorg.org
3  webmaster@smallorg.org   rich@smallorg.org
```

In Listing 11.4, line 1 shows an example of redirecting all mail for the domain smallorg.org to a single mailbox called mailbox@ispmail.net. This technique has become popular with ISPs because they can give a customer a single mailbox to deliver any messages destined to an entire domain. The messages can then be downloaded using the POP3 protocol (see Chapter 6, "POP3 Protocol") and redistributed to the proper userid on the domain mailserver (see Chapter 13, "Connecting the Mailserver to an ISP").

Line 2 shows an example of redirecting messages for one host to another. The %1 variable is used as a token to replicate the username in the first address. Thus, a message destined to prez@anotherorg.org would be redirected to prez@smallorg.org.

Installing and Configuring sendmail

CHAPTER 11

317

11

INSTALLING AND
CONFIGURING
SENDMAIL

Line 3 shows an example of redirecting a single user mailbox to another location.

Specify sendmail Options

Directive: `define`

The `define` directive is used to set specific option values in the sendmail configuration file. Many of the sendmail configuration options can be overridden using the `define` directive. The format of the `define` directive is

```
define(`option', `value')
```

where *option* is the option to be defined, and *value* is the new value for the option. Configuration file option names are usually preceded by `'conf'`.

The most common option that you may have to override for a Linux mailserver is the `SMART_HOST` option. This allows sendmail to declare a remote host that will receive any mail messages that are not for the local host. The format of the `SMART_HOST` options directive is

```
define(`SMART_HOST', `mailer:host')
```

where *mailer* is the mail protocol needed to transport the message, and *host* is the hostname of the relaying host.

Specify Alternate Mail Host Name

Directive: `MASQUERADE_AS`

The `MASQUERADE_AS` directive is used to allow sendmail to pretend to be something else. The format of the `MASQUERADE_AS` directive is

```
MASQUERADE_AS(`hostname')
```

where *hostname* is a fully qualified host and/or domain name. sendmail will replace the hostname value in all outgoing messages with the `MASQUERADE_AS` hostname value. This includes the RFC822 "`FROM:`" header fields in the message.

Although at first it may seem odd to want to pretend to be a different host, the `MASQUERADE_AS` directive is useful. It has become a common Internet occurrence to use domain names as email addresses. For example, the address `prez@smallorg.org` is "cleaner" than having to use `prez@mailhost1.smallorg.org`. The `MASQUERADE_AS` directive allows this to happen.

By using the domain name as the `MASQUERADE_AS` value, sendmail will replace the normal hostname of the mailserver with the domain name. Thus the `FROM:` header fields will show the cleaner address rather than the normal full hostname address. Of course the DNS MX record for the domain must point to the mailserver or the return address will not work properly (see Chapter 13, "Connecting the Mailserver to an ISP").

Define Message Transport Systems

Directive: **MAILER**

The MAILER directives define mail systems that will be used by sendmail to transport messages. Each protocol used to transport mail must be defined by a MAILER directive. The format of the MAILER directive is

```
MAILER(`mailer')
```

where *mailer* is the name of the mailer type used. Table 11.3 lists the MAILER types that are available in sendmail.

TABLE 11.3   sendmail MAILER Types

Mailer	Description
cyrus	Defines cyrus and cyrusbb mailers.
fax	Defines a facsimile mailer.
local	Defines the local and prog mailers. This is included automatically.
mail11	Defines the DECnet mail11 mailer.
phquery	Defines the phquery program.
pop	Defines the POP3 mailer
procmail	Defines the procmail mailer.
smtp	Defines the SMTP mailer.
uucp	Defines the UUCP mailer.
usenet	Defines the Usenet network news mailer.

All mailers used should be declared at the end of the macro file. Also, if you declare both the smtp and uucp mailers, you must declare the smtp mailer first or the uucp-dom (sending smtp formatted mail across a UUCP connection) function won't work properly.

Creating the sendmail.cf File

When the configuration macro file has been built, it can be run through the GNU m4 macro processor and the output redirected to a test configuration file. The format for doing this is

```
m4 test.mc > test.cf
```

The output of this command is the test.cf file, which is a complete sendmail configuration file. In the next section of this chapter, we will create some sample configuration files by running the m4 macro processor on our created macro file and redirecting the output to a test configuration file.

Afterwards, you can test the newly created configuration file using the sendmail program's –bt and –C options as shown in Chapter 10, "The sendmail Program." If the configuration file produces the results you want, back up the current /etc/sendmail.cf file and copy the new configuration file to that location. Because the sendmail program only reads the configuration file when it first starts up, you may need to send a SIGHUP signal to the currently running sendmail program to force it to read the new configuration file. Listing 11.5 shows an example of this procedure.

LISTING 11.5   Sending a SIGHUP to the sendmail Program

```
1  [carol@shadrach carol]$ su
2  Password:
3  [root@shadrach carol]# ps ax | grep sendmail
4  14061 ?        S     0:00 sendmail: accepting connections on port 25
5  26666 pts/0    S     0:00 grep sendmail
6  [root@shadradh carol]# kill -HUP 14061
7  [root@shadrach carol]# ps ax | grep sendmail
8  26667 ?        S     0:00 sendmail: accepting connections on port 25
9  26670 pts/0    S     0:00 grep sendmail
10 [root@shadrach carol]#
```

Sample sendmail Configurations

Creating sendmail configuration files using m4 macro files is simple and straightforward. Knowing what directives to include in the macro files for specific mailserver installations is the difficult part. This section describes several mailserver environments and sample macro files that would create configuration files necessary to process mail messages in the given environment.

Simple Linux Workstation Configuration

When a Linux workstation is connected to an office network, it must know how to send mail to other users on other workstations, as well as send mail to external users. The easiest way to accomplish this is to use a central mailserver that everyone sends mail to. This mail "hub" should handle the local in-house users' mailboxes, as well as be the mail gateway for the office to route any external mail to the ISP. Figure 11.3 shows how this scenario is set up.

Under this scenario, a Linux workstation forwards all mail messages directly to the mail hub, whether they are intended for local in-house users or external users. Listing 11.6 shows a sample sendmail macro file that can be used to generate a configuration file for the workstation.

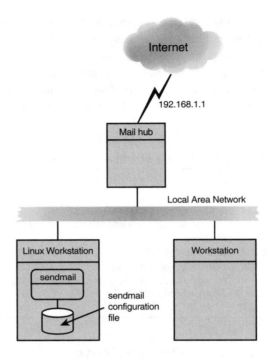

FIGURE 11.3
The Linux workstation mail setup.

LISTING 11.6   Sample Linux Workstation Macro File

```
1  divert(-1)
2  divert(0)
3  include(`/usr/lib/sendmail-cf/m4/cf.m4')dnl
4  OSTYPE(`linux')dnl
5
6  FEATURE(`nullclient', `[192.168.1.1]')dnl
```

In Listing 11.6, lines 1 through 4 show the standard macro file beginning directives. Line 6 uses the `nullclient` feature. This indicates that sendmail on this Linux system will forward all mail messages to the IP address `192.168.1.1`. This configuration is common for using a Linux workstation to send messages through a mailhub.

By saving the macro file in Listing 11.6 as `test1.mc`, a test sendmail configuration file is generated by typing

```
m4 test1.mc > test1.cf
```

Installing and Configuring sendmail

CHAPTER 11

321

11

INSTALLING AND
CONFIGURING
SENDMAIL

The output configuration file, test1.cf, can be tested using the sendmail program. Listing 11.7 demonstrates a test of this file.

LISTING 11.7   Testing the Linux Workstation Configuration File

```
1  [carol@shadrach carol]$ /usr/sbin/sendmail -bt -C test1.cf
2  ADDRESS TEST MODE (ruleset 3 NOT automatically invoked)
3  Enter <ruleset> <address>
4  > 3,0 rich
5  rewrite: ruleset   3   input: rich
6  rewrite: ruleset   3 returns: rich @ [ 192 . 168 . 1 . 1 ]
7  rewrite: ruleset   0   input: rich @ [ 192 . 168 . 1 . 1 ]
8  rewrite: ruleset   0 returns: $# nullclient $@ [ 192 . 168 . 1 . 1 ]
➥ $: rich @ [ 192 . 168 . 1 . 1 ]
9  > 3,0 rich@otherhost.org
10 rewrite: ruleset   3   input: rich @ otherhost . org
11 rewrite: ruleset   3 returns: rich @ otherhost . org
12 rewrite: ruleset   0   input: rich @ otherhost . org
13 rewrite: ruleset   0 returns: $# nullclient $@ [ 192 . 168 . 1 . 1 ]
➥ $: rich @ otherhost . org
14 >
15 [carol@shadrach carol]$
```

In Listing 11.7, line 1 shows the sendmail command used to test the newly generated configuration file. The sendmail test mode allows the mail administrator to perform what-if situations with the test configuration file. Line 4 shows a test using sendmail rules 3 and 0 on a local email address. Line 8 shows the final results from the sendmail configuration file. The message will be forwarded to the user rich on the remote host 192.168.1.1, just as we wanted. As a final test, a remote email address is tested in line 9. Line 13 shows that the result is for sendmail to forward the complete message to the 192.168.1.1 mail host. This behavior matches what we expected from the nullclient feature in the macro file. To exit the sendmail test mode, press Control+D. After you have a proper configuration file, you can replace the current configuration file—normally located at /etc/sendmail.cf—with the new one and restart the sendmail program.

Full-Time Internet Connection Mailserver

The second scenario is a Linux mailserver connected to the Internet all the time via a dedicated connection. Because the Internet connection is full time, this server can forward mail for external users directly to the destination mailserver as defined in the DNS MX record. Figure 11.4 shows how this scenario is set up.

Because the mailserver is on a dedicated Internet connection, precautions need to be made to ensure that spammers can't use the mailserver to forward their email messages. However, because this is the mail gateway for internal users to send mail out to the Internet, it should allow domain clients access to relay messages. Listing 11.8 shows a sample macro file that will produce the necessary sendmail configuration file.

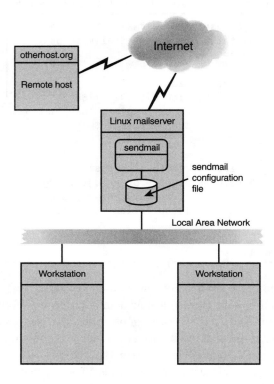

FIGURE 11.4

A Linux mailserver on a dedicated Internet connection.

LISTING 11.8   Sample Dedicated Linux Mailserver Macro File

```
1  divert(-1)
2  divert(0)dnl
3  include(`/usr/lib/sendmail-cf/m4/cf.m4')dnl
4  OSTYPE(`linux')dnl
5
6  FEATURE(`allmasquerade')dnl
7  FEATURE(`masquerade_envelope')dnl
8  FEATURE(`always_add_domain')dnl
9  FEATURE(`virtusertable')dnl
10 FEATURE(`local_procmail')dnl
```

Installing and Configuring sendmail

CHAPTER 11

323

11

INSTALLING AND
CONFIGURING
SENDMAIL

```
11 FEATURE(`access_db')dnl
12 FEATURE(`blacklist_recipients')dnl
13
14 MASQUERADE_AS(`smallorg.org')dnl
15
16 MAILER(`smtp')dnl
17 MAILER(`procmail')dnl
```

In Listing 11.8, lines 6 through 12 define features needed by the mailserver for this environment. Line 11 creates an access database that can contain the domain name or the subnet IP address of the local network. This allows local users to relay messages intended for external users through the mail gateway. Line 14 sets the masquerade name as the domain name of the organization. This sets all mail messages as coming from the domain name rather than the hostname. After using the m4 macro processor to generate a test sendmail configuration file as before, Listing 11.9 shows a test of the new configuration file.

LISTING 11.9   Testing the Dedicated Linux Mailserver Configuration File

```
1  [kevin@shadrach kevin]$ /usr/sbin/sendmail -bt -C test2.cf
2  ADDRESS TEST MODE (ruleset 3 NOT automatically invoked)
3  Enter <ruleset> <address>
4  > 3,0 rich@otherhost.org
5  rewrite: ruleset   3   input: rich @ otherhost . org
6  rewrite: ruleset  96   input: rich < @ otherhost . org >
7  rewrite: ruleset  96 returns: rich < @ otherhost . org >
8  rewrite: ruleset   3 returns: rich < @ otherhost . org >
9  rewrite: ruleset   0   input: rich < @ otherhost . org >
10 rewrite: ruleset 199   input: rich < @ otherhost . org >
11 rewrite: ruleset 199 returns: rich < @ otherhost . org >
12 rewrite: ruleset  98   input: rich < @ otherhost . org >
13 rewrite: ruleset  98 returns: rich < @ otherhost . org >
14 rewrite: ruleset 198   input: rich < @ otherhost . org >
15 rewrite: ruleset  95   input: < > rich < @ otherhost . org >
16 rewrite: ruleset  95 returns: rich < @ otherhost . org >
17 rewrite: ruleset 198 returns: $# esmtp $@ otherhost . org $:
   ➥ rich < @ otherhost . org >
18 rewrite: ruleset   0 returns: $# esmtp $@ otherhost . org $:
   ➥ rich < @ otherhost . org >
19 >
20 [kevin@shadrach kevin]$
```

In Listing 11.9, line 1 shows the command to test the new configuration file generated from the macro file in Listing 11.8. Line 4 shows testing a remote email address using rule sets 3 and 0. The final result is shown in line 18; the message would be sent directly to the receiving mail host using ESTMP, just as we wanted.

Part-Time Internet Connection Mailserver

The third scenario is using the Linux mailserver as a mail gateway with a dial-up PPP connection to the Internet. In this scenario, the Linux mailserver forwards any messages destined for external hosts to a common mail gateway, or "smart host." Figure 11.5 shows how this scenario is set up.

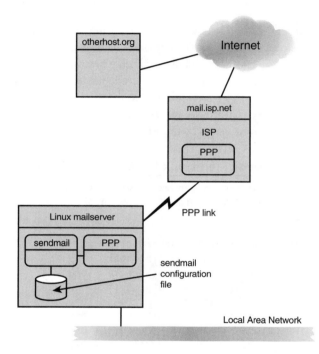

FIGURE 11.5

A Linux mailserver on a part-time Internet connection.

The main detail to configure in this scenario is the smart host necessary to forward any outgoing mail messages. Because the dial-up connection supports the IP protocol, you can still use SMTP to send messages to the smart host. Listing 11.10 shows a sample macro file that would create a sendmail configuration file to support this environment.

LISTING 11.10 Sample Part-Time Linux Mailserver Macro File

```
1   divert(-1)
2   divert(0)dnl
3   include(`/usr/lib/sendmail-cf/m4/cf.m4')dnl
4   OSTYPE(`linux')dnl
```

Installing and Configuring sendmail

CHAPTER 11

325

11

INSTALLING AND
CONFIGURING
SENDMAIL

```
 5
 6  FEATURE(`allmasquerade')dnl
 7  FEATURE(`masquerade_envelope')dnl
 8  FEATURE(`always_add_domain')dnl
 9  FEATURE(`virtusertable')dnl
10  FEATURE(`local_procmail')dnl
11  FEATURE(`access_db')dnl
12  FEATURE(`blacklist_recipients')dnl
13
14  MASQUERADE_AS(`smallorg.org')dnl
15
16  MAILER(`smtp')dnl
17  MAILER(`procmail')dnl
18
19  define(`SMART_HOST', `smtp:mail.isp.net')dnl
```

In Listing 11.10, lines 6 through 12 again define basic features that the Linux mailserver will use. Lines 6 and 7 instruct sendmail to use the masquerade name defined in line 14 for all messages. Line 19 differentiates this configuration example from the previous example in Listing 11.8. Instead of sending mail messages directly to the destination host, line 19 defines a smart host that all external mail will be forwarded to. Any mail not destined for the local host will be sent via SMTP to the host `mail.isp.net`. It is then the job of the smart host to forward the messages to the destination hosts. Listing 11.11 shows the results of the sendmail test of this configuration file.

LISTING 11.11   Testing the Part-Time Linux Mailserver Configuration File

```
 1  [lizzy@shadrach lizzy]$ /usr/sbin/sendmail -bt -C test3.cf
 2  ADDRESS TEST MODE (ruleset 3 NOT automatically invoked)
 3  Enter <ruleset> <address>
 4  > 3,0 rich@otherhost.org
 5  rewrite: ruleset   3   input: rich @ otherhost . org
 6  rewrite: ruleset  96   input: rich < @ otherhost . org >
 7  rewrite: ruleset  96 returns: rich < @ otherhost . org >
 8  rewrite: ruleset   3 returns: rich < @ otherhost . org >
 9  rewrite: ruleset   0   input: rich < @ otherhost . org >
10  rewrite: ruleset 199   input: rich < @ otherhost . org >
11  rewrite: ruleset 199 returns: rich < @ otherhost . org >
12  rewrite: ruleset  98   input: rich < @ otherhost . org >
13  rewrite: ruleset  98 returns: rich < @ otherhost . org >
14  rewrite: ruleset 198   input: rich < @ otherhost . org >
15  rewrite: ruleset  95   input: < smtp : mail . isp . net >
 ➥ rich < @ otherhost . org >
```

continues

LISTING 11.11   continued

```
16 rewrite: ruleset  95 returns: $# smtp $@ mail . isp . net $:
➥ rich < @ otherhost . org >
17 rewrite: ruleset 198 returns: $# smtp $@ mail . isp . net $:
➥ rich < @ otherhost . org >
18 rewrite: ruleset   0 returns: $# smtp $@ mail . isp . net $:
➥ rich < @ otherhost . org >
19 >
20 [lizzy@shadrach lizzy]$
```

In Listing 11.11, line 1 shows the sendmail test of the new configuration file. Line 4 shows the test sample of sending a message to a user on a remote mail host. After several iterations, line 18 shows the final results—the message is forwarded to the host `mail.isp.net` using SMTP, just as we configured it to do. That host will hopefully forward the message on to `otherhost.org` for us.

UUCP Connection Mailserver

The last scenario that will be examined is the situation where the Linux mailserver is connected to the ISP via a UUCP connection. Again, this scenario requires the mailserver to forward any external mail to a smart host. This time, the smart host is connected via UUCP, so it doesn't need complicated relay blocking features to stop spammers. Figure 11.6 shows how this scenario is set up.

For the UUCP connection to work, the ISP must be able to accept and spool all mail destined for the local Linux mailserver. This requires the ISP to host the mailserver's domain as a virtual domain. Listing 11.12 shows a sample macro file that can be used to create a sendmail configuration file to work in this environment.

LISTING 11.12   Sample UUCP Linux Mailserver Macro File

```
1   divert(-1)
2   divert(0)dnl
3   include(`/usr/lib/sendmail-cf/m4/cf.m4')dnl
4   OSTYPE(`linux')dnl
5
6   FEATURE(`allmasquerade')dnl
7   FEATURE(`masquerade_envelope')dnl
8   FEATURE(`always_add_domain')dnl
9   FEATURE(`local_procmail')dnl
10
11  MASQUERADE_AS(`smallorg.org')dnl
12
```

Installing and Configuring sendmail

CHAPTER 11

327

11

INSTALLING AND
CONFIGURING
SENDMAIL

```
13 MAILER(`smtp')dnl
14 MAILER(`procmail')dnl
15 MAILER(`uucp')dnl
16
17 define(`SMART_HOST', `uucp-dom:ispmail')dnl
```

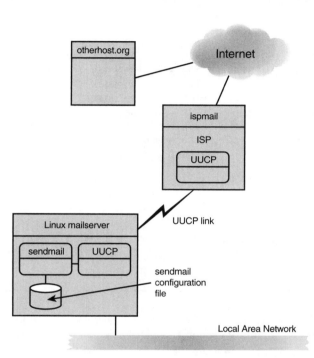

FIGURE 11.6
A Linux mailserver on a UUCP connection.

In Listing 11.12, lines 1 through 9 use the same features as the previous example in Listing 11.10. The main difference between these two scenarios is the addition of line 15 to define the UUCP mailer type and line 17 that defines the different smart host. The uucp-dom mailer type is used to transfer mail messages across a UUCP connection without rewriting the header file to match the UUCP method. This keeps the mail message headers intact to be forwarded by the smart host onto the Internet. After using the m4 macro processor to produce a test configuration file, Listing 11.13 shows the results of the sendmail test of this configuration file.

LISTING 11.13 Test of UUCP Linux Mailserver Configuration File

```
 1  [erin@shadrach erin]$ /usr/sbin/sendmail -bt -C test4.cf
 2  ADDRESS TEST MODE (ruleset 3 NOT automatically invoked)
 3  Enter <ruleset> <address>
 4  > 3,0 rich@otherhost.org
 5  rewrite: ruleset    3   input: rich @ otherhost . org
 6  rewrite: ruleset   96   input: rich < @ otherhost . org >
 7  rewrite: ruleset   96 returns: rich < @ otherhost . org >
 8  rewrite: ruleset    3 returns: rich < @ otherhost . org >
 9  rewrite: ruleset    0   input: rich < @ otherhost . org >
10  rewrite: ruleset  199   input: rich < @ otherhost . org >
11  rewrite: ruleset  199 returns: rich < @ otherhost . org >
12  rewrite: ruleset   98   input: rich < @ otherhost . org >
13  rewrite: ruleset   98 returns: rich < @ otherhost . org >
14  rewrite: ruleset  198   input: rich < @ otherhost . org >
15  rewrite: ruleset   95   input: < uucp-dom : ispmail > rich
16  ➥ < @ otherhost . org >
17  rewrite: ruleset   95 returns: $# uucp-dom $@ ispmail $:
➥ rich < @ otherhost . org >
18  rewrite: ruleset  198 returns: $# uucp-dom $@ ispmail $:
➥ rich < @ otherhost . org >
19  rewrite: ruleset    0 returns: $# uucp-dom $@ ispmail $:
➥ rich < @ otherhost . org >
20  >
21  [erin@shadrach erin]$
```

In Listing 11.13, line 1 again shows the sendmail command used to test the new configuration file, and line 4 shows the command used to test a remote email address using rule sets 3 and 0. The final results shown in line 19 indicate that the message will be forwarded to UUCP host ispmail using the uucp-dom protocol. This is exactly what we configured in the macro file. Again, we assume that the remote host ispmail will forward our message onto the final destination for us.

Summary

sendmail is a versatile MTA program that is available for the Linux platform. New versions can be downloaded from the Internet and installed without too much difficulty. After sendmail is installed, it must be properly configured to work in the desired environment. The GNU m4 macro processor can be used to create the sendmail configuration file from small macro files that define features desired in the configuration. Different mail environments require different configuration features and options. After the required features are defined, the configuration file can be built and the sendmail program can become operational.

Installing and Configuring POP3 and IMAP

IN THIS CHAPTER

After successfully installing the sendmail program, your Linux mailserver should be receiving email messages from other mail hosts. However, this only gets the messages to the Linux mailserver. It is still up to the individual email clients on the mailserver to retrieve their own mail.

Users who have physical access to the mail host can log in to an interactive session such as a console screen or an X Window session. When logged in to the mailserver, a user can use a Mail User Agent (MUA) program such as pine, elm, or kmail to access the local mailbox and manage their messages. These types of programs allow users to view and delete mail messages from an interactive session on the local mailserver.

Unfortunately, many users do not have physical access to the mailserver host. In fact, in most cases it is impossible for all users on the network to have physical access to read their email messages on the same mailserver. The next possible solution for remote email clients is to utilize the telnet or X terminal programs to establish a connection with the remote mailserver. Although this works, it is inefficient for reading mail messages. Both telnet and X terminal sessions create a large network overhead for just reading a few lines of text messages.

The best solution mail administrators have available are Mail Delivery Agents (MDAs). MDAs offer a method for remote users to access their mailboxes on the local mailserver without a large network overhead. The MDA can access the remote mailbox and download just the information necessary for the client computer to present the message to the user. Figure 12.1 shows remote clients accessing mail messages residing on the mailserver using an MDA.

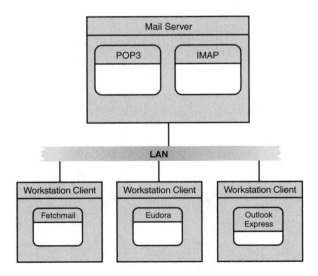

FIGURE 12.1
Remote network clients retrieving mail messages from server.

Two protocols that allow remote access of mailboxes were discussed in Chapter 6, "POP3 Protocol," and Chapter 7, "IMAP Protocol." The POP3 and IMAP protocols allow remote users to view and delete mail messages on the local mailserver from a remote workstation using an email client program. The Linux mailserver must have server software that supports either the POP3 or IMAP protocols to allow remote users access to their mailboxes.

This chapter describes two server software packages that allow the Linux mailserver to support the POP3 and IMAP protocols. The qpopper program allows the Linux mailserver to accept POP3 connections from remote hosts to access local mailboxes. The University of Washington IMAP program supports both the POP3 and IMAP protocols to access the local mailboxes.

Email Client Protocols

Although POP3 and IMAP programs perform similar functions, the methods they use to access mailboxes are totally different. Both protocols are used by client workstations to retrieve mail from the mailserver, but each protocol uses a different philosophy in how the mail messages are stored. This philosophical difference must be understood by the mail administrator because it is crucial to the operation of the mailserver.

This section compares and contrasts the two most common email client protocols to help the mail administrator decide which protocol(s) to implement and for what reasons.

POP3

The Post Office Protocol (POP) has been extremely popular. Currently, it is on its third official release version (thus the name POP3). Figure 12.2 demonstrates how the POP3 protocol can be used to retrieve mail from a mailserver.

The user's client computer can use the POP3 protocol to download messages from the user's mailbox on the mailserver to folders on the workstation. When downloaded, the message can be deleted from the mailserver, or the user can elect to keep the mail message on the mailserver. In either situation, the message is downloaded in its entirety for the user to be able to view it on the remote client computer using email client software.

The POP3 protocol is popular with Internet service providers (ISPs) who must maintain hundreds of email mailboxes on servers. The POP3 protocol allows the ISP to force the messages to be deleted from the server as they are downloaded, thus saving on server disk space. One unfortunate consequence of this scenario is that the user's mail is kept on the computer that he or she happened to check the mail from. If this is always the same computer, then there is not a problem. However, today many people must have the capability to check email messages from home as well as from the office. This is where POP3 becomes a problem. If the user checks for email at home and downloads 20 new messages, those messages will remain on the home PC. When the user gets to work, the messages will not be on the email server, and thus unobtainable. This is where IMAP comes in.

12

INSTALLING AND
CONFIGURING
POP3 AND IMAP

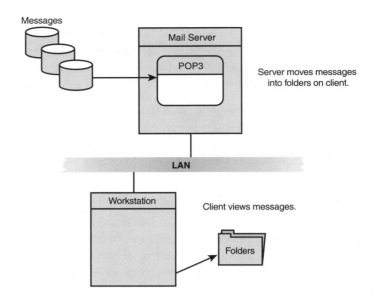

Figure 12.2
An overview of the POP3 protocol.

IMAP

The Interactive Mail Access Protocol (IMAP) has been a less-known protocol in the email world, but it is quickly gaining popularity. Currently, it is at release version 4 revision 1 (commonly called IMAP4rev1). Figure 12.3 demonstrates how the IMAP protocol works.

The main difference between the IMAP and POP3 protocols is where mail is located. For POP3, the mail messages are spooled on the mailserver but downloaded to the client for further manipulation. Often the messages on the server are deleted as soon as the client downloads them. In contrast, the IMAP protocol maintains all the messages in folders on the server. Each user has a default folder named the INBOX. New messages are placed in the INBOX to be read. Each time the client connects to the IMAP server, a listing of the INBOX messages can be obtained, and any of the messages can be retrieved—even from different client computers. This is a great advantage to users who must check mail from multiple workstations throughout the day. Also, separate folders can be created on the server to organize mail messages. These folders reside on the server, not on the client workstation. Although this is a great feature for remote email users, it makes life much more difficult for the mail administrator. Because all the mail messages are retained on the mailserver, server disk space becomes a crucial issue.

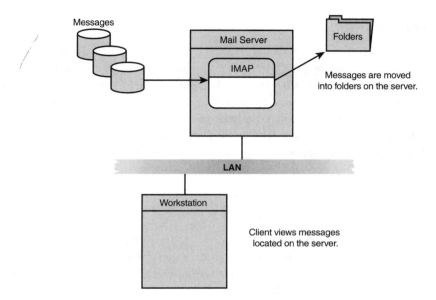

FIGURE 12.3
Overview of the IMAP protocol.

POP3 Versus IMAP

The choice of POP3 or IMAP is not mutually exclusive. Many sites run both email protocols to allow clients to retrieve mail using either method. It is common for in-house workstations to use the IMAP protocol to maintain messages on the mailserver, whereas dial-in clients use the POP3 protocol to read messages from the mailserver. When using this scenario, be careful that the dial-in clients using POP3 do not delete the messages from the server after they are downloaded to the workstation, or they will not be present for the IMAP sessions. This presents a "best of both worlds" scenario to the client. Unfortunately, this also presents a large administration overhead for the mail administrator.

The two software packages examined in this chapter exhibit behavior that is common for Linux POP3 and IMAP servers, to include encrypted passwords and the use of the shadow password file.

qpopper

The qpopper program is freeware originally released by the University of California at Berkeley, but now maintained by the Qualcomm corporation, that also supports the Eudora email client software (discussed in Chapter 15, "Configuring LAN Clients"). qpopper was written to provide POP3 server software for most types of UNIX servers. It works great on Linux. qpopper supports both the normal user/password POP3 logins and the APOP POP3 encrypted authentication. The user/password login feature also supports Linux shadow password files. The APOP feature supports encrypted passwords using a separate password database file that must be maintained separately by the mail administrator.

Information about qpopper can be found on its Web site at

```
http://www.eudora.com/freeware/servers.html
```

The current release version of qpopper is version 2.53. A beta version also is available for use—version 3.0b18. If you happen to come across a version of qpopper earlier than version 2.41, don't use it. Earlier versions contained some serious buffer overflow problems that could allow a hacker root access to your mailserver.

Downloading qpopper

The Qualcomm FTP site hosts the most current version of qpopper. The FTP server is located at `ftp.qualcomm.com`. The directory where qpopper is located is `/eudora/servers/unix/popper`. At the time of this writing, three qpopper distributions are in this directory—versions 2.53, 3.0b17, and 3.0b18. All three utilize the UNIX tar and compress utilities to compact the distribution files. Make sure that you are using the FTP `BINARY` mode and download the version that you want to use. For this example, the file `qpopper3.0b18.tar.Z` will be used:

```
ftp://ftp.qualcomm.com/eudora/servers/unix/popper/qpopper3.0b18.tar.Z
```

After the file is downloaded (the 3.0 beta version is a little more than 2.5MB), you can extract the source code files into a working directory:

```
tar -zxvf qpopper3.0b18.tar.Z
```

The Linux tar utility creates a subdirectory `qpopper3.0` and places the source code files in subdirectories beneath it.

Configuring qpopper

The qpopper program utilizes the configure program to examine the operating environment and create a Makefile that references the specific locations of the C compiler, libraries, and include files. The configure program also uses command-line parameters to change specific features that you may want to include in your implementation of the qpopper server. These will be described later in this section.

The default qpopper configure environment uses no extra command-line parameters and can be built by using the commands `./configure` and `make`. This creates a default POP3 server that does not recognize the APOP authentication method and also does not recognize the shadow password database if one exists. The qpopper executable program is called `popper` and is located in the `popper` subdirectory beneath the `qpopper3.0` directory. You will need to copy this program to a common location as the root user. The qpopper documentation recommends using the `/usr/local/lib` directory.

The popper program can use command-line parameters to modify the behavior of the POP3 server. Table 12.1 shows the available command-line parameters.

TABLE 12.1 popper Command-Line Parameters

Parameter	Description
-b	Changes the default directory for bulletins
-c	Changes all usernames to lowercase
-d	Enables debugging
-e	Sets POP3 extensions
-k	Enables Kerberos support
-s	Enables statistics logging
-t	Defines an alternate debug and log file
-T	Changes the default timeout waiting for reads
-R	Disables reverse client address lookups

The qpopper program uses the inetd program to execute. The inetd program listens for network connections and passes those connections to the appropriate program depending on the TCP or UDP port number that the connection is established on. The first part of the inetd configuration is to make sure that it recognizes the POP3 TCP port (number 110). This information is in the `/etc/services` file. The pertinent line should look like the following:

```
pop-3       110/tcp              # POP version 3
```

After ensuring that the `/etc/services` file supports POP3, the next step is to configure the inetd configuration file to support POP3. The inetd configuration file is `/etc/inetd.conf`. A line should be added to the configuration file that corresponds to the tag in the `/etc/services` line (`pop-3`) and identifies the program to start when a connection is established. The new line should look like the following:

```
#pop-3  stream  tcp nowait  root    /usr/local/lib/popper   popper -s
```

12

INSTALLING AND
CONFIGURING
POP3 AND IMAP

This `inetd.conf` entry assumes that the popper program is located in the `/usr/local/lib` directory and that statistics logging is enabled (the `-s` option). By default, statistics will be logged in the Linux default syslog file. On Mandrake Linux 6.0, this is the `/var/log/messages` file.

To activate the new `inetd.conf` settings, the currently running inetd daemon must be restarted. This can be accomplished by sending a `SIGHUP` signal to it. The following commands can be used to accomplish this:

```
[root@shadrach lizzy]# ps ax | grep inetd
  327 ?        S     0:00 inetd
12600 pts/2    S     0:00 grep inetd
[root@shadrach lizzy]# kill -HUP 327
[root@shadrach lizzy]#
```

You can test the qpopper installation by using the telnet program and connecting to port 110 on the Linux mailserver as shown in Listing 12.1.

LISTING 12.1   Sample POP3 Session

```
1  [erin@shadrach erin]$ telnet localhost 110
2  Trying 127.0.0.1...
3  Connected to localhost.
4  Escape character is '^]'.
5  +OK QPOP (version 3.0b18) at shadrach.smallorg.org starting.
6  QUIT
7  +OK Pop server at shadrach.smallorg.org signing off.
8  Connection closed by foreign host.
9  [erin@shadrach erin]$
```

In Listing 12.1, line 1 shows the user `telnet`ing to port 110 of the local host. Line 5 shows the greeting banner produced by the qpopper program.

The default qpopper configuration will work fine in some simple POP3 implementations running on basic Linux mailservers. However, other features can be implemented to make qpopper more versatile.

Shadow Password Support

A common Linux feature is shadow passwords. In a traditional Linux configuration, userids and passwords are kept in the `/etc/passwd` file. Unfortunately, this file must be readable by every user on the Linux system. This is so that the login program can authenticate new logon requests. This leaves the file vulnerable to hackers who can download the `/etc/passwd` file and run password cracking programs against it. Usually, users who use such unique passwords as their first names or the names of professional sports teams are the first to be cracked.

> ### Linux and Passwords
>
> Chapter 14, "Mailserver Administration," discusses maintaining Linux userids and passwords in more detail.

To combat this problem, many Linux distributions have incorporated the use of a shadow password file. The normal /etc/passwd file still contains userids, but now the encrypted passwords are stored in a separate file that can be made inaccessible to other users. When a shadow password file is used, programs that verify userids must be aware of its existence.

A way to determine whether your Linux setup is using shadow passwords is to look at the /etc/passwd file. Listing 12.2 shows a sample Linux password file from a system using shadow passwords.

LISTING 12.2   Sample Linux /etc/passwd File

```
1   root:x:0:0:root:/root:/bin/bash
2   bin:x:1:1:bin:/bin:
3   daemon:x:2:2:daemon:/sbin:
4   adm:x:3:4:adm:/var/adm:
5   lp:x:4:7:lp:/var/spool/lpd:
6   sync:x:5:0:sync:/sbin:/bin/sync
7   shutdown:x:6:0:shutdown:/sbin:/sbin/shutdown
8   halt:x:7:0:halt:/sbin:/sbin/halt
9   mail:x:8:12:mail:/var/spool/mail:
10  news:x:9:13:news:/var/spool/news:
11  uucp:x:10:14:uucp:/var/spool/uucp:
12  operator:x:11:0:operator:/root:
13  games:x:12:100:games:/usr/games:
14  gopher:x:13:30:gopher:/usr/lib/gopher-data:
15  ftp:x:14:50:FTP User:/home/ftp:
16  nobody:x:99:99:Nobody:/:
17  postgres:x:100:101:PostgreSQL Server:/var/lib/pgsql:/bin/bash
18  lists:x:500:500:BeroList:/dev/null:/dev/null
19  xfs:x:101:103:X Font Server:/etc/X11/fs:/bin/false
20  rich:x:501:501:Rich:/home/rich:/bin/bash
21  barbara:x:502:502:Barbara's logon id:/home/barbara:/bin/bash
22  katie:x:503:503:Katie's logon id:/home/katie:/bin/bash
23  jessica:x:504:504:Jessica's logon id:/home/jessica:/bin/bash
```

12

INSTALLING AND
CONFIGURING
POP3 AND IMAP

Listing 12.2 shows several userid listings in the /etc/passwd file. Colons (:) are used to separate the fields. The first field is the username. The second field is normally the encrypted password. In this file, though, the second field is always the letter x. This indicates a system that is using shadow passwords. On this particular system, the real password file is located at /etc/shadow. Listing 12.3 shows this file.

LISTING 12.3 Sample Linux /etc/shadow File

```
 1  root:$1$wkRtb3BgrTSWmezOiXx.ZGAtG/zGKU1:10863:0:99999:7:-1:-1:134537880
 2  bin:*:10863:0:99999:7:::
 3  daemon:*:10863:0:99999:7:::
 4  adm:*:10863:0:99999:7:::
 5  lp:*:10863:0:99999:7:::
 6  sync:*:10863:0:99999:7:::
 7  shutdown:*:10863:0:99999:7:::
 8  halt:*:10863:0:99999:7:::
 9  mail:*:10863:0:99999:7:::
10  news:*:10863:0:99999:7:::
11  uucp:*:10863:0:99999:7:::
12  operator:*:10863:0:99999:7:::
13  games:*:10863:0:99999:7:::
14  gopher:*:10863:0:99999:7:::
15  ftp:*:10863:0:99999:7:::
16  nobody:*:10863:0:99999:7:::
17  postgres:!!:10863:0:99999:7:::
18  lists:!!:10863:0:99999:7:::
19  xfs:!!:10863:0:99999:7:::
20  rich:LMQ0lb3GwZr1s:10863:0:99999:7:::
21  barbara:MDOb23ddXdgPP:10863:0:99999:7::
22  katie:$1$OR1Qdo1l$ggBH8mFNPGCBUUHMEjXWe1:10863:0:99999:7:-1:-1:
    ➥134537888
23  jessica:$1$XEd8PKaP$AhJre7HN3UBcKjB0GeL1d1:10882:0:99999:7:-1:-1:
    ➥134537872
```

Listing 12.3 shows that now the second field contains encrypted versions of the passwords for the users. To access the shadow password file, qpopper must be compiled to look for the shadow password file.

If you have previously compiled a version of qpopper, you must clean the object and executable files from the build directory. You can accomplish this by using the following command from the qpopper3.0 directory:

```
make clean
```

This command removes files that have been added or modified by the install script. The next step is to run the configure script with the parameter that includes shadow password support. The format of this command is

```
./configure --enable-specialauth
```

This re-creates the Makefile using parameters necessary for the GNU gcc compiler to add support for shadow password files. After the configure program finishes building the Makefile, you can then run the GNU make program against it to create a new `popper` executable program in the `popper` subdirectory. Again, you must copy this file to the location specified in the `inetd.conf` file as the root user. There is no need to restart the inetd daemon because the configuration file `/etc/inetd.conf` was not modified.

After copying the new executable popper file to the appropriate directory, you can test the configuration by `telnet`ing to port 110 and attempting to log in as a user. Listing 12.4 demonstrates an example of this.

LISTING 12.4   Sample POP3 Login Session

```
1  [riley@shadrach riley]$ telnet localhost 110
2  Trying 127.0.0.1...
3  Connected to localhost.
4  Escape character is '^]'.
5  +OK QPOP (version 3.0b18) at shadrach.smallorg.org starting.
6  USER riley
7  +OK Password required for riley.
8  PASS firetruck
9  +OK riley has 3 messages (1162 octets).
10 QUIT
11 +OK Pop server at shadrach.smallorg.org signing off.
12 Connection closed by foreign host.
13 [riley@shadrach riley]$
```

In Listing 12.4, line 1 shows a `telnet` session to port 110 (the POP3 port) of the local mailserver. Line 5 shows the greeting banner produced by qpopper, indicating that it is indeed up and running. In lines 6 and 8, the user enters his userid and password, and in line 9, qpopper accepts the login attempt and informs the user that he has three messages waiting to be downloaded.

APOP Authentication Support

As shown in Listing 12.4, the poor email client had to send his userid and password in clear text to the qpopper server. Had Riley been checking his mail from across the Internet, it is possible that this information could have been captured by a hacker and used for illegal purposes.

12

INSTALLING AND
CONFIGURING
POP3 AND IMAP

However, the POP3 protocol provides a solution for this problem.

As described in Chapter 6, POP3 can use alternative methods to authenticate a user. The qpopper program supports the APOP method of authenticating a user. To add this capability to the popper executable program, you must recompile the program.

First, you must remove the object and executable files that were created from any previous builds using the following command:

```
make clean
```

Next, you must run the configure script again, including parameters to define the location of the APOP password database and the userid of the APOP administrator:

```
./configure --enable--apop=/etc/pop.auth --with-popuid=pop
```

This creates a new Makefile using the values /etc/pop.auth for the authentication database location and the user pop being the database administrator. You can then create the new executables by using the GNU make command as before. With the APOP option, two executable files are created: popper and popauth.

As before, copy the popper executable file to the location specified in the inetd.conf file (such as /usr/local/lib). The popauth file created allows the APOP administrator to add users to the APOP authentication database specified in the configure command line.

To test the new qpopper configuration, you can telnet to port 110 and observe the new greeting banner. Listing 12.5, shows an example of a qpopper server using APOP authentication.

LISTING 12.5 Sample qpopper Greeting Banner Using APOP

```
1  [carol@shadrach carol]$ telnet localhost 110
2  Trying 127.0.0.1...
3  Connected to localhost.
4  Escape character is '^]'.
5  +OK QPOP (version 3.0b18) at shadrach.smallorg.org starting.
        ➥ <17166.940368317@shadrach.smallorg.org>
6  QUIT
7  +OK Pop server at shadrach.smallorg.org signing off.
8  Connection closed by foreign host.
9  [carol@shadrach carol]$
```

In Listing 12.5, line 1 shows the telnet command to connect to the POP3 service port. Line 5 shows the new greeting banner generated by qpopper. It differs from the greeting banner shown in Listings 12.1 and 12.4 in that it includes the APOP seed information. As described in Chapter 6, the APOP protocol requires a seed value to hash with a known secret word—in this case the password. The POP3 server supplies this seed value on the greeting banner. Both sides of the POP3 connection must know the secret word so that the hashed value can be matched. The qpopper server stores the secret words in the authentication database.

To create the APOP authentication database, as the root user enter the following command:

```
./popauth -init
```

This creates a new authentication database in the location specified (/etc/pop.auth in the example). The userid specified in the -with-popuid parameter is now the APOP administrator and can add users to the authentication database. One strange characteristic about qpopper is that after a userid is added to the authentication database, that user must use APOP authentication to connect to the POP3 server.

To add a new user to the authentication database, the APOP administrator can type the command

```
popauth -user user
```

where *user* is the Linux username of the user. The popauth program will query the administrator for a password for the user to be used for APOP authentication. This password can be different from the normal Linux login password. To remove a user from the authentication database the administrator can type

```
popauth -delete user
```

where *user* is the Linux username of the user to be removed. Individual users can change their APOP passwords by using the popauth command without any parameters.

qpopper Bulletins

Another feature that can be added to qpopper is the use of bulletins. Bulletins allow users the capability to send messages to all POP3 users. When a user connects via POP3 to the mailserver, qpopper checks the bulletin directory and determines which bulletins have not been read. Any unread bulletins are added to the normal mail messages for the user. The mail administrator can restrict who can send bulletins by controlling the access of the bulletins directory.

First, as before, if you have already compiled a version of qpopper, you must delete any existing object and executable files:

```
make clean
```

Next the configure program must be run with the bulletins parameter added. You can run the configure program with multiple parameters if you also need shadow password and/or APOP support as well as bulletins. The format for using bulletins with shadow password support would look like this:

```
./configure --enable-bulletins=/var/spool/bulls --enable-specialauth
```

12

INSTALLING AND
CONFIGURING
POP3 AND IMAP

where the `--enable-bulletins` parameter points to the directory where you want the bulletins to reside. After the configure script completes, you must run the GNU make utility to create the `popper` executable. When this completes, you must again copy the `popper` executable to the directory pointed to by the `inetd.conf` configuration file.

To use the bulletins feature, you must create a separate file for each bulletin and place them in the bulletins directory. The filenames should be in the format

nnnnn.string

where *nnnnn* is a five-digit number to identify the bulletin number, and *string* is text used to identify the bulletin. An example would be `00001.Test_Bulletin`. Bulletins must be numbered sequentially for qpopper to keep track of which bulletins each user has seen. When a POP3 client has downloaded the bulletin, it will not appear in the user's mailbox again. The text of the bulletin file must follow strict RFC 822 message formats. Listing 12.6 shows a sample bulletin.

LISTING 12.6   Sample qpopper Bulletin Text

```
1  From pop Wed Oct 20 18:25:00 1999
2  Date: Wed, 20 Oct 1999 18:25:00 (EST)
3  From: "Mail Administrator" <postmaster@shadrach.smallorg.org>
4  Subject: Test bulletin
5
6  This is a test of the Qpopper mail bulletin system.  This is only a test
7    Had this been a real bulletin you would have been instructed to do
8  something important, like log off of the system.
9  This is the end of the bulletin test.
```

The bulletin will be checked for download as long as it is in the bulletins directory. If you remove the bulletin file, new POP3 clients will not see the bulletin in their mail.

University of Washington IMAP

The most common POP3 and IMAP package used on the Linux platform was developed by the University of Washington. It includes both a POP3 server as well as an IMAP4rev1 server. This section describes how to install and configure the UW IMAP software to support remote POP3 and IMAP clients from your Linux mailserver.

Downloading and Installing UW IMAP

Many Linux distributions already come with a UW IMAP binary package. Mandrake Linux 6.0 uses package `imap-4.5-5mdk.i586.rpm`. To install this package, you can use the normal RPM package installer. The command for installing the package is

```
rpm -Uvh imap-4.5-5mdk.i586.rpm
```

The University of Washington currently supports a Web site for the IMAP software project. The URL of this site is

```
http://www.washington.edu/imap/
```

This site contains information about the UW IMAP project at the university, as well as links to the current release of UW IMAP—version 4.6. You can download the source code distribution of this version by the link provided at the Web site. Alternatively, you can also connect directly to the FTP site at `ftp.cac.washington.edu` and check the `/imap` directory for the current release version. A link named `imap.tar.Z` is always set to the current release version. By checking the FTP site, you can see that a beta test version of the next release, version 4.7, is also available for download. The source code distribution comes as a compressed tarred file—`imap-4.7.BETA.tar.Z`. Remember to use `BINARY` mode when retrieving the file.

When the source code distribution file is downloaded, it can be untarred into a working directory using the following command:

```
tar -zxvf imap-4.7.BETA.tar.Z
```

This produces a subdirectory named `imap-4.7.BETA` and places the source code in subdirectories underneath it.

The UW IMAP program does not have any feature options that are necessary to add at compile time like qpopper does. The main requirement for building the IMAP distribution executables is to know what type of system you are compiling the source code on and use the appropriate Makefile section. Table 12.2 shows common IMAP make options for Linux systems.

TABLE 12.2 UW IMAP make Options

Option	Description
lnx	Traditional Linux systems
lnp	Linux with Pluggable Authentication Modules (PAM)
sl4	Linux using `-lshadow` for passwords
sl5	Linux using shadow passwords
slx	Linux using `-lcrypt` for passwords

For Mandrake Linux 6.0 with shadow passwords enabled, you can use the `slx` option:

```
make slx
```

This compiles the source code and produces the IMAP executables located in the subdirectories in the distribution. The next step is to install and configure the individual pieces of IMAP.

Configuring UW POP3

For the UW POP3 server software to work properly it must be set up and configured after it is compiled. The first step is to copy the executables into a common directory. Because the ipop3d and imapd programs were written to be used by the tcpd wrapper program, it is best to locate them in the same directory—`/usr/sbin`. The ipop3d program is located in the `ipopd` subdirectory under the `imap-4.7.BETA` directory. Also included in this directory is a POP2 server—ipop2d. This is mainly for compatibility with older mail clients that do not support the POP3 protocol. If you are establishing a new email system, you should stick with the POP3 implementation. Plenty of new clients are available that use the POP3 protocol (see Chapter 15, "Configuring LAN Clients"). Make sure that you are the root user when copying the `ipop3d` file to the `/usr/sbin` directory or the copy will fail.

When the executable is placed in the proper directory, the inetd configuration files must be modified. The first file to modify is the `/etc/services` file. Make sure that the POP3 TCP port is configured. The POP3 line should look like this:

```
pop-3        110/tcp              # POP version 3
```

This indicates that the inetd program will monitor TCP port 110 and pass any connection attempts off to the program defined by the `pop-3` tag in the `/etc/inetd.conf` file.

The `/etc/inetd.conf` configuration file should indicate where the executables are located when a connection is passed off to it. The necessary POP3 lines in the `/etc/inetd.conf` file are

```
pop-3    stream  tcp     nowait  root    /usr/sbin/tcpd  ipop3d
```

These lines assume that the tcpd and ipop3d programs are both located in the `/usr/sbin` directory. The `pop-3` tag relates to the `pop-3` tag in the `/etc/services` file.

To activate the new `inetd.conf` settings, the currently running inetd daemon must be restarted. This can be accomplished by sending a `SIGHUP` signal to it. The following commands can be used for this:

```
[root@shadrach erin]# ps ax | grep inetd
  327 ?        S      0:00 inetd
12600 pts/2    S      0:00 grep inetd
[root@shadrach erin]# kill -HUP 327
[root@shadrach erin]#
```

With the inetd daemon restarted, you can now test the UW IMAP installation. Listing 12.7 shows an example of testing the POP3 server.

LISTING 12.7 Sample POP3 Session

```
1  [lizzy@shadrach lizzy]$ telnet localhost 110
2  Trying 127.0.0.1...
3  Connected to localhost.
4  Escape character is '^]'.
5  +OK POP3 localhost v7.63 server ready
6  USER lizzy
7  +OK User name accepted, password please
8  PASS SINGING
9  +OK Mailbox open, 5 messages
10 QUIT
11 +OK Sayonara
12 Connection closed by foreign host.
13 [lizzy@shadrach lizzy]$
```

In Listing 12.7, line 1 shows a telnet session to the POP3 port—110. Line 5 shows the greeting banner generated by the UW POP3 server, indicating that it is indeed running.

One optional feature that is available for the UW POP3 server is the capability to use APOP user authentication. The method of implementing APOP that UW POP3 uses is not as sophisticated as that of the qpopper POP3 server, but it serves its purpose.

If the UW POP3 server detects that the file /etc/cram-md5.pwd exists, it will support the APOP and CRAM-MD5 authentication protocols. Both methods use the same technique of hashing a seed value with a secret word to create the encrypted password used for authentication. As described in Chapter 6, the seed value is displayed on the POP3 greeting banner. Both the server and the client must already know the secret word that will be hashed with the seed value.

In the case of UW POP3, the secret words are stored in the /etc/cram-md5.pwd file. Each line of the file contains the username and the secret word that the user will use. Listing 12.8 shows a sample /etc/cram-md5.pwd file.

LISTING 12.8 Sample /etc/cram-md5.pwd File

```
1  rich      guitar
2  barbara   reading
3  riley     firetruck
```

continues

LISTING 12.8 continued

```
4  haley      starwars
5  katie      boxcar
6  jessica    sharks
```

As seen in Listing 12.8, the cram-md5.pwd database is a plain text database. To protect the passwords, make sure that the file is set to mode 600 so that other users cannot view it. This means that the mail administrator must have root access to modify passwords. Also, this means that users cannot modify their own passwords.

To check whether the APOP feature is available, telnet to the POP3 port. The new greeting banner should be present showing the seed value. Listing 12.9 shows an example of an APOP-enabled POP3 server.

LISTING 12.9 Sample APOP-Enabled POP3 Server Greeting Banner

```
1  [kevin@shadrach kevin]$ telnet localhost 110
2  Trying 127.0.0.1...
3  Connected to localhost.
4  Escape character is '^]'.
5  +OK POP3 v7.63 server ready <4d61.380e35cc@localhost>
6  USER kevin
7  +OK User name accepted, password please
8  PASS dinosaur
9  +OK Mailbox open, 0 messages
10 QUIT
11 +OK Sayonara
12 Connection closed by foreign host.
13 [kevin@shadrach kevin]$
```

In Listing 12.9, line 1 again shows a sample telnet session to the POP3 server port. This time, line 5 shows a different greeting banner than the example in Listing 12.7. Included in the greeting banner is the APOP seed value. Line 6 demonstrates a nice feature of the UW POP3 server implementation of APOP. Unlike qpopper, where if a user is defined as using APOP he cannot connect in any other way, UW POP3 will allow a user to connect using either the APOP or user/password methods. This is particularly good for users who may connect to the mailserver using different PCs and different email client software packages.

Configuring UW IMAP

Much like the POP3 server software, the UW IMAP software utilizes the inetd program. This requires new lines in the inetd configuration files to specify the actions for the IMAP server. The first line required is in the /etc/services file:

```
imap2      143/tcp     imap      # Interim Mail Access Proto v2
```

The preceding line was defined in my Mandrake Linux 6.0 configuration file. As you can tell, it was originally set up for the IMAP2 protocol. However, it uses an alias of imap, thus the inetd program will look for either tag in the `inetd.conf` file. (Mandrake also managed to get the comment wrong, too!)

The `/etc/inetd.conf` file should also be modified to contain the information necessary for the IMAP server. This is an example of what the configuration line should look like:

```
imap    stream  tcp     nowait  root    /usr/sbin/tcpd  imapd
```

This example assumes that the tcpd and imapd programs are located in the `/usr/sbin` subdirectory.

To activate the new `inetd.conf` settings, the currently running inetd daemon must be restarted. This can be accomplished by sending a SIGHUP signal to it as shown in the "Configuring UW POP3" section.

After the `inetd` daemon is restarted, you can test the installation of the IMAP server by `telnet`ing to the IMAP port—number 143. Listing 12.10 shows an example of this.

LISTING 12.10   Sample IMAP Session

```
1  [jessica@shadrach jessica]$ telnet localhost 143
2  Trying 127.0.0.1...
3  Connected to localhost.
4  Escape character is '^]'.
5  * OK localhost IMAP4rev1 v12.261 server ready
6  a1 LOGIN jessica sharks
7  a1 OK LOGIN completed
8  a2 SELECT INBOX
9  * 0 EXISTS
10 * 0 RECENT
11 * OK [UIDVALIDITY 940284862] UID validity status
12 * OK [UIDNEXT 2] Predicted next UID
13 * FLAGS (\Answered \Flagged \Deleted \Draft \Seen)
14 * OK [PERMANENTFLAGS (\* \Answered \Flagged \Deleted \Draft \Seen)]
        ➥ Permanent flags
15 a2 OK [READ-WRITE] SELECT completed
16 a3 LOGOUT
17 * BYE shadrach.smallorg.org IMAP4rev1 server terminating connection
18 a3 OK LOGOUT completed
19 Connection closed by foreign host.
20 [jessica@shadrach jessica]$
```

Summary

When mail is on the Linux mailserver, clients must have a way to retrieve it. The two most popular protocols used by remote clients to retrieve mail from mailboxes on mailservers are the POP3 and IMAP protocols. Each protocol has strengths and weaknesses. Two software packages that can be used on the Linux mailserver are the qpopper POP3 server, and the University of Washington POP3 and IMAP servers. These packages are easy to install and configure. Many software packages are available that allow remote clients to connect via POP3 or IMAP to the mailserver to check their mailboxes. Chapter 15, "Configuring LAN Clients," demonstrates how to configure client email software packages to connect with the POP3 and IMAP server programs. The next chapter discusses how to configure a complete Linux mailserver for different Internet environments.

Connecting the Mailserver to an ISP

IN THIS CHAPTER

Internet service providers (ISPs) offer several different methods that can be used to connect the Linux mailserver to the Internet. No one method is clearly better than the others are. The decision of which method to use often depends on external factors such as company resources or politics. The purpose of this chapter is to explain the Internet mail options available to a Linux mailserver administrator. This information should help prepare you to make an informed decision as to which method is best to implement in your particular office environment. After discussing the options available, this chapter offers four detailed examples to help you configure your Linux mailserver according to your Internet mail environment.

Preliminary Issues

Before any hardware is installed or any software is configured, some issues must be decided. Often this is the most difficult part of the mailserver installation. After the main questions are answered, it is fairly straightforward to choose the mailserver configuration that satisfies your office environment.

Three main issues must be addressed with the ISP before the mailserver can be configured and built:

- Domain name hosting
- Mail drop options
- Connectivity options

Each of these issues involves services that can be provided by the ISP. Each issue has multiple ways of being accomplished. All of these issues are discussed in the following sections.

Domain Name Hosting

The most important decision you can make as the mail administrator is how mail will be addressed to people in your organization. Email addresses and Web site addresses have come to be a hot item on the Internet. Companies often pay considerably more than the standard name registration fee to buy back a domain name being used by another organization.

In the past, the Network Information Center (NIC) was responsible for all domain name registrations. Recently, in an agreement with the US Department of Commerce, the NIC has allowed other companies to start handling domain name registrations. The process for obtaining a new domain name is still fairly simple. Connect to the Web site `http://www.networkso-lutions.com` and follow the directions. There is also a query feature that allows you to check whether your potential domain name is already in use. After you have purchased an appropriate domain name, you must decide how that domain name will be hosted on the Internet.

Local Hosting of Domain Names

If you are on a dedicated Internet connection (see "Dedicated PPP Connection" later in this chapter), you can also use the same Linux server to be the mailserver and to host the DNS domain records for your domain. Chapter 4, "DNS and Domain Names" discusses how to use the Linux named program and the files necessary for it to host your DNS domain.

One requirement for a DNS domain is that there must be at least two DNS servers for the domain. The tricky part of this requirement is that the two DNS servers should not share the same network connections or electrical power. This almost ensures that one of the servers must be offsite. With this requirement, it is often cost-prohibitive for a small organization to host its DNS domain. Fortunately, companies are willing to provide this service.

ISP Hosting of Domain Names

When negotiating with ISPs for your Internet service, one item of discussion will be the DNS domain hosting. Almost all ISPs provide this service as part of a connectivity package.

For a fee, most ISPs will register your domain name with the Network Information Center and host your DNS domain records on their servers. That means the NS records for your domain will point to the ISP's servers. Often, ISPs will contract with other ISPs to provide the secondary DNS domain services required. Thus, there will be several NS records for your domain that might point to several different ISPs.

The drawback to you is if you want to register individual host names on your network. Every time you want to register a new host name, you must go to your ISP and have the A and PTR records for the new hosts added to your domain database.

13

CONNECTING THE
MAILSERVER TO
AN ISP

Primary DNS Service

One trick that can be used to solve this problem is to configure the Linux server to be the primary DNS server for your domain, and allow the ISP to be the secondary DNS server. By using this scheme, you are in control of registering new hosts on your network.

Mail Drop Options

The second decision to make when thinking about connecting your mailserver to the Internet is how Internet email will get to your Linux mailserver. There are three common options to receiving Internet email. This section describes the pros and cons of each method.

Direct Mail Connection

The simplest method of receiving Internet email is for it to be directly delivered from the sending sites to your Linux mailserver. This method is available only if your Linux mailserver has a dedicated connection to the Internet or is connected to a network that has a dedicated connection.

The Linux mailserver must be running an SMTP server program such as sendmail or smail, and must have the proper IP network configuration to allow remote sites to establish SMTP connections. Wherever the DNS database for your domain resides, it will contain an MX record pointing to the IP address of your Linux mailserver as the mailserver for your domain. Internet hosts that want to deliver mail to your domain will query the DNS database to find the mailserver. If the Linux mailserver's IP address is the only MX record available for the domain, it must be running and able to accept SMTP connections or the mail messages might not be delivered.

Outbound mail is also delivered directly to the destination site using the sendmail program and SMTP. The advantage to this method is that mail is sent and delivered in realtime. There are no delays waiting for mail to be spooled from a central mail hub.

The disadvantage to this method is that the Linux mailserver must be available 24 hours a day, 7 days a week. Any downtime could mean the possible loss of mail. Downtime not only means server downtime, but also network connection downtime.

For many sites, it is not possible to maintain a 24-hour, 7-day-a-week connection to the Internet. Because of this, the next two methods were developed.

All Domain Mail to One ISP Mailbox

One of the nice features of ISPs is that they have hosts that are connected to the Internet 24 hours a day. It makes perfectly good sense to allow the ISP to host all the mail for your domain. This requires the DNS database to point the MX record for your domain to the ISP mailserver. This directs any Internet mail destined to your domain to the ISP mailserver. It is then the job of the ISP to place the mail for your domain in a location where your Linux mailserver can download it.

One method of doing this is to forward any message destined for a user on your domain to a special mailbox on the ISP mailserver. As shown in Chapter 11, "Installing and Configuring sendmail," it is possible to create a virtual user table entry to allow sendmail to forward all mail for a domain to a single mailbox (as shown in Listing 11.4).

The Linux mailserver can use the POP3 protocol to connect to the ISP mailserver as the userid related to the domain mailbox. Using this userid, the Linux mailserver can download all the mail destined for users in the domain. After the mail has been downloaded to the Linux mailserver, it must be parsed and delivered to the proper userids that the messages were originally intended for.

Although this method works, it is not always efficient and not always recommended. The mail distribution program must parse the RFC822 message headers to determine the proper destination userid. Sometimes the distribution program fails to recognize the proper recipient of the mail message. Also, some mail distribution programs have been known to mangle the original RFC822 header when they transfer the message to the appropriate userids, thus making return mail difficult if not impossible. The next method has a more robust way of delivering domain mail messages.

ISP Spools Domain Mail for Delivery

A better method of receiving mail messages for your domain is to use virtual mail hosting. The DNS database still points the MX record for your domain to the ISP mailserver. The sendmail program on the ISP mailserver can be configured to accept mail destined for your domain and spool it for delivery in a mail queue directory. Until the time your Linux mailserver connects to the ISP mailserver, the mail remains in the mail queue on the ISP mailserver.

By forwarding the mail via SMTP or UUCP, the RFC822 message headers are not adversely affected as they are in the previous method. This allows return address schemes to have a better chance of working properly.

After the mail is sitting in the ISP's mail queue, multiple methods can be used by the Linux mailserver to retrieve it. The most common method is for the Linux mailserver to establish an SMTP connection with the ISP mailserver and send the SMTP ETRN command. This command tells the ISP to establish an SMTP connection with the Linux mailserver and forward any mail that is destined for your domain name (refer to Chapter 5, "SMTP Protocol").

Connectivity Options

The third decision that must be made is how the Linux mailserver will connect to the ISP. Often ISPs offer a variety of methods to accomplish this. Although some ISPs might prefer one method to another, they are all valid methods for transferring mail messages to and from the Linux mailserver.

Often, other Internet connectivity requirements determine the choice of which method to use. For example, if other devices on your network must establish Internet connections, you might not want to use the UUCP protocol for mail. On the other hand, many companies use dedicated PPP connections for interactive Internet traffic and a separate UUCP connection for mail traffic. That way, mail transfers do not slow down interactive traffic. Again, resources and politics often play a vital role in this decision process. This section describes the methods that are available from most ISPs to connect a mailserver to the Internet.

Dedicated PPP Connection

A dedicated connection to the Internet is often the most desirable method to implement. Unfortunately, it is usually the most expensive. There are two methods of establishing a dedicated connection from the Linux mailserver to the Internet.

The first, and maybe most preferred, option is to use an external device to establish the connection. Often, ISPs provide small network routers to connect a client's internal network to the ISP network via either a dial-up or dedicated line. In this scenario, the Linux mailserver requires only a standard connection to the internal network to communicate with the Internet.

The second option is to use the Linux mailserver itself as the dedicated connection to the Internet. As described in Chapter 8, "PPP Protocol," a Linux mailserver is fully capable of using the pppd program to establish a PPP connection with an ISP server. By connecting a modem to the Linux mailserver, you can allow it to perform both the mailserver and IP routing functions for the network. In this scenario, it is better to use a PC with a large processor and as much memory as possible.

Dial-on-Demand PPP Connection

The next method of connecting the Linux mailserver to the Internet is to use a dial-on-demand PPP connection. A dial-on-demand PPP connection is established only when the Linux mailserver needs to transfer data. It does not need to be active 24 hours a day. This method is often the most economical method of connecting the mailserver to the Internet.

Special programming must be utilized to allow the mailserver to establish the PPP connection when needed. Usually the Linux diald program, discussed in Chapter 8, can be used along with the standard pppd program to detect outgoing IP traffic and automatically start the PPP link as necessary.

Dial-Up UUCP Connection

The last method of communicating with the Internet is by using the UNIX-to-UNIX CoPy (UUCP) protocol described in Chapter 9, "UUCP Protocol." ISPs are not always willing to support the UUCP protocol. Often, ISPs that do not have UNIX administrators onsite are unwilling to tackle UUCP connections.

On the other hand, many ISPs offer considerable discounts to customers who connect via UUCP only to transfer mail. You will have to check the ISPs in your area to decide whether UUCP is a valid option for you. There also are a few national ISPs that offer UUCP connectivity via 1-800 numbers. Be careful about connectivity charges however; some ISPs that support UUCP charge by the hour of connectivity time. If your organization is thinking about mailing lots of large file attachments, connectivity time might become a large hidden cost for you.

The biggest advantage to using the UUCP protocol to transfer mail is security. At no time during the UUCP session is your Linux mailserver connected directly to the Internet. This helps prevent hackers from attempting to access your server. The less opportunity hackers have to access your server the better.

Sample Mailserver Scenarios

The previous section outlined the different issues that should be considered by the mail administrator for a Linux mailserver. This section describes four Linux mailserver scenarios that incorporate some of these methods:

- Dedicated PPP connection to the Internet with direct mail
- Dial-on-demand PPP connection using a single ISP mailbox
- Dial-on-demand PPP connection using an ISP mail queue
- Dial-up UUCP connection using an ISP mail queue

Each of these scenarios includes sample configuration files for each piece that is required to implement the scenario. Remember that in each of these examples, fictitious hostnames and addresses are used. You must substitute the hostnames and addresses shown with ones suitable for your ISP environment.

Dedicated Connection with Direct Domain Mail

By far the easiest mail configuration scenario is using the Linux mailserver on a dedicated PPP connection to the Internet. As described earlier, there are two methods to use to obtain a direct connection to the Internet. Assuming that your internal network does not have a router connecting it to the Internet, your Linux mailserver must provide a PPP link. Figure 13.1 shows an example of how this network configuration would work.

In this scenario, you will want to configure the PPP link to connect at all times and the sendmail program to deliver mail directly to remote Internet hosts. Even though the PPP link is connected all the time, this scenario assumes that the ISP is providing all our DNS domain name services to the Internet so that the Linux mailserver does not have to. The following sections describe the configuration files necessary to implement this scenario.

PPP Link Configuration

As described in Chapter 8, the pppd program is used to establish a PPP connection to the ISP server. The pppd program requires a chat script that tells it how to connect to the remote server via the modem. Listing 13.1 shows a sample chat script that can be used to contact the ISP server.

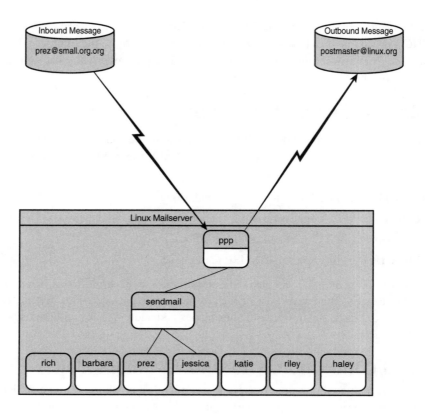

FIGURE 13.1
A Linux mailserver using a dedicated Internet connection.

LISTING 13.1   Sample pppd Chat Script `isp.chat`

```
1   ""
2   ATDT5551234
3   CONNECT
4   ""
5   "ogin:"
6   rich
7   "word:"
8   guitar
9   "rich]$"
10  "exec /usr/sbin/pppd silent modem crtscts proxyarp 10.0.0.100:10.0.0.2"
```

In Listing 13.1, line 2 should be replaced with the phone number required to call your ISP, and lines 6 and 8 should be replaced with the userid and password required to connect to your ISP. Line 9 should be replaced with the command-line prompt used by your ISP's server. Line 10 demonstrates the string required to start the pppd server on the ISP. Your ISP most likely has a different command string for you to use. Consult your ISP for the proper pppd command line to use. Save the chat script in a location that can be accessed only by the root user (remember: it contains your ISP userid and password).

After the chat script is created, you can run the pppd program to connect the Linux mailserver to the ISP server:

```
pppd ttyS1 38400 connect '/usr/sbin/chat -v -f /root/isp.chat'
        ➥modem crtscts defaultroute
```

Remember to replace `ttyS1` with the Linux device name of your modem and the `isp.chat` filename and `path` with your specific chat filename and path. After this command is run, the PPP link should be established. If you want, you can save the pppd command line as a script file. This makes it easier to execute if the PPP link drops for any reason.

To allow the Linux mailserver to correctly resolve Internet domain names, you must point the `/etc/resolv.conf nameserver` variable to the ISP's domain name server. The `/etc/resolv.conf` file can contain up to three `nameserver` variables. The line to define the `nameserver` should look like this:

```
nameserver     192.168.10.6
```

The IP address should point to the IP address of your ISP domain name server. This allows the sendmail program to properly identify domain names used in mail messages and to obtain the proper MX hosts for those domains.

sendmail Configuration

The sendmail configuration file for this scenario is about as easy as possible for sendmail. The main items that must be addressed in the configuration file are

- Send all mail using the domain name, not the hostname
- Send all mail directly to the destination host
- Use the procmail program to deliver local mail
- Allow local network users to relay mail to the Internet

Using these guidelines, the sendmail configuration macro file should look similar to the example shown in Listing 13.2.

LISTING 13.2 Sample sendmail Macro File `direct.mc`

```
1  divert(-1)
2  divert(0)dnl
3  include(`/usr/lib/sendmail-cf/m4/cf.m4')dnl
4  OSTYPE(`linux')dnl
5
6  FEATURE(`allmasquerade')dnl
7  FEATURE(`masquerade_envelope')dnl
8  FEATURE(`local_procmail', `/usr/bin/procmail')dnl
9  FEATURE(`access_db', `/etc/mail/access.db')dnl
10 FEATURE(`nocanonify')dnl
11
12 MAILER(`smtp')dnl
13 MAILER(`procmail')dnl
14
15 MASQUERADE_AS(`smallorg.org')dnl
```

In Listing 13.2, lines 6,7, and 15 define the masquerading feature that allows all outgoing mail to use the masquerade name (in this case, the domain name for the sample domain). This feature enables users to have email addresses that use only the domain name, such as prez@smallorg.org. Line 8 defines the procmail mail delivery agent for local mail, and line 9 defines the access.db hash database file to use to define the hosts allowed to relay mail through the server. You can use the m4 macro processor to create the new sendmail configuration file:

```
m4 direct.m4 > sendmail.cf
```

After the new configuration file is created, you can replace the old sendmail.cf configuration file located in the /etc directory with the new one generated by m4.

To allow local network clients to relay messages through the Linux mailserver (see Chapter 15, "Configuring LAN Clients"), you must create an access database that allows the local network addresses RELAY capabilities. Listing 13.3 shows the text version of this database.

LISTING 13.3 Sample sendmail Access Database `/etc/mail/access`

```
192.168.1          RELAY
```

Listing 13.3 assumes that the local IP network addresses are all in the 192.168.1.0 network. You must change this value to reflect your local IP network addresses. To create the new database from the text file, use the makemap utility:

```
makemap hash /etc/mail/access.db < /etc/mail/access
```

With the new sendmail configuration file and access database file in place, the sendmail program can be either started or restarted if it is already running. The sendmail command line should include the -q option to set a time period for checking the mail queue for new messages:

```
/usr/sbin/sendmail -bd -q30m
```

This allows the sendmail program to run as a background daemon process and to check the mail queue every 30 minutes for any mail that must be processed.

Automating the Mail Process

The sendmail program can be added as part of the automated startup scripts in the Linux system to start at boot time. Most Linux distributions already incorporate a startup script for sendmail. The linuxconf program can be used to add the sendmail program to the startup scripts. Figure 13.2 shows the linuxconf configuration screen for enabling the sendmail script at boot time.

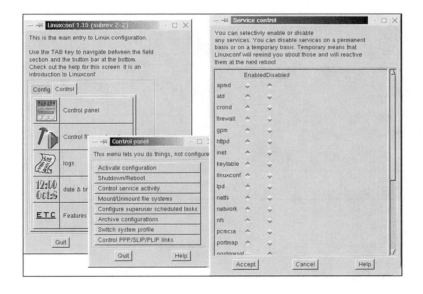

FIGURE 13.2
The linuxconf configuration screen.

Dial-on-Demand PPP Connection with One ISP Mailbox

The second scenario is often used by small organizations that do not have direct 24-hour access to the Internet. By using a dial-on-demand PPP connection, the mailserver can call the ISP server when outbound mail is detected and, at regular intervals, check for new inbound mail messages at the ISP. This scenario also assumes that the ISP will configure its mailserver to forward any mail destined to your domain to a single user mailbox on the system. The Linux fetchmail program is utilized to retrieve the mail from the ISP mailbox and distribute that mail to the proper local users on the Linux mailserver. Figure 13.3 shows how this network configuration works.

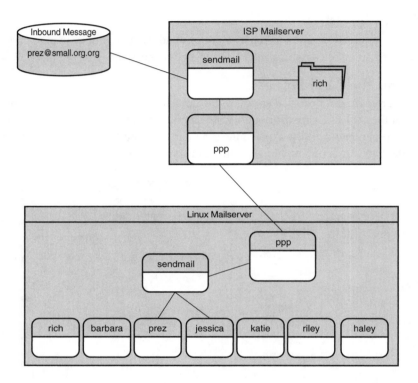

FIGURE 13.3

A Linux mailserver using a dial-on-demand PPP connection and one ISP mailbox.

PPP Link Configuration

The dial-on-demand PPP link configuration uses the same technique as the direct PPP link. The difference in this scenario is that the PPP link is started and stopped each time the mailserver needs to contact the ISP server. This feature requires the Linux diald program to start and stop the pppd service created in the previous scenario.

If your Linux distribution does not come with a binary distribution of the diald program, one can be obtained from the Web site `http://diald.unix.ch`. At the time of this writing, the current version of diald is `diald-0.99`. The following steps can be used to install the diald program:

1. Unpack the source distribution:

   ```
   tar -zxvf diald-0.99.tar.gz
   ```

2. Change to the new `diald-0.99` directory:

   `cd diald`

3. Run the GNU make program with the `depend` option:

   `make depend`

4. Run the GNU make program alone to compile:

   `make`

5. As root, run GNU make with the `install` option:

   `make install`

When diald is installed, you must create a configuration file for it. The diald configuration file is located at `/etc/diald.conf`. Listing 13.4 shows a sample diald configuration file.

LISTING 13.4   Sample `/etc/diald.conf` File

```
1  ###
2  # /etc/diald.conf - diald configuration
3  #
4  # see /usr/lib/diald for sample config files
5  #
6  mode ppp
7  connect '/usr/sbin/chat -f /root/isp.chat -t 35000'
8  connect-timeout 180
9  device /dev/ttyS1
10 speed 115200
11 modem
12 lock
13 crtscts
14 local 192.168.1.1
15 remote 192.168.1.2
16 dynamic
17 defaultroute
18 include /usr/lib/diald/standard.filter
19 fifo /etc/diald/diald.ctl
```

In Listing 13.4, line 7 defines the location of the same pppd chat script that was created in the previous scenario to start the PPP link. The diald program does not create the PPP session, it just automatically starts the existing pppd program when it detects network activity. Line 9 uses a modem connected to the Linux `/dev/ttyS1` port (DOS COM2). Refer to Chapter 3, "Installing Communication Devices in Linux," to determine where your modem is connected on your Linux system. Lines 14 and 15 define temporary IP addresses that are used to establish the PPP link between the ISP and the Linux mailserver. Line 18 defines the standard diald filter that determines when the PPP link is established and disconnected.

Only the root user can run diald. When diald is run, it automatically goes to background mode, watching for IP traffic to start the PPP link. After the IP traffic is finished, diald automatically disconnects the PPP link after 30 seconds.

The combination of diald and pppd allows the Linux mailserver to connect to the ISP whenever outgoing mail is detected. This includes mail relayed from the local clients to the ISP.

sendmail Configuration

As in the previous scenario, a new sendmail configuration file is built to incorporate the new configuration scenario. This scenario differs from the previous one in that this time the Linux mailserver can not deliver or receive messages directly from the remote hosts. This scenario relies on the use of a smart host to help the Linux mailserver forward mail messages. Any outgoing messages are stored in the mail queue until sendmail can contact the smart host. Incoming mail messages are stored in the mail queue of the ISP mailserver until the Linux mailserver connects to retrieve the mail via the fetchmail program.

The *smart host* is defined as the ISP mailserver that allows mail forwarding for your Linux mailserver. Listing 13.5 shows a sample sendmail configuration file that supports this scenario.

LISTING 13.5   Sample sendmail Macro File `dialup.mc`

```
1  divert(-1)
2  divert(0)dnl
3  include(`/usr/lib/sendmail-cf/m4/cf.m4')dnl
4  OSTYPE(`linux')dnl
5
6  FEATURE(`allmasquerade')dnl
7  FEATURE(`masquerade_envelope')dnl
8  FEATURE(`local_procmail', `/usr/bin/procmail')dnl
9  FEATURE(`access_db', `/etc/mail/access.db')dnl
10 FEATURE(`nocanonify')dnl
11
12 MAILER(`smtp')dnl
13 MAILER(`procmail')dnl
14
15 MASQUERADE_AS(`smallorg.org')dnl
16 define(`SMART_HOST', `smtp:mail.isp.net')dnl
```

As in the previous scenario, Listing 13.5 defines the domain name for the mailserver to masquerade as, and defines the procmail program as the local mail delivery program. The difference is in line 16. Line 16 defines the SMART_HOST as the ISP's mailserver. You should change the `mail.isp.net` hostname to point to your specific ISP mailserver. After the macro file is saved, it can be used by the m4 macro processor to generate a new `sendmail.cf` file (as shown in the previous example).

As in the previous scenario, for local network clients to be able to use the Linux mailserver as a mail relay, you must create the `access` database file and use the makemap utility to create the `access.db` hash file.

Also as in the previous scenario, you want to have the sendmail program run as a daemon in the background. This can be accomplished by adding the sendmail start script to the init scripts for the run level you plan to use for your Linux mailserver, or by using the linuxconf graphical program shown in Figure 13.2.

fetchmail Configuration

The fetchmail program is extremely versatile in retrieving mail messages from remote mailservers. For this scenario, the fetchmail program is configured to retrieve messages from a single mailbox on the ISP mailserver using the POP3 protocol.

After fetchmail retrieves the mail messages from the ISP mailserver, it must be able to parse the RFC822 header fields to determine the local user for whom the message is intended. This feature can be configured in the fetchmail configuration file.

Each user on the Linux mailserver has a unique fetchmail configuration file. The location of the file is `$HOME/.fetchmailrc`. In this scenario, the root user uses a fetchmail configuration file that is set up to log in to the ISP mailserver using the POP3 protocol with the ISP-assigned userid and password. Also, each local user who will receive mail from the Internet must be defined in the root user's `.fetchmailrc` file. Any mail retrieved by fetchmail that is not destined for a defined local user is stored in the mailbox of the userid running the fetchmail program (in this case, the root user). Listing 13.6 shows a sample `.fetchmailrc` file that can be used for this scenario.

LISTING 13.6   Sample `$HOME/.fetchmailrc` Configuration File

```
1   poll mail.isp.net with proto POP3
2     localdomains smallorg.org
3     no envelope
4     no dns
5     user "rich" with password "guitar" is
6        rich
7        barbara
8        katie
9      jessica
10     haley
11     riley
12     chris
13     matthew
14   here
```

In Listing 13.6, line 1 defines the ISP mailserver that fetchmail connects with to retrieve the domain mail. Line 1 also indicates to use the POP3 protocol for the connection. Lines 2 through 4 define options that are used for the connection. Line 2 indicates what domain fetchmail will look for as the local domain address in message headers. Thus, it recognizes the address prez@smallorg.org as the local mailserver user prez. Line 3 indicates not to use the X-Envelope-To: header field to parse the recipient address. These header fields are often added by MTAs as the mail passes from one site to another. They can be confusing to fetchmail. Line 4 indicates not to use DNS to confirm the identity of the sending host. Line 5 identifies the ISP mailbox userid and password that fetchmail uses to connect to the ISP mailserver. These should be provided by your ISP.

Lines 6 through 13 list all the local users on the Linux mailserver who can receive mail. Fetchmail parses the RFC822 message header fields and looks for these usernames. If one is found, fetchmail forwards the message to that local user. If the destination user does not match any of the local usernames listed, fetchmail delivers the message to the userid that ran fetchmail (the root user, in this scenario). It is the job of the mail administrator to add new local users to the list. Line 14 indicates that the local usernames are located on the local host on which fetchmail is running.

After the .fetchmailrc file is created and stored in the $HOME directory of the userid that will run fetchmail (for this example the root user), the program can be run. By typing **fetchmail** on the command line, the diald program should automatically start the PPP link, and fetchmail should automatically connect to the ISP mailserver and download any mail messages waiting in the common ISP mailbox. If this is successful, the next step is to automate the mail retrieval process.

Automating Mail Retrieval

After all the individual pieces of the Linux mailserver are configured, the next step is to automate the mail checking and retrieval process. The only function that must be performed at regular intervals is the fetchmail operation. The sendmail program should already be running as a background process.

Running the fetchmail operation at a regular interval can be accomplished by using the Linux cron utility. The cron utility reads a table containing lines of scripts to execute at specific times. Each user on the Linux system has a separate cron table. For this example, the root user will run the fetchmail program, so the root user's cron table must be modified. The method used to modify the table is the crontab utility. By logging in as the root user and typing **crontab -l**, you can view the existing cron table for the root user. To change the cron table, you must type **crontab -e**. This edits the cron table using the Linux vi editor.

To make the fetchmail program execute every 15 minutes, you would add the line shown in Listing 13.7 to the root user's cron table.

LISTING 13.7   Sample cron Entry for Fetchmail

```
0,15,30,45 * * * * /usr/bin/fetchmail
```

This line indicates that for every hour, day, week, and year at 0, 15, 30, and 45 minutes past the hour, the fetchmail program will be executed. You can modify this to suit your needs. Be careful not to check the ISP mailbox too often or the diald PPP link might not have a chance to properly drop between connections.

Dial-on-Demand PPP Connection with ISP Domain Mail Spooling

The third scenario also uses the dial-on-demand PPP connection to transfer mail messages to the ISP server. The difference in this scenario is that the domain mail for your domain is spooled to a mail queue on the ISP mailserver instead of being delivered to a single mailbox. Again, this is a feature of sendmail that the ISP must configure on its mailserver.

After the Linux mailserver establishes a PPP connection, it can establish an SMTP connection with the ISP mailserver and request that any mail in the mail queue be sent back to it using the SMTP ETRN command. As described in Chapter 5, the SMTP ETRN command instructs the ISP mailserver to create a second SMTP connection with the Linux mailserver and send any mail messages queued for delivery. This method does not alter the message headers as in the previous scenario. Figure 13.4 shows an example of this configuration.

PPP Link Configuration

The PPP link for this scenario is exactly like the previous scenario. To utilize dial-on-demand PPP connections, you must install the diald and pppd programs and use a `diald.conf` file similar to the one shown in Listing 13.4. The diald program runs as a background process and watches for IP traffic. Any outgoing messages trigger the diald program to start the PPP link. After the IP traffic stops, the diald program waits 30 seconds and then drops the PPP link. In this scenario, depending on your ISP server, you might have to extend the timeout value to ensure the ISP server has enough time to establish the SMTP connection back to the Linux mailserver. To do this, you can edit the `/usr/lib/standard.filter` file that comes with the diald program. The last line of the file should look like this:

```
accept any 30 any
```

This allows for the 30-second timeout. To increase the timeout, change the `30` to a value appropriate for your ISP environment and save the new file.

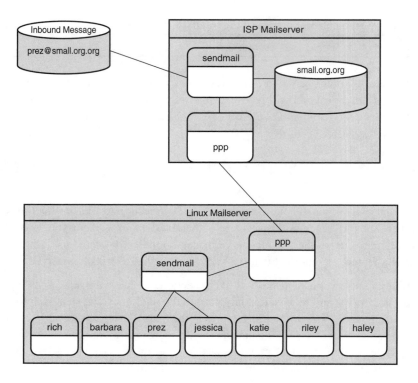

FIGURE 13.4

A Linux mailserver using a dial-on-demand PPP connection and the ISP spooling domain mail.

sendmail Configuration

Because the PPP link is not continually active, the sendmail program has to utilize the services of a remote smart host as in the last scenario. Also as before, sendmail should allow local clients to relay outbound messages through the Linux mailserver. With this scenario, you can use the same sendmail configuration file as the previous scenario. It should look similar to one shown in Listing 13.5: `dialup.mc`. Also, the access database should be created as shown in Listing 13.3 to allow remote network clients to relay SMTP mail through the Linux mailserver.

fetchmail Configuration

This scenario differs from the previous scenario in the method used to retrieve messages from the ISP mailserver. This time the fetchmail program must retrieve messages in the mail queue on the ISP mailserver.

To accomplish this task, fetchmail utilizes the SMTP ETRN command described in Chapter 5. Thus, the fetchmail program does not actually retrieve any messages; it instructs the ISP mailserver to initiate another SMTP connection back to the Linux mailserver and exits. Listing 13.8 shows a sample .fetchmailrc file that can be used to call the ISP using the SMTP ETRN command.

LISTING 13.8   Sample .fetchmailrc File for SMTP Mail

```
1   poll mail.isp.net with proto ETRN
2       localdomains smallorg.org
3       no dns
4       no envelope
```

In Listing 13.8, line 1 indicates the remote host to which to connect, and that fetchmail should use the SMTP ETRN command to initiate the mail transfer from the remote host. Line 2 indicates the alternative domain name as which the Linux mailserver will receive mail. You should replace that alternative domain name with your domain name. Lines 3 and 4 indicate that fetchmail will not use DNS to verify domain names in message headers and that it will not look at the X-Receive-To: RFC822 header field for recipients.

Automating Mail Retrieval

As in the previous scenario, this scenario must be able to automatically run the fetchmail program at set intervals to check the ISP for new mail. The easiest way to do this is to use the Linux cron utility. Again, a script file can be created similar to the one shown in Listing 13.7 and added to the cron table for the root user. As before, the cron table schedule can be set to check mail at the frequency that you choose. Each time the fetchmail program is run by the cron daemon, the diald program should initiate a PPP connection with the ISP mailserver.

Dial-Up UUCP Connection with ISP Domain Mail Spooling

The last scenario discussed uses the UUCP protocol to establish a connection with the ISP mailserver. Any outgoing mail is queued in the UUCP spool area on the Linux mailserver and transferred when the UUCP connection is established. Likewise, any inbound mail destined for the Linux mailserver is queued by the ISP mailserver and transferred when the UUCP connection is established. This is demonstrated in Figure 13.5.

UUCP Configuration

For the Linux mailserver to establish a UUCP connection with the ISP, UUCP software must be installed. The most common UUCP package available for the Linux platform is the Taylor UUCP package. Many Linux distributions come with a binary distribution package for Taylor UUCP. On Mandrake Linux 6.0, the package is called uucp-1.06.1-10mdk.i586.rpm. You can use the standard rpm package installer to install Taylor UUCP.

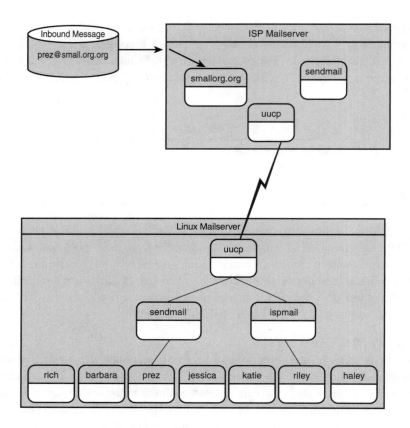

FIGURE 13.5

A Linux mailserver using a dial-up UUCP connection and ISP spooling domain mail.

If your Linux distribution does not include a binary distribution package for UUCP, you can download the source code from `sunsite.unc.edu` in the `/pub/Linux/systems/network/uucp` directory. The most current version available at that location is `uucp-1.05.tar.gz`. Chapter 9, "UUCP Protocol," details how to compile and install the source code package.

After the Taylor UUCP package is installed, it must be configured to support UUCP communications with the ISP UUCP server. Taylor UUCP requires four configuration files. The configuration files are normally located in the `/etc/uucp` directory. The first configuration file defines the UUCP nodename of the Linux mailserver. Listing 13.9 shows an example of the `config` file.

LISTING 13.9   Sample Taylor UUCP `config` File

```
nodename    smallorg
```

The next required file is the `sys` file. The `sys` file defines each remote UUCP site with which the Linux mailserver will communicate. For this example, the only site that must be entered is the ISP UUCP server. Listing 13.10 shows an example of the `sys` file.

LISTING 13.10   Sample Taylor UUCP `sys` File

```
1  system    ispmail
2  time      Any
3  phone     555-1234
4  port      modem
5  speed     38400
6  chat      ogin: rich word: guitar
```

In Listing 13.10, line 1 defines the remote UUCP node with which the Linux mailserver will communicate. You must replace this value with the name of your ISP UUCP server. Line 2 defines the times of day the server can connect. For this example, there are no restrictions when the two UUCP servers can connect. Line 3 defines the phone number required to connect to the ISP server. Again, you need to replace this value with the appropriate phone number for your ISP's UUCP server. Line 4 points to a definition in the `port` file to use for the connection. Line 5 defines the speed that is used on the connection. Line 6 defines the login chat sequence required to connect to the ISP UUCP server. You need to replace the userid and password with the correct ones for your ISP connection.

The third UUCP configuration file was alluded to in the `sys` file. The `port` file defines the modem ports that can be used by Taylor UUCP to attempt connections to the remote UUCP servers. Listing 13.11 shows an example of a `port` file.

LISTING 13.11   Sample Taylor UUCP `port` File

```
1  port      modem
2  type      modem
3  device    /dev/ttyS1
4  speed     38400
5  dialer    normal
```

In Listing 13.11, line 1 defines the port name referenced in the `sys` file. Line 2 defines the type of port used. In this case, the Linux mailserver uses a modem to connect to the remote UUCP server. Line 3 defines the device name of the modem. `ttyS1` defines the second COM port on the server. Line 4 again defines the modem speed used, and line 5 points to a dialer type from the `dial` file that is used to communicate with the modem.

The last UUCP configuration file is the `dial` file. The `dial` file is used to define the chat script used to communicate with the modem and dial the remote UUCP server. Listing 13.12 shows an example of the `dial` file.

LISTING 13.12   Sample Taylor UUCP `dial` File

```
1  dialer     normal
2  chat          "" ATZ OK ATDT\T CONNECT
```

In Listing 13.12, line 1 defines the dial type referenced by the port file. Line 2 defines the chat script necessary to dial the remote UUCP server's phone number. The `\T` variable is used to insert the phone number listed in the `sys` file.

When the Taylor UUCP configuration files are created, you should be able to establish a UUCP connection with the ISP UUCP server. To do this, you can use the command

```
/usr/sbin/uucico -s ispmail
```

where `ispmail` is the UUCP nodename of the ISP's UUCP server. When this command is entered, the modem should dial the ISP's UUCP server and establish a connection. The connection should drop quickly if there are no mail messages to transfer. The session should be logged in the UUCP `log` file, as specified by your particular Linux distribution. On Mandrake Linux, the UUCP log file is located at `/var/log/uucp/Log`.

sendmail Configuration

The sendmail configuration for this scenario is similar to the configurations used in the two previous scenarios. Because the Linux mailserver is not directly connected to the Internet, it must make use of a smart host to deliver any outgoing mail messages. The difference this time is that the Linux mailserver must use UUCP to connect to the smart host. Again, sendmail must also support relaying mail from local network clients. Listing 13.13 shows a sample macro file that can be used to create a `sendmail.cf` file.

LISTING 13.13   Sample sendmail Macro File Using UUCP

```
1  divert(-1)
2  divert(0)dnl
3  include(`/usr/lib/sendmail-cf/m4/cf.m4')dnl
4  OSTYPE(`linux')dnl
5
6  FEATURE(`allmasquerade')dnl
```

```
7  FEATURE(`masquerade_envelope')dnl
8  FEATURE(`local_procmail', `/usr/bin/procmail')dnl
9  FEATURE(`access_db', `/etc/mail/access.db')dnl
10 FEATURE(`nocanonify')dnl
11
12 MAILER(`smtp')dnl
13 MAILER(`procmail')dnl
14 MAILER(`uucp')dnl
15
16 MASQUERADE_AS(`smallorg.org')dnl
17 define(`SMART_HOST', `uucp-dom:ispmail')dnl
```

In Listing 13.13, lines 1 through 13 are the same as the previous two scenarios. Line 14 defines the UUCP mailer functions for sendmail. Line 17 defines a smart host, ispmail, which can be contacted using the uucp-dom protocol. This is a special format of the UUCP protocol that sendmail uses to transfer mail by using the UUCP protocol but retaining the SMTP headers of the messages.

As in the previous scenarios, the sendmail program should run in background mode. You can use the linuxconf program as shown in Figure 13.2 to set the sendmail program to start at boot time.

Automating Mail Retrieval

To make the mail process automatic, the UUCP connection must be established at a regular interval. As before, you can use the Linux cron utility to execute a script that initiates the UUCP connection to the ISP UUCP server. Again, you must use the crontab program to enter the scripts that cron will execute.

Two scripts can be entered into the cron table to execute at regular intervals. The uucico program is used to call the remote UUCP site. This can be set to call at set times throughout the day. To force uucico to call the remote UUCP host even if there are no queued jobs to transfer, you can manually create a poll file in the UUCP job queue area for the remote host. The poll file can be created just prior to execution of the uucico program. The uucico program deletes the poll file when it is finished. Listing 13.14 shows a sample script file that can be used to poll the ISP UUCP server.

LISTING 13.14   Sample UUCP cron File

```
14,29,44,59 * * * * /usr/sbin/touch /var/spool/uucp/ispmail/C./C.ispmailA0000
0,15,30,45, * * * * /usr/sbin/uucico -s ispmail
```

13

CONNECTING THE
MAILSERVER TO
AN ISP

The first entry in the script file creates a poll file for the remote UUCP host `ispmail`. You can substitute the UUCP nodename of the ISP UUCP server to create a poll file for your Linux mailserver. Similarly, the `uucico` command parameter should also be the UUCP nodename of the ISP UUCP server.

This configuration allows the Linux mailserver to call the ISP UUCP server every 15 minutes throughout the day. If you are paying for UUCP connection charges, you might want to set up several cron table entries to call uucico at one interval during business hours and at a less-frequent rate during non-business hours.

In this scenario, all mail is batched for delivery. Mail received by SMTP from the local clients is batched for transmission to the smart host. Mail received by the ISP mailserver from the Internet is stored in a UUCP queue until the UUCP connection is established.

Summary

This chapter defined some of the issues that a mail administrator must resolve before implementing a mailserver in the business network. There are many options to choose from regarding DNS name hosting, mail hosting, and ISP connectivity. This chapter also described four scenarios that demonstrated various configuration options available to use to transfer mail to and from the Internet via a Linux mailserver and an ISP. The direct Internet connection method is useful for sending and receiving mail in realtime. The dial-on-demand options are good for sending mail in realtime, but received messages are queued by the ISP and are downloaded by the Linux mailserver at set times. However, this option is usually inexpensive to implement. The last method examined was the use of the UUCP protocol to batch both outbound and inbound mail messages. Often, UUCP connections are all a small organization needs to support a solid Internet mail environment. Sometimes, a UUCP connection is the cheapest way to implement an Internet mail solution.

Mailserver Administration

IN THIS CHAPTER

Chapter 13, "Connecting the Mailserver to an ISP," described how to connect the Linux mailserver to the Internet using the Internet service provider. After everything has been configured and connected, mail will flow back and forth. Now your job as the mail administrator is done. Wrong. Your job has just begun.

The mail administrator must constantly be doing things with the mailserver. One of the most important tasks is userid maintenance. Another task is to watch the mailserver logs to determine whether things are going well. Depending on the type of Internet connectivity you chose, you might also have to constantly watch for hackers trying new and improved methods of breaking into your mailserver. You always need to be on the lookout for spammers flooding your mailboxes with useless mail, or trying to use your mailserver as an unknowing relay participant. The job of the mail administrator never ends. This chapter will describe some of the tools and techniques used by Linux mail administrators in maintaining a healthy mailserver.

Userid Maintenance

Each user who wants to receive mail via your mailserver must have a valid userid and password on the system. The mail administrator is continually adding and deleting userids. Depending on your organization, this can be either a daily task or a once-in-a-while task. Whichever it is, at some time you will need to add and delete userids. Also, don't forget about the occasional user who forgets his password—at some time, you will run across him, too.

Many Linux distributions include fancy graphical programs to assist in userid maintenance. The following section first describes the basics of Linux userids and passwords, and then examines some of the more popular Linux graphical userid maintenance programs.

The Linux Userid File

By default, Linux userids are stored in the /etc/passwd file. This file was discussed briefly in Chapter 12, "Installing and Configuring POP3 and IMAP." Listing 14.1 shows an example of a typical /etc/passwd file.

LISTING 14.1   Sample Linux /etc/passwd File

```
1   root:unaoBNGut6giH2:0:0:root:/root:/bin/bash
2   bin:*:1:1:bin:/bin:
3   daemon:*:2:2:daemon:/sbin:
4   adm:*:3:4:adm:/var/adm:
5   lp:*:4:7:lp:/var/spool/lpd:
6   sync:*:5:0:sync:/sbin:/bin/sync
7   shutdown:*:6:0:shutdown:/sbin:/sbin/shutdown
8   halt:*:7:0:halt:/sbin:/sbin/halt
```

```
9   mail:*:8:12:mail:/var/spool/mail:
10  news:*:9:13:news:/usr/lib/news:
11  uucp:*:10:14:uucp:/var/spool/uucppublic:
12  operator:*:11:0:operator:/root:/bin/bash
13  games:*:12:100:games:/usr/games:
14  man:*:13:15:man:/usr/man:
15  postmaster:*:14:12:postmaster:/var/spool/mail:/bin/bash
16  nobody:*:65535:100:nobody:/dev/null:
17  ftp:*:404:1:::/home/ftp:/bin/bash
18  rich:cLafgrY5tfHiw:501:101:Rich B.:/home/rich:/bin/bash
19  usenet:*:502:13:News master:/home/usenet:/bin/bash
20  bbs:*:503:200:BBS User:/home/bbs:/home/bbs:/bin/bash
21  barbara:*:504:100:Barbara B.:/home/barbara:/bin/bash
22  katie:*:505:100:Katie B.:/home/katie:/bin/bash
23  jessica:Ru7vx4rgypupg:506:100:Jessica B.:/home/jessica:/bin/bash
24  haley:WfNervHPbUxUk:507:100:Haley S.:/home/haley:/bin/bash
25  riley:VHA1qqu/pqjMU:508:100:Riley M.:/home/riley:/bin/bash
26  chris:5MLvL/waxN276:509:100:Chris W.:/home/chris:/bin/bash
27  matthew:nZF35ripKCbXQ:510:100:Matthew W.:/home/matthew:/bin/bash
28  alex:9QJ.MQWbSpBG.:511:100:Alex P.:/home/alex:/bin/bash
```

Listing 14.1 shows the common format of the /etc/passwd file. Each line represents information for one userid; the information is divided into fields separated by colons. The first field is the Linux username with which the user logs in. The second field is an encrypted version of the user's password. You'll notice that for some users the password field is just an asterisk (*). This is equivalent to locking the userid, as no combination of characters can be encrypted to just an asterisk. The third field is the userid number by which Linux tracks file access for the user. The fourth field is the group ID number assigned to the user. The next section describes Linux groups in detail.

The remaining fields further identify the user. The fifth field, a text identifier of the user, often contains the full name of the user to help document information for the mail administrator. The sixth field identifies the location of the user's default home directory. If your users are using the IMAP protocol to retrieve their mail (see Chapter 7, "IMAP Protocol"), each user must have a separate home directory. The Linux IMAP software uses the user's home directory as the default location to create new folders requested by the user. Each user must have the proper read and write permissions to the home directory.

The last field identifies the default Linux shell program the user will execute if she logs in interactively. For the purposes of a mailserver, it is safe to use the default Linux bash shell (/bin/bash) for this field. Some advanced mail administrators concoct complex login shells to prevent users from logging in interactively. Those techniques are beyond the scope of this book.

14

MAILSERVER
ADMINISTRATION

Shadow Passwords

You might have noticed one bad thing about the default Linux userid file—all users can read it. The logon programs run as the userid and need to be able to read the /etc/passwd file to compare the attempted password with the real password. Creative users can copy the password file and run commonly found cracker programs against it to determine the passwords of other users. This is a potentially bad situation (especially if senior managers use simple passwords so they can remember them).

To combat this problem, most Linux distributions offer the ability to use a shadow password file. The *shadow password file* is a separate file that contains the user's passwords and other related housekeeping information. Passwords are not kept in the /etc/passwd file. The shadow password file is not readable to normal Linux users, so they won't be able to copy the file and attempt to crack it. Listing 14.2 shows a sample shadow password file.

LISTING 14.2   Sample Linux Shadow Password File

```
1  root:$1$wkRtbOwr46TSWmezOiXx.ZGAtG/zGKU1:10863:0:99999:7:-1:-1:134537880
2  bin:*:10863:0:99999:7:::
3  daemon:*:10863:0:99999:7:::
4  adm:*:10863:0:99999:7:::
5  lp:*:10863:0:99999:7:::
6  sync:*:10863:0:99999:7:::
7  shutdown:*:10863:0:99999:7:::
8  halt:*:10863:0:99999:7:::
9  mail:*:10863:0:99999:7:::
10 news:*:10863:0:99999:7:::
11 uucp:*:10863:0:99999:7:::
12 operator:*:10863:0:99999:7:::
13 games:*:10863:0:99999:7:::
14 gopher:*:10863:0:99999:7:::
15 ftp:*:10863:0:99999:7:::
16 nobody:*:10863:0:99999:7:::
17 postgres:!!:10863:0:99999:7:::
18 lists:!!:10863:0:99999:7:::
19 xfs:!!:10863:0:99999:7:::
20 rich:LMQ0vbvbnZpZr1s:10863:0:99999:7:::
21 barbara:$1$OR1Qdo1l$GK/H8tjwPGCBUUHMEjXWe1:10863:0:99999:7:::
22 katie:$1$XEd8PKaP$AuwsgfeN3UBcKjB0GeL1d1:10882:0:99999:7:::
23 jessica:$1$ashasfha4hasfhasfhwr$asfgas44rgs:10885:0:99999:7:::
```

Listing 14.2 shows the common format of the shadow password file. On most Linux distributions, it is located at /etc/shadow. As in the normal /etc/passwd file, each line represents information for one userid. The information is divided into fields separated by colons. The first field is the username. This name should exactly match the username field in the /etc/passwd file. The second field is the encrypted password. You might notice a difference between the encrypted passwords in Listing 14.2 and the ones in Listing 14.1. The Linux system shown in Listing 14.2 was configured to use MD5 encryption of passwords. MD5 produces a stronger encryption than the standard UNIX password encryption technique that is used by default in Linux.

The shadow file itself can be used for more than just hiding passwords. Each of the other fields has special meanings when used by other Linux utilities. The third field shows the number of days after January 1, 1970, that the password was last changed. The fourth field contains a 0 for all the users in the example, indicating that they are all allowed to change their own passwords. Changing this to a 1 prevents a user from changing his own password. The fifth field shows the number of days after January 1, 1970, that the password will expire. All the fields in the example are set to high values that, for all practical purposes, will keep the passwords from expiring.

The sixth field indicates the number of days before your password expires that Linux will forewarn you of the expiration. The seventh field shows the number of days you have after the password expires before Linux prevents that userid from logging in. The eighth field is used for expired passwords, and contains the number of days since January 1, 1970, that a password has been out of use.

The downside to using a shadow password file is that any program which verifies userids needs to be compiled to use the file. This includes FTP, POP3, and IMAP servers. Fortunately, most common network software packages have this capability already.

Mail User Passwords

The mail administrator can use the Linux shadow password file features to control password usage among mail users. Just remember that most mail users do not log in to the Linux mailserver interactively, so changing a user password is often not an easy task.

14

MAILSERVER ADMINISTRATION

The Linux group File

The other important file employed in user administration, the /etc/group file, identifies usernames with groups. Assigning users to groups allows access to files for a large subset of users. Listing 14.3 shows a sample /etc/group file.

LISTING 14.3   Sample Linux /etc/group File

```
 1  root::0:root
 2  bin::1:root,bin,daemon
 3  daemon::2:root,bin,daemon
 4  sys::3:root,bin,adm
 5  adm::4:root,adm,daemon
 6  tty::5:
 7  disk::6:root
 8  lp::7:daemon,lp
 9  mem::8:
10  kmem::9:
11  wheel::10:root
12  mail::12:mail
13  news::13:news
14  uucp::14:uucp
15  man::15:
16  games::20:
17  gopher::30:
18  dip::40:
19  ftp::50:
20  nobody::99:
21  users::100:
22  postgres:x:101:
23  utmp:x:102:
24  lists:x:500:
25  floppy:x:19:
26  console:x:11:
27  xfs:x:103:
28  pppusers:x:230:
29  popusers:x:231:
30  slipusers:x:232:
31  slocate:x:21:
32  rich::501:
33  dba:x:502:
34  oinstall:x:503:oracle
35  oracle:x:504:
36  pop:x:505:
```

Listing 14.3 shows the common format for the Linux group file. Each line represents a different group; group information is divided into fields separated by colons. The first field is the group name. The second field is the group password. If this field is blank, no password is required to access group files. As shown in Listing 14.3, this group file uses shadow passwords (identified by the x). The third field is the group ID that identifies the group when members access files and directories. The fourth field lists userids with access to the group. In line 34, the userid `oracle` has access to the group `oinstall` besides having its own group, `oracle`. This demonstrates that a userid can be a member of multiple groups.

> ### Groups and Mail Users
>
> Linux groups are not commonly used in mailserver installations. It is often safest to designate a new group for each userid created, so that no accidental sharing of files can occur between users. Groups are useful for allowing mail users access to co-workers' mailboxes when necessary without having to grant special privileges.

Userid Maintenance Utilities

If your Linux system does not use shadow passwords, you can add and delete userids by editing the /etc/passwd file. However, this is not recommended; making mistakes in the /etc/passwd file can render your Linux system useless. It is best to use the user administration utilities to add and delete userids, whether you use shadow passwords or not.

The most common user administration utility in Linux is the useradd utility. The format of the useradd utility is

```
useradd [-c comment] [-d home_dir]
             [-e expire_date] [-f inactive_time]
             [-g initial_group] [-G group[,...]]
             [-m [-k skeleton_dir] | -M] [-s shell]
             [-u uid [ -o]] [-n] [-r] login
```

Table 14.1 describes the command parameters available for the useradd utility.

TABLE 14.1   useradd Parameters

Parameter	Description
-c	Adds a comment to the `passwd` file record
-d	The home directory
-e	The expiration date of the password
-f	The number of days after the password expires that it is disabled
-g	The default group
-G	A list of other groups to which the userid can belong
-m	Creates the user's home directory if it does not exist
-k *skeldir*	Uses an alternate `skel` directory

continues

14

MAILSERVER
ADMINISTRATION

TABLE 14.1 continued

Parameter	Description
-M	The user's home directory will not be created if it does not exist
-n	In Red Hat Linux variants, a group with the same name as the username will not be created
-r	Creates a system account rather than a user account
-s	Specifies the default logon shell
-u	Specifies a user ID number

Listing 14.4 shows an example of creating a new Linux user with the useradd utility.

LISTING 14.4 Creating a New User

```
 1  [root@shadrach /root]# useradd -c "Riley M." riley
 2  [root@shadrach /root]# cat /etc/passwd | grep riley
 3  riley:x:504:506:Riley M.:/home/riley:/bin/bash
 4  [root@shadrach /root]# cat /etc/group | grep riley
 5  riley:x:506:
 6  [root@shadrach /root]# ls -al /home/riley
 7  total 21
 8  drwx------    5 riley     riley        1024 Nov  1 16:48 .
 9  drwxr-xr-x    7 root      root         1024 Nov  1 16:48 ..
10  -rw-r--r--    1 riley     riley        1899 Nov  1 16:48 .Xdefaults
11  -rw-r--r--    1 riley     riley          24 Nov  1 16:48 .bash_logout
12  -rw-r--r--    1 riley     riley         230 Nov  1 16:48 .bash_profile
13  -rw-r--r--    1 riley     riley         434 Nov  1 16:48 .bashrc
14  -rw-r--r--    1 riley     riley        2626 Nov  1 16:48 .emacs
15  drwxr-xr-x    3 riley     riley        1024 Nov  1 16:48 .kde
16  -rw-r--r--    1 riley     riley        1416 Nov  1 16:48 .kderc
17  -rw-r--r--    1 riley     riley         185 Nov  1 16:48 .mailcap
18  -rw-r--r--    1 riley     riley        3846 Nov  1 16:48 .vimrc
19  -rw-r--r--    1 riley     riley         397 Nov  1 16:48 .zshrc
20  drwxr-xr-x    5 riley     riley        1024 Nov  1 16:48 Desktop
21  drwxr-xr-x    2 riley     riley        1024 Nov  1 16:48 tmp
22  [root@shadrach /root]#
```

In Listing 14.4, line 1 shows the useradd utility being used to create a new username, riley, with a text comment added to the comment field. The default userid value and login shell are used in this example. Line 3 shows the result in the /etc/passwd file. A new line is added for the new username with the next available userid (504) and the next available groupid (506). By default, the useradd utility created a default home directory of /home/riley. Also by default, the logon shell was set to /bin/bash. By listing the newly created home directory in line 6, you can see that several new files have been created already. This is definitely overkill for a simple email userid. Where did all these defaults come from?

By using the -D option on the useradd utility, you can view the defaults that useradd uses when creating a new user account. Listing 14.5 shows an example of this.

LISTING 14.5   Sample useradd -D Output

```
1  [root@shadrach /root]# useradd -D
2  GROUP=100
3  HOME=/home
4  INACTIVE=-1
5  EXPIRE=
6  SHELL=/bin/bash
7  SKEL=/etc/skel
8  [root@shadrach /root]#
```

In Listing 14.5, line 3 shows the default home directory location that useradd appends to the username to create the new directory. You can change this value if you want to create user home directories somewhere other than /home. The mail administrator might be most interested in line 7, which declares a directory that will be copied to the newly created user home directory. Listing 14.6 shows the contents of the /etc/skel directory.

LISTING 14.6   Sample /etc/skel Directory

```
1  [root@shadrach /root]# ls -al /etc/skel
2  total 23
3  drwxr-xr-x   5 root     root        1024 Sep 29 05:18 .
4  drwxr-xr-x  31 root     root        3072 Nov  1 16:48 ..
5  -rw-r--r--   1 root     root        1899 Apr 27  1999 .Xdefaults
6  -rw-r--r--   1 root     root          24 Jul 13  1994 .bash_logout
7  -rw-r--r--   1 root     root         230 Aug 22  1998 .bash_profile
8  -rw-r--r--   1 root     root         434 May 17 21:15 .bashrc
9  -rw-r--r--   1 root     root        2626 Apr 27  1999 .emacs
10 drwxr-xr-x   3 root     root        1024 Sep 29 05:18 .kde
11 -rw-r--r--   1 root     root        1416 May 17 14:44 .kderc
12 -rw-r--r--   1 root     root         185 May 18 10:16 .mailcap
13 -rw-r--r--   1 root     root        3846 May 11 12:49 .vimrc
14 -rw-r--r--   1 root     root         397 Apr 27  1999 .zshrc
15 drwxr-xr-x   5 root     root        1024 Sep 29 05:18 Desktop
16 drwxr-xr-x   2 root     root        1024 May 18 10:12 tmp
17 [root@shadrach /root]#
```

14

MAILSERVER ADMINISTRATION

Listing 14.6 looks suspiciously familiar. It is exactly the same directory as shown in Listing 14.4. The useradd utility took the contents of the /etc/skel directory and copied them to the user home directory when it was created. As you can see, there are lots of configuration files here that users logging in to the system from an X Window session will need, but almost none that an email client will need.

To make the user home directories simpler (especially if you are using the IMAP protocol to store mail folders in the users' home directories), you can move the template files from the /etc/skel directory. By leaving the /etc/skel directory empty, nothing will be copied into new users' home directories.

> ### CAUTION
>
> Although leaving the skel directory empty is preferred for mail users, other users (especially X Window users) might need those files and directories. If you are supporting a mixed environment, it might be easier to use the -k option in the useradd program and create a separate, empty skel directory just for mail users.

After the userids are created, each user must have a password to log in to the mailserver. Although the useradd program creates the user account, it does not create a password for it. By default, the user account is locked and not allowed to be used until a password is assigned. The passwd program is used to assign new passwords to userids. The format of the passwd program is

```
passwd username
```

where *username* is the username of the user you want to change the password for. To change passwords for users other than yourself, you must be logged in as the root user. The passwd program queries for a new password, and then repeats the query to ensure that no typos were made.

Graphical Userid Maintenance Utilities

Most Linux distributions that support a windowing environment include a graphical userid maintenance utility. For Mandrake Linux it is the kuser program. To use kuser, you will need to either log in as root, or use the su program to change your effective userid to the root user. Figure 14.1 shows the main kuser window.

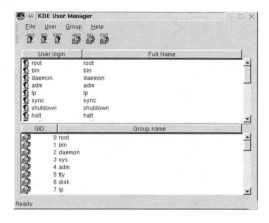

FIGURE 14.1
The kuser main window.

The main window displays the existing userids on the Linux system. The kuser program can be used to add, delete, and modify usernames. By selecting the Add button, and entering in a new username, the User properties window, shown in Figure 14.2, appears. The User properties window queries for the same values that were entered for the useradd program and the /etc/passwd file.

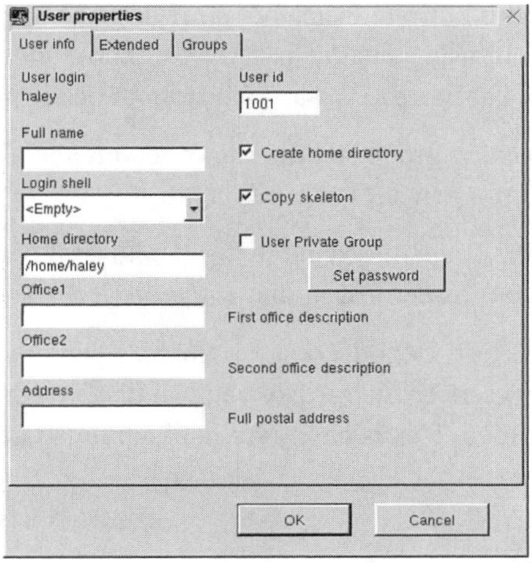

FIGURE 14.2
The kuser User properties window.

Clicking on the Extended tab reveals values present in the shadow password file /etc/shadow. Figure 14.3 shows the results of this action.

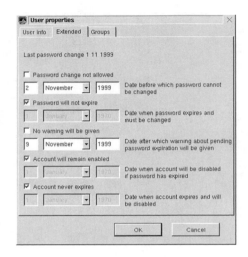

FIGURE 14.3

The kuser User properties Extended tab window.

Figure 14.3 shows fields that can be changed with the Extended User properties window. Dates can be entered in standard format instead of worrying about calculating the days since January 1, 1970. If you are not using shadow passwords, these fields will be unavailable for you to enter data. Figure 14.4 shows the Groups tab from the User properties window.

The Groups window lists existing groups on the Linux server, and allows the administrator to pick and choose which groups a new user will belong to.

Finally, Figure 14.5 shows the Properties window for the kuser program. This enables the administrator to set the defaults as defined in the -D option of the useradd program.

As shown in Figure 14.5, the Edit Defaults window enables you to set the default shell and home directories for all new users created. Also, you can disable copying the /etc/skel directory to the new home directories. This is handy for mail administrators.

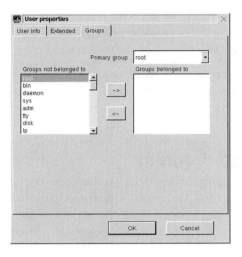

Figure 14.4
The kuser User properties Groups tab window.

Figure 14.5
The kuser Edit defaults window.

Monitoring the Mailserver

As the mail administrator, it is your responsibility to monitor the activity on the mailserver. Sometimes this is much easier said than done. There are often many things happening at the same time on the mailserver, and watching them all is difficult. You must be able to monitor the Internet connection to ensure that mail is properly flowing both into and out of the mailserver, as well as ensure that no hackers or spammers have discovered your mailserver and are attempting to take advantage of it. On the other side, you must monitor the POP3 and/or IMAP services to ensure your customers can properly access their mailboxes. Speaking of mailboxes, how's the disk space doing on the mailserver?

The mail administrator must monitor all these topics to ensure proper mail service for the office. Fortunately, the mail administrator has some help from Linux. This section discusses the Linux system logging programs that can help watch the mailserver activity and report any problems that may occur.

The Linux syslogd Program

The Linux system's syslogd program tracks events that occur on the system and logs messages for each event in system log files. As the mail administrator, you will be able to locate log files and track any problems that might appear there. You should get in the habit of scanning through the log files at least once a day to watch for possible system or security problems.

The syslogd program is normally started at boot time by an `init` script and quietly runs in background mode. Most Linux distributions start syslogd by default. You can check to see whether syslogd is running on your Linux system by using the command

```
ps ax | more
```

The syslogd program will show up in the list of processes running on your system. When syslogd starts, it reads a configuration file to determine what types of messages to log and how to log them.

The events that syslogd logs in the log files can be configured by the mail administrator. You can create as many different log files as you feel necessary. Each log file can contain information regarding particular types of system and program events. Table 14.2 shows the different event types available on the Linux system.

TABLE 14.2   syslogd Event Types

Event	Description
auth	Security/authorization events
authpriv	Private security/authorization events
cron	Cron daemon events
daemon	System daemon events
kern	System kernel events
lpr	Line printer events
mail	Mail program events

Event	Description
mark	Internal check
news	Network news program events
syslog	Internal syslogd events
user	User-level events
uucp	UUCP program events
localn	Locally defined events ($n = 0$ through 7)

Each event type has a hierarchy of message priorities. In Table 14.3, the priorities are listed from debug (the lowest priority) to emerg (the highest priority). Lower priorities mean smaller problems. Higher priorities mean bigger problems.

TABLE 14.3   syslogd Message Priorities

Priority	Description
debug	Debugging events
info	Informational events
notice	Normal notices
warning	Warning messages
err	Error condition events
crit	Critical system conditions
alert	System alerts
emerg	Fatal system conditions

The following sections describe the syslogd program and how to configure it to log events in log files.

syslogd Parameters

The format of the syslogd command is

syslogd *options*

where *options* is a list of options to modify the behavior of the syslogd program. Table 14.4 shows the options available to use with syslogd.

14

MAILSERVER ADMINISTRATION

TABLE 14.4 `syslogd` Options

Option	Description
`-a socket`	Specifies additional sockets to listen to for remote connections
`-d`	Turns on debugging mode
`-f config`	Uses the configuration file specified by `config`
`-h`	Forwards any remote messages to forwarding hosts.
`-l hostlist`	Specifies a list of hosts that are logged only by hostname
`-m interval`	Sets the `MARK` timestamp interval in the log file; Setting to `0` disables the timestamp
`-n`	Avoids auto-backgrounding
`-p socket`	Specifies an alternative socket to listen to for remote syslog connections
`-r`	Enables receipt of remote syslog connections
`-s domainlist`	Specifies a list of domain names that will be stripped off before logging.
`-v`	Prints syslogd version.

A Linux server has the capability of becoming a remote syslog server. By default, this option is turned off. By using the `-r` option for the syslogd program, the Linux server accepts syslog messages sent from remote hosts and logs them in its own log files. This technique is handy if you have several Linux servers and want to redirect their logs to a single place.

> **CAUTION**
>
> You should use the -r option with caution if you are directly connected to the Internet. A well-known hacker technique involves sending massive numbers of bogus syslog messages to a remote host's syslog port to flood the server and create a denial-of-service situation.

By default, the syslogd program reads a configuration file at startup to determine the actions that it should take for particular events. The next section describes the format of the `syslogd` configuration file.

syslogd Configuration File

The syslogd configuration file is located by default at `/etc/syslog.conf`. It contains directives that tell the syslogd program what type of events to log, and how to log them.

The format of the /etc/syslog.conf file is

```
event.priority     action
```

Each line in the /etc/syslog.conf file represents different actions. There are three actions that can be taken for events:

- Displaying the event message to the system console
- Logging the event message to a log file
- Sending the event message to a remote log host

The syslogd configuration file consists of combinations of events and actions that define the characteristics of the syslogd program. Listing 14.7 shows a sample /etc/syslog.conf file.

LISTING 14.7 Sample /etc/syslog.conf File

```
1  # Log all kernel messages to the console.
2  # Logging much else clutters up the screen.
3  kern.*                          /dev/console
4
5  # Log anything (except mail) of level info or higher.
6  # Don't log private authentication messages!
7  *.info;mail.none;authpriv.none          /var/log/messages
8
9  # The authpriv file has restricted access.
10 authpriv.*                      /var/log/secure
11
12 # Log all the mail messages in one place.
13 mail.*                          /var/log/maillog
14
15 # Everybody gets emergency messages, plus log them on another
16 # machine.
17 *.emerg                         *
18 *.emerg                         @meshach.smallorg.org
19
20 # Save mail and news errors of level err and higher in a
21 # special file.
22 uucp,news.crit                  /var/log/spooler
```

Listing 14.7 shows an /etc/syslog.conf file from a Mandrake Linux 6.0 system. Lines 1 and 2 start off by showing how to use comments within the configuration file. These lines are not processed by syslogd. Line 3 shows wildcard characters in the configuration, which indicates that all kernel event messages of any priority will be sent to the system console. Line 7 is a good example of a complex configuration.

14

MAILSERVER ADMINISTRATION

Multiple events can be configured for a single action line. A semicolon separates event and priority pairs. The first pair is `*.info`. This defines all events of priority `info` and higher. Remember that specifying a particular priority also specifies the priorities higher in the list.

The second pair, `mail.none`, might look confusing. You might be wondering why there is no `none` priority. This event pair excludes all mail events of any priority from the previous definition. The next pair, `authpriv.none`, does the same. This statement, in effect, logs all events except `mail` and `authpriv` events, of priority `info` and higher to the log file `/var/log/messages`.

Lines 10 and 13 define what is happening to the `authpriv` and `mail` events. Line 10 defines that all authpriv events of any priority get logged to a separate file `/var/log/secure`. Similarly, line 13 defines that all mail events of any priority get logged to a separate file named `/var/log/maillog`. This is an extremely handy way of parsing event messages by separating them into their own log files. As the mail administrator, you'll want to define a separate place to put all mail-related event messages to make it easier to spot mail problems on the system.

Line 18 shows an example of using a remote syslog server to log messages. Any emergency priority messages are sent to the remote host `meshach.smallorg.org`. If there is a serious error on the host, you might not get a chance to see the log file on it, so it is often a good idea to send these messages elsewhere (assuming that the serious error does not prevent the Linux system from sending the messages).

Watching for Hackers and Spammers

One of the most difficult jobs of the mail administrator is trying to protect the integrity of the mailserver. It is crucial that individual users' mail messages not be compromised in any way. Often the mail administrator can get clues about illegal activity from the log files. Listing 14.8 shows part of a sample `/var/log/maillog` file from a Mandrake Linux mailserver.

LISTING 14.8 Sample Log File with SMTP Session

```
1  Nov  2 19:09:12 shadrach sendmail[5365]: NOQUEUE: "wiz" command from
➥ [192.168.1.15] (192.168.1.15)
2  Nov  2 19:09:14 shadrach sendmail[5365]: NOQUEUE: "debug" command from
➥ [192.168.1.15] (192.168.1.15)
```

Listing 14.8 shows two attempts to access the sendmail program via the network. Both times the hacker attempted to use the archaic sendmail hacker commands "`wiz`" and "`debug`" that have long since been disabled. By reading the log file, you can determine the source address from which the commands were sent. It is proper Internet protocol to inform your ISP of this illegal attempt on your Linux mailserver. With any luck the ISP can track down the source of the hacking attempts.

Besides sendmail event messages, you might also find other types of mail messages in the /var/log/maillog log file. Listing 14.9 shows an example of a client trying to log in to the POP3 server.

LISTING 14.9   Sample Log File with POP3 Session

```
1  Nov  2 16:24:49 shadrach ipop3d[5373]: port 110 service init from
➡ 192.168.1.15
2  Nov  2 16:24:49 shadrach ipop3d[5373]: Login failure user=rich
➡ host=[192.168.1.15]
3  Nov  2 16:24:52 shadrach ipop3d[5373]: AUTHENTICATE LOGIN failure
➡ host=[192.168.1.15]
4  Nov  2 16:24:52 shadrach ipop3d[5373]: Command stream end of file while
➡ reading line user=??? host=[192.168.1.15]
5  Nov  2 16:24:55 shadrach ipop3d[5374]: port 110 service init from
➡ 192.168.1.15
6  Nov  2 16:24:55 shadrach ipop3d[5374]: Login failure user=rich
➡ host=[192.168.1.15]
7 Nov  2 16:24:58 shadrach ipop3d[5374]: AUTHENTICATE LOGIN failure
➡ host=[192.168.1.15]
```

Listing 14.9 shows the log file for the mail events generated by a mail user who did not know his password. Notice how in lines 2 and 6 the POP3 server program generated warning messages regarding the failed login attempts that include the source IP address of the site attempting to log in. Had this been a real hacker, your ISP could attempt to trace the IP address back to determine where the hacker was trying to log in from.

Summary

Administrating a mailserver is more than just installing software. Userids must be created and maintained to allow users to connect and read their mail messages. Linux provides several methods of manipulating userids. The useradd program is a console-based tool that can add and modify userids. The kuser program is a graphical tool that can be used to manipulate userids. Both produce the same results—userids are kept in the /etc/passwd file, and, optionally, the /etc/shadow file contains the user passwords. The mail administrator is also responsible for watching the Linux syslogd log files for improper behavior, both from the server and from users. Any hardware or software problems will be logged in the log file, and should be addressed as quickly as possible to prevent unnecessary server downtime. Attacks on the server can also be monitored by closely watching mail events. Excessive bad logins and invalid connection attempts are clues either that one of your users is going to call you with a problem, or that someone is trying to hack into your mailserver.

14

MAILSERVER
ADMINISTRATION

Configuring LAN Clients

IN THIS CHAPTER

After the Linux mailserver is configured and operational, the next step is to allow network clients to access their mailboxes on the server. First, the network clients must be configured to work in an IP environment on the network. This chapter describes the steps necessary to install Microsoft Windows 95, 98, and NT 4.0 workstations on the network. This chapter also describes the software required to connect to the Linux mailserver from the workstation clients. As discussed in Chapter 6, "POP3 Protocol," and Chapter 7, "IMAP Protocol," several client software packages are available to read mail messages from the mailserver. Because this book relates to creating an email environment as inexpensively as possible, this chapter discusses only email client software packages that are freely available, such as

> Netscape Navigator
>
> Outlook Express
>
> Eudora Light

Both Netscape Navigator and Outlook Express are parts of larger, more complex programs. Although they are good products, they tend to only work well on high-end Pentium workstations. They also tend to use up a lot of disk space on the workstation. Eudora Light is an excellent package for offices that have older, underpowered workstations, such as 486s, or workstations that do not have a lot of available disk space.

There are also other free email client software packages available besides those discussed in this chapter. The three packages described are representative of POP3 and IMAP client software packages. If you find another email client package available on the Internet, you can use these packages for comparison purposes to determine what features meet the requirements for your office mail system.

Requirements for a LAN Client

The mail administrator must make several decisions when choosing email client software. Much like choosing a method of connecting the mailserver to the Internet, choosing an email workstation client package often comes down to political decisions. This section describes the technical requirements that an email client should meet in order to properly read mail messages from the Linux mailserver. One of the political decisions that this section assumes is that the user workstations are running the Microsoft family of operating systems: Windows 95, 98, and NT 4.0. Similar features are also required for workstations running either an Apple- or UNIX-based operating system. Another assumed political decision is that the Linux mailserver is running either POP3 or IMAP server software. Chapter 6 discusses how to configure a POP3 server, whereas Chapter 7 discusses how to configure an IMAP server.

> ## Windows 2000
>
> At the time of this writing, Microsoft's newest operating system, Windows 2000, has not officially been released. The details available with the beta release versions of Windows 2000 indicate that the information presented in this chapter will also apply to a Windows 2000 workstation installation. If in doubt please consult the Windows 2000 documentation.

Network Connection

The most basic requirement for a network client is a connection to the network. To accomplish this, the client workstation must have some type of network card installed. Microsoft Windows 95, 98, and NT workstations all support the use of network cards to connect to a local network. Additionally, some kind of network system must be in place in the organization to connect the network workstations and Linux mailserver together. 100MB Ethernet hubs or switches are often used to connect network devices. For a small office network that is used primarily for email and maybe some file sharing, older (and cheaper) 10MB hubs will work just fine.

Microsoft Windows 95 and 98 Network Card Setup

Installing a network card in a Windows 95 or 98 computer is often an easy job. Windows 95 and 98 utilize the plug-and-play feature to autodetect new network cards that are inserted in the computer. After the network card is detected, the Install Wizard walks you through the steps necessary to load the appropriate drivers. If your network card was not detected, you can manually add it using the Network function available in the Control Panel. Figure 15.1 shows the Windows 95 and 98 Network window.

If the network card was detected at boot, it appears in the list of Configuration items. If not, you can click the Add button to install the network card. The Select Network Component Type window should appear, asking you what to add. Select the Adapter icon and then click the Add button.

After selecting the Add button, you should get the Select Network adapters window shown in Figure 15.2. From here, you can either select one of the adapters defined in Windows 95 or 98 or you can click the Have Disk button to use the driver disk that came with your network adapter. After the driver loads, Windows 95 or 98 should recognize your network card. You can determine that your card is recognized by observing the main Network window shown in Figure 15.1.

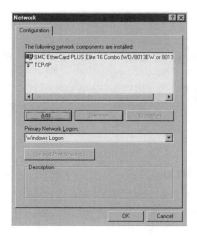

FIGURE 15.1
The Windows 95 and 98 Network window.

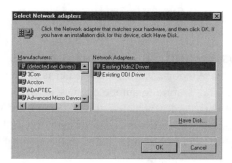

FIGURE 15.2
The Windows 95 and 98 Select Network adapters window.

Existing Drivers

Often if a workstation is upgraded from Windows 3.1 to Windows 95 or 98, any pre-existing NDIS or ODI drivers are migrated to the Windows network setup (as shown in Figure 15.2). This does not produce the most efficient network configuration. If your network card supports Windows 95 or 98 drivers, use those instead of the NDIS or ODI driver.

Microsoft NT 4.0 Workstation Network Card Setup

Installing network cards in a Microsoft Windows NT 4.0 workstation is not as easy as for Windows 95 and 98 workstations. Windows NT 4.0 does not support the plug-and-play architecture, so the network card must be manually added. As with Windows 95 and 98 workstations, you can access this function from the Network function in the Control Panel window. Figure 15.3 shows the main Network window.

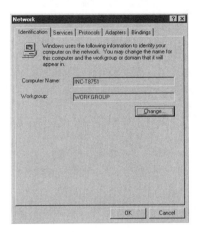

FIGURE 15.3
The Windows NT 4.0 workstation Network window.

You must select the Adapters tab to view the current network cards installed or to add a new network card. Figure 15.4 shows the Adapters tab of a Windows NT 4.0 workstation.

Clicking the Add button causes the Select Network Adapter window to appear. From the Select Network Adapter window, you can either select a preconfigured Windows NT driver for your network card or select the Have Disk button to use the driver disk that came with your network card. Figure 15.5 shows the Select Network Adapter window. After installing the appropriate driver for your network card, Windows NT 4.0 workstation should now recognize the network card. This can be determined by observing the Adapters tab shown in Figure 15.4.

IP Address

The second item that must be configured on the client workstation is a valid IP address for your network. The workstation must use the IP protocol to communicate with the Linux mailserver. Configuring an IP address for a workstation is a relatively simple task. Many networks have network administrators who manually assign IP addresses. Other networks have

15

DHCP servers that automatically assign an IP address as the workstation boots up. You will have to consult your network administrator to determine which method your network uses. If you are the network administrator, that should not be a problem.

FIGURE 15.4

The Windows NT 4.0 workstation Network Adapters window.

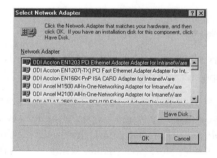

FIGURE 15.5

The Windows NT 4.0 workstation Select Network Adapter window.

If your network does not already have an IP address scheme, you must decide on one to use. The most common scheme for local networks is to use the Internet class B public IP domain: 192.168.0.0. This is an address range set aside by the Network Information Center to be used for local networks not directly connected to the Internet or connected through an IP proxy server (see Chapter 19, "IP Routing with Linux"). You can then choose to use either the entire 192.168.0.0 address range or a subset of it; for example, just the 192.168.1.0 network. This determines the subnet mask that you will use on your workstations. Each workstation on the network should use the same subnet mask. The most common method is to use a subnet of `192.168.1.0`, with a subnet mask of `255.255.255.0`. This allows for 254 hosts on the network.

After the IP address scheme has been determined for your network, each device on the network must have its own address. The following sections describe how to configure an IP address on Microsoft Windows 95, 98, and NT 4.0 workstations.

Microsoft Windows 95 and 98 IP Configuration

Configuring an IP address on a Windows 95 or 98 workstation is a simple task. First, you must ensure that the TCP/IP protocol is added to the networking software. The IP address function can be accessed from the Network function on the Control Panel. Figure 15.1 showed the Network window for a Windows 95 or 98 workstation.

To add TCP/IP protocol support to the workstation, you can click the Add button in the main Network window. This produces the Select Network Component Type window discussed earlier. From there, you can select the Protocol icon and click the Add button. This produces the Select Network Protocol window shown in Figure 15.6.

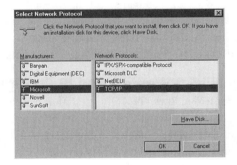

FIGURE 15.6
The Windows 95 and 98 Network Select Network Protocol window.

From this window, you can click once on the Microsoft icon, select the TCP/IP icon. This will install the TCP/IP protocol on the Windows 95 or 98 workstation. You might need to insert the Windows 95 or 98 media with which you installed the operating system as new files are loaded onto the system.

The next step is to configure the IP address necessary to communicate on your network. By selecting the TCP/IP icon on the main Network window, you will see the TCP/IP Properties window shown in Figure 15.7.

15

FIGURE 15.7

The Windows 95 and 98 Network TCP/IP Properties window.

Within the TCP/IP Properties window, you can select the method by which the workstation will receive an IP address: either automatically by a DHCP server on your network or manually by specifying an IP address and subnet mask in the appropriate fields. After you click the OK button, these values will take effect after the workstation reboots.

Microsoft Windows NT 4.0 Workstation IP Configuration

Configuring an IP address for a Windows NT 4.0 workstation uses a similar technique as for Windows 95 and 98 workstations. You must first select the Network function from the Control Panel window to get the Network window shown in Figure 15.3. From that window, you must select the Protocols tab to view the installed protocols on the workstation. Figure 15.8 shows an example of the Network Protocols window.

If the TCP/IP protocol does not appear in the Network Protocols list, you must click the Add button to install it. This produces the Select Network Protocol window shown in Figure 15.9. Select the TCP/IP icon to install the protocol. You might have to insert the media disk that was used to install the operating system because Windows NT must install several new files to support the TCP/IP protocol.

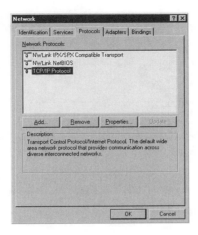

FIGURE 15.8

The Windows NT 4.0 workstation Network Protocols window.

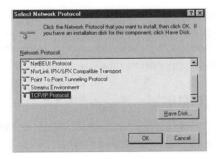

FIGURE 15.9

The Windows NT 4.0 workstation Select Network Protocol window.

After the TCP/IP protocol is installed, you can return to the main Network window and select the Protocols tab. Now the TCP/IP protocol should appear as an installed protocol, as shown in Figure 15.8. Now, you can select the TCP/IP icon and click the Properties icon to display the Microsoft TCP/IP Properties window shown in Figure 15.10.

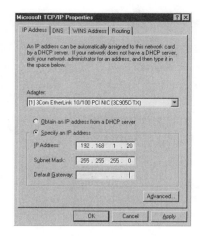

FIGURE 15.10

The Windows NT 4.0 workstation Microsoft TCP/IP Properties window.

The Microsoft TCP/IP Properties window enables you to select the method that the Windows NT 4.0 workstation will use to obtain an IP address: either automatically by using a DHCP server on your network or manually by specifying an IP address and subnet mask in the appropriate fields. You can click the Apply button for these values to take effect immediately.

Netscape Messenger

After the network card and IP protocol are configured for the workstation, you must install an email client software package to enable the user to connect to the Linux mailserver and read mail messages. This section covers installing and using the Netscape Messenger email client software.

Netscape Messenger is part of a larger software package, Netscape Communicator. Netscape Communicator includes Web browsing and Web page creation software as well as email client software. If your network clients will not do any Web browsing, this software package might be overkill. However, it does have the nice feature of being able to use either the POP3 or IMAP protocols to retrieve mail from the mailserver.

Downloading Messenger

The Netscape Communicator software package is freely available for downloading from Netscape's home page at http://www.netscape.com. You can also order a CD-ROM that contains the latest version of the software package. If you are planning to install lots of network clients, it might be easier to obtain the CD-ROM version of the software.

At the time of this writing, the latest version of Netscape Communicator is version 4.7. You can also directly download the software from the `ftp.netscape.com` FTP site using the userid `anonymous`, and your email address as the password. Currently, Communicator 4.7 is located in the directory

```
/pub/communicator/english/4.7/windows/windows95_or_nt/complete_install
```

When there, you can use the `BINARY` FTP mode to download the file `cc32e47.exe`, which is the self-extracting installation file for Netscape Communicator version 4.7.

Installing Messenger

Installing the Netscape Communicator software is easy. If you downloaded the program from the Web site or the FTP site, you can double-click the `cc32e47.exe` icon from Windows Explorer to start the installation process. If you are installing Communicator from a CD-ROM, the installation program automatically starts when you insert the CD. After the initial InstallShield progress screens, the main Netscape Communicator Setup screen appears.

After clicking the Next button and agreeing to the licensing agreement, the Setup Type window appears. From this window, you can choose how to load the Communicator program. The Typical install option installs the complete package—about 44MB. If you do not need all the fancy multimedia player software used in the Web browser, you can select the Custom install option and opt not to install those pieces to save some disk space. Either option will install the main Netscape Communicator software that you need.

After selecting the type of install you want, the InstallShield wizard asks a few more house-keeping questions, and then verifies that you want to install using the options you selected. After clicking the Install button, InstallShield copies the Netscape Communicator files to the location you selected.

After the installation program is complete, a new program group should appear on the workstation's Program list for Netscape Communicator, as well as a new desktop icon for the Communicator package. To access the Netscape Messenger program directly, select it from the Netscape Communicator program group.

Configuring Messenger

The first time you run Netscape Messenger, it asks you to create a profile. Profiles are used to track individual configuration information that is created while using Communicator. After clicking the Next button, Messenger asks for a specific profile name to use. If only one person will use the workstation, you can select the default profile. If more than one person will use the workstation, you can create a separate profile for each user so that they can all access their own mail. Netscape user profiles, although a nice feature, do not provide any privacy between users on the same workstation. You should remember that profiles are not protected and any user can access any other user's profile.

Windows Default Mail Applications

After the profile has been created, Messenger asks whether you want Netscape Messenger to be the default mail application for the workstation. If Messenger is the only mail application you are to use, select Yes. If you have another mail application, select No.

To start Netscape Messenger, select it from the Programs Start menu item. Figure 15.11 shows the main Netscape Messenger window that will appear.

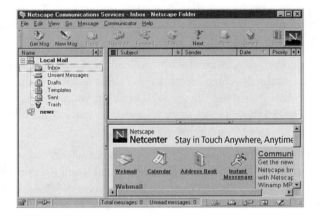

FIGURE 15.11

The Netscape Messenger main window.

To configure Messenger for your Linux mailserver, you must go to the Edit, Preferences menu option. The Preferences window will appear, allowing you to modify the settings within Messenger.

By clicking the Mail Servers menu item, the Mail Servers configuration window appears, as shown in Figure 15.12.

To configure Messenger to access the Linux mailserver, click the Add button. The Mail Server Properties window shown in Figure 15.13 enables you to configure the details for the remote Linux mailserver. You must select the type of access you need: either POP3 or IMAP. Additional configuration information is required depending on which type of email server access you select. Remember that for POP3 connections, all mail messages are downloaded to the local workstation; for IMAP connections, the mail messages remain on the mailserver at all times. You might notice the options available for each method change. For a POP3 server, Messenger asks whether you want to delete the message from the server after downloading. In this environment, that is probably the best thing to do. For an IMAP server, Messenger enables you to configure any predefined folders that are available on the mailserver.

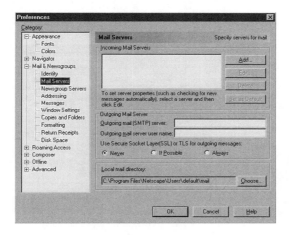

FIGURE 15.12
The Netscape Messenger Mail Servers configuration window.

FIGURE 15.13
The Netscape Messenger Mail Server Properties window.

After creating a default mailserver, Messenger is ready to connect to the server and retrieve new mail messages. To send messages from this workstation, you must configure the Outgoing Mail Server parameters as shown in Figure 15.12. The Outgoing mail (SMTP) server address field is the IP address of the Linux mailserver. This configuration uses the Linux mailserver to relay outgoing messages from the workstation to the Internet or other local network users. Remember to configure the sendmail program on the Linux mailserver to allow local workstations to relay mail messages (see Chapter 13, "Connecting the Mailserver to an ISP"). Also, you must set your identity in Messenger using the Edit, Preferences menu item, and selecting the Identity option as shown in Figure 15.14. You should enter the email address of the person using the workstation in the email address field. This string is used as the return address in all outgoing messages.

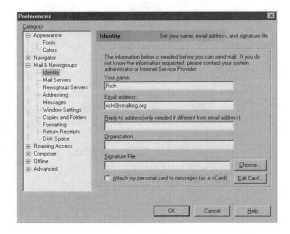

FIGURE 15.14

The Netscape Messenger Identity configuration window.

Using Messenger

After configuring Messenger for the local Linux mailserver, you can use it to send and receive mail. After you click on the Get Msgs icon at the top of the main window, Messenger will ask for your password, and then attempt to connect to the Linux mailserver and retrieve any messages in your INBOX folder using the mail protocol that you specified. If you specified the IMAP protocol, Messenger will show a separate INBOX for the remote Linux mailserver (remember that the IMAP protocol keeps the messages on the mailserver). Either way, new messages will appear in the INBOX folder. The message headers are shown in the list on the rightmost side. By clicking on the message header, the body will appear in the lower window. Messenger supports messages sent in HTML format by displaying them as a Web page in the window.

Sending messages is just as easy. Clicking on the New Msg button produces the Composition window shown in Figure 15.15. The top section specifies the recipients of the message. You can change a recipient from a To: to a CC: or BCC: by clicking on the To: icon. As in received messages, Messenger supports sending HTML-formatted messages. By default, Messenger attempts to convert the message to text format if the receiving mail host can not accept HTML-formatted mail. You can change the default behavior by using the Edit, Preferences menu item and selecting the Formatting option from the Mail & Newsgroups area. Messenger also supports attaching binary files to messages using the MIME encoding method. This greatly simplifies file transfers between people within the office.

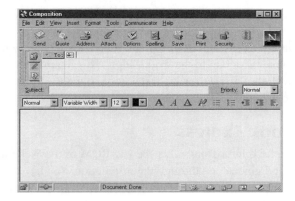

FIGURE 15.15
The Netscape Messenger Composition window.

The Netscape Messenger mail package is a good email client package. Its support of both POP3 and IMAP protocols makes it extremely versatile. Unfortunately, the large installation size of Netscape Communicator can sometimes be a problem with small offices that might have underpowered workstations to support.

Microsoft Outlook Express

Another popular free email software package is Microsoft Outlook Express. This is a trimmed-down version of the standard Microsoft Outlook email program often used with the Microsoft Exchange email server. Much like Netscape Messenger, Microsoft Outlook Express is a piece of a larger software package; in this case, Internet Explorer. Internet Explorer version 5.0 is the default Web browsing software in the Windows 98 operating system. This section describes how to get and install the Microsoft Internet Explorer package and how to configure and use the Outlook Express package with a Linux mailserver.

Downloading

The Microsoft Internet Explorer software package is freely available for downloading from Microsoft's home page at `http://www.microsoft.com`. From there, you can also order a CD-ROM that contains the latest version of the software package. Again, if you are planning on installing many network clients, it might be easier to spend the few dollars and obtain a CD-ROM version of the software.

At the time of this writing, the current version of Internet Explorer is version 5.0. The Internet Explorer 5.0 package includes Outlook Express version 5. It is available from a link on Microsoft's Web home page. Unlike the Netscape installation in which you download the complete install file, Microsoft's installation does things a little bit differently. All you download is a setup file: `ie5setup.exe`. That file does not contain the entire installation for Internet Explorer. When you run the `ie5setup.exe` program, it uses a Web connection to download the rest of the Internet Explorer program to the workstation. This requires each workstation to be able to communicate with the Internet for the installation to work. If that is not the case with your office network, you should request Internet Explorer on CD-ROM.

Installing Outlook Express

When you install Internet Explorer from either the CD-ROM or the Web page install, the Install Wizard appears and guides you through the installation. You have the option of installing just the Web browser software or the complete package. To get the Outlook Express software, you must install the complete package. The complete Internet Explorer package takes about 17MB of disk space.

After the Install Wizard is complete, Internet Explorer reboots the system. When the system starts up, the Install Wizard completes a few more tasks and then starts the Internet Connection Wizard to enable you to configure the software for your Internet and mail environments.

Configuring Outlook Express

After rebooting, the Internet Connection Wizard window appears. It offers you several choices of how to connect to the Internet. Select the option to manually configure the Internet connection. The wizard steps you through defining your network connection. Select the local area network (LAN) option because that is how you will connect to the Linux mailserver.

When the Internet connection part is completed, the Internet Connection Wizard asks whether you want to set up an Internet mail account. You can answer Yes to this question to configure your Linux mailserver account in Outlook Express. As in the Netscape Messenger installation, Outlook Express queries for specific information regarding the Linux mailserver: your username, email address (including domain name), and server address. Remember to enter the proper domain name for your email address or your messages might not have the proper return address on them.

Outlook Express also gives you the option of using either the POP3 or IMAP protocols to connect to the mailserver. Remember that when you select the IMAP option, all the mail messages remain in folders on the Linux mailserver. The POP3 option downloads the messages to the local workstation. It is advisable to not allow Outlook Express to remember the password for the user account on the Linux mailserver. This could be a security risk if other people have access to the workstation.

After Outlook Express is configured, you can go back and change the mailserver settings by using the Tools, Accounts menu item. This produces the Internet Accounts dialog box shown in Figure 15.16.

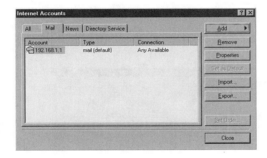

FIGURE 15.16
The Microsoft Outlook Express Internet Accounts dialog box.

By clicking the Properties button, values can be changed for the mailserver connection. By clicking the Add button, a new mailserver connection can be defined. Figure 15.17 shows the Properties dialog box for the mailserver connection.

The General tab contains information about the name and email address that the user will be using in mail messages. The Servers tab contains information about the type of mailserver (POP3 or IMAP) and the network addresses of the inbound and outbound mail servers. The IP address of the Linux mailserver should be used in both these fields. Again, remember to configure the sendmail program on the Linux mailserver to allow local network users to relay SMTP messages, or the outbound mail function on Outlook Express will not work.

Using Outlook Express

The first time you attempt to connect to the Linux mailserver, Outlook Express will query for the password needed to connect to the Linux mailserver mail account. Figure 15.18 shows the connection dialog box.

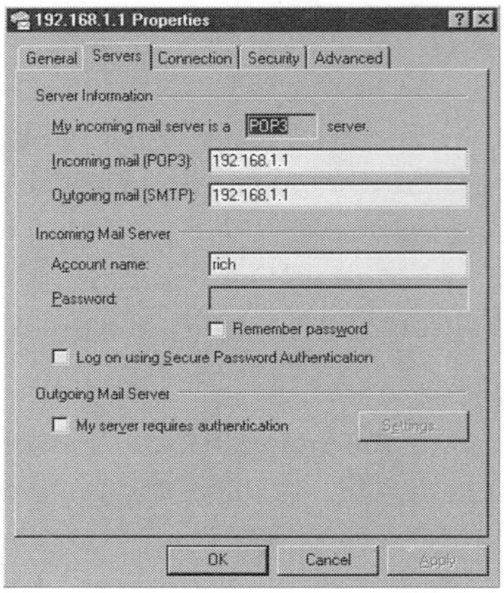

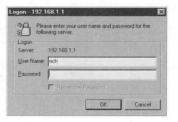

FIGURE 15.17

The Microsoft Outlook Express mailserver Properties dialog box.

FIGURE 15.18

The Microsoft Outlook Express connection dialog box.

After entering the appropriate password, Outlook Express connects to the Linux mailserver and retrieves any messages waiting for the user. The basic layout of Outlook Express is similar to that of the Netscape Messenger package. As shown in Figure 15.19, message headers are listed in a small window at the right side of the main window. The message body is displayed in a window beneath the headers list. Separate mail folders are listed on the left side. If you select the IMAP protocol to retrieve messages from the mailserver, the mailserver folders are listed separate from the local workstation folders. Thus, for IMAP servers, the Inbox for the server is different than the Inbox on the workstation.

To compose new messages, click the New Mail icon at the top of the main window. The New Message window shown in Figure 15.20 appears. You can enter the recipient email names in either the To: or Cc: line. You must use the full domain email name of the recipients when entering addresses here. If you want, you may enter addresses into the Outlook address book, assigning nicknames to fully qualified domain email addresses to simplify things. As with Netscape Messenger, Outlook Express enables you to send and receive HTML-formatted mail messages. Also, Outlook Express supports binary file attachments to messages by clicking the Attach icon at the top of the New Message window.

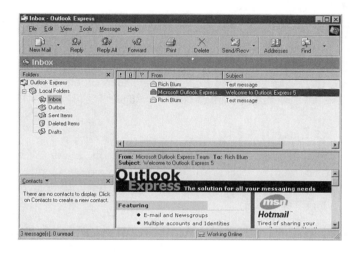

FIGURE 15.19

The Microsoft Outlook Express main window.

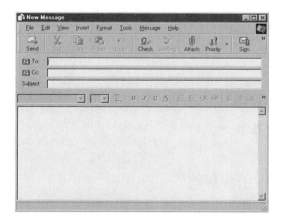

FIGURE 15.20

The Microsoft Outlook Express New Message dialog box.

The Microsoft Outlook Express email client is a nice email tool to have in the office. If your office does not do Web browsing, there might be too much overhead though with this package. As with the Messenger package, Internet Explorer is not for offices that must support workstations that are a little underpowered. The next package described solves this problem.

Qualcomm Eudora Light

The Qualcomm corporation was already mentioned before in this book. Chapter 6 discussed using the Qpopper POP3 server program for the Linux mailserver. Qualcomm maintains the Eudora Pro email client package as well. Besides the Eudora Pro package, Qualcomm produces a free version of Eudora Pro called Eudora Light. This section describes how to download, install, and use the Eudora Light email client package.

Downloading Eudora Light

The Eudora Light software package can be downloaded from the Eudora Web site at `http://www.eudora.com/eudoralight/`. You must fill in a short questionnaire before you are allowed to download the software. If you are not into completing questionnaires, you can FTP the file from the Eudora FTP server:

`ftp://ftp.eudora.com/eudora/eudoralight/windows/english/306/eul306.exe`

The file is about 4.6MB in size. As before, remember to use the `BINARY` FTP mode when downloading. The `eul306.exe` file contains the complete Eudora Light installation program, so it can be copied and used on any workstations that must have email client software installed.

Installing Eudora Light

Eudora Light uses InstallShield to install the software, so installation is easy. By running the `eul306.exe` program, InstallShield begins. There are a few questions that you will have to answer first. One screen prompts you to select either the 16-bit or 32-bit version of Eudora Light. If you are using Windows 95, 98, or NT you should select the 32-bit version.

After the InstallShield program is finished, there should be a new program group, named Eudora Light, in the program listing that contains the Eudora Light executable program icon.

Configuring Eudora Light

After Eudora Light is installed, it can be configured. Start Eudora Light by clicking on the Eudora Light program icon from the Eudora Light program group in the program listing. The main client window appears as shown in Figure 15.21.

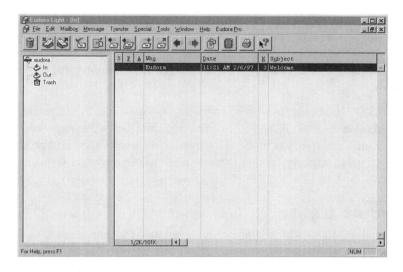

FIGURE 15.21
The Eudora Light main client window.

To get to the configuration window from the main client window, select the Tools, Options menu items. The Options window shown in Figure 15.22 appears.

FIGURE 15.22
The Eudora Light Options window.

Several options must be configured for Eudora Light to work properly with the Linux mailserver. First, you must select the Checking Mail icon to configure basic information on where your mailbox is located. As shown in Figure 15.22, you must enter your username and the IP address of the Linux mailserver in the POP account field. One nice feature of Eudora Light is that it supports encrypted POP authentication methods. As shown in the figure, this example uses the APOP authentication method. Remember that the POP3 server must also be configured to support the APOP authentication or the client will not be able to log in to the POP3 server.

After the Checking Mail fields have been completed, you must select the Sending Mail icon to configure how Eudora Light will send messages. As in the other software packages, use the IP address of the Linux mailserver as the SMTP server. Also as before, ensure that the sendmail program on the Linux mailserver is configured to relay SMTP messages from clients on your local network.

Using Eudora Light

The first time you use Eudora Light, it asks for the password to your account on the Linux mailserver. After you enter your password, Eudora Light attempts to connect to the mailserver and download any new messages. To check for new messages after you have logged in to the mailserver, click the Check Mail icon at the top of the main window.

The main window shown in Figure 15.21 shows the message headers in the rightmost window and the mailbox folders in the leftmost window. To view a message, double-click the message header. The message header list will be replaced with the message body. To return to the Inbox listing, double-click the In icon on the left side.

To compose a new message, click the New Message icon at the top of the main window. This produces the New Message window shown in Figure 15.23.

In the New Message window, you can insert recipient addresses in the To: and Cc: lines. As in Messenger and Outlook, you can configure commonly used email addresses in the Address Book to simplify adding them to email messages. Unlike Messenger and Outlook, Eudora does not support mail in HTML format. It does, however, support binary file attachments like the other packages.

Eudora Light is a nice lightweight email client package that can meet the basic email needs of any office. It works great for offices that might have some older underpowered workstations still in use.

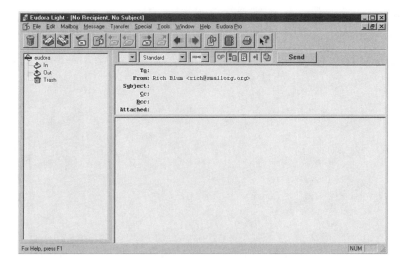

FIGURE 15.23
The Eudora Light New Message window.

Summary

Installing network clients to communicate with the Linux mailserver on the office network requires two things: a network card and an IP address. You can use the Control Panel Network function to install the network card in a Windows 95, 98, or NT 4.0 workstation. Also, you can use the Network function to install the TCP/IP protocol and assign an IP address to the workstation. Besides network services, workstation should have some kind of POP3 or IMAP client software to connect to the Linux mailserver. Many high-quality products are available for free. Three software packages described in this chapter are Netscape Messenger, Microsoft Outlook Express, and Qualcomm Eudora Light. All three packages allow the workstation to connect to the Linux mailserver by using either the POP3 or IMAP protocol, to process mail messages on the server, as well as to send messages through the mailserver to other mail recipients.

Advanced Topics

PART

III

IN THIS PART

Supporting Dial-In Clients

IN THIS CHAPTER

If this were a perfect world, there would be no hunger, no war, and no dial-in mail clients. Unfortunately, you have to live with all three. As a Linux mail administrator, it will most likely be your job to support clients who want to read their mail messages from a remote location outside of the office network. The easiest way to accomplish this task is for the Linux mailserver to support dial-in PPP clients (see Chapter 8, "PPP Protocol"). After a remote client establishes a PPP connection with the Linux mailserver, the client can behave just as if it were connected through the local network. This means running one of the email client packages discussed in Chapter 15, "Configuring LAN Clients." This chapter describes some methods to support users dialing in with Windows 95, 98, or NT 4.0 workstations to read their mail messages on the Linux mailserver.

Configuring Dial-In Modems

If you use a separate modem to support dial-in customers, Linux must first be able to recognize and handle the modem in dial-in mode. Chapter 3, "Installing Communication Devices in Linux," discussed methods of connecting a modem to a Linux mailserver. The following section describes the software details required to enable the Linux mailserver to support remote clients dialing into the modem.

Using inittab

After you have installed the modem and created a Linux device, you should ensure that the Linux mailserver recognizes the modem device and is capable of establishing a session on it. All Linux devices used for logging in to the system require an entry in the /etc/inittab file.

The /etc/inittab file is used by Linux to execute specific processes at specific init run-levels. In this situation, the /etc/inittab file defines the Linux devices where users can log in and know how to handle each individual device. The init program reads the /etc/inittab file and spawns the required programs to listen to the indicated devices for login attempts. Listing 16.1 shows an example of an /etc/inittab file.

LISTING **16.1**   Sample /etc/inittab File

```
1  # inittab        This file describes how the INIT process should set up
2  #                the system in a certain run-level.
3  #
4  # Author:        Miquel van Smoorenburg, <miquels@drinkel.nl.mugnet.org>
5  #                Modified for RHS Linux by Marc Ewing and Donnie Barnes
6  #
7  # Default runlevel. The run-levels used by RHS are:
8  #  0 - halt (Do NOT set initdefault to this)
9  #  1 - Single user mode
```

```
10 #   2 - Multiuser, without NFS (The same as 3, if you do not have networking)
11 #   3 - Full multiuser mode
12 #   4 - unused
13 #   5 - X11
14 #   6 - reboot (Do NOT set initdefault to this)
15 #
16 id:3:initdefault:
17 # System initialization.
18 si::sysinit:/etc/rc.d/rc.sysinit
19 l0:0:wait:/etc/rc.d/rc 0
20 l1:1:wait:/etc/rc.d/rc 1
21 l2:2:wait:/etc/rc.d/rc 2
22 l3:3:wait:/etc/rc.d/rc 3
23 l4:4:wait:/etc/rc.d/rc 4
24 l5:5:wait:/etc/rc.d/rc 5
25 l6:6:wait:/etc/rc.d/rc 6
26
27 # Things to run in every runlevel.
28 ud::once:/sbin/update
29
30 # Trap CTRL-ALT-DELETE
31 ca::ctrlaltdel:/sbin/shutdown -t3 -r now
32
33 # When our UPS tells us power has failed, assume we have a few minutes
34 # of power left.  Schedule a shutdown for 2 minutes from now.
35 # This does, of course, assume you have powerd installed and your
36 # UPS connected and working correctly.
37 pf::powerfail:/sbin/shutdown -f -h +2 "Power Failure; System Shutting Down"
38
39 # If power was restored before the shutdown kicked in, cancel it.
40 pr:12345:powerokwait:/sbin/shutdown -c "Power Restored; Shutdown Cancelled"
41
42# Run gettys in standard runlevels
43 1:12345:respawn:/sbin/mingetty tty1
44 2:2345:respawn:/sbin/mingetty tty2
45 3:2345:respawn:/sbin/mingetty tty3
46 4:2345:respawn:/sbin/mingetty tty4
47 5:2345:respawn:/sbin/mingetty tty5
48 6:2345:respawn:/sbin/mingetty tty6
49
50 # Set serial line for modem
51 s1:2345:respawn:/sbin/uugetty ttyS0 38400 vt100
52
53 # Run xdm in runlevel 5
54 x:5:respawn:/usr/bin/X11/xdm –nodaemon
```

The format of each record in the `inittab` file is

```
id:runlevels:action:process
```

where `id` is a unique ID within the `inittab` file used to identify the action, `runlevels` is a list of `init` run levels when the action will be taken, `action` is the `init` action that will be performed on the process, and `process` is the specific program that will be run. In Listing 16.1, lines 43 through 48 demonstrate this format. These lines define the virtual terminals present in most Linux distributions. They use the standard `mingetty` program to monitor the appropriate tty line. Each record represents one tty line. They are set to the `respawn` action, which "respawns" a new terminal session when you log off. You might also notice that `tty1`, the main console screen, is started at all run levels, but `tty2` through `tty6` only start at run level 2. In Linux, `init` run level 1 is considered the single user mode, thus only one terminal session is required.

Line 51 defines the dial-in modem on the Linux mailserver. It specifies the `inittab` id `s1`, which is activated on `init` run levels 2, 3, 4, and 5. The `respawn` action indicates that the process defined will be restarted by init whenever the process terminates. The program can then be restarted automatically after a user terminates the dial-in session. The `uugetty` program will be run. It also contains a few command line parameters included in the line to define its behavior. The `uugetty` program handles any login attempts coming in on the modem connected to device `/dev/ttyS0` (because of the command line parameter `ttyS0`).

The `uugetty` program can be used to monitor dial-in lines and establish logins, as well as for dial-out sessions. It uses UUCP-style lock files to determine whether the modem is already in use. The `uugetty` program also can initialize the modem device and listen for login attempts by default when it `respawns` after a session. When a connection is made to the modem, `uugetty` will send a login prompt and pass the login data to the `login` program. The following section describes the `uugetty` program in more detail.

The uugetty Program

The format of the `uugetty` command line is

```
uugetty  [-d  defaults_file]  [-a]  [-h]  [-r delay] [-t
         timeout] [-w waitfor] line [speed [type [lined]]]
```

Table 16.1 describes the different parameters that are available for the `uugetty` command line. These parameters can be used when using `uugetty` in the `/etc/inittab` file, as shown in Listing 16.1.

TABLE **16.1**   uugetty Parameters

Parameters	Description
-d defaults	Defines the location of a defaults file
-h	Does not force a hang-up when it starts
-r delay	Waits for a single character and then waits the specified number of delay seconds
-t timeout	Causes uugetty to exit if no login name is given for timeout seconds
-w waitfor	Causes uugetty to wait for the specified string of characters
line	Specifies the /dev/line to monitor
speed	Specifies the /etc/gettydefs speed definition
type	Specifies the termcap terminal definition
lined	Specifies the line discipline

The minimum parameters that uugetty needs to operate is the line parameter, which tells it which device to monitor. In Listing 16.1, uugetty monitors device /dev/ttyS0, or COM1 on the PC, expecting to talk to the modem at 38400 speed, and expecting a connection with a remote workstation using the VT100 terminal emulation protocol. The terminal emulation protocol is important if uugetty is configured to clear the terminal screen or send a greeting banner (more on that later).

Each line of the configuration file defines a variable representing an action for uugetty. The format of the lines is

NAME=value

where *NAME* is a string variable representing the action, and *value* is the value that is assigned to the action. Table 16.2 shows the actions that can be defined in the configuration file.

TABLE **16.2**   uugetty Configuration File Variables

Variables	Description
SYSTEM=name	Defines the system name for the @S substitution
VERSION=string	Defines the version name for the @V substitution
LOGIN=name	Defines the program used to log in the client
INIT=string	Defines the initialization string sent to the modem
ISSUE=string	Defines a greeting banner sent to the remote terminal
CLEAR=value	Clears the remote terminal screen if value=YES

continues

TABLE 16.2 continued

Variables	Description
HANGUP=value	Same as -h parameter if value=NO
WAITCHAR=value	If value=YES, waits for character from device before continuing
DELAY=seconds	Adds a delay after WAITCHAR character is received before continuing
TIMEOUT=number	Same as -t parameter
CONNECT=string	Defines an expected string sequence to receive from the modem for a connection
WAITFOR=string	Defines a string of characters to wait for
ALTLOCK=line	Defines an alternative line to check and lock
ALTLINE=line	Defines an alternative line to initialize
RINGBACK=value	Enables ringback mode if value=YES
SCHED=range1 range2 ...	Defines a schedule when the line can enable logins
OFF=string	Defines a string to send to the modem when turning it off

By creating configuration files for each modem line, you can customize the behavior of uugetty depending on the type of modem or dial-in required for a particular device. A sample configuration file is shown in Listing 16.2.

LISTING 16.2 Sample /etc/conf.uugetty Configuration File

```
1  CLEAR = YES
2  HANGUP=YES
3  INIT="" ATS0=1\r OK
4  ALTLOCK=modem
5  ALTLINE=modem
6  TIMEOUT=60
```

In Listing 16.2, line 1 indicates that the uugetty program will attempt to clear the screen of the remote terminal when it establishes the connection. Line 2 indicates that uugetty will attempt to hang up the line when it starts up (in case the previous session did not force a hang-up). Line 3 demonstrates a sample initialization chat script. This string sets the modem to answer after one phone ring (ATS0=1), and expects a response of "OK" back from the modem. Lines 4 and 5 define an alternative device name to check for locks on. Many Linux distributions use a link named /dev/modem that points to the actual tty name. It can be confusing if some programs lock the tty line and some lock the /dev/modem link. These lines cause uugetty to check both. The last line indicates that uugetty will wait 60 seconds after answering the line for the user to try to log in to the system. After 60 seconds, it will exit the program.

You might have noticed some special codes in Listing 16.2 and Table 16.2. uugetty defines such special codes to be used in configuration files and in the command line as a shorthand method for defining variables or actions. Table 16.3 shows the codes that can be used.

TABLE **16.3**   uugetty Special Codes

Code	Description
\\	Backslash
\b	Backspace
\c	Prevents newline
\f	Formfeed
\n	Newline
\r	Carriage return
\s	Space
\t	Tab
\nnn	ASCII character with octal value nnn
@B	Baud rate
@D	Current date
@L	Line
@S	System name
@T	Current time
@U	Number of currently signed-on users
@V	Version
@@	Single @ character

These codes can come in handy, especially when customizing greeting banners for the uugetty line. By default, the standard banner sent to a remote device produced when uugetty connects is located in the file /etc/issue. This file can be customized to report specific information using the special uugetty codes.

PPP Scripts

After the remote user logs in to the mailserver, he must be able to establish a PPP session to run the email client software across the modem line. As described in Chapter 8, Linux can act as a PPP server using the pppd program. After the client's workstation chat script logs him in to the mailserver, it must then run the pppd program on the mailserver to establish the PPP session. Usually, the pppd program requires a lot of command line parameters to be used for it to work properly. If you must support dial-in access for non–computer-literate clients, this might not be an easy thing to accomplish. Expecting a user to type

```
pppd silent modem crtscts proxyarp 192.168.1.100:192.168.1.2
```

when he establishes a connection might be a little too much. Fortunately, there is an easier way to get pppd to recognize all the necessary parameters without unduly burdening your users.

The pppd program recognizes configuration files where command line parameters can be placed to simplify the pppd command line. When pppd starts, it checks the configuration files and processes any parameters there just as if they were entered on the command line. The default location for the pppd configuration file is /etc/ppp/options. Listing 16.3 shows a sample pppd configuration file.

LISTING **16.3**   Sample /etc/ppp/options File

```
1  lock
2  silent
3  modem
4  crtscts
5  proxyarp
6  192.168.1.100:192.168.1.2
```

When the pppd parameters are saved in the configuration file, all the user needs to enter at the command prompt is the pppd program name. In Listing 16.3, line 6 assigns a static IP address to the dial-in device. If you are supporting multiple dial-in devices, this will not work. Each dial-in device will be assigned the same static IP address, which will not be good. To solve this problem you can remove the IP address assignment from the /etc/ppp/options file, and use separate /etc/ppp/options.ttyxx files for each tty line xx that supports a dial-in modem. The individual options files can then each assign a different static IP address.

One final word about the pppd program. In Listing 16.3, line 5 shows the proxyarp command line parameter, which enables the remote device to connect to other IP devices on the network that the Linux mailserver is connected to. This feature can come in handy if there are other devices on the office network to which you need to support dial-in access. If you prefer that your dial-in clients be restricted to just the Linux mailserver, you can remove the proxyarp command line parameter from the configuration file. The dial-in client can then connect only to the Linux mailserver.

Revisiting the mgetty Program

One problem with using the uugetty program to support dial-in lines is that each client must construct a chat script for logging in to the mailserver and executing the pppd program.

Microsoft Windows 95, 98, and NT 4.0 workstations support automatic PPP authentication in their dial-up software. It would be nice if the Linux mailserver could use this feature to enable a Windows client to establish the PPP session without having to use a complicated chat script. There is a way it can—it is called the `mgetty+sendfax` program.

Chapter 8 discussed the `mgetty+sendfax` program written by Gert Doering. `mgetty` has the capability to autodetect an incoming fax or PPP connection on the modem. You can use this feature to seamlessly support dial-in Windows 95, 98, and NT 4.0 workstations. The home Web page for `mgetty+sendfax` is

```
http://alpha.greenie.net/mgetty/
```

The latest official release is version 1.0.0. The latest beta test release is version 1.1.21. Many Linux distributions include a binary distribution package for `mgetty+sendfax`. You can also download a version of `mgetty+sendfax` from the `sunsite.unc.edu` FTP site in the `/pub/Linux/system/serial` directory.

Installing mgetty

If your Linux distribution includes an RPM binary package for `mgetty+sendfax`, you can install it using the RPM package installer:

```
rpm –Uvh mgetty-sendfax-1.1.14-9mdk.i586.rpm
```

If you elected to download a version of `mgetty+sendfax`, you must unpack and compile the source code. The following steps can be taken to accomplish this task:

1. Untar the `mgetty+sendfax` source code distribution:

    ```
    tar -zxvf mgetty+sendfax-1.0.0.tar.gz
    ```

2. Change directory to the newly created `mgetty-1.0.0` directory.

3. Edit the `policy.h-dist` file to match your desired environment, and copy it to `policy.h`.

4. Run the GNU `make` utility.

5. Run the GNU `make` utility with the parameter `testdisk`.

6. Change to the root user and run `make install` to place the binary executables in their proper locations.

After compiling and installing mgetty, you can use it in the `/etc/inittab` file as a controlling process for the modem line. The format of the `mgetty` command is

```
mgetty [options] ttydevice
```

where [*options*] are `mgetty` options that control the behavior of the modem line and *ttydevice* is the Linux tty line that `mgetty` will monitor. Table 16.4 shows the options available for `mgetty`.

TABLE 16.4   mgetty Command-Line Options

Option	Description
-x LEVEL	Sets debugging level to LEVEL
-s SPEED	Sets line speed to SPEED
-a	Tries to autodetect the modem connection speed
-k SPACE	Sets number of kbytes required in the incoming fax spool directory to SPACE
-m 'EXPECT SEND'	Sets a modem initialization chat script
-r	Used to indicate a direct line
-p LOGIN_PROMPT	Sets the login prompt for the modem line
-n RINGS	Sets the number of rings before mgetty will answer the modem
-D	Locks modem to data mode
-F	Locks modem to fax mode
-R SEC	Enables ring-back mode—callers must call twice
-i 'issue'	Specifies an issue file to display on a connection
-S 'FAX DOC'	Specifies a default fax document to send to polling fax machines

A sample /etc/inittab line using mgetty will look like this:

s1:12345:respawn:/sbin/mgetty -D -s 38400 -n 4 ttyS0

The sample line shows the mgetty program being used for a data connection on line /dev/ttyS0. It is set to a constant baud rate of 38400, and is set to answer after the fourth ring.

One word of caution about mgetty: Unlike the uugetty program that must set the modem to autoanswer mode, mgetty listens for the RING string when the phone rings and picks up the line. This is handy, in that sometimes with uugetty the process might hang, but the modem might still answer the line. With mgetty, it is up to mgetty to answer the line. If mgetty hangs, it will not answer the phone. The oddity with this scenario is that if your modem has an autoanswer LED on it, it won't be lit. Don't worry; that is not a problem, but a feature of mgetty.

To configure mgetty to autodetect a PPP connection requires settings in the mgetty configuration file as well as a new file to control the PPP access. The following section describes the steps necessary to configure mgetty to autodetect PPP connections.

Configuring mgetty for Automatic PPP Support

Enabling automatic PPP connections from Windows clients starts with the mgetty configuration file. The default location for the configuration file is /etc/mgetty+sendfax/

`login.config`. If you build the `mgetty` executable yourself from the source code, you can change this location.

The `login.config` file tells `mgetty` how to handle the different types of connection attempts that it detects. Listing 16.4 shows a sample `login.config` file.

LISTING 16.4   Sample `/etc/mgetty+sendfax/login.config` File

```
1   # login.config
2   #
3   # This is a sample "login dispatcher" configuration file for mgetty
4   #
5   # Format:
6   #       username userid utmp_entry login_program [arguments]
7   #
8   # Meaning:
9   #       for a "username" entered at mgettys login: prompt, call
10  #       "login_program" with [arguments], with the uid set to "userid",
11  #       and a USER_PROCESS utmp entry with ut_user = "utmp_entry"
12  #
13  # username may be prefixed / suffixed by "*" (wildcard)
14  #
15  # userid is a valid username from /etc/passwd, or "-" to not set
16  #  a login user id and keep the uid/euid root (needed for /bin/login)
17  #
18  # utmp_entry is what will appear in the "who" listing. Use "-" to not
19  #  set an utmp entry (a must for /bin/login), use "@" to set it to the
20  #  username entered. Maximum length is 8 characters.
21  #
22  # login_program is the program that will be exec()ed, with the arguments
23  #  passed in [arguments]. A "@" in the arguments will be replaced with the
24  #  username entered. Warning: if no "@" is given, the login_program has
25  #  no way to know what username the user entered.
26  #
27  #
28  # SAMPLES:
29  # Use this one with my Taylor-UUCP and Taylor-UUCP passwd files.
30  #  (Big advantage: tuucp can use the same passwd file for serial dial-in
31  #   and tcp dial-in [uucico running as in.uucpd]). Works from 1.05 up.
32  #
33  #U*     uucp    @        /usr/lib/uucp/uucico -l -u @
34
35  #
36  # Use this one for fido calls (login name /FIDO/ is handled specially)
37  #
```

continues

LISTING 16.4   continued

```
38 # You need Eugene Crosser's "ifmail" package for this to work.
39 #  mgetty has to be compiled with "-DFIDO", otherwise a fido call won't
40 #  be detected.
41 #
42 /FIDO/ uucp    fido     /usr/local/lib/fnet/ifcico @
43
44 #
45 # Automatic PPP startup on receipt of LCP configure request (AutoPPP).
46 #  mgetty has to be compiled with "-DAUTO_PPP" for this to work.
47 #  Warning: Case is significant, AUTOPPP or autoppp won't work!
48 #  Consult the "pppd" man page to find pppd options that work for you.
49 #
50 #  NOTE: for *some* users, the "-detach" option has been necessary, for
51 #        others, not at all. If your pppd doesn't die after hangup, try it.
52 #
53 #  NOTE2: "kdebug 7 debug" creates lots of debugging info. If all works,
54 #        remove those!
55 #
56 /AutoPPP/ -    ppp     /usr/sbin/pppd auth -chap +pap login modem crtscts lock
57 proxyarp
58
59 #
60 #
61 # An example where no login name in the argument list is desired:
62 #  automatically telnetting to machine "smarty" for a given login name
63 #
64 #telnet-smarty  gast     telnet /usr/bin/telnet -8 smarty
65 #
66 # This is the "standard" behavior - *dont* set a userid or utmp
67 #  entry here, otherwise /bin/login will fail!
68 #  This entry isn't really necessary: if it's missing, the built-in
69 #  default will do exactly this.
70 #
71 *         -         -         /bin/login @
```

In Listing 16.4, line 56 shows the entry that is required for mgetty to autodetect a PPP connection. The configuration file is case sensitive, so make sure that the /AutoPPP/ header is entered exactly as shown or mgetty will not recognize it. The line also includes the pppd command exactly as it would be entered if using pppd from the command prompt. If you already have entered pppd command line parameters in a pppd configuration file, you do not need to enter them here as well. Line 71 is important. It instructs mgetty on what to do if it does not autodetect a special signal such as a fax or PPP connection. In this case it assumes that it must be a normal terminal connection and passes it to the login program to produce the standard login prompt.

The next step needed to enable automatic PPP connections is a method to authenticate userids and passwords automatically. You might notice that one of the parameters used in the pppd command line in line 56 is +pap. This instructs mgetty to use pppd's PAP authentication method when initializing the PPP connection. Chapter 8 describes the PAP authentication in detail.

For pppd to use PAP authentication, there needs to be a password file that contains userids and passwords of users who will dial into the Linux mailserver. The default location of the file is /etc/ppp/pap-secrets. Listing 16.5 shows a sample pap-secrets file.

LISTING 16.5 Sample /etc/ppp/pap-secrets File

```
1  # Secrets for authentication using PAP
2  # client          server  secret              IP addresses
3  rich      *        guitar  192.168.1.100
4  barbara       *          aslsign  192.168.1.100
5  katie     *        boxcar  192.168.1.100
6  jessica   *        clifford  192.168.1.100
```

Each line in the pap-secrets file represents information for a separate user. The format of the pap-secrets file is

client   server   secret   addresses

where *client* is the username that the user is assigned, *server* is the server that this entry applies to, *secret* is the password entered into the Microsoft dial-in software, and *addresses* is the local IP address that the user can use. In Listing 16.5, an asterisk (*) is used to enable the client username to be used on any server that the user connects to. This feature is generally used if the client dials out to several different servers and needs a different secret word for each server. The IP address field can also be left blank if you do not know what IP address will be assigned to the user, such as if there are multiple dial-in lines.

mgetty Log Files

After configuring the mgetty and pppd software, you can test it out by connecting with a Microsoft Windows 95, 98, or NT 4.0 workstation (see the following sections for Windows configuration information). When a client connects, or attempts to connect, mgetty produces an entry in a log file. On the Red Hat, Mandrake, and Caldera Linux distributions, the log file is located in /var/log/mgetty.log.ttyxx, where xx is the tty line that the mgetty process is monitoring. Listing 16.6 shows a sample mgetty log file.

LISTING **16.6**   Sample `/var/log/mgetty.log.ttyS0` File

```
1  11/07 07:16:13 yS0  mgetty: experimental test release 1.1.14-Apr02
2  11/07 07:16:13 yS0  check for lockfiles
3  11/07 07:16:13 yS0  locking the line
4  11/07 07:16:14 yS0  lowering DTR to reset Modem
5  11/07 07:16:14 yS0  send: \dATQ0V1H0[0d]
6  11/07 07:16:15 yS0  waiting for ``OK'' ** found **
7  11/07 07:16:15 yS0  send: ATS0=0Q0&D3&C1[0d]
8  11/07 07:16:15 yS0  waiting for ``OK'' ** found **
9  11/07 07:16:16 yS0  waiting...
10 11/07 07:16:16 yS0  checking if modem is still alive
11 11/07 07:16:16 yS0  mdm_send: 'AT' -> OK
12 11/07 07:16:16 yS0  waiting...
13 11/08 07:16:27 yS0  checking if modem is still alive
14 11/08 07:16:27 yS0  mdm_send: 'AT' -> OK
15 11/08 07:16:28 yS0  waiting...
16
17 11/08 07:44:10 yS0  waiting for ``RING'' ** found **
18 11/08 07:44:10 yS0  waiting for ``RING'' ** found **
19 11/08 07:44:16 yS0  waiting for ``RING'' ** found **
20 11/08 07:44:22 yS0  waiting for ``RING'' ** found **
21 11/08 07:44:46 yS0  send: ATA[0d]
22 11/08 07:44:46 yS0  waiting for ``CONNECT'' ** found **
23 11/08 07:44:59 yS0  send:
24 11/08 07:44:59 yS0  waiting for ``_'' ** found **
25 11/08 07:45:02 ##### data dev=ttyS0, pid=10089, caller='none',
➥ conn='38400/ARQ/2
26 6400 LAP-M', name='', cmd='/usr/sbin/pppd', user='/AutoPPP/'
```

In Listing 16.6, lines 1 through 12 show the log entries generated by starting mgetty. The date, time, and device name are all logged on the lines. Lines 13 through 15 show the periodic checks that mgetty makes to ensure that the modem is still operating properly. mgetty continues checking the line until a connection is made. In line 17, the first sign of activity appears. mgetty detects the first RING string from the phone line. This particular mgetty is set on the command line parameters to answer after the fourth ring (one method used to fool war dialers). As shown in line 21, after mgetty receives the fourth phone RING, it issues the ATA command to instruct the modem to pick up the line, and then waits for a CONNECT string from the modem. Lines 25 and 26 show the end result of the connection: mgetty detected a PPP signal, and started the pppd program.

After viewing the mgetty log and determining that mgetty detected a PPP connection, you can then look at the pppd program log to determine if pppd was able to establish a connection. In the Red Hat, Mandrake, and Caldera Linux distributions, the pppd program sends its event logs to the /var/log/messages file. Listing 16.7 shows sample entries from the pppd program after mgetty has established the modem connection.

LISTING **16.7**   Sample pppd Log Entries in /var/log/messages

```
1   Nov  8 07:45:02 shadrach mgetty[10089]: data dev=ttyS0, pid=10089,
➥ caller='none'
2   , conn='38400/ARQ/26400 LAP-M', name='', cmd='/usr/sbin/pppd',
➥ user='/AutoPPP/'
Nov  8 07:45:04 shadrach kernel: CSLIP: code copyright 1989 Regents
➥ of the University of California
4   Nov  8 07:45:04 shadrach kernel: PPP: version 2.2.0 (dynamic channel
➥ allocation)
5   Nov  8 07:45:04 shadrach kernel: PPP Dynamic channel allocation code
➥ copyright 1995 Caldera, Inc.
6   Nov  8 07:45:04 shadrach kernel: PPP line discipline registered.
7  Nov  8 07:45:04 shadrach kernel: registered device ppp0
8  Nov  8 07:45:04 shadrach pppd[10089]: pppd 2.3.5 started by ppp, uid 0
9  Nov  8 07:45:04 shadrach pppd[10089]: Using interface ppp0
10 Nov  8 07:45:04 shadrach pppd[10089]: Connect: ppp0 <--> /dev/ttyS0
11 Nov  8 07:45:06 shadrach PAM_pwdb[10089]: (ppp) session opened for
➥ user rich by (uid=0)
12 Nov  8 07:45:06 shadrach pppd[10089]: user rich logged in
13 Nov  8 07:45:07 shadrach pppd[10089]: found interface eth0 for proxy arp
14 Nov  8 07:45:07 shadrach pppd[10089]: local  IP address 192.168.1.1
15 Nov  8 07:45:07 shadrach pppd[10089]: remote IP address 192.168.1.100
16 Nov  8 07:45:10 shadrach pppd[10089]: CCP terminated by peer
17 Nov  8 07:45:10 shadrach pppd[10089]: Compression disabled by peer.
18 Nov  8 07:51:19 shadrach pppd[10089]: LCP terminated by peer
19 Nov  8 07:51:22 shadrach pppd[10089]: Hangup (SIGHUP)
20 Nov  8 07:51:22 shadrach pppd[10089]: Modem hangup
21 Nov  8 07:51:22 shadrach PAM_pwdb[10089]: (ppp) session closed for
➥ user shadrach.smallorg.org
22 Nov  8 07:51:22 shadrach pppd[10089]: Connection terminated.
23 Nov  8 07:51:23 shadrach pppd[10089]: Exit.
24 Nov  8 07:53:03 shadrach kernel: PPP: ppp line discipline successfully
➥ unregistered
```

In Listing 16.7, line 1 shows the mgetty log entry indicating that a PPP session was detected. Lines 3 through 7 indicate that the Linux kernel loaded the PPP kernel support software dynamically when the PPP connection was detected. Lines 8 through 17 show the pppd program starting and attempting to run through the configured command line parameters. Line 12 shows that the remote userid was detected and that the authentication method was successful. Line 13 indicates that the proxy arp command line parameter was used and that now the remote client has access to the local network via the `eth0` network device on the Linux mailserver. In lines 14 and 15, the `pppd` program assigns an IP address of `192.168.1.100` to the remote client. After the PPP session has ended, line 18 indicates that the remote client has initiated a disconnect signal on the PPP Link Control Protocol, and lines 19 through 23 show the `pppd` program terminating the PPP session. In line 24, the Linux kernel unregisters the PPP kernel support.

Configuring Windows 95 and 98 Dial-Up Networking

The first step to using PPP dial-up support on a Windows 95 or 98 workstation is to ensure that you have a modem installed. You can select Start, Settings, Control Panel, Modems to view the installed modems, or to add a new modem. Figure 16.1 shows this window.

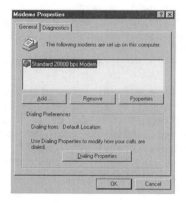

FIGURE 16.1
The Windows 95 and 98 Modems Properties window.

After selecting the modem type installed and loading the drivers, use the Windows Wizard to configure a new Dial-Up Networking (DUN) session. Run the Windows Explorer program and select the Dial-Up Networking icon to start the wizard. Follow the instructions in the wizard to create a new connection using a configured modem. Figure 16.2 shows a sample wizard window.

After creating the new DUN session, you must enter the phone number required to connect to the remote server. When the wizard finishes, the new DUN session will appear as an icon in Windows Explorer under the Dial-Up Networking section. The Entry name will match the name you gave it in the wizard configuration. Figure 16.3 shows the connection window that appears when you double-click the DUN session icon.

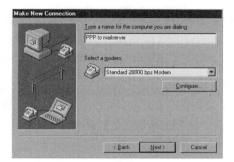

FIGURE 16.2
The Windows 95 and 98 New Connection wizard window.

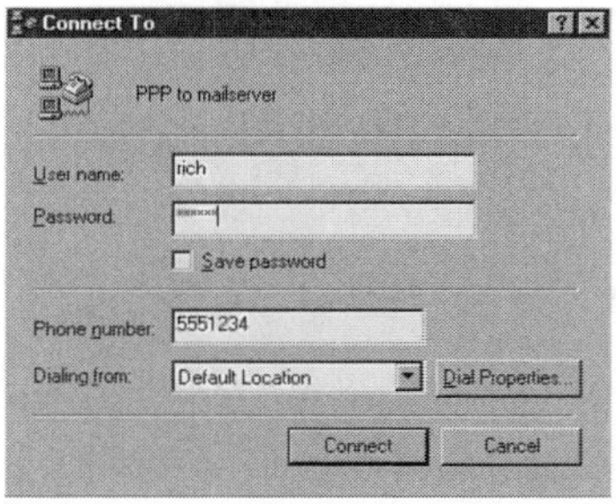

FIGURE 16.3
The Windows 95 and 98 Dial-Up Networking Connection window.

After typing in your assigned username and password, click the Connect button. If all goes well, the Windows workstation will dial the Linux mailserver and establish a PPP session. If the Windows workstation dials the Linux mailserver but fails to establish a PPP session, you can check the Linux log files as described in the previous section to determine where the problem might be. Most often it is a problem with the /etc/ppp/pap-secrets file.

After the PPP session is established, an icon of two terminals appears in the Windows system tray. Each terminal will flash when data is transmitted in its respective direction. The email client software package can then be started to connect to the Linux mailserver.

To stop the PPP session, you must right-click the DUN icon in the system tray and select the Disconnect menu item. The workstation modem will hang up the phone connection. The Linux mailserver will also reset the modem and respawn the mgetty process to wait for another incoming call.

Configuring Windows NT 4.0 Dial-Up Networking

Configuring the Windows NT 4.0 Dial-Up Networking software is similar, but different from, the configuration of Windows 95 and 98 software. Again, the first step is to ensure that you have a modem installed on the workstation. By selecting the Modem icon in the Control Panel area, you will see the Modems Properties window shown in Figure 16.4.

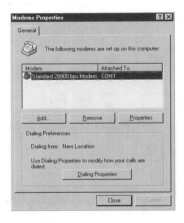

FIGURE 16.4

The Windows NT 4.0 workstation Modems Properties window.

As with the Windows 95 and 98 software, you can view the current modem configuration, or add a new modem using the Add button. After the modem is configured, you can begin to configure the Dial-Up Networking information. To select the Dial-Up Networking feature, double-click the Dial-Up Networking icon in Windows Explorer. If Dial-Up Networking has not been installed, the main installation window, shown in Figure 16.5, is displayed.

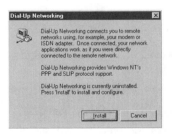

FIGURE 16.5

The Windows NT 4.0 workstation Dial-Up Networking installation.

To start the installation wizard, click the Install button. To properly communicate with the remote PPP server, the Dial-Up Networking software must recognize the modem. The first dialog box shown, Add RAS Device, enables you to select the modem that will be used to dial into the remote server. Figure 16.6 shows the Remote Access Setup window that enables you to select which modem will be used to connect to the remote PPP server.

FIGURE 16.6
The Windows NT 4.0 workstation Remote Access Setup.

After the modem is selected, the Dial-Up Networking software is installed on the workstation. You will need to use the media with the Windows NT 4.0 workstation software to install the necessary files to support Dial-Up Networking services. When the installation is complete, the wizard will reboot your workstation.

After the workstation is rebooted, you can select the Dial-Up Networking icon from Windows Explorer. Unlike Windows 95 and 98, which have a separate icon for each DUN session, Windows NT 4.0 workstation just uses one icon to access the DUN software. The first time you select the DUN software, it starts a wizard to help you add a new session to the phonebook. The New Phonebook Entry Wizard main window is shown in Figure 16.7.

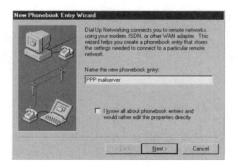

FIGURE 16.7
The Windows NT 4.0 workstation New Phonebook Entry Wizard.

After following the wizard and entering the phone number information for the new PPP session, the main Dial-Up Networking software window is displayed (see Figure 16.8).

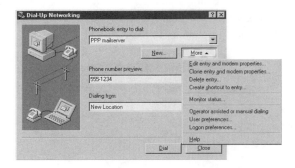

FIGURE 16.8

The Windows NT 4.0 workstation Dial-Up Networking main window.

The main window shows the drop-down choice box that enables you to select configured sessions in the phonebook. You will need to select the Edit Entry or Modem Properties menu item to configure the new phonebook entry. The Edit Phonebook Entry window appears, as shown in Figure 16.9. You must select the Server tab to modify the connection entries.

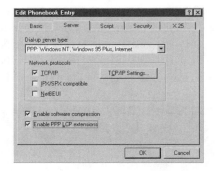

FIGURE 16.9

The Windows NT 4.0 workstation Edit Phonebook Entry window.

The last entry that needs to be modified in this section is under the Security tab. For the PPP authentication to work correctly, you must select the Accept Any Authentication Including Clear Text method of authentication.

For the Dial-Up Networking software to connect to the Linux mailserver, you must select the PPP Dial-Up server type. Ensure that the TCP/IP protocol check box is checked. You can also enable compression and the PPP LCP extensions. The Linux pppd program supports both of these functions. Figure 16.10 shows the PPP TCP/IP Settings window.

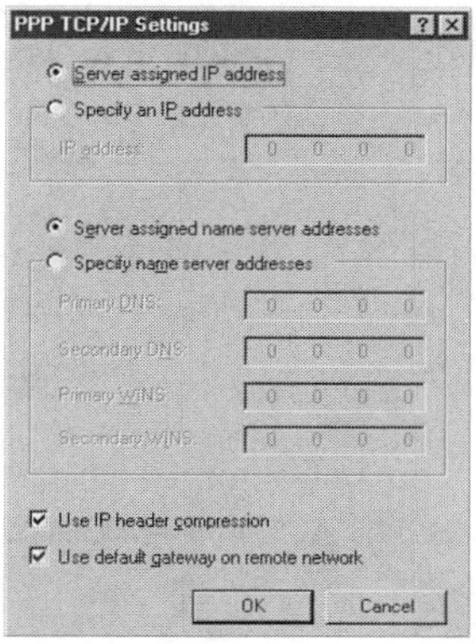

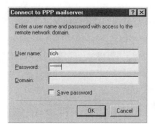

FIGURE 16.10
The Windows NT 4.0 workstation PPP TCP/IP Settings window.

Depending on the configuration of the Linux mailserver pppd program, either you will have to assign static IP and DNS server addresses to the Windows NT workstation, or you can enable the pppd program to assign the address. Also, you can check the check boxes to enable IP compression and to use the default gateway on the Linux mailserver.

After the configuration parameters are finished, you can go back to the Dial-Up Networking main window shown in Figure 16.8, select the phonebook entry for the Linux mailserver, and click the Dial button. This produces the Dial-Up Networking Connect window, as shown in Figure 16.11. After entering the appropriate username and password, click the OK button to enable DUN to attempt to connect to the Linux mailserver.

FIGURE 16.11
The Windows NT 4.0 workstation Dial-Up Networking Connect window.

As with the Windows 95 and 98 DUN, when the connection is established, an icon appears in the system tray indicating that the connection has been made. The two bars indicate sending and receiving packets across the PPP link.

After the PPP connection has been established, you can start the email client software package and connect to the Linux mailserver using the POP3 or IMAP protocols to retrieve your mail messages. When you are finished, you can right-click the DUN icon in the system tray and select Close from the menu items. This stops the PPP session and disconnects the modem connection.

One nice extra feature on the Windows NT 4.0 workstation is the addition of the Dial-Up Networking Monitor. By right-clicking on the DUN icon in the system tray, you can select the Open system monitor menu item. This produces the Dial-Up Networking Monitor window shown in Figure 16.12.

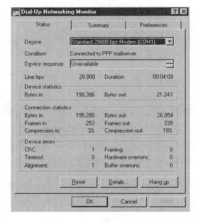

FIGURE 16.12
The Windows NT 4.0 workstation Dial-Up Networking Monitor.

The Dial-Up Networking Monitor helps determine how your PPP client is behaving by showing you statistics on the amount of traffic that has gone across the PPP connection, as well as the number of errors that it has encountered. You can also keep tabs on the compression rates being used on the PPP session if you enabled compression on both the Windows NT 4.0 workstation and the Linux mailserver pppd program.

Sharing a Modem

Depending on the method you use to connect to the Internet, supporting dial-in clients can be a tricky thing to do. If you use one modem for a dial-on-demand PPP connection, it is possible to share the same modem to support dial-in clients as well as the normal dial-on-demand PPP connection. But, be careful. Having lots of dial-in clients connect might severely impede the `diald` program from being able to use the modem to dial out.

If you are sharing a modem, you might want to limit the amount of time that each dial-in client is connected to the modem. The protocol that your dial-in clients use to retrieve mail will make a big difference. From a connection-time point of view, it will be better for remote users to use the POP3 protocol to quickly download messages and disconnect from the server, rather than using the IMAP protocol and having to linger on the modem while they read their mail. Of course this defeats one of the reasons for using the IMAP protocol—that remote users won't download messages at home and then not have them at work.

This creates a dilemma for the mail administrator. Often it is easier to add a second modem and a second dial-in phone line to support dial-in clients, rather than try and deal with the issues of a shared modem.

One trick commonly used by mail administrators is connecting to an ISP with a two channel ISDN line. Chapter 3 describes the use of an ISDN line with an ISDN modem. Under normal traffic, the ISDN modem can use the two B data channels to provide 128kbps throughput to the ISP. However, the mail administrator can configure a second phone line on one of the channels to accept incoming phone calls and send them to an analog modem connected to the Linux mailserver.

When a remote dial-in client connects to the second line, the ISDN service automatically drops the ISP connection to just one channel at 64 kbps, and enables the dial-in connection. Although this might affect performance of outbound connections, it won't totally stop the ISP connection when a remote client dials in.

Summary

This chapter dealt with the topic of supporting remote dial-in clients. There are several methods to use to enable clients to be able to read and send mail messages from a workstation that is not connected to the network. This chapter described how to support dial-in clients using a modem connected to the Linux mailserver. Besides the standard modem configuration, Linux needs a program to monitor the modem for new inbound connections. This can be accomplished with either the `uugetty` program or the `mgetty` program. Both enable users to log in with a chat script and execute the `pppd` program to start a PPP session with the Linux mailserver. The `mgetty` program has the added benefit of detecting a PPP session from a client and using the PAP authentication method to log the user in to the system and to start the `pppd` program automatically. This chapter also covered how to configure Microsoft Windows 95, 98, and NT 4.0 workstations to use the Dial-Up Networking feature to establish a PPP session with the Linux mailserver. This enables a remote dial-in client to run standard email client software just as if she were directly connected to the local network.

Mail Aliases and Masquerading

IN THIS CHAPTER

Now that the Linux mailserver is up and running smoothly and all your network and dial-in clients are reading and sending messages flawlessly, it is time to experiment with some fancier email services. This chapter discusses two special features of an office email server. The first feature is the use of email aliases that can be used for special events or purposes. The second feature is the use of masquerading, which allows you to support multiple email servers from the main office Linux mailserver.

The .forward File

One method of creating email aliases is the .forward file. The .forward file is a simple way of redirecting mail to alternative addresses. This function is illustrated in Figure 17.1.

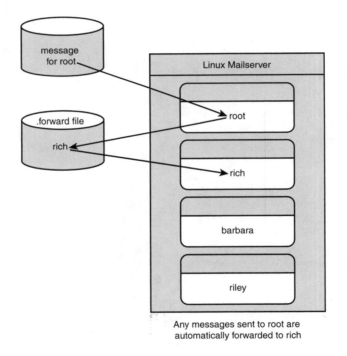

Any messages sent to root are
automatically forwarded to rich

FIGURE 17.1

The .forward file.

Each user can have a file named .forward in his or her home directory on the server. When the mail program receives a message for a user, it first checks for the presence of the .forward file. If the .forward file is present, the message is sent to any addresses in the .forward file, rather than to the actual user mailbox. Notice that there can be multiple email addresses listed in the `.forward` file, each one listed on a separate line. The mail program will forward the single message to each email address listed.

This feature can come in handy in a couple of different situations. If a user has to change email addresses for some reason (such as getting married), you can leave the old email address active for awhile and use the `.forward` file to point to the new address. That way the user can receive mail for both email addresses, but only has to log in as the new email addressee to retrieve the messages.

Also, if an employee leaves the organization, you can keep his or her email address active for awhile and create a `.forward` file. That `.forward` file can be used to forward any mail that comes to the old email address to the new email address at the other organization (provided that the employee's new organization has Internet email).

Another great use of `.forward` files is as a simple mail list. Mail lists allow multiple email recipients to receive the same message with the sender having to send to only one location. Mail lists are explained in greater detail in Chapter 18, "Mail Lists." Although there are more sophisticated methods to use to create mail lists, the `.forward` file will do the trick in a pinch. By creating a special account for the mail list, you can create a `.forward` file that contains the email addresses of all the participants in the mail list. Participants do not necessarily have to be local email users. Fetchmail also forwards messages to remote users, if possible.

As an example, assume you want to create a mail list called `officenews`. You want any message sent to the `officenews` email address to be forwarded to everyone in the local office, plus a few special customers who have email addresses on remote systems. First, you must create the Linux account, complete with the home directory `/home/officenews`. In the home directory for the new username, you can create a `.forward` file as shown in Listing 17.1.

LISTING 17.1   Sample `.forward` File

```
1  rich
2  barbara
3  katie
4  jessica
5  riley
6  haley
7  matthew@othercompany.com
8  christopher@othercompany.com
9  frank@secondcompany.com
10 melanie@secondcompany.com
```

With this configuration, sending a message to `officenews@smallorg.org` will result in all the email addresses shown in Listing 17.1 receiving a copy of the message. In Listing 17.1, lines 1 through 6 show users on the local Linux mailserver. Lines 7 through 10 show users on remote mail hosts who will also receive the message.

Aliases

A great feature of the sendmail program is the ability to create email aliases for usernames. It is often desirable to use special email addresses for special events. An example is to have a special email address called `register@smallorg.org` to which customers send messages to register in a special event. Without sendmail aliases, you have to create a new Linux userid for the `register` username, and either have someone in the office log in and check that mailbox on a regular basis or use the `.forward` file to redirect messages to a different userid.

With aliases, you don't have to create a separate mailbox for the new username. You can assign an alias name of `register` and point it to an existing email user. Any messages sent to the email address `register` are automatically redirected by sendmail to the user to whom the alias points.

sendmail aliases File

All sendmail aliases used on the Linux mailserver are listed in a common file. The `aliases` file is normally located at `/etc/aliases`, but can be changed in the `sendmail.cf` file. The `aliases` file points alias email names to real addresses, programs, or files. Each alias is listed on a separate line in the configuration file. Each of these four functions uses a different line format:

- Format 1:

  ```
  name:    name_1, name_2, name_3,
  ```
- Format 2:

  ```
  name:    ¦program
  ```
- Format 3:

  ```
  name:    file
  ```
- Format 4:

  ```
  name:    :include:filelist
  ```

The first format of the alias allows an email alias to point to one or more actual email addresses. The format of this `aliases` line is shown as Format 1, where `name` is the alias name and `name_1`, `name_2`, and so on, are the addresses to which the message will be sent instead of the original name. One or more different addresses can be used for the alias. Each email address listed receives a copy of the message.

Mail Alias Conventions

The email alias address for each of the different formats created in the `aliases` file must always be a local address on the Linux mailserver. You cannot create an alias with a remote mail address (that is, `alias@otherhost.com`). The address to which the alias points can be a remote address if needed.

The second format of the alias allows an alias email address to point to a program that can be executed. The format of this alias line is shown as Format 2 above, where `program` is the full pathname of a program that can process the message. This feature is described in more detail in Chapter 18. The Majordomo mail list program uses this feature to pass email messages to the Majordomo program for processing.

The third format of the alias allows for messages to be stored in a designated file. In this alias line `file` is a full pathname pointing to a text file. Any messages sent to the email address name are spooled to the given text file. For this feature to work properly, the proper read/write Linux system permissions must be set on both the text file and the directory where the text file is located.

The last format of the alias line (shown as Format 4) allows messages to be forwarded to a list of email address contained in a file. In this alias line `filelist` is the full pathname of a file that can contain a list of email addresses. This has the same effect as listing each email address on the aliases line separated by commas, as in the first format. This format might be easier to manipulate if you have a large mail list that changes frequently.

Listing 17.2 shows a sample `aliases` file from a Mandrake Linux 6.0 system.

LISTING 17.2   Sample `/etc/aliases` File

```
1  #
2  #   @(#)aliases 8.2 (Berkeley) 3/5/94
3  #
4  #  Aliases in this file will NOT be expanded in the header from
5  #  Mail, but WILL be visible over networks or from /bin/mail.
6  #
7  #  >>>>>>>>>>  The program "newaliases" must be run after
8  #  >> NOTE >>  this file is updated for any changes to
9  #  >>>>>>>>>>  show through to sendmail.
10 #
11
12 # Basic system aliases -- these MUST be present.
```

continues

LISTING 17.2   continued

```
13 MAILER-DAEMON:   postmaster
14 postmaster: root
15
16 # General redirections for pseudo accounts.
17 bin:        root
18 daemon:     root
19 games:      root
20 ingres:     root
21 nobody:     root
22 system:     root
23 toor:       root
24 uucp:       root
25
26 # Well-known aliases.
27 manager:    root
28 dumper:     root
29 operator:   root
30
31 # trap decode to catch security attacks
32 decode:     root
33
34 # Person who should get root's mail
35 root:       rich
36
37 # Program used to auto-reply to messages
38 auto-test:    |/home/rich/auto-test
39
40 # Send all messages to a text file
41 saveme:     /home/rich/test.txt
42
43 # Send all messages to remote site
44 rich:         rich@othercompany.com
45
46 #Create a simple multi-user mail list
47 officenews:          :include:/home/rich/office.txt
```

In Listing 17.2, lines 13 through 32 redirect any mail for various standard Linux system usernames to the root user. This is usually a good idea to ensure no one is trying to hack into the system using one of the default system usernames. If these userids are not aliased to root, any mail messages generated to them are lost. Line 35 is also a good idea. It redirects any mail for the root user to a common username that should log in to the system on a regular basis. Remember: If you are a good system administrator, you should not be logging in as the root user very frequently.

Line 38 demonstrates redirecting messages to a program. The program must be shown with its full pathname so that the shell can find it. Line 41 demonstrates using a text file to store any messages sent to an address. Remember to be careful about read/write permissions for the file.

Line 44 demonstrates that although the alias name must be local to the Linux mailserver, the names it aliases do not have to be. As with the .forward file, you can redirect a mail message for a user to another email account on a completely different system. This is a handy feature to use when users move to different email machines within the organization or if they leave the organization for another company.

Line 47 demonstrates the use of a mail list text file in the aliases file. The file /home/rich/office.txt is a plain text file that lists email addresses similar to the .forward file shown in Listing 17.1. When a message is received for the officenews alias, the office.txt file is checked and the message is sent to all email addresses present in that file.

newaliases Program

The /etc/aliases text file is where the mail administrator must enter new alias names, but it is not the file that the sendmail program actually uses when it processes mail. The real aliases file (as far as sendmail is concerned) is located in /etc/aliases.db. The aliases.db file uses a hashed database feature similar to other sendmail files such as the mailertable file described in Chapter 10, "The sendmail Program."

To create the aliases.db file, sendmail uses a special command-line option. The option used is -bi. When sendmail is run with the -bi option, it reads the /etc/aliases text file and creates the /etc/aliases.db database file. When the sendmail program is installed, it creates a special executable—newaliases—that performs the sendmail executable with the -bi function. Any time changes are made to the /etc/aliases text file, the newaliases program must be run.

Masquerading

Just as at a masquerade party, mail masquerading is pretending to be someone you are not. This section describes techniques that can be used by sendmail to accept mail destined for a different location, and also how to send mail pretending to be someone else.

Single-Host Masquerading

Chapter 13, "Connecting the Mailserver to an ISP," demonstrated one use of single-host masquerading. Often it is desirable to allow the Linux mailserver to accept mail addressed to the actual domain name. Under normal circumstances, the Linux mailserver sends and receives mail only for its particular host name. If the mailserver's host name is mail1, it sends and receives all mail messages with the fully qualified domain name of `mail1.smallorg.org`. To address mail to users on that system, you have to use the full host name in the mail address:

`username@mail1.smallorg.org`.

For the Linux mailserver to accept messages addressed directly to the domain, two things must be present. First, the DNS MX record for the domain must point to a specific mailserver—either the ISP mailserver or the local Linux mailserver, depending on the Internet connectivity. This informs remote hosts that a mailserver will accept mail addressed to the domain name; in this case, `smallorg.org`. The DNS server database for the domain is discussed in Chapter 4, "DNS and Domain Names." A DNS record for using the Linux mailserver as the domain mailserver would look something like this:

```
smallorg.org    IN MX    10    mail1.smallorg.org
```

This DNS record points remote hosts wanting to send mail to the `smallorg.org` domain directly to the `mail1.smallorg.org` host (the Linux mailserver). That solves the problem for inbound mail.

The other piece of this puzzle is the outbound mail from the Linux mailserver. Even though it receives messages from the Internet for the `smallorg.org` domain, the Linux mailserver still sends outbound messages with its full host name in the return address header field. This could be confusing. This is where sendmail masquerading saves the day.

sendmail masquerading allows outbound messages to change their return address header fields to match the desired return location (such as the domain name). Even though the message is sent from the mailserver, the return addresses will have the domain name instead of the host name. To enable masquerading in sendmail, you must add it to the configuration file.

As discussed in Chapter 11, "Installing and Configuring sendmail," the method used to change the sendmail configuration file components is to create an m4 macro file and use the GNU m4 macro processor program to create a new sendmail configuration file. The macro directive used to allow sendmail to masquerade as a different site is

`MASQUERADE_AS(domain)`

where `domain` is the domain name you want sendmail to use for the return address in the message header fields. Note that this feature changes only the return addresses in the message header fields. If you want the complete message envelope to have the masqueraded domain name as well, you must use another special sendmail feature:

`FEATURE(`masquerade_envelope')`

Other sendmail features can also be used to fine-tune masquerading on the mailserver. Table 17.1 lists the sendmail masquerading features.

TABLE 17.1   sendmail Masquerading Features

Feature	Description
masquerade_envelope	Masquerades the envelope sender and recipient
allmasquerade	Causes recipient addresses to be masqueraded also
limited_masquerade	Selectively uses the masquerade feature
masquerade_entire_domain	Uses masquerading on multiple domain names defined by MASQUERADE_DOMAIN

Multi-Host Masquerading

In larger offices, it is sometimes beneficial to split the mailserver function into several small servers rather than having one large server. The idea behind the multi-server network is that there is one server that acts as the central email hub, while other servers can support clients connecting in to read and send mail messages. This takes some load off the main mailserver, but unless you are dealing with hundreds of users, it is usually more hassle than benefit. Of course, there are times when multiple email servers are the result of political reasons rather than technical reasons. Figure 17.2 shows an example of a multi-server email network.

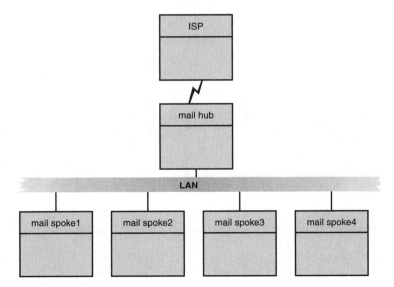

FIGURE 17.2

A multi-server email network.

The main Linux mailserver still uses one of the standard configurations discussed in Chapter 13 to connect to the ISP to transfer mail destined for the Internet. Each individual spoke Linux mailserver should be configured to use the main hub mailserver as its smart host. Each spoke server should use the normal sendmail masquerading features to change the return address of users to match the domain name.

Using this configuration simplifies outbound messages because no matter what spoke server the user is located on, the return email address is always the same (assuming that no two spoke servers have the same username). However, in this scenario inbound messages become a problem. For example, suppose that a spoke mailserver called `spoke1.smallorg.org` has a user called `frank`. All outbound messages from `spoke1.smallorg.org` are sent through the hub mailserver—called `hub.smallorg.org`—to the ISP for delivery. By using masquerading, the return address for `frank` will be `frank@smallorg.org`. Figure 17.3 demonstrates this example.

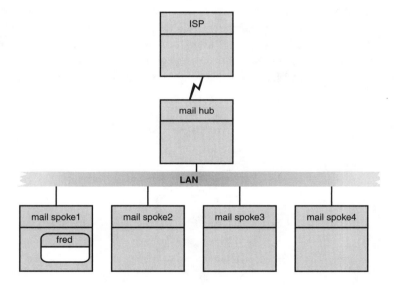

FIGURE 17.3

An example of an outbound message from a spoke mailserver.

So far, so good. The outbound message passes from the spoke server to the main hub server, to the ISP, out to the Internet. Now, what about the return inbound message? Assume for this scenario that the DNS mail record for the domain points to the ISP, which then spools mail for the main hub mailserver to collect at predetermined intervals. After the main hub mailserver collects the messages, it must determine which spoke mailserver the messages should be forwarded to. Figure 17.4 demonstrates this scenario.

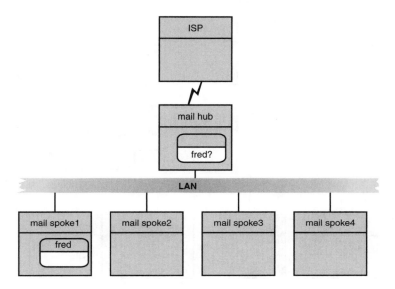

17

FIGURE 17.4
A failed inbound message for a spoke mailserver user.

If the return message were addressed to frank@spoke1.smallorg.org, the main hub's job would be easy. However, in this example (and in real life), the return message is addressed to frank@smallorg.org. The main hub (hub.smallorg.org) is set to masquerade as smallorg.org. Because the main hub thinks that it is the smallorg.org domain, it assumes that frank must be a local user on hub.smallorg.org. Of course this is not the case, so the message will be returned as being undeliverable. Ouch.

One method that can be used to solve this problem is to use the aliases file on hub. smallorg.org. By entering an alias for frank and pointing it to frank@spoke1.smallorg.org, the return message will get to the proper mailserver for frank to be able to read it. Although this method works, it tends to be a little clunky. By utilizing another feature of sendmail called *virtual hosting*, frank's mail can be forwarded to the proper spoke mailserver and then, hopefully, to frank's mailbox.

Virtual Hosting

Virtual hosting allows sendmail to read a user table that tells it how to redirect inbound mail messages. This table is similar to the aliases file, but is more robust in its options. Figure 17.5 demonstrates how the virtual user table operates.

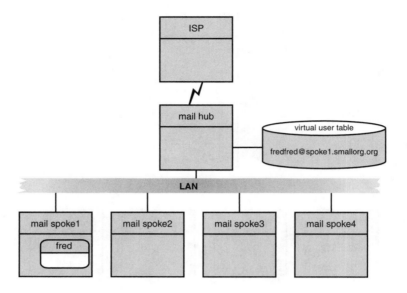

FIGURE 17.5

Mail forwarding using the virtual user table.

First, you must create a new sendmail configuration file for the main hub mailserver. To use virtual hosting, you must add the `virtusertable` feature to the macro file. It should look like this:

```
FEATURE(`virtusertable', `hash /etc/virtusertable')
```

After regenerating the sendmail configuration file with the m4 macro processor, restart the sendmail process on the server.

The next step is to create the virtual user table that directs sendmail how to forward messages. Again, much like the `aliases` file, the virtual user table is a text file that must be converted into a hash database file.

The text version of the file can be created at

```
/etc/virtusertable
```

Each mail user should be on a separate line. The format of the virtual user table lines is

```
virtaddress Tab⁖ realaddress
```

where `virtaddress` is the virtual user address for which sendmail will receive messages and `realaddress` is the actual address to which sendmail will forward the messages. There must be a Tab character separating the two values. Listing 17.3 shows an example of a virtual user table.

LISTING 17.3   Sample `/etc/virtusertable` File

```
1  frank@smallorg.org[Tab⇥]frank@spoke1.smallorg.org
2  melanie@smallorg.org[Tab⇥]melanie@spoke1.smallorg.org
3  haley@smallorg.org[Tab⇥]haley@spoke2.smallorg.org
4  riley@smallorg.org[Tab⇥]riley@spoke2.smallorg.org
5  katie@smallorg.org[Tab⇥]katie@spoke3.smallorg.org
6  jessica@smallorg.org[Tab⇥]jessica@spoke3.smallorg.org
7  rich@smallorg.org[Tab⇥]rich
8  barbara@smallorg.org[Tab⇥]barbara
```

In Listing 17.3, lines 1 and 2 demonstrate users who are on the `spoke1.smallorg.org` mailserver. When the main `hub.smallorg.org` mailserver receives a message destined for `frank@smallorg.org`, that message is automatically forwarded to `frank@spoke1.smallorg.org`. Similarly, in lines 3 and 4, users on the `spoke2.smallorg.org` server also receive their Internet mail via the `hub.smallorg.org` mailserver. This continues for all the spoke servers in the local network. Each time a new user is added to a spoke server, a new user entry must be added to the virtual user table. Also remember that no two spokes can use the same username.

Lines 7 and 8 are a little different. They demonstrate a deliberate definition of local users on the `hub.smallorg.org` mailserver. By default, if a username does not appear in the virtual user table, sendmail assumes that the username is a local user. Lines 7 and 8 are therefore unnecessary, but sometimes it helps to include obvious things for documentation purposes.

After the `/etc/virtusertable` file is created, it must be converted into the hash database format that sendmail uses. The makemap program is used for this. The format of the `makemap` command is

```
makemap hash /etc/virtusertable < /etc/virtusertable
```

This might seem like an odd format, but the makemap program creates a separate file—`/etc/virtusertable.db`—from the text file. Each time the virtual user table is changed, the makemap program must be rerun.

Besides forwarding individual users' addresses to the proper mailservers, the virtual user table can be used for other purposes. Listing 17.4 shows some alternative entries that can be in the `/etc/virtusertable` file.

17

MAIL ALIASES AND MASQUERADING

LISTING 17.4   Alternative `/etc/virtusertable` Entries

```
1  rich@smallorg.org[Tab↹]rich@othermail.com
2  @acct.smallorg.org[Tab↹]acct
3  baduser@smallorg.org[Tab↹]error:nouser No such user
4  register@smallorg.org[Tab↹]rich
5  officenews@smallorg.org[Tab↹]officenews
6  @smallorg.org[Tab↹]%1@neworg.org
```

In Listing 17.4, each line represents a different feature that the virtual user table can support. Line 1 demonstrates a feature similar to the `aliases` file by forwarding messages for the email address `rich` to an email account on a remote Internet mailserver.

Line 2 demonstrates a feature with which your ISP is probably very familiar. This feature allows all mail for a particular domain to be sent to a single mailbox on the server. This is a handy method to use to support remote subordinate offices that can dial into the main Linux mailserver to retrieve mail messages for the subdomain `acct.smallorg.org`. Chapter 13 details how to break the messages out of the single mailbox to deliver them to individual users on the remote mailservers.

Line 3 demonstrates a nice feature of the virtual user table. If you want to deliberately generate an error message for a specific email address, you can add it to the table. Line 4 shows the redirection of an alias email account to a valid local user account on the mailserver.

Line 5 shows how the virtual user table can work hand-in-hand with the `aliases` file. By creating an alias of `officenews` as described previously, the virtual user table can redirect messages sent to the alias address at the domain address to the local alias. If the alias is a list file as previously described, all email addresses in the list receive a copy of the message.

The last example in line 6 shows a unique way of redirecting mail messages. If for some reason you need to redirect messages for an entire domain, the format shown in line 6 will come in handy. This format redirects any address in the `smallorg.org` domain to the `neworg.org` domain. The usernames remain intact; only the domain names are changed.

Summary

This chapter covered some advanced methods of using office email systems. Often it is desirable to create temporary email accounts for special events or activities that describe the function. The sendmail program allows the use of email aliases to redirect messages sent to a nonexistent user to a regular email account. The `/etc/aliases` file contains the text version of the aliases used by the sendmail program. To convert the text file to the hash database file used by sendmail, run the newaliases program. Each time the `/etc/aliases` file is changed, the newaliases program must be run to activate the changes. Another advanced feature of sendmail is the use of masquerading. By using masquerading, multiple hosts can use the same domain name as the return address from email messages. For this to work properly, a central mail hub should be created that uses the sendmail virtual user table feature. By using the virtual user table, the main mail hub can map generic usernames from the domain to specific usernames on the specific spoke mailservers.

Mail Lists

IN THIS CHAPTER

In the previous chapter, the different uses of email aliases were discussed. One use for aliases is to generate a simple mail list—a single email address that can replicate the received message to multiple email accounts. Although this is a nice feature of the `aliases` file, it is far from the full-blown mail list features that many people are accustomed to on the Internet. This chapter discusses how to implement a full mail list system on the Linux mailserver that can support advanced user and administrator features for both local and remote mail users on multiple mail lists.

Features of a Full Service Mail List

As a subscriber, you might already be familiar with mail list servers. If you have ever had to send a message to a mail list with the word *subscribe* in the body of the message, you probably have interacted with a large mail list system. The ability of remote users to request a subscription is just one feature of real mail list servers. This section describes some of the common features found in various mail list servers.

Open and Closed Mail Lists

When you want to become a member of a mail list, you must first send a message asking to subscribe. The mail list server can use several different options to handle new subscription requests.

In an open mail list, anyone is allowed to subscribe. No checks are made to authenticate the email address requesting the subscription. This is the simplest type of mail list to administer, as there are almost no functions that need administering. There is one drawback to this feature. You are assuming that the email address requesting the subscription is the actual person that is subscribing. Sometimes this can be dangerous. Just like pranksters who send in magazine subscription cards with other peoples' names on them, pranksters can subscribe other peoples' email addresses to a mail list without the latter knowing.

To combat this situation, most mail list server programs allow open mail lists, but confirm the actual subscription. When a request to subscribe to the mail list is received, the server sends a message back to the email address requesting the subscription, asking that the address reply with a confirmation message. Often a special ID code is used, making it difficult to fake the return confirmation message. When a proper return confirmation message is received, the email address is added to the subscription list.

In a closed mail list, all subscription requests go to a special email address called the *list owner*. New email addresses are not added to the mail list unless the mail list owner sends a message okaying the addition. The mail list owner then has complete control over who is allowed access to the mail list.

Moderated and Unmoderated Mail Lists

Users can send messages to the mail list to be forwarded to all other members of the list. In an unmoderated mail list, messages are not checked for content or other issues. Any member of the list can send any message to the list and it is automatically forwarded to every member of the list.

Some mail list owners get a little scared with this feature. You might want or need to control the content of messages sent to list members. A moderated mail list lets the list owner screen all messages before they are sent to list members. If the list owner does not want the message forwarded, he can stop the message. If the message is okay, it will be sent to the list as normal. This feature creates a large amount of work for the list owner. Depending on the scope of the mail list, it might be a necessary job.

Remote Administration of Mail Lists

Sophisticated mail list server software packages frequently offer an extremely nice feature: the capability to remotely administer the mail list. Most packages enable the list owner to create a special password to access administration functions on the mail list. When the owner has access, she can then change the configuration of the mail list server via email messages sent to the mail list. Because the configuration is accomplished via email, the list owner can be any-where in the world, as long as she can still send email messages to the server. This is a nice feature to have if the mail list server is located remotely from the mail list owner.

Each mail list has a separate configuration file that can be maintained by the mail list owner. Features—such as whether the list is open or closed, and moderated or unmoderated—can be configured and changed remotely without any work having to be done on the mail list server.

Digests of Mail Lists

Full-service mail list servers can also compact received messages into digests. You can config-ure the mail list server to create digests of messages sent to the list daily, weekly, or monthly. A user can request to receive the digests rather than the individual messages. If the mail list generates lots of messages each day, this can be a nice feature to add. Sometimes it is better to receive just one large message at the end of the day rather than lots of small messages scattered throughout the day. Mail lists that are time sensitive (where responses are generated often) might not be good candidates for digests.

Archives of Mail Lists

Archives are files that contain previous messages sent to the mail list. The list owner can select an archive period to use—daily, weekly, monthly, or yearly. All messages sent to the list in the set time period are also saved to an archive file. New members of the list can request to receive archives of past messages. The mail list server can produce lists of available archive files, and members can select which files to receive via email.

Introducing Majordomo

Majordomo is a popular mail list server package, written by Brent Chapman. Majordomo supports all the mail list features mentioned in the previous section. It consists of a set of Perl programs(which use the sendmail `aliases` file to manipulate messages) and a system of configuration files and directories for the mail lists, digests, and archives.

The Majordomo program can be implemented on Linux mailservers with minimal effort. You will need to do some configuration work to enable the sendmail program to work with Majordomo, and to ensure that the mail list is properly secure from hackers. This section describes the steps necessary to get a Majordomo mail list server up and running.

Downloading Majordomo

Some Linux distributions include a binary distribution package for Majordomo. Caldera's OpenLinux Linux distribution includes a Majordomo RPM file.

CAUTION

Users of OpenLinux 2.2 are warned that a bug has been discovered in the Majordomo distribution of that release. If you are using OpenLinux 2.2, don't use the Majordomo RPM distribution on the CD. A fixed version can be downloaded from Caldera's Web site at `http://www.calderasystems.com`.

If your Linux does not include a binary distribution of Majordomo, or you want to get the latest version, you can download it from the Internet. Many different UNIX and Linux sites have Majordomo distributions available for download. At the time of this writing, Great Circle Associates hosts the official Majordomo Web and FTP sites. The Web site is located at

`http://www.greatcircle.com/majordomo/`

Software can be downloaded at its FTP site

`ftp.greatcircle.com`

in the `/pub/majordomo` directory. The file `majordomo.tar.gz` always points to the most current version of Majordomo (at this writing, version 1.94.4). Remember to change to BINARY FTP mode before downloading the file to your Linux server.

Installing Majordomo

After the distribution package has been downloaded, you can begin the installation of Majordomo. Because the Majordomo program is distributed as source code, you will need the GNU C compiler installed on your Linux system. There are several steps that are required to install Majordomo.

Creating a Majordomo Userid

For security purposes, Majordomo must be installed from a separate userid. Otherwise, the Perl programs will run as the root user and create possible vulnerabilities. The new userid must belong to a Linux group that is considered trusted by the sendmail mail program, because it must interact with the sendmail program. To determine which groups are trusted by sendmail, view the sendmail configuration file `/etc/sendmail.cf` and look for the `'T'` configuration lines. Listing 18.1 shows the pertinent lines from a Mandrake Linux 6.0 system.

LISTING 18.1 Sample `/etc/sendmail.cf` File

```
1  #####################
2  #   Trusted users   #
3  #####################
4
5  # this is equivalent to setting class "t"
6  #Ft/etc/sendmail.ct
7  Troot
8  Tdaemon
9  Tuucp
```

Listing 18.1 shows the trusted users for sendmail on the Linux mailserver. As shown in line 6, sendmail can also be configured to read the trusted users from a file named `/etc/sendmail.ct`. Currently the `root`, `daemon`, and `uucp` groups are trusted by sendmail on this server.

For this example, the userid `majordomo` and group `daemon` were chosen as the Majordomo installation account. The Majordomo distribution file was copied to the Majordomo home directory. To extract the software from the file, type

```
tar -zxvf majordomo.tar.gz
```

This creates the subdirectory `majordomo-1.94.4` and installs the Majordomo source code files. Next, you must modify the Makefile to reflect your particular installation of Majordomo.

Edit the Majordomo Makefile

The Makefile directs what features the Majordomo program will have when it is compiled. Listing 18.2 is a partial listing of the Makefile.

LISTING 18.2   Partial Listing of Majordomo Makefile

```
1   #$Modified: Wed Aug 27 17:52:25 1997 by cwilson $
2   #
3   # $Source: /sources/cvsrepos/majordomo/Makefile,v $
4   # $Revision: 1.63 $
5   # $Date: 1997/08/27 15:56:21 $
6   # $Header: /sources/cvsrepos/majordomo/Makefile,v 1.63 1997/08/27 15:56:21
7     cwilson Exp $
8 #
9
10 #   This is the Makefile for Majordomo.
11 #
12 #------------- Configure these items ---------------#
13 #
14
15 # Put the location of your Perl binary here:
16 PERL = /usr/bin/perl
17
18 # What do you call your C compiler?
19 CC = gcc
20
21 # Where do you want Majordomo to be installed?  This CANNOT be the
22 # current directory (where you unpacked the distribution)
23 W_HOME = /usr/local/majordomo
24
25 # Where do you want man pages to be installed?
26 MAN = $(W_HOME)/man
27
28 # You need to have or create a user and group which majordomo will run as.
29 # Enter the numeric UID and GID (not their names!) here:
30 W_USER = 507
31 W_GROUP = 2
32
33 # These set the permissions for all installed files and executables (except
34 # the wrapper), respectively.  Some sites may wish to make these more
35 # lenient, or more restrictive.
36 FILE_MODE = 644
37 EXEC_MODE = 755
38 HOME_MODE = 751
39 # If your system is POSIX (e.g. Sun Solaris, SGI Irix 5 and 6, Dec Ultrix
40 # MIPS, BSDI or other 4.4-based BSD, Linux) use the following four lines.
41 # Do not change these values!
42 WRAPPER_OWNER = root
43 WRAPPER_GROUP = $(W_GROUP)
44 WRAPPER_MODE = 4755
45 POSIX = -DPOSIX_UID=$(W_USER) -DPOSIX_GID=$(W_GROUP)
```

```
46 # Otherwise, if your system is NOT POSIX (e.g. SunOS 4.x, SGI Irix 4,
47 # HP DomainOS) then comment out the above four lines and uncomment
48 # the following four lines.
49 # WRAPPER_OWNER = $(W_USER)
50 # WRAPPER_GROUP = $(W_GROUP)
51 # WRAPPER_MODE = 6755
52 # POSIX =
53
54 # Define this if the majordomo programs should *also* be run in the same
55 # group as your MTA, usually sendmail.  This is rarely needed, but some
56 # MTAs require certain group memberships before allowing the message sender
57 # to be set arbitrarily.
58 # MAIL_GID =    numeric_gid_of_MTA
59
60 # This is the environment that (along with LOGNAME and USER inherited from
61 # the parent process, and without the leading "W_" in the variable names)
62 # gets passed to processes run by "wrapper"
63 W_SHELL = /bin/sh
64 W_PATH = /bin:/usr/bin:/usr/ucb
65 W_MAJORDOMO_CF = $(W_HOME)/majordomo.cf
66
67 # A directory for temp files..
68 TMPDIR = /usr/tmp
```

18

Several lines in the Makefile shown in Listing 18.2 need to be modified to suit your particular Linux environment. Line 16 defines where Majordomo can find the Perl program. As the Majordomo scripts are written in Perl, you must have Perl installed on your Linux system, and Majordomo must know how to find it. A popular scripting program language developed by Larry Walls, Perl is included with almost all Linux distributions. Line 19 defines the C compiler used on the Linux system. For most Linux distributions, the GNU C compiler, gcc, is included.

Besides the compilers, you must specify the location where Majordomo will be installed. Line 23 defines the home directory for the Majordomo program. Don't get this confused with the home directory for the majordomo userid. They are not the same. They can be the same, but it is easier if you select another location that can be used for the scripts and configuration files. I've selected the /usr/local/majordomo location. You will have to create this directory as the root user, and can change the owner to the majordomo user with the command

```
chown majordomo.daemon /usr/local/majordomo
```

You will have to replace majordomo.daemon with the userid and the groupid under which you chose to install Majordomo. Speaking of that, the majordomo userid and groupid in the Makefile also need to be. Lines 30 and 31 specify these values to the Majordomo program. You can log in as the majordomo userid and type the command **id** to determine the userid and groupid. In the samples, the majordomo userid was 507, and the daemon groupid was 2. Remember, the Makefile is looking for the numerical values, not the text names.

Creating and Editing the majordomo.cf File

The main configuration file, majordomo.cf, controls the behavior of the Majordomo installation. To create a new configuration file, you can copy the template file sample.cf located in the majordomo-1.94.4 directory to majordomo.cf in the same directory. Listing 18.3 shows a sample majordomo.cf file.

LISTING 18.3 Sample majordomo.cf File

```
1  #
2  # A sample configuration file for majordomo.  You must read through this
3  # and edit it accordingly!
4  #
5
6  # $whereami -- What machine am I running on?
7  #
8  $whereami = "smallorg.org";
9
10 # $whoami -- Who do users send requests to me as?
11 #
12 $whoami = "Majordomo\@$whereami";
13
14 # $whoami_owner -- Who is the owner of the above, in case of problems?
15 #
16 $whoami_owner = "Majordomo-Owner\@$whereami";
17
18 # $homedir -- Where can I find my extra .pl files, like majordomo.pl?
19 # the environment variable HOME is set by the wrapper
20 #
21 if ( defined $ENV{"HOME"}) {
22      $homedir = $ENV{"HOME"};
23 } else {
24      $homedir = "/usr/local/majordomo";
25 }
26
27 # $listdir -- Where are the mailing lists?
28 #
29 $listdir = "$homedir/lists";
30
31 # $digest_work_dir -- the parent directory for digest's queue area
32 # Each list must have a subdirectory under this directory in order for
```

```
33 # digest to work. E.G. The bblisa list would use:
34 #      /usr/local/mail/digest/bblisa
35 # as its directory.
36 #
37 $digest_work_dir = "/usr/local/mail/digest";
38
39 # $log -- Where do I write my log?
40 #
41 $log = "$homedir/Log";
```

There are several variables that must be set in the `majordomo.cf` file. Line 8 defines the `$whereami` variable, which is the address used for return messages. If sendmail on the Linux mailserver is using masquerading, the return address will be the domain name as shown in line 8. If not, the return address will be the fully qualified hostname. Lines 12 and 16 define the `$whoami` and `$whoami_owner` variables based on the `$whereami` variable. You should not need to change these values.

The `$homedir` variable shown on line 24 is important. It must point to the Majordomo program home directory that you configured in the Makefile. This is where Majordomo will look for the Perl scripts as it processes list messages. Line 29 defines the `$listdir` variable. This indicates where Majordomo will store the information for the mail lists. The default location is a subdirectory called `lists` that is located in the Majordomo home directory.

In line 37, `$digest_work_dir` defines where the mail list digest files will be kept. If you are planning on using the digest feature of Majordomo, you might need to change this value and create the new subdirectory. Remember that digest files contain the full text of all messages sent during a particular time period. You might need to use an area that has a fairly large amount of disk space, depending on the number of mail list messages you generate. The last variable described is the `$log` variable in line 41. Majordomo logs all transactions with the mail list server in a log file. You can change the location of this file to match your Linux distribution's current log file directory, such as `/var/log/majordomo.log`.

Using the GNU make Utility for Majordomo

After the Makefile and `majordomo.cf` files are configured, you can use the GNU make utility to build the Majordomo executable files. This requires three steps:

1. Run `make wrapper` to verify that the wrapper program will compile cleanly.

2. Run `make install` as the `majordomo` userid to install the Majordomo scripts and executables in the Majordomo home directory.

3. Run `make install-wrapper` as the root userid to install the wrapper program `setuid` root.

At this point you can run the wrapper program and test the Majordomo installation. Log in as a user without any special rights, and change to the Majordomo program's home directory (/usr/local/majordomo, for this example). From there, type

./wrapper config-test

This runs the wrapper program and tests the configuration. Listing 18.4 shows the partial output generated by the wrapper program.

LISTING 18.4   Output from Wrapper Configuration Test

```
1 ---------------------- end of tests ----------------------
2
3
4 Nothing bad found!  Majordomo _should_ work correctly.
5
6 If it doesn't, check your configuration file
7    (/usr/local/majordomo/majordomo.cf)
8 closely, and if it still looks okay, consider asking the majordomo-users
9 mailing list at "majordomo-users@greatcircle.com" for assistance.  Be sure
10 and fully specify what your problems are, and what type of machine (and
11 operating system) you are using.
12
13 Enjoy!
```

Listing 18.4 shows the final few lines of the long output that the config-test generates. As you can tell, this Majordomo configuration passed the tests.

Creating sendmail Aliases for Majordomo

After successfully installing the Majordomo software, you must configure sendmail to recognize the mail lists. Majordomo processes mail lists using the sendmail aliases file (see Chapter 17, "Mail Aliases and Masquerading"). For the default Majordomo configuration, add the lines shown in Listing 18.5 to the /etc/aliases file.

LISTING 18.5   Majordomo Alias Lines

```
1  #  Majordomo aliases
2  majordomo:   "|/usr/local/majordomo/wrapper majordomo"
3  owner-majordomo:    rich,
4  majordomo-owner:    rich
```

After new entries are made to the aliases file, you must run the newaliases program for sendmail to recognize them. In Listing 18.5, line 2 shows the alias majordomo being redirected to the wrapper program with the command line parameter of majordomo. This tells sendmail to run the wrapper program when it receives a message.

There is one trick to using aliases to run the wrapper program. Some sendmail installations use the smrsh feature, as described in Chapter 11. This restricted shell refuses to execute programs unless they appear in a special directory owned by the root user. If your sendmail configuration is using the smrsh feature, it will refer to the directory where you can place the executable files that sendmail is allowed to run. On Mandrake Linux 6.0, it is the /etc/smrsh directory. By copying the wrapper program from the normal location (/usr/local/majordomo/wrapper, in this example) to the /etc/smrsh directory, sendmail will be able to run the wrapper program.

Lines 3 and 4 are support aliases. If a list member has difficulties with the mail list, he can send mail to the mail list owner asking for help, advice, and so on. These addresses will point to the real email address of the mail list owner.

Testing the Majordomo Installation

You can easily create a test mail list to see whether the installation is correct. First, you must create a dummy list file in the Majordomo lists directory, as specified in the majordomo.cf file. In this example, the location is /usr/local/majordomo/lists. You can create the test file using the command

```
touch /usr/local/majordomo/lists/test
```

After the file is created, you can send the Majordomo 'lists' command to the majordomo alias to receive a listing of the available mail lists. Listing 18.6 shows an example of this.

LISTING 18.6   Sample Test of Majordomo Installation

```
1   [rich@shadrach rich]$ echo 'lists' | mail -v majordomo
2   majordomo... aliased to "|/usr/local/majordomo/wrapper majordomo"
3   "|/usr/local/majordomo/wrapper majordomo"... Connecting to prog...
4   "|/usr/local/majordomo/wrapper majordomo"... Sent
5   [rich@shadrach rich]$ mail
6   Mail version 8.1 6/6/93.  Type ? for help.
7   "/var/spool/mail/rich": 1 message 1 new
8   >N  1 Majordomo@smallorg.org  Thu Nov 18 18:51  23/736   "Majordomo results"
9   &
10  Message 1:
11  From Majordomo-Owner@smallorg.org  Thu Nov 18 18:51:35 1999
12  Date: Thu, 18 Nov 1999 18:51:34 -0500
13  X-Authentication-Warning: shadrach.smallorg.org: majordomo set sender to
14  Majordomo-Owner@smallorg.org using -f
15  To: rich@smallorg.org
16  From: Majordomo@smallorg.org
17  Subject: Majordomo results
18  Reply-To: Majordomo@smallorg.org
19
```

continues

LISTING **18.6**   continued

```
20 --
21
22 >>>> lists
23 Majordomo@smallorg.org serves the following lists:
24
25   test
26
27 Use the 'info <list>' command to get more information
28 about a specific list.
29
30 &
```

In Listing 18.6, line 1 shows an example of sending the `'lists'` command to Majordomo. The `-v` command line option puts the Linux mail program in verbose mode so you can see what is happening. Lines 2 through 4 show the results of the mail message. Line 2 indicates that sendmail recognized the alias. Line 3 shows sendmail attempting to contact the wrapper program. Line 4 shows that sendmail was successful in passing the message off to the wrapper program. After the message is sent, you can check the mailbox for the user that sent the message for Majordomo's reply. Lines 5 through 30 show the resulting mail message returned from Majordomo, indicating that there is one mail list available on the Majordomo server. Of course, this is not totally true because you have not configured the mail list properly.

As a final check of the Majordomo system, the command that you sent to Majordomo will have been logged in the Majordomo log file. Check the log to see whether it made it. The following line appeared in the `/usr/local/majordomo/log` file of the sample server:

```
Nov 18 18:51:34 smallorg.org majordomo[28128] {Rich
➥<rich@shacrach.smallorg.org>} lists
```

The log file indicates the time, email address, and the command entered. Frequent checking of the Majordomo log file helps in spotting any unauthorized activity with the mail list server.

Configuring a Majordomo Mail List

With the Majordomo program installed, you will next configure actual mail lists. First, you must create an empty file that will be used to hold the email addresses in the list. The name of the file must match the name of the mail list. This example will use the mail list name office-news. After the file is created, you must ensure that it has the proper access modes set. sendmail will complain if it tries to use an alias list that is group writable, or is in a directory that is group writable. The commands to create the file and change the permissions are

```
touch /usr/local/majordomo/lists/officenews
chmod 755 /usr/local/majordomo/lists
chmod 644 /usr/local/majordomo/lists/officenews
```

Next, create an information file for the mail list. Majordomo will use the mail list information file when someone requests information on the mail list, or subscribes to the mail list. The information file will be in the form `list.info`, where `list` is the mail list name. For this example, the information file is `/usr/local/majordomo/lists/officenews.info`, and contains a simple text description of the mail list.

Each mail list requires several entries in the sendmail `aliases` file, depending on which features you want the mail list to support. Table 18.1 shows the aliases that can be used for a mail list named `list`.

TABLE 18.1   sendmail Aliases Used for a Majordomo Mail List

Alias	Description
list	The mail list alias
list-outgoing	Actual list of subscribers
owner-list	Administrator of the mail list
list-request	Address for Majordomo requests
list-approval	Person who approves postings in moderated lists
list-digest	Address for digest lists
list-digest-request	Address for digest requests

Listing 18.7 shows a sample entry for the `officenews` mail list. This list will be a simple, no-frills mail list. The mail list will be open to the public, and no digests or archives will be created.

LISTING 18.7   Sample Mail List Alias Entries

```
1  #officenews mail list entries
2  officenews:      "|/usr/local/majordomo/wrapper resend -l officenews
➥ officenews-list"
3  officenews-list:        :include:/usr/local/majordomo/lists/officenews
4  owner-officenews:       rich,
5  officenews-owner:       rich
6  officenews-approval:    officenews-owner
7  officenews-request:     "|/usr/local/majordomo/wrapper majordomo –l
➥ officenews"
```

As usual, remember to run the newaliases program as root after adding the new aliases. At this point the mail list will be operational, but not configured. You can create a configuration file by emailing the mail list from an email address that is either local or remote to the mail list server. Majordomo will automatically create a default configuration file and mail it back to you. Listing 18.8 shows an example of this operation, plus a partial listing of the return message.

LISTING 18.8   Partial Sample Mail List Configuration Request

```
1  [rich@shadrach rich]$ mail officenews-request
2  Subject:
3  config officenews officenews.admin
4  .
5  Cc:
6  [rich@shadrach rich]$ mail
7  Mail version 8.1 6/6/93.  Type ? for help.
8  "/var/spool/mail/rich": 1 message 1 new
9  >N  1 Majordomo@shadrach.s  Thu Nov 18 16:25 400/16764 "Majordomo results"
10 &1
11  From Majordomo-Owner@shadrach.smallorg.org  Thu Nov 18 16:06:05 1999
12  Return-Path: <Majordomo-Owner@shadrach.smallorg.org>
13  Received: (from majordomo@localhost)
14     by shadrach.smallorg.org (8.9.3/8.9.3) id QAA28433;
15     Thu, 18 Nov 1999 19:06:05 -0500
16 Date: Thu, 18 Nov 1999 19:06:05 -0500
17 Message-Id: <199911182106.QAA28433@shadrach.smallorg.org>
18 X-Authentication-Warning: shadrach.smallorg.org: majordomo set sender to
➥ Majordomo-Owner@smallorg.org using -19 f
20 To: rich@smallorg.org
21 From: Majordomo@smallorg.org
22 Subject: Majordomo results
23 Reply-To: Majordomo@smallorg.org
24 Status: R
25
26 --
27
28 >>>> config officenews officenews.admin
29 admin_passwd        =   officenews.admin
30 administrivia       =   yes
31 advertise           <<  END
32 announcements       =   yes
33 approve_passwd      =   officenews.pass
34 archive_dir         =
35 comments            <<  END
36 date_info           =   yes
37 date_intro          =   yes
38 debug               =   no
39 description         =
40 digest_archive      =
41 digest_issue        =   1
42 digest_maxdays      =
43 digest_maxlines     =
44 digest_name         =   officenews
```

```
45 digest_rm_footer      =
46 digest_rm_fronter     =
47 digest_volume         =    1
48 digest_work_dir       =
49 get_access            =    list
50 index_access          =    open
51 info_access           =    open
52 intro_access          =    list
53 maxlength             =    40000
54 message_footer        <<   END
55 message_fronter       <<   END
56 message_headers       <<   END
57 moderate              =    no
58 moderator             =
59 mungedomain           =    no
60 noadvertise           <<   END
61 precedence            =    bulk
62 purge_received        =    no
64 reply_to              =
64 resend_host           =
65 restrict_post         =
66 sender                =    owner-officenews
67 strip                 =    yes
68 subject_prefix        =
69 subscribe_policy      =    open+confirm
70 taboo_body            <<   END
71 taboo_headers         <<   END
72 unsubscribe_policy    =    open
73 welcome               =    yes
74 which_access          =    open
75 who_access            =    open
```

In Listing 18.8, line 1 shows the mail list owner sending an email message to the officenews-request address. All mail list commands will be sent to the -request version of the list name. Normally any message sent to the list name will be automatically forwarded to everyone on the list. Majordomo contains a program called resend that can be used to screen incoming messages and bounce any messages that appear to be Majordomo commands sent to the list name by mistake. This greatly reduces the annoyance of seeing new members' subscribe commands forwarded to everyone on the list.

Line 3 shows the format that is used to request a configuration file for the mail list. The third parameter on the line is the mail list administrative password. The default password for any mail list is *list*.admin, where *list* is the mail list name. After receiving the message, Majordomo sends a return message. The return address includes the complete configuration file created by Majordomo. The configuration file is stored in the `lists` directory as `list.config`, where `list` is the mail list name.

Lines 29 through 75 show the configuration variables that can be changed in the configuration file. The explanatory comments have been removed from the original message. You can read the actual return message to get an idea of what each of the configuration parameters control. To change the configuration, you can save the message, change the configuration parameters, and mail the new configuration file back to the mail list using the `newconfig` command. The first line of the return message will have the format

```
newconfig    list    adminpasswd
```

where `list` is the list name and `adminpasswd` is the administrative password for the mail list. After the `newconfig` line, the normal configuration file with your changes will start.

Listing 18.9 shows some common variables that will be changed from the default configuration file.

LISTING 18.9   Configuration File Changes for Mail List

```
1   admin_passwd = newpassword
2   approve_passwd = newpasswd
3   description = A mail list used to distribute general office news
4   subscribe_policy = open
5   who_access = list
```

Most of the default values will work fine in a general mail list as this example shows. Please remember to change the administrator password for the new mail list. In Listing 18.9, line 4 changes the default subscription policy. The default policy is `open+confirm`, which is for an open mail list, but members must confirm their subscription requests by responding to a message sent by Majordomo. This example uses a simple open policy, which allows anyone to subscribe to the list, and doesn't verify email addresses. If this was a mail list that contained sensitive company information, you might want to use a closed subscription policy wherein the mail list owner must confirm each subscription to the mail list. Line 5 restricts who can issue the `'who'` command to receive a listing of mail list members; only current list members can issue the command. Listing 18.10 shows the results of using this parameter for a non-member.

LISTING 18.10   Sample `'who'` Command

```
1   [melanie@shadrach melanie]$ echo 'who' | mail officenews-request
2   [melanie@shadrach melanie]$ mail
3   Mail version 8.1 6/6/93.  Type ? for help.
4   "/var/spool/mail/melanie": 1 message 1 new
```

```
5  >N  1 Majordomo@smallorg.o  Thu Nov 20 16:40  20/744    "Majordomo results"
6  &
7  Message 1:
8  From Majordomo-Owner@smallorg.org  Thu Nov 18 20:40:54 1999
9  Date: Thu, 18 Nov 1999 20:40:53 -0500
10 X-Authentication-Warning: shadrach.smallorg.org: majordomo set sender
➥ to Majordomo-Owner@smallorg.org using -f
11 To: melanie@smallorg.org
12 From: Majordomo@smallorg.org
13 Subject: Majordomo results
14 Reply-To: Majordomo@smallorg.org
15
16 --
17
18 >>>> who
19 **** List 'officenews' is a private list.
20 **** Only members of the list can do a 'who'.
21 **** You [ Melanie <melanie@smallorg.org> ] aren't a member of list
➥ 'officenews'.
22
23 &
```

In Listing 18.10, line 1 shows the user melanie sending a 'who' command to the mail list server to retrieve a list of members. Lines 18 through 21 show the results that were mailed back to melanie. Because the 'who' mail list command was configured as private—for list members only—melanie is restricted from viewing the mail list.

That completes the installation and configuration of the Majordomo mail list server. The next section describes how email clients can use the new mail list server.

Using Majordomo

Majordomo makes tasks simple for general users. Subscribing, posting new messages, and unsubscribing are very straightforward. However, there are more complicated commands for advanced features, such as retrieving digests and archive files, as well as managing the mail list remotely.

The first step in becoming a mail list member is to request a subscription. Subscription requests are sent to the -request form of the mail list name. Majordomo ignores the subject line, so it can be left blank. The body of the message will contain a single line with the word subscribe in it. Depending on the list mode, you will receive either a confirmation of the subscription, or a message, which you must return to join the list. Listing 18.11 shows a sample subscription session.

18

MAIL LISTS

LISTING 18.11   Sample Mail List Subscription Session

```
1  [rich@shadrach rich]$ mail officenews-request
2  Subject:
3  subscribe
4  .
5  Cc:
6  [rich@shadrach rich]$ mail
7  Mail version 8.1 6/6/93.  Type ? for help.
8  "/var/spool/mail/rich": 3 messages 3 new
9  >N  1 Majordomo@smallorg.o  Fri Nov 19 04:42  44/1625   "Welcome to
➥ officenews"
10 N   2 Majordomo@smallorg.o  Fri Nov 19 04:42  18/696    "SUBSCRIBE
➥ officenews "
11 N   3 Majordomo@smallorg.o  Fri Nov 19 04:42  18/613    "Majordomo results"
12 &
13 Message 1:
14 From owner-officenews@smallorg.org  Fri Nov 19 04:42:56 1999
15 Date: Fri, 19 Nov 1999 04:42:56 -0500
16 X-Authentication-Warning: shadrach.smallorg.org: majordomo set sender to
➥ owner-officenews@smallorg.org using -f
17 To: rich@smallorg.org
18 From: Majordomo@smallorg.org
19 Subject: Welcome to officenews
20 Reply-To: Majordomo@smallorg.org
21
22 --
23
24 Welcome to the officenews mailing list!
25
26 Please save this message for future reference.  Thank you.
27
28 If you ever want to remove yourself from this mailing list,
29 you can send mail to <Majordomo@smallorg.org> with the following
30 command in the body of your email message:
31
32     unsubscribe officenews
33
34 or from another account, besides rich@smallorg.org:
35
36     unsubscribe officenews rich@smallorg.org
37
38 If you ever need to get in contact with the owner of the list,
39 (if you have trouble unsubscribing, or have questions about the
40 list itself) send email to <owner-officenews@smallorg.org> .
```

```
41 This is the general rule for most mailing lists when you need
42 to contact a human.
43
44  Here's the general information for the list you've subscribed to,
45  in case you don't already have it:
46
47 Welcome to the smallorg.org officenews mail list.
48
49 This mail list is used to help keep you informed about general information
50 that is happening in the organization.  Please post any announcements to
51 this mail list.  Unauthorized use of this mail list is prohibited.
52
53 &
```

In Listing 18.11, lines 1 through 5 show the user `rich` sending a message to the `officenews-request` mail alias to subscribe to the mail list. Users can also send requests to the `majordomo` alias, but the desired list name must follow the command so that Majordomo knows which mail list you are requesting. Lines 6 through 11 show the mail messages that are returned in response to the command. Line 11 shows the message that is returned confirming that Majordomo received the subscription message. Line 10 is a message that is sent to the mail list owner (which also happens to be `rich`) that a new member has subscribed to the mail list. Line 9 is the message returned by Majordomo confirming that the user is now a member of the mail list. Lines 13 through 53 show the text of this message. Notice that Majordomo gives full instructions on how to unsubscribe from the mail list in lines 28 through 36. Lines 47 through 51 reproduce the `officenews.info` file that was created for the mail list.

Mail List User Commands

Several commands can be sent to the `-request` mail alias requesting actions from the mail list server. The following commands are available to users.

subscribe Command

As shown in Listing 18.11, the `subscribe` command lets new members request subscriptions to the mail list. The format of the command is

`subsscribe <list> [<address>]`

where `list` is the list name and `address` is the email address that you want to add to the mail list. If you are sending the message to the `list-request` version of the alias, you can omit the `list` parameter. Also, if you want to subscribe the email address that you are sending the message from, you can omit the `address` parameter. You are allowed to subscribe a different email address. The results depend on the subscription policy configuration of the mail list.

unsubscribe Command

The opposite of the `subscribe` command is `unsubscribe`, which removes an email address from a mail list. The format of this command is

```
unsubscribe <list> [<address>]
```

where, again, the *list* and *address* parameters are optional.

get Command

The `get` command is used to retrieve a file from the mail list. The format of this command is

```
get <list> filename
```

where *filename* refers to a file that is in the mail list. This command is used when a mail list is archived. The mail list member can retrieve an archive file by issuing the `get` command with the desired archive name.

index Command

The `index` command is used to return a list of files that are available in the mail list. The format of this command is

```
index <list>
```

The `index` command is used in conjunction with the `get` command when using mail list archives. The `index` command will return a list of the archive files available for retrieval.

which Command

The `which` command is used to determine which mail lists on the Majordomo server an email address is a member of. The format of the which command is

```
which [<address>]
```

If you want information regarding the email address from which you are sending the request, you can omit the address parameter. Majordomo will return a message listing all the mail lists to which you belong.

who Command

The `who` command can be used to retrieve a listing of the members currently subscribed to the mail list. The format of the who command is

```
who <list>
```

As seen in Listing 18.10, the `who` command can be restricted to only members of the list.

info Command

The `info` command is used to retrieve the information file for the mail list. The format of the command is

`info <list>`

The information retrieved is the text from the file `list.info` located in the Majordomo `lists` directory.

intro Command

The `intro` command is used to retrieve the introduction text message that is sent to new users. The format for this command is

`intro < list>`

lists Command

The `lists` command is used to retrieve a listing of all the mail lists on the Majordomo server. The format of this command is

`lists`

help Command

The `help` command returns a message that lists all the user commands available in Majordomo. No list-specific information is returned in the `help` command.

end Command

The `end` command is used to tell Majordomo to stop processing commands in the message. This command is used mainly when extra text appears at the end of an email message, such as when users have an email client package that includes an automatic signature block at the bottom of the message. The `end` command will appear on a line by itself at the end of the command section of the message.

Mail List Owner Commands

The designated owner of the mail list has more commands available that can be used to control the operation of the mail list. All of the commands are sent as normal email messages to the `-request` form of the mail list. This feature greatly simplifies the list's administration. Anyone from anywhere can become the owner of a mail list. Owners are not restricted to having physical contact with the mail list server. Also, the mail list owner does not need a log-in userid for the system on which the mail list is running. This section describes these owner commands in more detail.

18

MAIL LISTS

approve Command

The `approve` command is used in closed mail lists to approve subscriptions of new members. The command format is

```
approve password subscribe/unsubscribe< list> < address>
```

where *password* is the administrative password for the list, `subscribe/unsubscribe` is the action to approve, *list* is the mail list name, and *address* is the email address to approve.

config Command

The `config` command is used to retrieve a copy of the mail list configuration file, `list.config`. The format of this command is

```
config <list> password
```

mkdigest Command

The `mkdigest` command is used in mail lists that use the digest feature to create a new digest. Digests can be created as frequently as needed. The command format is

```
mkdigest <list> password
```

If there is a lot of traffic in the mail list, sometimes it is desirable to create digests more frequently than is configured in the mail list settings. The `mkdigest` will force Majordomo to create a new digest.

newconfig Command

The `newconfig` command is used to create a new configuration file with the parameters sent. The command format is

```
newconfig <list> password
```

Following the command will be the text of the new configuration file. Majordomo will replace the existing configuration file with the new one, and automatically follow the new configuration guidelines. This feature allows the mail list owner to completely change the configuration of the mail list with a single email message. This is extremely handy when administering a mail list from a remote location.

newinfo Command

The `newinfo` command is used to change the text in the `list.info` file via email. The format for this command is

```
newinfo <list> password
```

The text immediately following the `newinfo` command will be the desired text of the new information file. Majordomo will replace the `list.info` file with the text sent. This is another handy remote administration feature.

passwd Command

The `passwd` command is used to change the mail list password. The format of the `passwd` command is

```
passwd < list> old-passwd new-passwd
```

This command can cause some confusion. Normally, the mail list password is stored in the `list.config` file, which can be modified using the `newconfig` command. Alternatively, if you do not want to mess with sending a new configuration file, you can use the `passwd` command to change just the password. However, this command does not replace the password present in the configuration file. It creates a new file, `list.passwd`, that indicates the new password. If the password in the configuration file does not match the password in the password file, both passwords become active.

writeconfig Command

The `writeconfig` command is used to reformat the existing configuration file to the original format. The command format is

```
writeconfig < list> password
```

This command can be used when the configuration file is hopelessly scrambled, possibly because of errors when using the `newconfig` command. As you can only retrieve the existing configuration file, you might not be able to fix them using `newconfig`. The `writeconfig` command attempts to reformat the existing configuration file back to the original format.

Summary

One nice feature of mailservers is the capability to create a mail list that users can subscribe to. Mail lists can handle large numbers of members and seamlessly deliver messages. One mail list package available for the Linux platform is the Majordomo program. Majordomo can manage multiple mail lists on a single server. Mail lists range from publicly open, unmoderated mail lists to closed, restricted mail lists. Mail list digests and archives can be created to help simplify message retrieval. Majordomo also enables remote administration of mail lists, so the mail list owner does not require physical access to the mail list server. User commands are kept simple to make subscribing, posting, and unsubscribing to mail lists easy for non-technical list members.

18

MAIL LISTS

IP Routing with Linux

IN THIS CHAPTER

This book is intended to help network mail administrators install and configure a fully working Internet email server using the Linux operating system. You may be wondering why then is the last chapter about IP Routing. When deciding the platform to implement an office email server on, there are many decisions to consider. Many other valid operating systems can be used to implement third-party software to provide email services (although none of them includes email software like Linux). A feature that is often implemented when configuring an office network is the capability for locally connected office workstations to have full access to the Internet. Some operating systems (such as Microsoft Windows NT 4.0 server) allow this functionality from within the operating system. Others (such as Windows 95) require third-party software packages to support this functionality.

If you have made the decision to use the Linux operating system to provide your Internet email services, you may also be wondering whether Linux can also provide connectivity to the Internet for your office workstations. It can. This chapter describes how you can use the Linux mailserver to connect the office workstations to the Internet and at the same time provide Internet email services for your office.

Methods of Network Connectivity Using Linux

Two different methods can be used to connect network workstations to the Internet using the Linux server:

- Obtain a range of valid Internet IP addresses and use the Linux server as an IP routing device.
- Use a public IP address range and use the Linux server as an IP masquerading device.

The first method requires that each device on the network have a valid Internet IP address in a network that is routable from the Internet. The Linux server acts as a normal IP router to transfer IP packets from the local office network through the ISP network to the Internet.

You can obtain valid Internet IP addresses for the office network in two ways. One way is to register for a block of IP addresses from the Network Information Center (NIC). The other way is by the ISP allowing the office network to use a subset of its assigned IP addresses. Registering a block of IP addresses from the NIC is an expensive method. There has been a lot of talk about the NIC running out of IP network addresses due to organizations taking large blocks of addresses but not using them. Often an ISP will subnet its IP network address block and allow each client to use some IP addresses from its own block of assigned addresses. Unfortunately, this will not work if you intend on connecting more than five or six workstations to the office network because most ISPs do not give out large quantities of IP addresses.

The second method is the more common approach. The local network is assigned IP addresses from the public IP network address space—192.168.0.0. Using this IP address range, network connectivity can be established between the network workstations and the Linux mailserver on the local network. However, devices in the public IP network are not routable from the Internet. The idea of the public network addresses is that they can be used by anyone not on the Internet without worrying about routing problems because they cannot be reached from the Internet.

The Linux server can solve this problem by using IP masquerading. When the Linux server connects to the ISP, it is assigned a valid Internet IP address either dynamically or statically. The Linux server can then masquerade the IP addresses from the local office workstation with its own valid Internet IP address before sending the packets out into the Internet. The receiving Internet host can reply to the packet, which can be routed back to the Linux server. The Linux server must then be able to put the original office network IP address on the packet and forward it to the proper workstation.

The Linux mailserver can support either method of Internet connectivity for workstations connected to the office network. The following sections describe how this can be accomplished.

Local Network Has a Valid Internet IP Address Range

When the office network has been assigned valid Internet IP addresses, IP masquerading is not needed. The Linux mailserver can act as a normal IP router forwarding packets between the office network and the Internet. Figure 19.1 shows an example of a local office workstation connecting with a remote host on the Internet using the Linux server as a router.

A remote Internet host can send IP packets directly to the local workstation because the workstation's IP network is routable from the remote network. The Linux server must have IP forwarding enabled in the kernel to work as a router. In Figure 19.1, a network client with address 5.6.8.2 wants to talk to a remote host with address 1.2.3.4. Using routing in the local mailserver, the process involves the following:

1. Client sends packet to remote host 1.2.3.4.
2. Local mailserver forwards packet to the ISP server with address 5.6.7.8 on the client network side.
3. ISP server routes the packet through the Internet to the remote host at address 1.2.3.4 and indicates a response to 5.6.8.2.
4. The remote host receives the message and replies through the Internet to address 5.6.8.2.

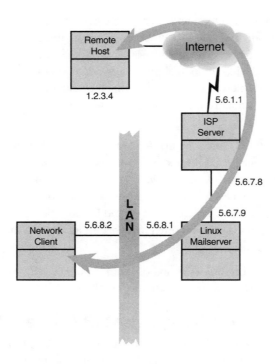

FIGURE 19.1

Local workstations using Internet IP addresses.

5. The ISP server recognizes the packet as one to be directed to local address `5.6.8.2` and forwards it.

6. The local mailserver recognizes the packet as one for a local client and forwards it to `5.6.8.2`.

If the kernel does not have IP forwarding enabled, you must recompile the kernel to enable it.

To determine whether your Linux kernel has IP forwarding enabled, you can check for the file `/proc/sys/net/ipv4/ip_forward`. By setting the `ip_forward` file to the value of `'1'`, IP forwarding is enabled. To accomplish this, as the root user type the following:

```
echo '1' > /proc/sys/net/ipv4/ip_forward
```

NOTE

With the popularity of IP forwarding and masquerading, most modern Linux distributions include support for IP forwarding by default. If your Linux kernel does not have IP forwarding installed, you must recompile the kernel to include it. Several good Sams Publishing books are available that describe the details on how to reconfigure the Linux kernel.

CAUTION

Use caution when changing the Linux kernel. Any mistakes could leave your Linux server unbootable.

Using the Linux server as a router is a nice feature, but risks are involved. After the Linux server is configured to route IP network traffic from your office network to the Internet, traffic from the Internet can also get to your office network. I repeat—*traffic from the Internet can also get to your office network*. This leaves your office network open and vulnerable to various attacks by hackers on the Internet. Depending on what types of devices are on your network, this may or may not be a large concern for you.

Another nice feature of Linux is that since version 1.3, kernel firewall support code has been built into the kernel. You can use this feature to help reduce the chances of unauthorized hackers gaining access to devices on your network by implementing the firewall code.

Firewalls help filter certain types of packets from entering or leaving the office network. Using a firewall, you can prevent remote hosts from establishing connections to internal office devices. Also, you can prevent internal office devices from accessing certain remote hosts. This is accomplished by using a Network Address Translation (NAT) table that is maintained in the kernel. IP address pairs are entered into the table by programs that use rules. Each rule is constructed to create an entry in the NAT. As each packet is received, Linux examines the NAT table to determine whether the packet should be forwarded or dropped.

Two software packages for Linux are used to assist in configuring the kernel NAT table. The ipfwadm package is a popular package that can be used with the 1.3 to 2.0 kernels. In kernel version 2.1, new features were added to the NAT table. If your Linux distribution is using either the 2.1 or newer kernels, you can use the ipchains software package to utilize new

19

**IP ROUTING
WITH LINUX**

features such as faster masquerading and packet rejecting (sending an ICMP reject packet back to the original host). Both packages are explained in detail later in the "Using ipfwadm" and "Using ipchains" sections.

By setting up a firewall, you can configure the software to block attempts by hackers to initiate connections to devices on your network. This is not intended to be a substitute for proper system administration. You must always monitor the Linux system log files to watch for intruders. Firewalls can be compromised.

Local Network Is Using a Public IP Address Range

As described earlier, using a public IP address range in the local office network requires a little more work from the network administrator. Figure 19.2 shows an example of how this scenario works.

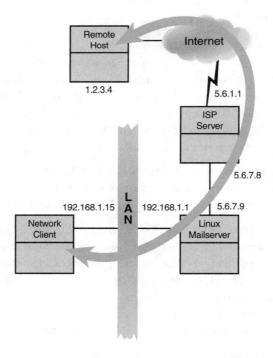

FIGURE 19.2
Local workstations using public IP addresses.

Because the local workstations do not have valid Internet IP addresses, the Linux server must be configured to masquerade the addresses used on the local office network devices when they request connections to remote Internet hosts. IP masquerading support has been built into the Linux kernel since version 1.3, and upgraded in version 2.1. In Figure 19.2, a network client with address 192.168.1.15 wants to talk to a remote host with address 1.2.3.4. Using masquerading, the dialog would involve the following:

1. Client sends packet to remote host 1.2.3.4.

2. Local mailserver forwards packet to the ISP server with address 5.6.7.8 on the client network side. The message masquerades the sending address as itself—address 5.6.7.9— not the workstation address.

3. ISP server routes the packet through the Internet to the remote host at address 1.2.3.4 and indicates a response to 5.6.7.9.

4. The remote host receives the message and replies through the Internet to address 5.6.7.9.

5. The ISP server recognizes the packet as one to be directed to local address 5.6.7.9 and forwards it.

6. The local mailserver identifies the packet as one for a local client and forwards it to 192.168.1.15.

Like the firewall feature, masquerading must be compiled into the Linux kernel. Also like the firewall, the kernel maintains an internal table of connections where it can map the original local network device addresses with an assigned port number from its Internet IP address. This feature is added to the Network Address Translation (NAT) table. IP packets coming from the local network device are added to the NAT and assigned a port number on the existing IP address of the Linux server.

To determine whether IP masquerading is installed in your Linux kernel, check for the file /proc/net/ip_masquerade. If it is present, IP masquerading is compiled in the kernel. Also, for IP masquerading to work, IP forwarding must be enabled as described in the previous section. If not, you must recompile the Linux kernel and add it. As before, use caution when recompiling the Linux kernel. Mistakes can result in an unusable Linux server.

To set up masquerading, you can use the same software packages as setting up the firewall. The ipfwadm and ipchains software packages mentioned earlier are both capable of inserting and deleting IP addresses into the kernel NAT table for masquerading. The following sections describe these two software packages in detail.

19

IP ROUTING
WITH LINUX

Using ipfwadm

The ipfwadm package helps manipulate the internal Linux kernel NAT table. The ipfwadm program is maintained by the X/OS company. Some basic information is available at its Web site:

```
http://www.xos.nl/linux/ipfwadm/
```

> **NOTE**
>
> Most Linux distributions before the version 2.1 kernel include a binary distribution package for ipfwadm. The most current version of ipfwadm at the time of this writing is version 2.3.0. It can be downloaded from the X/OS FTP site:
>
> ```
> ftp://ftp.xos.nl/pub/linux/ipfwadm/ipfwadm-2.3.0.tar.gz
> ```
>
> When downloaded, it can be unpacked and compiled to create the binary executable file ipfwadm.

ipfwadm uses rules to manipulate the NAT table addresses. You must run ipfwadm each time you want to add or delete an address from the NAT. ipfwadm uses rules to manipulate the NAT addresses. The rules are divided into four categories:

- IP packet accounting rules
- IP input firewall rules
- IP output firewall rules
- IP forwarding firewall rules

Each category has its own list of rules. Rules are implemented in the order in which they are entered, so be careful with rules that may override other rules. The format of the ipfwadm command is as follows:

```
ipfwadm category command parameters [options]
```

The *category* indicates the type of rules being entered. Table 19.1 shows the current category types.

TABLE 19.1   `ipfwadm` Category Types

Category	Description
-A	IP accounting rules
-I	IP input firewall rules
-O	IP output firewall rules
-F	IP forwarding firewall rules
-M	IP masquerading administration

Only one category can be specified per line. Each category relates to the `ipfwadm` category rule list. The `-M` category is used to list rules relating to the IP masquerading rules. This helps simplify administration of masquerading features.

Commands are used to add, delete, or modify the rules listed on the command line. Table 19.2 lists the commands available for each of the categories (except the `-M` category).

TABLE 19.2   `ipfwadm` Command Types

Command	Description
-a [policy]	Append one or more rules
-i [policy]	Insert one or more rules to the beginning of the rule list
-d [policy]	Delete one or more rules from the selected rule list
-l	List all the rules in the list
-z	Reset the counters
-f	Flush the selected rule list
-p policy	Change the default rule policy
-s tcp tcpfin udp	Change the timeout values used for masquerading
-c	Check whether an IP packet would be accepted
-h	Display the list of commands

The `policy` parameter relates to one of three policy types: `accept`, `deny`, or `reject`. The `accept` policy allows the specified packets to be forwarded. The `deny` policy prevents the specified packets from being forwarded. The `reject` policy also prevents the specified packets from being forwarded, but also returns an ICMP error packet to the sending address.

The parameters are used to further define actions taken in the commands. Table 19.3 shows the valid parameters that are used.

19

IP ROUTING
WITH LINUX

TABLE 19.3   `ipfwadm` Parameter Types

Parameter	Description
`-P` *protocol*	The protocol to check
`-S` *address[/mask]*	Source address(es) to check
`-D` *address[/mask]*	Destination address(es) to check
`-V` *address*	Optional address of an interface via which a packet is received
`-W` *address*	Optional name of an interface via which a packet is received

The addresses specified can be either a single IP address, or a subnet of IP addresses using a subnet mask that is specified. The mask is specified as a number of bits turned on. Thus a mask of 24 relates to a subnet mask of `255.255.255.0`.

The options are additional features that can be specified for the rules. Table 19.4 shows the available options that can be used.

TABLE 19.4   `ipfwadm` Option Types

Option	Description
`-b`	Bi-directional mode
`-e`	Extended output
`-k`	Match TCP packets with ACK bit set
`-m`	Masquerade packets for forwarding
`-n`	Numeric output
`-o`	Turn on logging of packets
`-r` *[port]*	Redirect packets to a local socket
`-t` *andmask ormask*	Masks used to modify the IP type-of-service
`-v`	Verbose output
`-x`	Expand numbers
`-y`	Match start-of-session packets

The most common options used are the `-m` option, which turns on masquerading, the `-o` option, which creates an entry in the kernel log file for each packet that matches the rule, and the `-y` option, which can be used to prevent connections from being established. Be careful when using the `-o` option because it could easily generate huge log files. Often it is used with the `-y` option to log when remote hosts attempt to connect to internal office workstations.

The `ipfwadm` commands are entered into the NAT table as they are entered at the command line. Unfortunately, they disappear when the Linux server is rebooted. Thus, when you find a configuration that you like, you should create a script file that can be run at boot time to re-create the rules. Listing 19.1 shows a sample script to start IP masquerading on the Linux server.

LISTING 19.1   Sample `ipfwadm` Script for Masquerading

```
1   /sbin/ipfwadm -F -p deny
2   /sbin/ipfwadm -F -a -m -S 192.168.1.0/24 -D 0.0.0.0/0
```

In Listing 19.1, line 1 shows the `ipfwadm` command to change the default policy to deny. The default policy is used when no matching rules are found. It is best to make the rules default to deny forwarding. Line 2 implements the masquerading feature. The `-a` command indicates that the rule will be appended to the IP forward firewall rule list. The `-m` option indicates that packets that pass the rule will be masqueraded when forwarded. The `-S` parameter indicates the source network address and mask that will be used in the rule. The mask of `24` indicates the top 24 bits will be used as a subnet mask. This creates a subnet mask of `255.255.255.0`, matching the network subnet mask for the office network. The `-D` parameter indicates the destination address and mask that will be used. This rule modifies the NAT to accept any packet from the `192.168.1.0` network that is destined for any other network and forwards it to the external PPP link using masquerading. Thus, all the office network workstations' packets should be masqueraded and forwarded to the Internet.

Using IP masquerading as shown in Figure 19.2, all outbound IP packets from the office network would use the Linux mailserver's IP address. To help differentiate the sessions, the Linux mailserver dynamically assigns a new TCP port number to each session.

This rule does not perform any firewall functions. To enable a basic firewall, you can add another `ipfwadm` line similar to this:

```
/sbin/ipfwadm -F -a deny -P tcp -W ppp0 -y -o
```

This command creates a NAT entry that blocks any TCP connection requests coming from the `ppp0` line, which should be the connection to the ISP. As an extra feature, it also will log any connection attempts made by remote clients. With this rule, no one from the Internet should be able to establish a connection with any device on the office network. If you have a device such as a Web server on the office network, you can be more specific and create a rule to allow Web traffic to the server but block all other connections. Remember that entering the rule to allow the Web traffic should precede the rule that blocks all traffic, or else it will be nullified. Addresses are placed in the NAT in the order that the rules are entered, and are also processed that way.

19

IP ROUTING
WITH LINUX

After a script is configured to meet your masquerading and firewall filtering needs, you can add it to the `init` scripts in the directory appropriate for your run level.

Using ipchains

In the Linux 2.1 kernel, the NAT table was expanded to provide for increased functionality. Because it was made backward-compatible, the ipfwadm program can still be used to modify the NAT, but to take advantage of the new functionality, a newer program was created. For Linux kernels version 2.1 or higher, the ipchains program is used to add and delete NAT table addresses. The ipchains program was written and is maintained by Rusty Russell. The main ipchains Web site is located at

```
http://www.rustcorp.com/linux/ipchains
```

> **NOTE**
>
> Most Linux distributions that use version 2.2 or higher kernel include a binary distribution of ipchains. The most current version of ipchains at the time of this writing is version 1.3.9. It can be downloaded from the following FTP site:
>
> ```
> ftp://ftp.rustcorp.com/ipchains/ipchains-1.3.9.tar.bz2
> ```
>
> When downloaded, it can be unpacked and compiled to create the binary executable file `ipchains`.

Besides the ipchains program, three scripts can be used to simplify ipchains administration—`ipchains-save`, `ipchains-restore`, and `ipchains-wrapper`. The `ipchains-wrapper` script can be used if you are currently using an `ipfwadm` script and want to convert to ipchains after upgrading your Linux kernel. If you are installing firewall and masquerade features for the first time, you will not need this script.

> **NOTE**
>
> The scripts can also be downloaded from the following FTP site:
>
> ```
> ftp://ftp.rustcorp.com/ipchains/ipchains-scripts-1.1.2.tar.gz
> ```

The `ipchains-save` and `ipchains-restore` scripts will be discussed in the "Saving the NAT Configuration" section.

The ipchains program works similar to the ipfwadm program in that it manipulates rules in four different categories in the NAT table. The four categories that ipchains uses are as follows:

- IP input chain
- IP output chain
- IP forwarding chain
- User-defined chains

The ipchains program uses the concept of chaining rules together to filter packets as they pass through the Linux server. Remember, rules are created to give system administrators a concrete method to use to manipulate the NAT. Figure 19.3 shows a graphical picture of how the rule chains are configured. The rules are stored in the NAT as IP address pairs, not as rules per se.

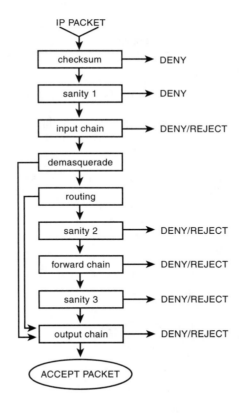

FIGURE 19.3

ipchains rule processing.

The processes shown in Figure 19.3 control how packets are processed in the Linux server. Table 19.5 describes these processes.

TABLE 19.5   ipchains Packet Filtering Processes

Process	Description
checksum	Checks for corrupted packets
sanity1	Checks for malformed packets
input chain	Firewall input chain check
demasquerade	If reply to a masqueraded packet, must be converted back to original packet address
routing	Destination checked to see whether it is local or needs to be forwarded
sanity2	Checks for malformed packets
forward chain	Firewall forward chain check
sanity3	Checks for malformed packets
output chain	Firewall output chain check

The packet must successfully pass each of the appropriate processes listed in Table 19.5 before it is accepted to be processed either on the local host or forwarded to a remote host.

The input, forward, and output chains use rules set in the NAT table by the ipchains program. The format of the `ipchains` command varies depending on the category used. The formats that `ipchains` can use are as follows:

```
ipchains -[ADC] chain rule-specification [options]
ipchains -[RI] chain rulenum rule-specification [options]
ipchains -D chain rulenum [options]
ipchains -[LFZNX] [chain] [options]
ipchains -P chain target [options]
ipchains -M [ -L | -S ] [options]
```

The first parameter is the command that controls the function that `ipchains` performs. Table 19.6 lists the commands available to use.

TABLE 19.6   ipchains Command Types

Command	Description
-A	Append one or more rules
-D	Delete one or more rules
-C	Checks the packet against selected chain
-R	Replace a rule in the selected chain

Command	Description
-I	Insert one or more rules as the given rule number
-L	List all rules in selected chain
-F	Flush the selected chain
-Z	Zero the counters for all chains
-N	Create a new user-defined chain
-X	Delete selected user-defined chain
-P	Set the policy for the chain
-M	View the current masqueraded connections

The next parameter is the chain name. This can be either one of the system chains—input, output, or forward—or a user-defined chain name created using the -N command. User-defined chains are often used to help simplify complex rules.

ipchains Rules

The rule specification consists of parameters that specify the actions taken in the rule. Table 19.7 lists the available specifications.

TABLE 19.7   ipchains **Parameter Types**

Parameter	Description
-p *protocol*	The protocol to check
-s *address[/mask]*	Source address to check
--source-port *port*	Source port to check
-d *address[/mask]*	Destination address to check
--destination-port *port*	Destination port to check
--icmp-type	ICMP type to check
-j *target*	Target to jump to if packet matches
-i *name*	Interface name
-f	Rule refers to fragment packets

There are six special targets that the -j option can jump to when a packet matches the rule. Targets themselves are not actual entities. They are used to help create a concrete description for the mail administrator to use when creating rules. The NAT still tracks packets by IP address pairs and will still either pass or block packets based on the IP address pairs.

19

IP ROUTING
WITH LINUX

The additional features included in the newer Linux kernel help support features such as masquerading and redirection. Table 19.8 lists the available targets.

TABLE 19.8   `ipchains` Target Types

Target	Description
ACCEPT	Allows packet to pass
DENY	Prevents packet from passing
REJECT	Prevents packet from passing and returns ICMP error to sender
MASQ	Masquerades forward packets
REDIRECT	Sends packet to local port instead of destination
RETURN	Drops out of chain immediately

Besides parameters, additional options are used to further define the rule. Table 19.9 lists the available options.

TABLE 19.9   `ipchains` Option Types

Option	Description
-b	Bi-directional mode
-v	Verbose output
-n	Numeric output
-l	Turn on logging
-o *[maxsize]*	Copy matching packets to user space device
-m *markvalue*	Mark matching packets
-t *andmask xormask*	Masks used to modify the IP packet type-of-service field
-x	Expand numbers
-y	Only match start-of-session packets

As each `ipchains` command is entered, the NAT table is modified accordingly. When the server is rebooted, the NAT table resets and any changes made previously are lost. To solve this problem, `ipchains` uses two script files to save the NAT table in a file that can be read back into the NAT table at boot time.

Saving a NAT Configuration

The `ipchains-save` script is used to save the existing NAT table configuration into a file specified. The format of the `ipchains-save` command is

```
ipchains-save > filename
```

where *filename* is the name of the file where you want to save the NAT table configuration. You must be logged in as the root user to execute this command. To restore the NAT table, you can create an initialization script that uses the `ipchains-restore` script. The format of the `ipchains-restore` command is

```
ipchains-restore < filename
```

where *filename* is the full pathname of the location where the original NAT table configuration was stored. Again, this command should be run as the root user, preferably during the server initialization scripts.

Enabling Masquerading

Listing 19.2 shows an example of `ipchains` commands that can be used to enable masquerading on a Linux server.

LISTING 19.2   Sample `ipchains` Commands for Masquerading

```
1  /sbin/ipchains -P forward DENY
2  /sbin/ipchains -A forward -i ppp0 -j MASQ
```

In Listing 19.2, line 1 sets the default policy for the forward chain to deny. Line 2 appends a rule to the forward chain. Any packets forwarded to the ppp0 interface will be passed to the masquerading target first. This assumes that the ppp0 line is the connection to the ISP. To add firewall features, you can add another command:

```
/sbin/ipchains -A input -i ppp0 -l -y -j DENY
```

This command denies any TCP start-of-session packet coming into the input chain on the ppp0 interface. Assuming that the ppp0 interface is the Linux server's connection to the ISP, this prevents Internet hosts from establishing connections with hosts on the office network. The use of the -l option allows any connection attempt to be logged in the kernel log file. By carefully monitoring the log files, the system administrator can detect unauthorized attempts by hackers to connect to internal workstations and hosts.

Configuring Network Clients for Routing

After the Linux server has been properly configured to allow routing and/or masquerading to the Internet, the local network workstations must be configured to use the router. The network workstations must know the IP address of the Linux server to be able to forward packets through the Linux server to the Internet.

For the workstation to properly forward packets to the Linux server, the network must operate with a single network address and subnet mask. The subnet mask defines how many bits of the IP address are used to define the network portion of the address. Workstations use this information to determine when they need to forward packets to the router, and when they can send them directly to the destination host.

If you obtained the office network from the ISP or the NIC, you will not have any choice in these values. They should be given to you by the ISP. If you selected the public IP address scheme for your office network, you have a choice of how much of the address space you want to use as the network portion. Table 19.10 shows different ways the 192.168.0.0 public IP address range can be separated into network addresses and host addresses.

TABLE 19.10   Subnetting the 192.168.0.0 Network

Mask	Number of Workstations
255.255.240.0	4094
255.255.248.0	2046
255.255.252.0	1022
255.255.254.0	510
255.255.255.0	254
255.255.255.128	126
255.255.255.192	62
255.255.255.224	30
255.255.255.240	14
255.255.255.248	6
255.255.255.252	2

The most common (and easiest) method is to use the 255.255.255.0 subnet mask. This provides that the first three octets in the IP address define the network. Each workstation on the network must have the same first three octet values. Thus you can use 192.168.1 as the network address and assign IP addresses from 1 to 254 to workstations on the office network (remember that the 255 address is for broadcasts and can't be used on a workstation).

Chapter 15, "Configuring LAN Clients," discusses the details required to configure network cards and IP addresses on Microsoft Windows 95, 98, and NT 4.0 workstations. Figure 19.4 shows the TCP/IP Properties window for a Windows 95 client.

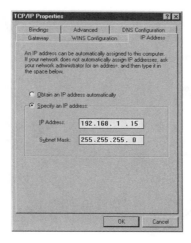

FIGURE 19.4

The Microsoft Windows 95 and 98 TCP/IP Properties window.

The workstation IP address and subnet mask are configured in the IP Address tab. The default gateway address must be configured from the Gateway tab. The default gateway address will be the IP address of the Linux server.

Windows NT 4.0 workstations require a similar configuration. Figure 19.5 shows the Microsoft TCP/IP Properties window from a Windows NT 4.0 workstation.

All three necessary parameters can be entered into the IP Address tab area. Again, the default gateway address will be the IP address of the Linux server.

After these values are entered into the network configuration of the workstation, the workstation should be able to contact remote Internet hosts via the Linux server.

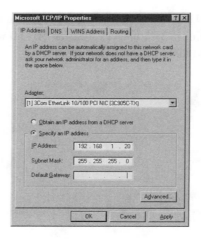

FIGURE 19.5

The Microsoft Windows NT 4.0 workstation TCP/IP Properties window.

Summary

Although not an email function, IP routing is often a requirement for local office networks connecting to the Internet via an ISP. The Linux mailserver can also be configured to route network traffic from the office network to the Internet. If the office network uses valid Internet IP addresses, the Linux server can be configured to forward packets "as-is" to the ISP. If the office network uses public IP addresses, the Linux server must be capable of performing masquerading. Masquerading allows the Linux server to use its own valid Internet IP address in place of the public IP addresses that the network workstations use. This way, remote Internet hosts can properly return IP packets to the Linux server, which in turn can convert them back to the public IP addresses for the workstations. In both scenarios, the Linux server can also perform firewall functions to help protect the office network from outside hackers. The Linux `ipfwadm` and `ipchains` commands can be used to implement both firewall and masquerading functions. Both commands modify rules set up in the Linux kernel to instruct it how to handle packets. After the Linux server is configured to route packets from the office network to the Internet, workstations on the office network must be configured to use it as the default gateway. All the Microsoft workstation operating systems allow for IP subnet masks and default gateways to be configured into the TCP/IP software configuration. By using the Linux mailserver's IP address as the default gateway, local office workstations can connect to the Internet.

At this point, you should be comfortable with the aspects of Linux mailserver administration and maintenance. But the job of the mail administrator never ends. There are many new technologies appearing on the horizon that will enhance the use of email in the office. One such technology that is getting more press is the Lightweight Directory Access Protocol (LDAP). This allows a single point of authentication for all network services, including email. Many companies are experimenting with this feature, and some work has been started in the Linux world to support LDAP. This and many other new technologies should keep you busy as the office mail administrator.

INDEX

A

The IT site
you asked for...

It's
Here!

InformIT is a complete online library delivering
information, technology, reference, training, news,
and opinion to IT professionals, students,
and corporate users.

Find IT Solutions Here!

www.informit.com

InformIT is a trademark of Macmillan USA, Inc.
Copyright © 2000 Macmillan USA, Inc.

Windows 95/98/NT/2000 Installation Instructions

1. Insert the CD-ROM disc into your CD-ROM drive.
2. From the Windows 95 desktop, double-click on the My Computer icon.
3. Double-click on the icon representing your CD-ROM drive.
4. Open the readme.txt file for descriptions of Third Party products.

Linux and Unix Installation Instructions

These installation instructions assume that you have a passing familiarity with UNIX commands and the basic setup of your machine. As UNIX has many flavors, only generic commands are used. If you have any problems with the commands, please consult the appropriate man page or your system administrator.

1. Insert CD-ROM in CD drive.
2. If you have a volume manager, mounting of the CD-ROM will be automatic. If you don't have a volume manager, you can mount the CD-ROM by typing

   `Mount -tiso9660 /dev/cdrom   /mnt/cdrom`

   NOTE: /mnt/cdrom is just a mount point, but it must exist when you issue the mount command. You may also use any empty directory for a mount point if you don't want to use /mnt/cdrom.
3. Open the readme.txt file for descriptions of Third Party products.

By opening this package, you are agreeing to be bound by the following agreement:

You may not copy or redistribute the entire CD-ROM as a whole. Copying and redistribution of individual software programs on the CD-ROM is governed by terms set by individual copyright holders.

The installer and code from the author(s) are copyrighted by the publisher and author(s). Individual programs and other items on the CD-ROM are copyrighted by their various authors or other copyright holders. Some of the programs included with this product may be governed by the GNU General Public License, which allows redistribution; see the license information for each product for more information.

Other programs are included on the CD-ROM by special permission from their authors.

This software is provided as is without warranty of any kind, either expressed or implied, including but not limited to the implied warranties of merchantability and fitness for a particular purpose. Neither the publisher nor its dealers or distributors assume any liability for any alleged or actual damages arising from the use of this program. (Some states do not allow for the exclusion of implied warranties, so the exclusion may not apply to you.)